INTERNATIONAL
HANDBOOK
OF
BROADCASTING
SYSTEMS

INTERNATIONAL HANDBOOK OF BROADCASTING SYSTEMS

Edited by
PHILIP T. ROSEN

GREENWOOD PRESS
New York • Westport, Connecticut • London

Library of Congress Cataloging-in-Publication Data

International handbook of broadcasting systems.

Includes index.
1. International broadcasting—Handbooks, manuals,
etc. I. Rosen, Philip T., 1946–   .
HE8689.6.I54   1988   384   87–29986
ISBN 0-313–24348–4 (lib. bdg. : alk. paper)

British Library Cataloguing in Publication Data is available.

Library of Congress Catalog Card Number: 87–29986
ISBN: 0–313–24348–4

First published in 1988

Greenwood Press, Inc.
88 Post Road West, Westport, Connecticut 06881

Printed in the United States of America

The paper used in this book complies with the
Permanent Paper Standard issued by the National
Information Standards Organization (Z39.48–1984).

10   9   8   7   6   5   4   3   2   1

To Jackie, Philip, and Beana

CONTENTS

ABBREVIATIONS

ABC	American Broadcasting Company;
	Australian Broadcasting Commission, later the Australian Broadcasting Corporation
ABT	Australian Broadcasting Tribunal
AIR	All Indian Radio
ARD	(Arbeitsgemeinschaft der Öffentlich-rechtlichen Rundfunkanstalten der Bundesrepublik Deutschland.) Radio and television program supplier organized jointly by the West German states to operate their regional radio and their first and third TV networks
BBC	British Broadcasting Corporation
BRT	Belgische Radio en Televisie
CATV	Community antenna television
CBS	Christian Broadcasting System (Korea);
	Columbia Broadcasting System (United States)
DBS	Direct broadcasting satellite;
	Dong-A Ilbo Broadcasting System (Korea)
FRCN	Federal Radio Corporation of Nigeria
IBA	Independent Broadcasting Authority (Great Britain);
	Israel Broadcasting Authority
ITV	Independent Television
KBS	Korean Broadcasting Station, later the Korean Broadcasting System

MBC	Munhwa Broadcasting Corporation
NBC	National Broadcasting Company (United States);
	Nigerian Broadcasting Corporation
NHK	Nippon Hoso Kyokai
NTA	Nigerian Television Authority
ORF	Austrian Broadcasting Corporation
PBS	Palestine Broadcasting Service (Israel);
	Public Broadcasting Service (United States)
PTT	Post, Telephone, and Telegraph
RAI	Italian Radio Audition
RTBF	Radio et Television Belge-Française
SBC	Swedish Broadcasting Corporation
SBS	Special Broadcasting Service (Australia)
SRG	Switzerland Broadcasting network
ZDF	Zweites Deutsches Fernsehen (West German Broadcasting network)

ACKNOWLEDGMENTS

This handbook represents a collective undertaking involving a multitude of scholars, librarians, archivists, government officials, and broadcasters. From its inception to its conclusion countless individuals gave willingly of their time, energy, and talent. To enumerate this august group would necessitate an additional volume entitled *Who's Who in International Broadcasting*.

Nevertheless, failure to thank several individuals who supported this endeavor would be remiss. First and foremost, very special thanks are due the twenty-eight contributors who prepared original chapters specifically for the handbook. This work culminates their efforts, and they deserve special acknowledgment. This distinguished group of broadcast scholars, area specialists, and practitioners enthusiastically embraced the project and diligently worked with the editor to complete it.

On a more personal note, Forrest and Ellen McDonald have guided my career from the beginning and continue to establish the standard for scholarship in the field of American history. The continued support and friendship of Ken Hagan (U.S. Naval Academy), Terry Sharrer (Smithsonian Institution), and William Keppler and Dennis Edwards (University of Alaska, Anchorage) have been vital to this endeavor. Cynthia Tiedeman of Xerox Alaska has provided invaluable technical expertise for the production of the manuscript.

Finally, any listing of acknowledgments would be sorely deficient that did not mention the substantial contributions of Jackie, Philip, and Beana. Some four hundred years ago, Francis Bacon wrote: "He that hath wife and children hath given hostages for fortune; for they are impediments to great enterprises." Bacon was never more wrong.

INTRODUCTION

It is a current conceit voiced in communications writings and at national conferences that we live in the age of the communications and information revolution. The observation comes over half a century late. Our so-called communications revolution actually occurred over sixty years ago, as these twenty-eight contributors point out time after time. Of course, the adaptation of an existing technology to broadcasting (a technological adjustment) did begin a dynamic process that continues to evolve and unfold. But while pundits and conference keynoters rhapsodize about broadcasting and its indelible stamp on every facet of society, its study continues to offer ample opportunity to the scholar interested in large amounts of unpublished or even unexplored material.

The field of international broadcasting presents an excellent case in point. American undergraduate education almost completely ignores it. Even within the professional schools of communications, as the International Committee of the Broadcast Education Association has observed, "International aspects receive far less priority than the typical 'bread and butter' course." The same situation exists today as in 1983 when Professor Laurence Day commented in the autumn issue of the *Journalism Educator*, "Most colleges and universities have such weak and peripheral international communications programs that it wouldn't occur to administrators to equip them with anything more than shirt-tail services of an instructor for a class or two."

So be it. Why would one care? What value would the average individual glean from any knowledge of such a seemingly esoteric and perhaps exotic subject? First, one must consider the commonalities expressed by this collected group of scholars. The nations they represent form a diverse collection of large and small, developing and industrialized, wealthy and not so well endowed. Yet one reads repeatedly of the current state of major transformation brought on by technological development. The theme of conservative marketplace philosophy appears throughout these chapters, but one sees countries experiencing the ubiquitous and intrusive proliferation of technology. While a conflict over degree or implementation of government control of broadcasting may exist, in any particular nation, including the United States, an even greater concern for the maintenance of national identity and cohesion pervades these pages. It is ironic that the very technology welcomed by many nations as a means of reaching a dispersed and heterogeneous populace now threatens to homogenize that same populace into a marketplace for mass entertainment and consumption. Even in nations regulating their industry by a strict public service standard, that mass audience is now demanding a new market orientation and thereby changing the shape of society forever. And in that change lies the threat of an even greater revolution. The degree to which we understand the forces at play in this process and the various national responses to it may well affect our future as well as that of generations to come.

Some material does already exist to aid the serious scholar or casual student. Sidney Head, for example, is a pioneer in the field of international broadcasting. He has edited a study on *Broadcasting in Africa: A Continental Survey of Radio and Television* (1974), a series of volumes produced by Temple University Press on communications in developing nations, and more recently has authored a comparative study entitled *World Broadcasting Systems: A Comparative Analysis* (1985). In addition, other scholars have conducted research in the field. Worthy of note are Burton Paulu, Douglas Boyd, Donald Browne, and Walter Emery. Finally, several international organizations have commissioned studies on the media of various nations, including the International Institute of Communications (London), Asian Mass Communication Research and Information Center (AMIC-Singapore), and UNESCO. Despite these efforts, however, much study is yet to be done to overcome the general theme of neglect and indifference to this most important subject. International broadcasting·is a field sorely in need of the scholarly touch.

Until now, there has been a lack of comprehensive reference works on international broadcasting systems. Of course, this attempt to summarize developments in a single volume or even several volumes is, if not next to impossible, certainly a daunting task. This offering represents merely the first step in such an enterprise.

In planning for the handbook, every effort was made to select nations representative of various regions and continents, political systems, and cultural traditions. This commendable goal was later influenced by the pragmatic consideration of the ready availability of competent scholars and practitioners proficient in the English language who could set aside other projects and contribute to this work.

To ensure uniformity throughout the work, each contributor was provided specific instructions regarding content, structure, and style. With one or two minor exceptions, each selection covers the following material: history of radio and television, government regulation, economic structure, programming, broadcast reform and alternative structures, new technologies, and a conclusion/forecast.

The handbook is intended as a reference work for students, scholars, and practitioners. At present no reference work exists where one can readily ascertain what the broadcasting structure is in a given nation and how it came to be. By filling this void, we hope that our work will make a substantial contribution to the field of international broadcasting.

INTERNATIONAL
HANDBOOK
OF
BROADCASTING
SYSTEMS

AUSTRALIA

Jeffrey M. Rushton

HISTORY

Australia comprises an island land mass of some 7,682,300 square kilometers, an area almost as extensive as the United States (excluding Alaska) but supporting a population of only 15.4 million inhabitants, slightly less than that of New York State. Australians, in the main, are for historical, climatic, and economic reasons domiciled in the capital cities. In 1984 almost 70 percent of the population was so distributed.

There are four considerably diverse broadcasting sectors serving this population, providing it with radio and television services—the commercial, national, and public sectors, and the Special Broadcasting Service. Together they form the Australian broadcasting system, one which has evolved over a period of more than sixty years since the first commercial radio station went on the air in Sydney on November 13, 1923.

That station's call sign, 2SB, like the majority of early Australian call signs, represented the initials (in this case reversed) of the licensee company, Broadcasters Sydney Pty Ltd. 2SB, like several other stations during that early period, was a sealed-set operation, providing its programs to subscribers who paid the license to be part of an exclusive audience. These subscribers also paid a license fee to the Australian government for the same privilege. As commercial services sluggishly developed over the next year, the government encouraged the establishment of a new "A"-class station, basically state funded but allowed to accept limited advertising. These "A"- class outlets represented the germ of the national sector.

By 1928 very serious consideration was being given to the formalizing of a completely government-funded national broadcasting operation. In June 1932 the Australian Broadcasting Commission (ABC)—now the Australian

Broadcasting Corporation—was created to "serve all sections and to satisfy the diversified tastes of the public." While it lacked a formal charter as such, it was modeled very closely in concept on the British Broadcasting Corporation.

Australia enjoyed its "golden days" of radio during the mid–1930s through to the mid–1950s, and the first real threat to radio as a medium came in 1956 with the introduction of national and commercial monochrome television services. It took another nineteen years before color (using the PAL system) was officially introduced.

In 1974 a new broadcasting interest was recognized with the establishment of the public broadcasting sector. The misleading title given to this sector by the legislators unfortunately confuses people, particularly those who may be interested in the comparative study of broadcasting systems. Public broadcasters in Australia provide radio programs to meet the needs and interests of particular community groups—for instance, they have been licensed to provide services for the print-handicapped, for ethnic community interests, and for specialist music interests. Some are providing educational programs, but mainly in the area of continuing education.

In 1978 the government, affirming its recognition of the reality of a multicultural society, created the Special Broadcasting Service (SBS). Its two radio stations, 2EA and 3EA (Ethnic Australia), provide services in more than fifty different languages. Late in 1980 two television outlets located in Sydney and Melbourne were operating and transmitting programs in a wide range of languages, including English. When English is not the scripted language, English subtitles, generally produced locally by SBS, are provided for English-speaking viewers.

REGULATION

The maintenance, development, and regulation of the Australian broadcasting system are responsibilities exercised by the Australian (federal) government. State and local governments exercise few powers in relation to the broadcasting system; however, as with any other business operation, it is necessary for licensees to observe local government ordinances controlling such things as mast heights, building construction, staff amenities, and fire standards.

The principal legislation, the Broadcasting and Television Act of 1948, empowers the minister of communications to regulate the broadcasting system. The steps taken to introduce new stations to the system demonstrate that the regulatory mechanism is not uniform for the four sectors.

Planning proposals for the national sector (ABC) and the SBS either originate within the broadcasting organizations themselves or arise as a direct result of government initiatives. Planning proposals for new commercial services arise as business decisions in the public sector, generally as the result of community initiatives. In each of the four cases, the planning proposal is subjected to technical consideration by the Department of Communications. If found to be feasible on these grounds, it is allocated a frequency and placed in the department's planning register available for public comment for thirty days.

At this stage the disparate procedures apply. Once public comment has been received, planning for new ABC and SBS outlets is transacted internally through direct negotiation between each of these two instrumentalities and the minister's department. To date there has been no formal structure established to enable the other two sectors, or indeed the public at large, to put forward formal submissions commenting on or critically appraising the government's plans for these two services. In other words, no regulatory mechanism at this critical stage requires government accountability for its planning policies in relation to the two publicly funded sectors.

On the other hand, the minister's planning role for new commercial and public stations is far more open to public scrutiny and involves the Australian Broadcasting Tribunal (ABT), an independent statutory authority with extensive regulatory powers vested in it under the Broadcasting and Television Act of 1948. Following the thirty-day public comment stage, if the minister decides that a planning proposal for a commercial or public station should proceed, it is passed on to the ABT for determination through the processes of a public inquiry. The ABT decides whether commercial or public licenses should be granted.

It should be noted that neither the ABC nor the SBS are licensed broadcasting operations. They are publicly funded government instrumentalities empowered to provide radio and television services under the act.

Commercial and public broadcasters are licensed to provide radio and television services, although at present no public broadcaster has yet been licensed to operate a television outlet. The government's communications platform, however, supports a development of this kind.

As licensed broadcasters, commercial and public operators have their licenses reviewed for renewal every three years. A few years ago the ABT commonly approached these through a public hearing process. Because most licensees do act responsibly and are genuinely serving their communities, the tribunal now more often than not renews licenses administratively, without a public hearing. Renewals for capital-city commercial radio and television stations are still heard publicly.

Whether there should be any triennial consideration of the government-funded ABC or whether SBS services should continue broadcasting over their dedicated frequencies is not questioned. To be fair, however, in 1986 the government conducted an extensive public inquiry into the whole operation of ABC and continued to pursue, again through an independent public inquiry, a major review of the SBS.

The ABT also determines program requirements that commercial and public broadcasters must observe. These standards are a condition of the license, and, theoretically at least, failure to observe them puts the security of the license at risk.

The Radio and Television Program Standards are quite separate, and the ABT endeavors to keep them under review. A public process also has been developed to facilitate amendments to the standards. The ABT publishes a notice of proposed amendments to the standards and invites public comment. Depending on the nature and extent of public reaction to the proposals, the ABT either proceeds with the amendments or reconsiders its position. If the proposal involves a highly sensitive aspect of programming, the tribunal may conduct a public hearing to allow community testimony.

The ABC and SBS traditionally had held that they too observe these program standards as a minimum benchmark. Be that as it may, neither of these sectors is required to demonstrate compliance.

Commercial radio and television operators also must observe advertising guidelines determined by the ABT. Again, while there is a similarity between the standards observed by commercial radio and television broadcasters, it is acknowledged that in structuring these guidelines the tribunal has endeavored to consider the distinctive nature of each of the two media.

As mentioned earlier, the public sector may not advertise as such. Sponsorship announcements are permitted, and these must be broadcast in accordance with ABT guidelines.

In 1977 the ABT conducted an extensive public inquiry into the concept of self-regulation for commercial broadcasters. In many ways the inquiry proved disappointing and undisciplined, culminating in a hurriedly written report that failed to address the brief. To date the inquiry has had but minimal effect on the size of the force deployed by the government and its agencies in regulating the broadcasting system. In fact, the inquiry chose largely to overlook considerable evidence indicating that the commercial radio and television industries for many years had observed, of their own volition, a range of codes and standards. They still do—and without any prompting by the ABT, the government itself, or any other group or agency.

For instance, the commercial radio and television operators have developed procedures whereby special divisions operating within the two industry associations—the Federation of Australian Radio Broadcasters (FARB) and the Federation of Australian Commercial Television Stations (FACTS)— check advertisements for adherence to the ABT's standards as well as local laws that might relate to the sale of the particular product or service being promoted.

Much of the regulatory mechanism, both government applied and industry initiated, has been ad hoc—at times almost a knee-jerk reaction to problems. Successive governments, regardless of political persuasion, have consciously avoided enunciating an overall national communications policy for Australia.

Probably the most significant policy review was the 1976 government inquiry into the Australian broadcasting system conducted by the Department of Post and Telecommunications (now the Department of Communications). There were no public hearings, but over six hundred submissions were presented for consideration. The inquiry report, known as the Green Report (after the departmental head F. J. Green who led the investigation) made several recommendations covering the planning, licensing, and funding of the Australian broadcasting services. In fact, the Australian government accepted many of the recommendations. Undoubtedly the most important was to abolish the Australian Broadcasting Control Board and to appropriate its technical and planning functions to the department. Its licensing and regulatory responsibilities became the prime concern of the new statutory authority, the ABT.

ECONOMIC STRUCTURE

The broadcasting and television act's ownership and control provisions limit the number of commercial radio and television licenses that can be controlled by any one person or licensed company. These provisions represent a fascinating, yet time-consuming study in their own right. In broad summary the complex situation is as follows: For commercial radio, section 90C of the act prohibits a prescribed interest in a license for

- more than one metropolitan commercial broadcasting station in any state;
- more than four metropolitan commercial broadcasting stations in Australia;
- more than four commercial broadcasting stations in any one state; and
- more than eight commercial broadcasting stations in Australia.

For commercial television, section 92 of the act prohibits a prescribed interest in a license for

- each of three or more licenses;
- each of two or more licenses for stations in a territory; and
- each of two or more licenses for stations in a state and within a radius of fifty kilometers of the general post office in the capital city of the state.

The act also treats a shareholding interest representing more than 15 percent of the voting rights or paid-up capital of a company as conferring a prescribed interest—potential control. In television, where shareholdings, in practice, are more widely spread, 15 percent may amount to a prescribed interest in some situations.

Each year in its annual report the ABT (and before it the Australian Broadcasting Control Board) publishes a complete listing of commercial radio and television licensee companies. Such a listing does not include the shareholding interests within these concerns, although in recent years much independent and careful research has been done.

In terms of revenue, during the 1982–83 financial year the following results were achieved:

Commercial radio—136 stations

Total revenue: $221,329,306
Total expenditures: $186,912,496
Net results before tax after license fee: $34,416,810
Net results after tax after license fee: $19,548,769

Commercial television—50 stations

Total revenue: $816,047,905
Total expenditures: $725,983,690
Net results before tax after license fee: $90,064,215
Net results after tax after license fee: $51,327,339

Commercial radio and television licensees are required to pay license fees in accordance with the Broadcasting Stations License Fees Act of 1964 and the Television Stations License Fees Act of 1964. Fees are payable on each anniversary of the date of commencement of a license and are calculated according to a series of complex formulas based on gross earnings. In the 1982–83 financial year, the following fees were paid to the Australian government: commercial radio, $3,676,626; and commercial television, $36,682,103.

During the same period, the Australian government funded the ABC to the extent of $274,175,000 and the SBS to $28,875,000. Direct basic government assistance to the public broadcasting sector amounted to $150,000. To put these figures into some perspective, they should be seen in relation to the nation's gross domestic product, which over the same period was $185,457,000.

Management and administrative practices in Australian broadcasting vary dramatically from sector to sector. Traditionally, the ABC had imposed upon it a management structure, personnel policies, and procedures that were associated with the public service. Until July 1, 1983, when the new Australian Broadcasting Corporation came into being, the administrative parameters were set out in the broadcasting act. With the advent of the corporation a new measure was introduced—the Australian Broadcasting Corporation Act—that includes provisions that are designed to remove some of the earlier administrative restrictions and provide for more organizational flexibility.

The corporation has a board of eight directors, including a chairperson, to which is answerable the chief executive officer—the managing director. That body appoints the managing director. The panel is responsible to Parliament and the minister of communications. The ABC is allowed considerable freedom in staffing arrangements; yet ABC staff members enjoy most of the benefits associated with public service employment.

The SBS has a similar structure to that of the ABC, but more modest. It is governed by a part-time chairperson and six part-time members appointed by the government. The service is managed by an executive director appointed by the governor-general of Australia. The staff of the SBS is employed directly under the provisions of the Public Service Act, which, administratively, places them in the more general public service category.

The management and administrative structures of public broadcasting stations vary considerably from station to station. In general terms, the policies of each station are developed by the station's part-time board and implemented by the manager of the station (usually a full-time employee) supervising a part-time staff. In addition, several of the public broadcasting stations operate in association with college and university campuses. In these circumstances, students frequently participate in the operation.

The commercial sector is comprised of radio and television businesses competing with each other for a greater share of the advertising dollar. They are operated according to conventional business practices, selling the commodity of airtime for advertising. Like any other private enterprise they seek the maximum return on investment, and the concept of profitability directs most decisions.

The commercial sector depends on advertising as its prime source of income. As mentioned earlier, certain constraints do apply to advertising, the principal ones being the Radio and Television Advertising Standards determined by the ABT. Advertising time standards also apply. For television, between the hours of 7:00 and 10:00 P.M. a maximum of eleven minutes of advertising may be broadcast each hour. Outside of these hours the basic hourly maximum is thirteen minutes. In either case no more than four advertisements are permitted in any program break. Commercial radio's time standards simply state that a licensee is entitled to transmit advertisements up to a maximum of eighteen minutes in every hour. Commercial radio and television broadcasters have chosen to disperse commercial content throughout their programming rather than to subscribe to the practice of providing for substantial blocks of advertising.

The training of broadcasters in Australia represents a subject for study in its own right. Private radio-announcing schools operate in capital cities training young announcers, who usually commence their careers in country stations with the hope that they will be discovered by one of the larger metropolitan operations.

In 1973 the Australian Film and Television School (AFTS) was established to provide advanced training in film and television production. It, too, is an independent statutory authority and in 1980 assumed a role in radio training. Through its full-time and open programs it provides courses in key areas of film and television production for directors, producers, writers, editors, and cameramen. In radio it has provided courses for broadcasters for all sectors.

In recent years the Federation of Australian Radio Broadcasters (FARB), in association with the University of New South Wales, has developed in-service training programs for senior management from the commercial radio industry. These short-term residential courses have had wide acceptance. The ABC for many years organized its own staff training and development programs for radio and television broadcasters.

PROGRAMMING

When the ABC was established in 1932, it was expected to provide adequate and comprehensive programming with a view to developing national unity and expressing a national identity. When it became a corporation, the ABC was given a charter that requires it to

1. provide innovative and comprehensive radio and television services of a high standard;
2. develop programs that contribute to a sense of national identity, inform and entertain, and reflect the cultural diversity of the Australian community;
3. create radio and television programs of an educational nature;
4. promote Australia's musical, dramatic, and other performing arts; and
5. transmit to other countries radio and television programs of news, current affairs, entertainment, and cultural enrichment.

The final stipulation relates to the overseas service, Radio Australia, operated by the ABC. As well as locally produced material, the ABC transmits a considerable amount of radio and television features imported from the United Kingdom.

The commercial television sector is committed to a more populist approach, providing, under Australian program requirements, almost 50 percent locally produced material. Locally produced television programs were once scorned by audiences, but today the local product dominates the lists of top-rated television series.

As with commercial television, advertising exerts a significant influence on the objectives and programming of the commercial radio industry. Commercial broadcasters cannot perform their function unless they are profitable. The need to be profitable acts as a spur to commercial managements to provide programs of wide popular appeal. They program to distinctive formats designed to appeal to specific demographic segments of the available radio audience. The most common demographic target usually is a specific age group, although socioeconomic characteristics (housewives, motorists) also dictate some commercial radio formats.

In single-station country markets, commercial radio stations usually provide programs that match, as far as possible, the characteristics of their audiences according to the particular time of day, the objective being to provide, in the course of a day, something for everybody.

The SBS, quite early in its history, developed a set of guidelines that illustrate that sector's underlying policy of providing radio and television programs for Australia's ethnic community. The guidelines exhort the state to

1. provide a medium for presenting to non-English-speaking residents of Australia entertainment, news, and other information in their own languages;
2. assist those from other cultures to maintain those cultures and to pass them on to their descendants and to other Australians;
3. provide information and advice on the rights and obligations of residence in Australia and on other matters to assist the non-English-speaking migrant to settle speedily, happily, and successfully;
4. encourage and facilitate the learning of English;
5. assist in promoting mutual understanding and harmony between and within ethnic groups and the English-speaking community;
6. avoid political partisanship.

In fulfilling this policy, the SBS broadcasts for 126 hours a week in 51 languages through radio station 3EA serving Melbourne and Geelong, and for 126 hours a week in 53 languages through 2EA serving Sydney, Newcastle, and Wollongong. It transmits multicultural television programs for 55 hours a week through its outlets in Sydney and Melbourne.

Public broadcasting stations, generally speaking, serve particular community interests. There are, for example, two classical music stations, several contemporary music outlets, stations providing programs consisting of a mix of popular music and community affairs, and other services for ethnic minorities.

There are two Christian-oriented facilities and a station with a link with a university union. This station serves mainly young tertiary-educated adults. There are ten others with licenses held by educational institutions; seven of these, as part of their output, provide programming for adult and continuing education.

Under the broadcasting act, licensees (not the ABC or the SBS) are required to broadcast or televise Divine Worship or other matter of a religious nature during such periods as the ABT determines and, if the ABT so directs, shall do so without charge. The ABT is quite liberal in its interpretation and administration of this section of the act; but public and commercial licensees, at their license renewals, are expected to demonstrate that they have observed the act's provisions in this regard. It should be mentioned that the ABC and SBS also provide religious features. The ABC has a department specifically dedicated to producing religious radio and television fare.

The ABC also has an education department that provides radio and television programs of an educational nature for children from preschool age through to senior secondary-school levels. The majority of these programs are produced by the corporation in Australia, but some relevant series are imported, principally from the United Kingdom. The ABC, in addition, provides educational radio and television programming of a less formal kind and of interest to a range of age groups.

The SBS also broadcasts informal educational material, as do individual public facilities, particularly those licensed to educational organizations. The commercial sector carries substantial amounts of informational fare, but because of the nature of its programming policies, these radio and television spots are generally intended for wider audience appeal.

In 1986 the tribunal developed new standards for children's television that commercial licensees are required to observe. Under these new rules commercial licensees must (each weekday)

1. continue the existing requirement that set aside the 4:00 to 5:00 P.M. weekday period for quality, age-specific children's programs;
2. ensure that 50 percent of those programs transmitted in a year be first-release Australian features;
3. limit the repetition of those programs and prohibit the practice of back-to-back scheduling of episodes or programs in the same series on the same day; and
4. transmit a minimum of eight hours of first-release Australian children's drama each financial year.

The commercial television industry opposed the extension of these standards.

BROADCAST REFORM

Over the past twelve or so years the Australian broadcasting system has been the subject of significant reforms. During that period the system has grown from two sectors to four sectors with the advent of public broadcasting and the SBS, both the result of government responding to reform movements.

As mentioned earlier, the government's own reform efforts flowed from its 1976 inquiry into the Australian broadcasting system (the Green Inquiry). A major outcome of that investigation was the establishment of the ABT, which through its public inquiry process enabled reform groups to air their grievances and enunciate their policies.

There is no doubt that many of these efforts have resulted in modifications to the system. As well as the Green Inquiry, the government precipitated reforms by conducting a range of other studies during this period. In addition, the government also initiated lesser, yet still important, examinations into a variety of systemic issues including localism, satellite program services, and cable and subscription television for Australia.

NEW TECHNOLOGIES

In 1985 Australia gained its first communications satellite, AUSSAT, put into orbit by the space shuttle. The establishment of a communications satellite system will be of considerable significance to Australia's remote and outback communities. Initially, the ABC will be a major user of this system and will reticulate its television service to 300,000 Australians who currently do not receive any television programs. The ABC's FM radio service will also be provided to these Australians via the satellite. In short, the satellite system will offer a range of broadcasting alternatives to those sectors wishing to make use of it for transmitting and relaying radio and television programs.

In 1982 the ABT conducted an inquiry initiated by the government into cable and subscription television services. Among other things, it recommended that Australia introduce cable television services (CTU) and subscription television (RSTV) as soon as practicable.

The Department of Communications has also continued to monitor and analyze communications developments, both overseas and within Australia. In the past year it has reviewed teletext, fiber optics, cellular radio, local area networks, satellite and cable television services, and earth station and switching technologies.

CONCLUSION/FORECAST

Australia is about to enter a new broadcasting era. Broadcasters know that new legislation is imminent; a series of policy-neutral amendments to the Broadcasting and Television Act of 1948 will render the legislation service-based rather than maintain an act that provides for the licensing of separate technical facilities. These particular amendments have wide industry support. Other amendments to the 1948 act have been foreshadowed that will make the ABT's powers, particularly in relation to its program and advertising standards, more definitive and less confusing.

In this situation, greater responsibility will be given to individual licensees in the administration and programming of their stations, and they will be called to public account at their license renewal inquiries. There should be a growth in the number of commercial radio stations using the FM mode in country areas, and thus there should be a demand for additional staff resources. The national sector, because it is publicly funded, will continue to be the subject of public scrutiny as its critics and supporters assess its performance with particular reference to its new charter. The same will apply to the SBS.

Overall, the system seems fragile. Hopefully, governments in the immediate future will not blindly accept new technologies before assessing whether they are appropriate for the nation. In this regard, the government's recent decision to postpone consideration of the introduction of cable and subscription services is encouraging. In a similar vein, it is hoped that future governments will resist the temptation to intrude directly at a political level in the development of communications policies and plans.

BIBLIOGRAPHY

Armstrong, Mark. *Broadcasting Law and Policy in Australia.* Sydney: Butterworths, 1982.

Armstrong, Mark, Michael Blakeney, and Ray Watterson. *Media Law in Australia.* London: Oxford University Press, 1983.

Australia. Broadcasting Control Board. *Frequency Modulation Broadcasting.* Melbourne: Australian Broadcasting Control Board, 1972.

———. Broadcasting Tribunal. "Satellite Program Services." *Inquiry into the Regulation of the Use of Satellite Program Services by Broadcasters.* Canberra: Australian Government Publishing Service, 1984.

———. Broadcasting Tribunal. *Self Regulation for Broadcasters: A Report on the Public Inquiry into the Concept of Self Regulation for Australian Broadcasters.* Canberra: Australian Government Publishing Service, 1977.

———. Department of Communications. *Localism in Australian Broadcasting: A Review of the Policy.* Canberra: Australian Government Publishing Service, 1984.

———. Department of the Media. *Public Broadcasting: Report by the Working Party to the Minister for the Media.* Canberra: Australian Government Publishing Service, 1975.

———. Postal and Telecommunications Department. *Australian Broadcasting: A Report on the Structure of the Australian Broadcasting System and Associated Matters.* Canberra: Australian Government Publishing Service, 1976.

Australian Advertising Industry Council. *Self Regulation in Australian Advertising.* Sydney: Australian Advertising Industry Council, 1982.

Barnes, Shenagh, and Michael Blakeney. *Advertising Regulation.* Sydney: The Law Book Company Limited, 1982.

Brown, A. *Australian Media Ownership.* Queensland: University of Queensland Press, 1977.

Dix, Alex et al. *The ABC in Review: National Broadcasting in the 1980s.* 5 vols. Canberra: Australian Government Publishing Service, 1981.

Harrison, Kate. *Press and Television Interests in Australian Commercial Radio.* Sydney: Federation of Australian Radio Broadcasters, 1982.

Inglis, K. S. *This Is the ABC: The Australian Broadcasting Commission, 1932–1983.* Carlton: Melbourne University Press, 1983.

McLean, F. C. *Report on Independent Inquiry into Frequency Modulation Broadcasting.* Canberra: Australian Government Publishing Service, 1974.

O'Dwyer, Brendan, ed. *Broadcasting in Australia, Today's Issues and the Future: Proceedings of the National Conference Held in July 1980 at the Australian National University.* Canberra: Center for Continuing Education, 1980.

Thomas, Alan. *Broadcast and Be Damned: The ABC's First Two Decades.* Carlton: Melbourne University Press, 1980.

Walker, R. R. *The Magic Spark: The Story of the First Fifty Years of Radio in Australia.* Melbourne: Hawthorn Press, 1983.

White, Brian. *White on the Media.* Melbourne: Cassell Australia, 1975.

AUSTRIA

Benno Signitzer and Kurt Luger

HISTORY

The Austrian Broadcasting Corporation (ORF) celebrated its sixtieth anniversary in 1984. This presented an occasion for assessing the history of broadcasting that has reflected the political, social, and economic developments of the nation. Both communications researchers and the ORF used this event to evaluate the medium as it came of age in the mid-1980s. Of course, such an evaluation took into consideration the dynamic and important effect television has had on Austrian history. In fact, television has come to be the most pervasive of all the media in the postwar era. Whatever the time lag may have been in the past, today Austria is certainly a full-fledged broadcasting nation.

The inception of radio as an organized activity occurred on October 1, 1924. The organizational unit responsible for radio's first operation was called Radio Verkehrs AG (RAVAG). From the very first transmission, the interest groups that were to determine the development of broadcasting in Austria to the present exercised considerable influence. These organizations included domestic and foreign economic groups such as the banking and equipment industry, political parties, government, and private citizens.

Technical and programming operations of the 1920s were characterized by a host of activities including the evolution from studio-based productions to outdoor transmissions. In 1925 the first broadcast from the Salzburg Festival took place. Shortly thereafter, transmissions occurred from stations in Munich, Zurich, and Prague. In 1928 the one hundredth anniversary of Franz Schubert's death marked the beginning of European programming exchanges, with more than forty-five stations commemorating the event by simultaneous broadcasts. By 1933 programs from the Salzburg Festival had become a regular feature of European programming schedules. These efforts enjoyed great success with listeners all over Europe.

The late 1920s also witnessed the first experiments with shortwave transmissions, the use of recorded music, and the first direct (live) coverage of political, cultural, and sporting events. In short, the period 1924 to 1929 is often nostalgically referred to as "the good time of beautiful ole RAVAG," symbolizing an epoch of pioneering creativity and relative freedom from outside encroachment.

With the establishment of an authoritarian regime in 1933, the deterioration of radio began. At the same time, the pressure by Nazi Germany had been continually stepped up, which ultimately led to the *Anschluss* of 1938. Acutely aware of radio's potential as a propaganda weapon, Joseph Goebbels incited a veritable "radio war" against Austria during the period 1933 to 1938, which prompted the Austrian government to jam these broadcasts. Powerful transmitters near Munich sent massive Nazi propaganda over the airwaves into Austria that rallied support for "Greater German" aspirations. By 1938 the struggle for Austria's independence had failed. With the occupation by German forces, RAVAG was turned into an integral part of the propaganda department of the Nazi government. Organizationally, radio became part of the "Greater German Broadcasting" entity, which was centrally controlled by the Berlin headquarters. RAVAG personnel was purged and streamlined among ideological and racist lines. Some of the provincial stations that had enjoyed a certain measure of autonomy in the past (such as Salzburg and Innsbruck) were integrated into neighboring units in Munich and Stuttgart. Listening to foreign broadcasts was considered a crime punishable by death.

Immediately after Austria's liberation in 1945, some of the early broadcast pioneers of the 1920s began to set up a new system that operated under the supervision of the Allied Powers—the United States, the Soviet Union, Great Britain, and France. This situation continued until 1955 when Austria regained its full independence and sovereignty. During the period 1945 to 1955 the occupation powers exercised a considerable measure of control over the development of postwar broadcasting. They used the medium for their own political purposes and imposed their respective national models of media philosophy and organization. The Western models certainly have had a greater effect on the further development of Austrian broadcasting than any other scheme. Eventually, it was the British model of a publicly chartered organizational arrangement (British Broadcasting Corporation) that finally prevailed and continues to function as a guideline to broadcasting in Austria. Throughout the occupation, the restitution of broadcasting to full Austrian control had been frequently promoted by the Austrian authorities. Finally, this goal was reached in 1955 when the occupational powers left the nation.

In 1957 the legal and organizational foundation for broadcasting in post-

war Austria was created by the federal government. This coincided with
the introduction of television, which has operated in the same organizational
model as radio ever since. The period after 1957 was not only characterized
by the development of television but also by public disenchantment with
the influence of the two large political parties (the Conservative People's
party and the Socialist party), which united in the so-called Grand Coalition
from 1945 to 1966. The coalition exercised considerable control over the
operation of broadcasting, including interference in personnel and programming decisions. In 1964 public disapproval of these intrusive practices
reached an all-time high and resulted in a public referendum separating
broadcasting from partisan political influence. In this effort the independent
newspapers played a key role. Intending to reduce the influence of broadcasting and its competition as an advertising medium, the newspapers
pushed the referendum through the political process. The election led to a
restructuring of the Austrian Broadcasting Corporation (ORF). Since then
it has enjoyed a considerable measure of political and economic independence from governmental domination. A second reorganization followed in
1974, giving the ORF the status of an autonomous financial body. In effect,
the federal constitutional law of July 10, 1974, safeguarded the independence of the broadcasting corporation from government interference. In
addition, the law promoted objectivity and impartiality in news reporting,
the multiplicity of opinion, balanced programming, and the independence
of ORF employees. Broadcasting had come of age.

REGULATION

Broadcasting in Austria is based on a publicly chartered national institution, the Austrian Broadcasting Corporation (ORF). The essential traits
of its organizational and legal structure include the following components:

1. Radio and television are organized under a single broadcasting structure.
2. The Austrian Broadcasting Corporation is a publicly chartered unit modeled after
   the British Broadcasting Corporation and is obliged to work according to the
   principle of "public service."
3. The ORF is a legal monopoly.
4. Local participation is required through the existence of provincial ORF stations,
   one for each of the nine provinces.

The Austrian Broadcasting Corporation was established by two separate
measures: the federal constitutional law of 1974 and the Broadcasting Act
of 1974 entitled "Tasks and Operation of Austrian Broadcasting." The
constitutional law, ensuring the independence of broadcasting, defined the
medium to include both wireless and cable operations. The ORF is thus
seen as an entity of "public service" that has to follow certain basic guide-

lines to ensure objectivity, impartiality, multiplicity of opinion, balanced programming, and the freedom of journalistic expression.

Operational standards concerning the organization of the agency and the overall framework of programming are specified in the 1974 Broadcasting Act. The act provides the basis for the broadcasting monopoly by issuing a license for broadcasting operation to only one organization, the Austrian Broadcasting Corporation (ORF).

The legal seat of the ORF is Austria's capital, Vienna. The ORF is endowed with a "juridical personality" and is to be operated on a nonprofit basis. In advertising matters the ORF follows the commercial code. The broadcasting act states further that the ORF is to produce at least two television and three radio programs (one of the latter is to be produced by the provincial ORF outlets). Furthermore, specific guidelines concerning the range of program content include comprehensive information for the public, educational features, limitations on advertising, and restrictions on objectionable entertainment fare.

The ORF is headed by a director general. Program planning is the responsibility of the director for radio and two directors for television. Each of the nine regional studios has its own provincial director. Furthermore, the technical and commercial departments have their own managers. The directors of radio and television are appointed by the board of trustees, a body with thirty-five members. Of these, six are nominated by the government on the recommendation of the parliamentary parties and in direct proportion to their representation in the lower house of Parliament. The provinces nominate one member each, the government appoints nine additional members, six are picked by the representatives of the radio and television subscribers' association, and five are chosen from the central employees' council of the ORF.

There are two more official bodies within the ORF: the radio and television subscribers' organization, comprising thirty-five members, and the auditing commission, which carries on the annual review of the ORF operations.

The exercise of the federal administration's legal supervision of the ORF is the responsibility of a special commission for the implementation of the radio and television act. This panel consists of seventeen members, of whom nine must be judges, while four are appointed by the representatives of the radio and television subscribers and four by the ORF's central employees' council.

As early as 1973 editorial statutes were ratified containing provisions for safeguarding the impartiality of news reporting and the independence of journalists in the ORF. The relevant legislation states explicitly that the ORF must respect "the independence and autonomous responsibility of all staff members involved in program production and the freedom of journalist staff in carrying out the duties assigned to them." In addition, editorial guidelines have to be established for journalists guaranteeing professional independence, legal protection, and participation in all personnel and substantive decisions affecting them.

ORF's organizational and control structure is designed to ensure that all significant views in society are fully and fairly represented in Austrian broadcasting. As can be seen, the ORF's intricate administrative structure is an attempt to develop the ideal balance between social responsiveness and political independence.

It should be noted, however, that the requirements of this ideal are not often met. For one thing, social representation is largely defined in terms of established groups and organizations, not the population at large. Second, partisan politics remains strong, and existing political relationships usually prevail in personnel, programming, and management decisions. Finally, the so-called "social and economic partnership" strongly affects broadcasting in terms of defining the parameters of such basic notions as objectivity and balance, but also in the area of personnel decisions. In sum, an evaluation of the ORF's basic organizational and administrative philosophy would include the following generalization: while the concept of a public charter has its inherent merits in that it has shielded broadcasting from the more overt commercial and political pressures and essentially has succeeded in maintaining and reflecting existing power relations in society, it has tended to perform poorly when broadcasting's purpose is to promote social, political, and cultural innovation and to extend democracy beyond established boundaries.

ECONOMIC STRUCTURE

The ORF is by far the largest media corporation in Austria, with more than 3,200 employees and several thousand freelance workers. In 1985 its revenue reached 5.4 billion Austrian schillings (approximately U.S. $360 million).

The ORF is financed by the collection of fees from radio and television subscribers, legally termed "program remuneration." The rate of remuneration is determined by a board of trustees so as to ensure, in accordance with the relevant provisions of the broadcasting act, that cost-covering conditions are maintained in the ORF's discharge of its public duties. Regulations make allowance for the inclusion of paid advertising time in the ORF's programming, with a special clause barring commercial spots from one of the radio programs. Generally, daily advertising time is limited to 120 minutes on radio and 20 minutes on television. Television advertisements appear in blocks between programs; they do not interrupt the individual features.

More than one-third of the ORF revenue was raised from advertising, 57 percent from subscription fees, and the rest from other sources, such as selling broadcasting rights. Approximately half of the expenditures are devoted to personnel costs such as salaries and pension funds, the other half to direct program expenditures and other costs.

By October 1, 1985, there were 2.6 million radio and 2.4 million television subscribers in Austria. With this accomplishment, the saturation point has been reached. The "program remuneration" varies from province to province due to regional taxation policies. On the average, the monthly fee is 170 Austrian schillings (U.S. $11.30).

Due to the mountainous terrain in the Eastern Alps, it is necessary to operate a great number of broadcasting transmitters for which the ORF has responsibility. This factor, as well as the disadvantages of a restricted and limited market of only 2.7 million households (leading to extremely low advertising rates and a small audience), has resulted in one of Europe's highest subscription fees. In these circumstances, low-income groups are exempt from paying the tax.

PROGRAMMING

The ORF broadcasts about 139 hours of radio and 20 hours of television every day. On a yearly average, about 28 percent of the airtime is entertainment, 17 percent information, and 16 percent educational/cultural features. Almost half of a viewer's time devoted to television is used for entertainment, 16 percent for informational programs, and 7 percent for educational/cultural fare.

In 1984, 39 percent of the television programs consisted of domestic ORF productions, 35 percent were purchased from foreign companies, and 25 percent were repeats (which in ORF statistics are listed separately; at least half of the repeats are to be considered foreign productions). The proportion of foreign programs is more than 40 percent of the total transmission time and about 60 percent during prime time. These figures include coproductions in which Austrian television participates.

Facing growing competition from satellites, cable television, and home video as well as from private radio stations across the borders, the ORF strategy concentrates on two aims: first, the improvement and expansion of specific national and regional information; and second, the purchase or coproduction of foreign entertainment, especially movies and light entertainment such as soap operas and series.

At present, half of all the programs are produced by the ORF-TV (repeats included). About 20 percent of the budget is used for Austrian-made entertainment programs that fill only 10 percent of the entire transmission time. Twenty-five percent of this transmission time is used for purchased movies and serials that only amount to 4 percent of the budget. To keep costs low, the ORF is buying inexpensive series-type programs, many of them of West German, English, or U.S. origin. Observers have called this a creeping "self-commercialization" of the public broadcasting system.

ORF-TV has had to compete with both public and private television stations in neighboring nations in terms of over-the-air operations, and with foreign satellites and cable programs. No less than one-third of the Austrian audience can receive foreign television programs over the air. In addition, some 300,000 Austrian households receive German and Swiss public television programs as well as those from the private satellites "Sky Channel" and "Sat 1" via cable. The commercial satellite programs contain mostly entertainment fare.

Austrian radio is more decentralized than is radio in most other European countries. Each of the nine provincial outlets transmits nine hours of regional programs daily. The two other radio channels broadcast nationally, some of their programs being produced in Vienna, some of them as regional contributions to the national broadcasts.

Only three out of the nine Austrian provinces have more than 1,000,000 inhabitants, and five have less then 500,000. The respective radio markets thus serve fairly small audiences. In provinces where the regional programs face competition from private radio stations operating from Italy, the ORF radio programs have become more popularized with more light and local content.

NEW TECHNOLOGIES

New communication technologies have been introduced to Austria since the beginning of the 1980s. In general, this development has occurred under cautious auspices in a still largely regulated environment. Part of this approach is due to the policy of ORF monopoly, part to the economic restrictions of a small market.

There are some 200 registered cable operators serving some 300,000 community antenna television (CATV) households. The overwhelming majority of these systems are small sized; only four of them serve larger communities. The cable operators are restricted by federal regulations that only allow simultaneous transmission of the ORF and other foreign programs but that do not allow program production and transmission by the cable systems themselves (thus defending the ORF monopoly).

Teletext, a supplementary service by the ORF, reaches about 5 percent of the TV households, which is about half the share of the CATV penetration. The introduction of teletext did not require special legislation, as it has been considered to fall clearly within the scope of broadcasting activities.

The pilot videotext phase by 1985 had given way to regular operation. This was made possible by the successful conclusion of negotiations involving the Post, Telephone, and Telegraph (PTT) and the social and economic partners on such issues as consumer and data protection. Respective draft legislation began preparation.

As far back as 1981 the ORF announced fairly ambitious plans concerning a joint satellite television project with the Swiss. Budgetary considerations have in the meantime led to a more modest involvement in a joint satellite of the three public broadcasting networks—SRG (Switzerland), ZDF (West Germany), and ORF—called 3-SAT. From a legal and regulatory viewpoint, a satellite is to be considered just like any other terrestrial transmitter licensed by the PTT. The setting up and operation of the transmitter remains in the sole domain of the ORF monopoly, and this holds true for satellite projects as well. In 1986 the ORF considered participation in the West German direct broadcasting satellite (DBS) "TV-SAT" to be launched during the next two years.

Home video's growth rate has been truly remarkable; penetration increased from 3 percent of the households in 1982 to 11 percent in 1985. In addition, some 6,000 video films were available in some 400 video rental shops.

BROADCAST REFORM

Broadcast reform and criticism is as old as the medium itself. From the beginning of radio, different societal forces have attempted to influence both its structure and program content. In the past, various reform groups and political parties have centered their criticism around such themes as political bias, high culture versus low culture, personnel policies and decisions, lack of representation for social groups, and lack of audience participation.

In fact, as far back as the 1920s attempts at alternative patterns of radio use and philosophy were made by the so-called "Free Radio Association," founded in 1924. This organization focused on furthering the interests of the worker class. Organized in more than one hundred local groups, its roughly 20,000 members explored possibilities for participatory radio use including critical comment on RAVAG programs and guidelines for political use of the new medium.

Throughout most of its development, Austrian broadcasting has been characterized by a tension between attempts at professionalism on the part of journalists and program producers on the one hand and bureaucratic restrictions on the other. While such tensions between organizations and professions are quite common in many fields, in Austria the situation is even more complex, as bureaucracies very often manifest themselves as mechanisms of party control. So it has been with the ORF. At its worst, the concept of public broadcasting has been misused as a license for political interference in a narrow partisan sense.

Nevertheless, many observers would still value the potential benefits of a public broadcasting system higher than its possible disadvantages. The issue of the broadcasting monopoly lies at the heart of the contemporary debates over the future of broadcasting and the entire communication system in Austria.

CONCLUSION/FORECAST

Broadcasting policy in Austria is designed to successfully confront competition from space, cable, and video. Such efforts include the following:

1. Development of a corporate identity within the ORF system
2. Organizational streamlining that involves both centralization of decision-making processes and more regionalization of television programming
3. Broad attempts at making all ORF programs more popular with viewers and listeners
4. Emphasis on highlighting the "Austrianness" in program production
5. Localization of radio production and programming
6. Large-scale buying of rights for some 1,200 feature films, most of them originating in the United States.
7. Reducing competition over advertising by means of an agreement with the Newspaper Publishers' Association (including a three-year commitment not to alter the existing balance of influence between electronic and print media)
8. Pilot engagement in satellite activities

In other terms, the ORF seems ready to steer a cautious line between maintaining the public service ideal and self-commercialization. By developing this strategy, the ORF hopes to survive in new circumstances where it will no longer be in a position of controlling the market. Public access, however, has not figured into the strategic consideration of the ORF management.

Notwithstanding the strong influence of the state sector, there is no coherent and coordinated public policy on the media and technology. Certain elements of such a policy have nevertheless begun to surface. These include such items as state support for programs of high technological development with a view to keeping abreast of technological innovation; maintenance of a declared commitment to the ORF monopoly; keeping a delicate balance between publicly organized broadcasting and the privately owned printed press industry; and attempts toward a definition of national interest in media and communications matters with some protectionist elements in the field of foreign trade. One expression of such national interest considerations is certainly the 1985 agreement between the ORF and the Austrian Newspaper Publishers' Association, which is designed to reduce ruinous competition over advertising income.

The above-mentioned major involvement of the government should not disguise the fact that the very dynamics behind communications developments has originated outside Austria. The multinational electronics industry is the driving force with the ultimate goal of turning each and every Austrian television set into a multifunctional home terminal.

BIBLIOGRAPHY

Fabris, Hans Heinz, ed. *Auswirkungen der Einführung neuer Medien in Österreich.* Vienna: Bohmann, 1984.
Fabris, Hans Heinz, K. Luger, and B. Signitzer. "Das Rundfunksystem Österreichs." In *Internationales Handbuch für Rundfunk und Fernsehen.* Hamburg: Hans-Bredow Institut, 1986.
Institut für Publizistik und Kommunikationswissenschaft der Universität Salzburg. *Massenmedien in Österreich—Medienbericht I, II, III.* Vienna: Internationale Publikationen Gesellschaft, 1977, 1983, 1986.
Lenhardt, H. *Teure neue Medien.* Salzburg: Salzburger Landespresseburo, 1983.
Luger, K. "Der Österreichische Rundfunk im Zeitalter der neuen Medien." In *Österreichisches Jahrbuch für Kommunikationswissenschaft,* no. 3 (Vienna: Bohlau, 1986), 71–92.
Luger, K., and H. Pürer. "Rundfunk in Österreich." In *Praktischer Journalismus in Zeitung, Radio und Fernsehen,* edited by H. Pürer. 377–90. Salzburg: Kuratorium für Journalistenausbildung, 1985.
ORF. *Almanach 1983.* Vienna: ORF, 1983.
Signitzer, B. "Österreich im internationalen Mediensystem—Beziehungen und Abhängigkeiten." In *Rundfunk und Fernsehen* 30, no. 1: (1985): 33–46.
Signitzer, B., and W. Amanshauser. "Austria Seeking an Answer to Sky Channel." *Intermedia* 12, no. 3 (1986): 6–7.
Signitzer, B., and K. Luger. *Radio in Austria.* Comparative Studies on the Socioeconomic Aspects of National Communications Systems. Paris: UNESCO, 1983.

BELGIUM

G. Fauconnier and Dirk De Grooff

HISTORY

The history of radio in Belgium began with the inauguration of the French-language station, Radio-Belgique, on November 24, 1923. Radio-Belgique was founded by SBR, the first Belgian company to specialize in the production of radio receivers. Initially, the station primarily transmitted music, setting aside some time for press reports. Gradually time devoted to newscasts increased. Radio-Belgique also sold commercial spots to private firms and to political and ideological groups.

Five years later, in 1928, the first Dutch-language broadcaster, Vlaamse Radio-Vereniging (VRV), was established in Antwerp. Meanwhile, the most important ideological groups in Belgium were also preparing their own radio stations—in 1929 the Katholieke Vlaamse Radio-Omroep (KVRO) and the Socialistische Arbeiders Radio-Omroep voor Vlaanderen (SAROV) started to broadcast. Somewhat later, the Liberale Radio-Omroep (Librado) and the Vlaams Nationale Radio-Vereniging (VLANARA) began.

In official circles the concept of a public station gained favor. The law of June 18, 1930, cleared the path, and on July 1, 1930, the Belgisch Nationaal Instituut voor Radio-Omroep/Institut National de Radio Diffusion (NIR/INR) started up. The broadcast law stipulated the NIR/INR to be a national institute that would utilize the services of existing broadcasters. The law further required complete impartiality in news reporting and prohibited advertising. Furthermore, the law prescribed the sources of income for the NIR/INR—in addition to gifts, legacies, loans, and subsidies from public administration, the NIR/INR would also receive a state grant equal to 90 percent of the radio tax. There was one director general and one director for each language group for the "spoken" broadcast.

Simultaneously with the NIR/INR, about sixteen local and private radio stations began operating. By the early 1930s they had developed into commercial radio outlets. At the beginning of World War II their broadcasting licenses were withdrawn by the Regie van Telegrafie en Telefonie (RTT, Telegraph and Telephone Administration), and a few weeks later the German occupying forces started to use them to jam BBC broadcasts.

During the war the national stations were also seized. In 1942 the government-in-exile in London founded the Belgische Nationale Dienst voor Radio-Omroep (BNRO), over which it maintained control. After the war the BNRO was abolished, and by the law of September 14, 1945, the NIR/INR received a commission to resume broadcasting. For the first time, regional stations were established under the authority of the NIR/INR. Broadcasting licenses for the private stations were not renewed, and these organizations gradually disappeared.

Between 1945 and 1953 the NIR/INR expanded enormously. Production and program capabilities doubled. German-language Belgians received their own broadcasting times in 1948 under the alternating management of the NIR (later the BRT, Belgische Radio en Televisie) and the INR (later the RTBF, Radio et Television Belge-Française. In 1955 a third outlet started, though on a very modest scale. These broadcasting initiatives occurred in a period fraught with financial difficulties. The arrival of television in 1953 further exacerbated the situation by severely draining radio personnel.

The official start of television on October 31, 1953, culminated two years of technical preparation. It had been preceded by a tug-of-war between the Flemish and the Walloons regarding the choice of a picture norm. The French-speaking Belgians chose the French 819-line form, while the Flemish opted for the 625-line standard used by the other European nations. Ultimately, in compromise Belgian television sets were fitted for both norms; consequently, the sets cost more than those in surrounding countries.

Broadcast time in 1953 amounted to twelve hours per week. In Antwerp and Liege, relay transmitters were built to direct the NIR/INR national stations to serve 6 million Belgians. Of these 6 million, 15,000 had television sets. By 1956 there were already 72,000 sets, while in the 1958 season, when signals could be received throughout the entire nation, 130,000 families had televisions, on which, by the way, they were taxed.

Seven years after the first television transmissions, it was ruled that the new medium deserved its own legal status and should no longer be regulated under the radio law of June 18, 1930. The broadcast law of May 18, 1960, abolished the NIR/INR and created the Belgische Radio en Televisie for Dutch programs (BRT), Radio et Television Belge for French programs (RTBF), and the Instituut van de Gemeenschappelijke Diensten (Institute of Common Services). They formed three separate institutions, an early sign of a growing trend toward cultural autonomy for the two communities. This cultural autonomy was carried through to administration, finances, technology, and world communications with the law of July 21, 1971, which stipulated that radio and television came under the authority of the cultural councils.

Also in 1971, three years later than in neighboring nations, color television was introduced in Belgium. In that same year (for the first time), public stations were confronted with a large and rapidly expanding number of competing cable television stations.

The law of February 18, 1977, again extended cultural autonomy by dissolving the unitary Instituut van de Gemeenschappelijke Diensten and dividing its personnel and equipment between the BRT and the RTBF. In addition, a new public institute was established, the Belgisches Rundfunk- und Fernsehzentrum für deutschsprachige Sendungen (BRF, Belgian Radio and Television Center for German-Language Transmissions) for the German-speaking Belgians from the East Cantons. Each of the three agencies, BRT, RTBF, and BRF, is now an independent public institution with its own legal status and managing board of directors chosen by the respective cultural councils.

In 1977 the BRT and the RTBF doubled their offerings; from that time Belgium has had four nationally distributed television channels—BRT 1 and 2 and RTBF 1 and 2.

REGULATION

In Belgium radio and television are cultural matters under the authority of the Flemish or the French community in application of the constitution and of the special law of August 8, 1980. Broadcasting of communications from the national government, transmission of commercial advertising, regulation and assignment of frequencies, and the system of the right of reply remain the domain of the national legislature.

The law of February 18, 1977, states that the stations are obliged to broadcast eight hours of communications from the government per month without charge. The right to reply is regulated in the law of June 23, 1961, while the assignment for frequencies is prescribed in the decree of April 9, 1965.

With regard to commercial advertising, the law of May 18, 1980, remains in force. This law regulates the organization of stations. Section 3 states, "It is forbidden for the institutes to transmit broadcasts that have the character of commercial advertising."

With these exceptions, broadcasting regulation comes under the authority of the two communities. The decree of December 28, 1979, regulates the status of the Dutch-language station BRT, while that of the French-language RTBF is determined by the decree of December 12, 1979. These decrees regulate both the authority, the organization, and the structure of the stations. In addition, these decrees contain specifications regarding delegation of broadcast time to organizations and foundations and to political parties so that by law no monopoly is assigned to the BRT and the RTBF (or the BRF). The national stations are obliged to give third parties the opportunity to make their own television programs by providing personnel and material support. These organizations must be noncommercial associations or foundations with the sole objective of broadcasting programs intended to provide information or opinions regarding current events. The amount of airtime for these third parties is specified by the king each year in a decree discussed with the executive councils of both the Dutch and French communities.

Although commercial advertising is forbidden on the BRT and the RTBF, the French executive council promulgated a decree in 1983 regulating commercial announcements on radio and television. The decree stated that advertising may not contain trademarks or names of private concerns. In practice, there are promotional messages from public institutions or nonprofit organizations (professional groups, social, cultural, and scientific societies, and athletic organizations). On the same day, another decree was approved that facilitated the introduction of pay television in the Walloon portion of the nation.

At the end of the 1970s the phenomenon of "free radio" became very popular in Belgium. In a short time, over 1,000 of these local radio stations emerged throughout the nation. Since in Belgium public broadcasting has a de facto monopoly on the transmission of radio and television programs, these free radio operations conducted business illegally. After over a decade, the authorities are busy recognizing these outfits on the basis of decrees issued by the Flemish and Walloon regional governments. These decrees provide conditions to be satisfied by the local radio facilities in exchange for government recognition. The most important include ownership by a nonprofit organization, technical equipment conforming to the technical specifications of the decree of August 20, 1981, and independence from political parties, professional organizations, and commercial groups.

Finally, in June 1985 a decree was approved permitting advertising on the free radios. The 1985 action restricted advertising to time blocks of a maximum of seven minutes per hour and prohibited advertising having any political, trade union, religious, or philosophical slant.

Regulating the transmission of radio and television programs via cable is reserved to the national legislature. The decree of December 24, 1966, concerning cable distribution still provides the basic structure for all cable activities. This decree contains stipulations regarding authorization, technical specifications, rates and taxes, and program restrictions.

This decree also states that each distribution network must transmit all the programs of the BRT and the RTBF simultaneously and integrally. The distributor may carry the broadcasts of other television outlets if they are licensed in the nation where the station is established. Interestingly enough, commercial advertising is still prohibited.

In Wallonia the decree of May 1976 (amending the 1966 law) allowed distribution of strictly cultural programs by local broadcasting associations. As of 1986 a dozen networks have received permission to do so.

Although the 1966 decree prohibited the distribution of advertising, this is not applied in practice. Programs from foreign commercial stations are carried on the network. "Cutting" advertising contained in these programs would be very expensive and ultimately would be charged back to the cable subscriber. The RTT, therefore, tolerates the distribution of foreign features interspersed with advertising.

ECONOMIC STRUCTURE

The BRT, RTBF, and BRF are public institutions, each with its own legal status. Each organization is managed by a board of directors, the members of which are chosen for specific terms by the cultural councils of the respective communities. The minister of the cultural community can participate in meetings of the board of directors with a consultative vote. Moreover, the BRT, RTBF, and BRF are financially controlled by the state. The institutes receive their income from the funds that the councils of each cultural community allocate to broadcasting. These funds consist of a particular percentage of the money the state collects each year from taxes on radio and television sets. Furthermore, the stations can have income from loans contingent on prior approval, from the sale of publications, and from the rental of productions, as well as from fees for services provided to third parties. (The institutes promote such services as the production, broadcasting, and sale of programs, the establishment, maintenance, and use of the technical infrastructure and the transmission of programs via cable and satellite.)

In addition, the RTBF can establish and operate regional production centers and associated stations. In short, the three broadcasting organizations are important service enterprises and are interwoven closely with the economic life of the nation.

It is impossible to categorize "free radio" stations in Belgium. Sprouting like weeds since the end of the 1970s, they have begun from diverse political, cultural, ideological, and commercial motivations with diverse resources and people. Since broadcasting commercial advertising had been expressly prohibited, most of the "free radio" stations initially depended on contributions from local sponsors or raised money through a host of projects including dances, contests, and appearances. Before advertising became allowed, however, many local outfits inserted surreptitious advertising in their broadcasts, even suffering prosecutions in some cases. After commercials were permitted on "free radio" stations, virtually all of them began to advertise. Although forbidden to do so by the government, many of the "free radio" outlets then formed national networks with common advertising management. Such chains were often run by newspaper or magazine publishers.

Since the first cable network appeared in the late 1960s, purely private companies (50 percent), government agencies run by the municipalities (35 percent), and mixed outfits with participation of both the municipal authorities and private organizations—mostly gas and electrical companies—(15 percent) have operated in Belgium. While the distributors provide their services for payment, the state secretary for the Telegraph and Telephone Administration determines maximum connection and subscription rates. Besides the annual cable connection fee a fixed charge is added (1985: BF 500) to cover the copyright costs paid by the cable operators to various authors' organizations.

PROGRAMMING

The public stations, the BRT, and the RTBF each have several radio networks that broadcast continuously and try to complement each other as much as possible. Each network puts programs together according to special criteria proper to each channel. For example, the BRT 1 and the RTBF 1 primarily feature news and interpretation, press reviews, sports reports, traffic information, and the like. The BRT 2 and the RTBF 2 support various regional stations that broadcast regional news and background information. Music is popular on these outlets as well. The BRT 3 and the RTBF 3 are the so-called cultural outlets that offer more serious oral presentations along with a great deal of classical music. The newest stations, the Flemish (BRT) outlet "Studio Brussel" and the French-language (RTBF) Channel 21, are directed to listeners who live or work in Brussels. Both facilities feature popular music and game shows along with information about Brussels. Finally, within the BRT radio services there is also the Wereldomroep, (World Broadcasting) outlet providing informational programs for Belgians living outside the nation as well as features for non-Belgians.

Nonpublic radio station programming consists largely of popular music, general and local news, and local advertising. General news is mostly compiled, although more local outlets are taking their news from newspaper publishers, who send the information to associated "free radio" stations via telex or videotext, generally in exchange for mention of the newspaper in the broadcasts.

National television programming services are divided into different departments, each of which are again split up into several production centers. At the BRT, for example, this division encompasses culture (art, youth broadcasts, leisure time, and sciences), entertainment (talk and game shows, light music, serious music, and drama), programming and services (program purchases, production facilities, and program editing), information (news, interpretation, and sports), and instructive telecasts (adult education, school features, and guest programs). In addition to these program departments, there are also technical services and administrative and financial services.

Approximately 65 percent of the total production volume is produced by its own staff or in collaboration with external producers.

In general, BRT programming has a "national character," with the exception of a small number of features. Because the RTBF has a number of regional production centers of its own, including Liege and Charleroi, its "regionalization" is more advanced than that of the BRT. Moreover, in Wallonia, local, noncommercial television programs have been allowed to be distributed via cable since 1976. As regards programming, the present twelve local television outlets focus on regional matters, including cultural activities, features for the unemployed, and adult education.

About 2.7 million Belgian households, or about 83 percent of all television owners, are connected to cable. Belgium is thus the most densely cabled nation in the world. Cable distribution in Wallonia and Flanders includes the following:

- 4 national stations: BRT 1, BRT 2, RTBF 1, and RTBF 2
- 2 Dutch stations: NOS 1 and NOS 2
- 3 French stations: TF 1, A 2, and FR 3
- 3 West German stations: ARD, WDR, and ZDF
- 1 Luxembourg station: RTL
- 5 British stations: BBC 1, BBC 2, ITV, Channel 4, and Sky Channel.

The competition of this broad offering for the national stations comes primarily from the stations that transmit in the national languages, namely NOS 1 and NOS 2 for the BRT, and RTL and, to a lesser extent, TF 1, A 2, and FR 3 for the RTBF.

BROADCAST REFORM

Political wrangling on broadcast policy in Belgium, as in many other European nations, is as old as the broadcasting system itself. Some policymakers, primarily the liberals, find the public broadcasting system obsolete, posing a kind of threat to free expression of opinion and objectivity in news.

Advertising dominates discussions regarding the medium, however. It is not surprising that concern for this problem has increased considerably in recent years, since Belgian television viewers are deluged with commercials from foreign stations distributed via cable. Advertising often focuses directly on the Belgian consumer, while in Belgium itself all forms of commercial advertising are forbidden.

The print media in particular have recently provided major participation in the discussions on broadcast advertising and the breakup of the broadcast monopoly. In 1981 and 1982 the Belgian Association of Daily Newspaper

Publishers and the National Federation of News Weeklies studied the consequences of the introduction of broadcast advertising on the written press
and the possibilities for the daily newspapers and weekly magazines to
participate in a commercial station still to be created. The studies showed
that a commercial outlet in Flanders could achieve an annual turnover of
BF 1.9 billion. They also concluded that 85 percent of these promotional
expenditures would be taken from the written press. Since then, the publishers have stubbornly asserted that they must be actively involved in the
establishment of a commercial facility. Although all the publishers agreed
in principle, there was no unanimity about the way in which the written
press should manage an outlet or on the financial share each newspaper or
group of newspapers would have in the new enterprise. Thus two camps
of publishers were formed, each with its own syndicate: OTV (Onafhan-
kelijke Televisie Vlaanderen, Independent Television Flanders) and VMM
(Vlaamse Media Maatschappij, Flemish Media Company).

The publishers of the French-language newspapers have also been seeking
to stem the loss of revenue, which has been flowing to the Luxembourg
RTL for a number of years. On April 24, 1985, the French-language newspapers, which had formed an investment company, Audiopresse, concluded
a cooperative agreement with RTL. The agreement stipulates that the newspapers will provide forty-five minutes of primarily regional news daily on
RTL. In exchange, Audiopresse will share in the advertising income of RTL,
some BF 120 million per year. Audiopresse also has shares in RTL.

In spite of several attempts by the last Christian Democrat and Liberal
government coalition and the pressure of interest groups like the press,
opposition parties, led by the Socialists, have as yet been able to prevent
the introduction of a commercial station. It is thus unlikely that any drastic
changes will take place in the Belgian media landscape in the near future.

NEW TECHNOLOGIES

Because Belgium has such a high degree of cable penetration, it is particularly attractive for new foreign stations who want to distribute their
programs via the Belgian cable network, possibly first via the satellite and
afterwards with cable. At present, Italian Radio Audition (RAI) programs
are already being transmitted via satellite to Belgium; also, the signal from
the commercial British station Sky Channel is received in Wallonia and
distributed by some cable outfits.

The RTBF has received permission from the Walloon regional government
to operate a pay television channel. This is not as yet permitted in Flanders,
but in October 1985 the Netherlands' pay television outlet FilmNet/ATN
received permission from the Flemish regional government to enter the
Flemish cable networks.

There are many other applicants, like the English Music Box, preparing to enter the Belgian living room via cable. In any case, there is still enough room on the cable. Gradually, stronger amplifiers are being placed on the networks with a capacity of 230 to 270 or even 300 MHz, so that the capacity of the present network can be expanded to 450 MHz, with room for at least thirty channels without the user having to utilize any setup converter.

In 1980 teletext broadcasts were begun on both the BRT and the RTBF, but the two stations selected different technical television norms. The BRT chose the British CEEFAX system; the RTBF took the French ANTIOPE standard. In 1985 about 190,000 Flemish households had reception apparatus adapted to teletext, while only a few hundred Walloon families had an ANTIOPE decoder. It should be noted that French decoders were significantly more expensive than the British ones in the initial years.

Both stations offer a teletext packet of about 150 pages with national and international news, weather and road information, stock exchange quotations, radio and television program schedules, and a cooking section. Both teletext packets also have a press review supplied by the daily newspapers via the national press agency, Belga. Both teletext services intend to expand their information packet in the future with, for example, regional news reports. The undertitling of programs for deaf viewers will also be systematically increased.

CONCLUSION/FORECAST

Public broadcasting in Belgium has existed for more than fifty years and, in all probability, will continue to fulfill an important educational, informative, and entertainment function for the next fifty years. It is unlikely, however, that it will be able to maintain its monopoly position. On the one hand, the bastion of public broadcasting is constantly and ever more frequently the subject of criticism from the political parties, particularly with regard to the objectivity of news reporting. This criticism not only relates to the operation of the stations but generally leads to challenging the broadcast monopoly itself. This monopoly of public broadcasting is, in practice, broken every day by new cable stations from abroad, sometimes financed by advertising. In a few years direct satellite reception may follow. While nonpublic radio stations already compete with national radio stations, in the very near future foreign broadcasters, pay television channels, and video and satellite television will certainly skim off some of the Belgian viewers and advertisers.

In light of the ever more pressing demands of the advertising-bearing media for protection of the national commercial market (the written press, for example) and of the national audiovisual industry for the promotion of its own industrial sector, it may be expected that one or perhaps more commercial stations will soon be licensed and established in Belgium.

BIBLIOGRAPHY

Boon, G. *De omroep: Radio en televisie in Nederlandstalig België.* Brussels: BRT, 1984.

De Groof, J., and J. Vermeire. *Administratieve en technische normen i.v.m. tele- en radioverbindingen.* Brussels: CEPESS, 1984.

De Groof, J., et al. *Over ether en inkt, bijdragen over de media.* Brussels: CEPESS, 1983.

De Grooff, D. *Medialand 2000.* K.V. Leuven: Center for Communications Sciences, 1982.

De Grooff, D., and R. Adriaens. *Abonnée-omroep.* K.U. Leuven: Center for Communications Sciences, 1983.

De Grooff, D., and G. Fauconnier. *Teletekst en Viewdata.* K.U. Leuven: Center for Communications Sciences, 1980.

Fauconnier, G. "Serving Two Cultures: Local media in Belgium." In *World Communications, A Handbook*, edited by G. Gerbner and M. Siefert. New York: Longmans, 1983.

Herroelen, P. *Eén, twee, . . . veel? Kroniek van 20 jaar Belgische radio en televisie.* Leuven: Acco, 1982.

————. *La régionalisation de la radio-télévision de service public, organisation, et programmes.* Brussels, RTBF, 1983.

Op de Beek, J., ed. *Omroepen in de woestijn.* Leuven: Kritak, 1977.

Van Laeken, W., ed. *Dossier omroep.* Leuven: Kritak, 1977.

Verhofstadt, D. *Het einde van het BRT-monopolie.* Antwerp: Kluwer, 1982.

BRAZIL

Omar Souki Oliveira

HISTORY

During the celebrations of Brazil's one hundredth year of independence, President Epitácio Pessoa became the first person there to have his voice broadcast. He was heard by a few listeners in Rio de Janeiro and São Paulo, the two major cities in the nation. On that same evening, September 7, 1922, directly from the municipal theater of Rio de Janeiro, the Brazilian opera, O Guarani, was broadcast live, in concert.

It was only on April 20 of the following year, however, that the first radio station in Brazil, the Rádio Sociedade do Rio de Janeiro (PRA–2), was officially established. It was installed with 2,000 watts of power by Rio de Janeiro and São Paulo Telephone Company, Westinghouse International, and Western Electric.

Radio listening soon became the favorite pastime of well-to-do Brazilians. During the 1920s the stations were called radio societies and were supported by membership contributions. Small groups cultivated the technological innovation, contributing with money, helping to produce programs, writing to outlets, playing their musical instruments, singing, talking, and listening. Thus the first decade of radio in Brazil was enjoyed by a fairly small number of elite groups, who treated it as a hobby. Most Brazilians did not have access to the medium then, due to the high prices of receivers.

In the 1930s, however, radio's history was drastically changed by the introduction of commercials and increased accessibility of receivers. Variety shows, rádio novelas (soap operas), music, and news entertained as well as informed the population, which was largely concentrated on the Atlantic coast. The airwaves became a conduit for cultural, social, and political messages uniting the vast land, roughly the size of the continental United

States. Radio's unifying power was facilitated by the common usage of one national language, Portuguese.

During its second decade of existence, radio was used as a political tool by the critics of the Getúlio Vargas regime. In response, Vargas started nationwide broadcasts of political messages. He instituted "A Hora do Brasil" (The Hour of Brasil), a mandatory program retransmitted by all radio outlets in the nation, every day, from seven to eight in the evening. Daily messages about the government and its actions were broadcast nationwide. Although the program never has ceased to exist, its popularity has consistently deteriorated. Tourists visiting Brazil often wonder why most radios are turned off between seven and eight in the evenings.

More recently, the Empresa Brasileira de Rádio e Televisão Radiobrás (Brazilian Corporation of Radio and Television), was created to coordinate government-owned stations. Radiobrás broadcasts to the distant rural regions of Brazil, trying to appeal to the third of the population living in the countryside. Its alternative programming is not intended to compete with privately owned facilities.

Most of Brazilian broadcasting, however, is in private hands. Among the commercial stations, the most popular for many years was the Rádio Nacional of Rio de Janeiro. It was determined to cover the entire nation with its mediumwave and shortwave bands. In the 1950s, during a national promotion, the station received 19,125,056 letters.

Radio has consistently grown in Brazil, and by the late 1970s the popularity of FM radio was increasingly due to the expanding market for FM receivers. New stations emphasize current musical hits, which include a great number of international songs. There are also formated FM stations. Some, such as Rádio Inconfidência of Belo Horizonte, play only popular Brazilian music.

The great days of radio lasted throughout the 1950s, ignoring the introduction of television. The first television station in Brazil, TV Tupi of São Paulo, started operation on September 18, 1950. The station's owner had to import one hundred sets and distribute them to public places because their price was well above what most people could afford. Consequently, the new medium was not able to pose an immediate threat to radio's supremacy.

As with radio, the first decade of television was enjoyed mostly by those few who could afford the expensive sets, which had to be imported from the United States or Europe. Audiences were rather small; therefore, sponsors were not convinced that television was worthy of much advertising money.

Yet in the mid–1950s Brazilian television accidentally found what it called *garotas-propaganda* (advertising girls). They were attractive women who advertised products on television. The first commercials of that kind were quite successful; thus they dominated advertising until the mid–1960s. Many of these young women became famous and developed popular careers in theater, film, and television dramas. Live advertising, though, gradually faded out with the arrival of spots, jingles, and videotaped commercials.

At the same time, more affordable television sets were made in Brazil, and audiences gradually preferred the new medium. As audience size increased, television's advertising power became evident. Domestic and international corporations switched to television for their major advertising campaigns. Radio had to change its format to mostly music and news, drastically reducing its budget, in order to overcome TV's competition.

During the late 1960s two important commercial television stations were installed: TV Globo and TV Bandeirantes. They became the dominant national networks. TV Globo, however, was able to hold more than 60 percent of the audience. While it accepted a Time-Life partnership and introduced advanced marketing strategies, TV Bandeirantes suffered a series of setbacks, including a major fire in 1968 that ruined its brand-new studios.

By the mid–1970s Rede Globo was the largest television network in the nation and the fourth in the world. Currently, its fifty affiliated and owned stations reach most of Brazil's 120 million inhabitants. Its soap operas have been exported to neighboring nations, to Portugal, and to the Spanish International Network (SIN) in the United States.

As the new television stations flourished, TV Tupi, the first station in the nation, had its license suspended in 1980. Its financial situation was so chaotic that employees were not paid for several months. The federal government withheld the station's right to operate and made its channels available to two other broadcasting corporations.

TV Studios and TV Manchete were created from the ashes of TV Tupi. The former joined the Sistema Brasileiro de Televisão (SBT), a national network, and the latter formed its own chain. Since 1981 four television networks have competed for Brazilian audiences: Rede Globo, Rede Bandeirantes, Rede Manchete, and Sistema Brasileiro de Televisão.

The broadcast media are now an integral part of national life in Brazil. The recent launching of two domestic communications satellites will further enhance their possibilities of reaching even the most distant corners of the vast territory.

REGULATION

The first attempt to control broadcasting in Brazil was made in 1930 with the creation of the Comissão Técnica do Rádio (Technical Commission of Radio), which clearly considered broadcasting the privilege of the state. A broader telecommunications code, however, only appeared in 1962. Yet broadcast regulations and their interpretations were under military siege from 1964 to 1984.

After the military took power in 1964, ousting a democratically elected president, three major legal instruments were used to regulate communications in Brazil: Lei de Segurança Nacional (National Security Law), Lei de Imprensa (Press Law), and the Codigo Nacional de Telecomunicações (National Code of Telecommunications). The security law was introduced by the military to eliminate from the media any content that could be dangerous to the "security" of the nation. Therefore, during the military years there was prior censorship of both the print and broadcast media. Prohibition of certain topics was often made by telephone calls from the federal police or other security organizations.

Apparently contradicting the security law, the press law acknowledged freedom of expression and explicitly recognized individual rights to receive and diffuse information without previous censorship. Nonetheless, this part of the press law was often disregarded by the government, which preferred, in many instances, to use the security law, especially when content was critical of its authoritarian practices.

The press law applied to both print and broadcast communication. It established that the electronic media are a concession of the state, which reserves for itself the right to use them. In legal terms this meant that radio and television stations are subject to censorship at any time. It also stated that only Brazilian citizens are entitled to own communication channels. The use of war propaganda and social or political subversion, and the diffusion of ethnic or class prejudices are not tolerated by the law.

The third legal instrument used by the military was the national code covering telecommunications created in 1962 and altered five years later, when the Ministry of Communications was created. Under this ministry two major organizations were established with the duty of implementing the norms of the national code, Contel or Conselho Nacional de Telecomunicações (National Council of Telecommunications) and Dentel or Departamento Nacional de Telecomunicações (National Department of Telecommunications). The council is responsible for the supervision of programs and their content regarding information, entertainment, and commercials, while the department is in charge of administering, supervising, and controlling the Brazilian telecommunications system.

The telecommunications code of 1962 emphasized the need for educational and cultural content in Brazilian broadcasting. The commercial use of the airwaves was allowed by the statute as long as it did not interfere with the educational and cultural goals previously established. Therefore, it was mandatory that stations devote 5 percent of their programming to news and five hours per week to the broadcasting of educational features. Advertising was limited to fifteen minutes every broadcast hour.

After 1964 the council and department were occupied by military officers or persons appointed by them. Subsequently, the 1962 code was altered by a series of decrees regarding penalties, administrative process, telecommunications crimes, licensing, and the need for the recording of programs. Thereafter, the fining of radio and television stations by the department became almost a daily occurrence. Presence of offensive programs, operation of unlicensed equipment, and broadcasting of programs "injurious" to state or federal authorities were some of the reasons offered for fining outlets.

Throughout the authoritarian years of Brazilian political life, telecommunications regulations were shaped to a large extent by the will of the military. During the early months of 1985, however, the nation returned to civilian rule, and chances for more democratic regulations appeared. Several documents were presented to the new regime suggesting guidelines for telecommunications policies. These proposals were an attempt to include the needs of the larger sectors of the Brazilian population within the context of new laws. The existing codes, however, have not yet been altered by the newly established government.

ECONOMIC STRUCTURE

Apart from the few radio and television stations owned by the state and federal governments, the overwhelming majority of broadcast services in Brazil are privately owned. The commercial stations are entirely supported by the selling of advertising time, mediated in most cases by advertising agencies.

The customers of such agencies have been the Brazilian government, multinational corporations, and domestic enterprises, whose paid commercials have supported Brazilian broadcasting. Currently, Brazil's gross domestic product (GDP) surpasses $200 billion, and the nation has the seventh largest market in the world. Roughly $1.5 million a year are spent on commercials. Federal and state governments have been the major advertisers, followed by cigarette companies and banking institutions. Also, enterprises such as Gessy Lever, Volkswagen, Nestlé, Anakol, and General Motors have been among the ten largest advertisers in the nation.

Radio, since its early days, has been used to introduce new consumer products to Brazilians. Jingles, slogans, and announcers became the most valuable part of programming. As early as 1928 the international advertising agencies started to arrive in Brazil. First came N. W. Ayer, followed by J. Walter Thompson, Standard Advertising, and McCann Erickson. They designed commercial campaigns for General Electric, Kodak, Coca-Cola, Goodyear, and Ford, among many other international concerns.

The financial support provided by these corporations promoted radio's instant growth across the nation. From 1931 to 1940, 56 new radio stations were installed, and in the following decade radio expanded even faster with the creation of 255 new facilities. Whole shows were sponsored by large corporations and acquired the industry's name. Examples of this trend were the "Reporter Esso" (Esso Reporter) and the soap operas sponsored by Colgate-Palmolive, and Standard Brands.

In 1950 television was introduced to a nation with approximately 52 million inhabitants, and by the early 1960s television's advertising potential had been unveiled. It then absorbed 24 percent of all promotions in Brazil. This figure was increased to 33 percent with the introduction of TV Globo a few years later. The new television station started charging advertising slots according to the popularity of the program in which they were inserted. The larger the audience for a certain feature, the more expensive were its commercial spots. Hence the search for large audiences gradually became the major goal of Brazilian television networks.

Program distribution across the nation and homogenization of programming have been the two main consequences of this search for larger numbers of viewers. Distribution of features is made by affiliate stations in different regions, and to minimize costs, production has been centralized in the two major centers, Rio de Janeiro and São Paulo. Consequently, high technical quality and a pervasive entertaining approach tend to characterize the majority of offerings.

In short, broadcasting is a growth industry in Brazil, now responsible for more then 60 percent of all advertising expenditures. In spite of the educational and cultural goals established in national regulations, it is evident that the electronic media are mostly concerned with the selling of commercial spots.

To support this lucrative enterprise, more than sixty universities train communication professionals. As demand for their skills grew, model schools such as the Escola de Comunicações e Artes (School of Communications and Arts) of São Paulo University and the Departamento de Comunicação Social (Social Communication Department) of the Federal University of Minas Gerais have been established. These institutions tend to provide a diverse curriculum in the humanities combined with professional training. The market for these professionals, though, is limited to the industrialized urban areas in the southern parts of the nation.

PROGRAMMING

Due to the commercial nature of Brazilian broadcasting, most of its program content is geared toward entertainment, trying to appeal to large audiences. Government regulations, however, mandate that at least 5 percent of a station's programming be devoted to information and an average of five hours per week be allocated to education. In addition, religious programs have been often presented to attract some sectors of the population. Entertainment, news, education, and religious features constitute the bulk of broadcasting content.

Before television, the *show de auditório* (variety show) and the *rádio novelas* (radio soap operas) tended to dominate radio's programming. Both genres were extremely popular, attracting at times 90 percent of the audience. The variety shows were typically broadcast live from a theater. A variety of styles were mixed on stage, including game shows, prizes, singers, and humor. The soap opera explored national myths and kept audiences entertained as they followed their hero through his or her internal or external struggles.

Although radio no longer broadcasts those two genres, they were successfully adapted for television. As radio gradually switched to more music and news on the hour, television continued the presentation of variety shows and soap operas at more sophisticated levels. "Fantastico" of the Globo network became one of television's counterparts for radio's variety shows. Although taped, the feature is essentially a variety show presenting a combination of documentaries, musical presentations, new scientific discoveries, humor, sports, and film reviews. Following the general trend of early radio, "Fantastico" does not search for any kind of depth. The sensationalistic aspect of news is explored, and the irony of daily or seemingly irrelevant events is dealt with. To compare with Globo's hit, the newly installed Manchete network produced "Programa de Domingo" (Sunday Program), which tends to give a more in-depth treatment of issues and keeps sensationalism at a minimum. Both shows are highly elaborate productions using the latest techniques and the best talents available. They are broadcast every Sunday from 8 to 10 in the evening.

Equally sleek are Brazilian *telenovelas*, broadcast during the week from 8:30 to 9:00 after the evening news. Their major source of inspiration is either national literature or contemporary living. "A Escrava Isaura" (Isaura, the Slave) and "Gabriela" were adaptations of famous novels and have achieved unprecedented popularity not only in Brazil but in many other nations of Latin America. "Malu, Mulher" (Malu, Woman) and "Dancing Days" depicted social transformations in urban Brazil and achieved similar success when exported to neighboring countries.

Although prime-time television is dominated by *telenovelas* and variety shows, nearly 60 percent of total programming is imported. Some of the most popular foreign shows are "Bonanza," "Kojak," "Lancer," "Search," and "Dallas." The great majority of imported programs, though, are used as fillers during unpopular schedules.

Television news programs are presented every weekday from 8:00 to 8:30 in the evening. Since 1969 these features have been able to reach most of the territory due to a system of terrestrial microwave links. Some networks have reporters stationed in the major capitals of the world, and their presentation of the news resembles U.S. or European professionalism.

Although not a major part of broadcasting, educational programs are required by law in both radio and television. All AM radio outlets are required to broadcast the government's "Projeto Minerva" (Minerva Project). This educational program is aimed at the less educated sectors of the population and attempts to lower the nation's 30 percent illiteracy rate. It is presented daily from 8:00 to 8:30 in the evening. Television stations use either imported or nationally produced educational features. Among the favorite imported programs is "Sesame Street" in Portuguese. A widely acclaimed Brazilian production is "Sitio do Pica Pau" (The Yellow Woodpecker Ranch), which appears to be even more popular than the imported shows.

Religious programs appear also in these two versions, imported and made in Brazil. Among the most popular religious programs are "Jimmy Swaggart" and "Rex Humbard" with subtitles in Portuguese. There are also domestically produced features of a similar nature, representing the Catholic, Pentecostal, and Baptist interpretations of the Bible.

Overall, Brazilian broadcasting can be characterized by a growing tendency of centralization and homogenization of production. Although this approach to programming seems to suit the networks' marketing interests, it has also been accused by the critics of not reflecting the Brazilian social and cultural diversity.

BROADCAST REFORM

Dissatisfaction with the existing broadcast system in Brazil has led intellectuals, professionals, and even some authorities to give support to and participate in illegal broadcasting activities. In addition, legal channels have also been used to exercise pressures toward change in communications legislation.

The leading state in pirate stations seems to be São Paulo. Several of its major cities have had, for a number of years, popular FM radio stations operating without licenses. These stations appeared as a response to the limited program choice available under the commercially oriented system. They do not broadcast for profit and often use homemade equipment. The programming is alternative music, presenting a variety of styles from hard rock and Brazilian country to classical.

TV Livre (Free TV) constitutes the most recent development along the lines of alternative broadcasting. A group of intellectuals in São Paulo, supported by some local government authorities and helped by electronic technicians, have built their own "free" station. With less than $4,000 spent in equipment they were able to defy the federal law, producing programs about their local community with indigenous talents and interviews with disillusioned actors. August 15, 1985, was the date planned for its first transmissions in the city of Sorocaba (320,000 inhabitants). Federal surveillance was so tight that they had to postpone their transmissions or run the risk of having their equipment confiscated.

Pirate broadcasters claim that they are trying to fill the existing communications gaps. Communities in the interior of Brazil constantly receive prefabricated programs portraying lifestyles in the cities of Rio de Janeiro and São Paulo. Supporters of the pirate stations say local people want to see their own daily concerns aired through television and wish to experience programming that reflects their realities and values.

Another challenge to the status quo comes from several documents produced by important social sectors in Brazil. The papers, proposing changes in the existing communications legislation, were prepared by the Centro de Comunicação e Cultura (CEC, Center of Communication and Culture) of Brasília, Federação Nacional de Journalistas (FENAJ, National Federation of Journalists), Associação Brasileira de Ensino e Pesquisa da Comunicação (ABEPEC, Brazilian Association for the Teaching and Research of Communication), Partido Movimento Democratico Brasileiro (PMDB, Brazilian Democratic Movement party), the Catholic church, writers, artists, professionals in several areas, and labor union leaders.

The fundamental theme is the need to achieve democracy in Brazilian society. This goal would not be achieved, they argue, without a democratic communications policy. On the other hand, it is stressed that the military used mass-media regulations to exercise authoritarian control for twenty years.

In general, the documents include the following items as necessary for the achievement of a democratic communications policy: participation of all sectors of society in their elaboration, broad access of media to information sources, and egalitarian distribution of messages across diverse social strata. The concept of information as an individual right appears in most documents, and the social responsibility issue is common to all. The proposals indicate that the broadcasting institutions owe to society the responsibility of broadcasting in the public interest.

It is, however, too early to predict the actual outcome of such developments on future legislation. Many of the key individuals of the previous administration still hold public positions, and decision making within the Ministry of Communications remains controlled by individuals who were appointed by the military.

NEW TECHNOLOGIES

Brasilsat I, the first Brazilian communications satellite, was launched on February 8, 1985, and Brasilsat II was placed in orbit by August of the same year. These domestic satellites will double the broadcast capabilities in the nation. Given the continental size of Brazilian territory, this new technology increased the possibilities of linking the entire country from its border in Argentina in the south to the Amazon region in the north.

Currently, Brazil has to rent transponders in the Intelsat in order to reach the distant regions of its territory. Seven of them are used for telecommunications purposes. Two are utilized by the Globo and Bandeirantes networks, and the others are used for information, telex, and government services.

The renting of these transponders cost over $8 million to Brazil. The two domestic satellites came into operation by the end of 1985 to replace the services now provided by Intelsat. Government plans projected fifty-one earth stations operating within two years.

The growth of earth stations for commercial use increased to literally explode within the next three years. By 1985, Globo and Bandeirantes already had sixty-eight earth stations for commercial use. The additional satellite service allowed integration of the other two networks, thereby fostering explosive growth.

One of the most important applications for satellite technology is education. The government is considering the possibility of connecting the schools in the northern states, where education levels are the lowest, and upgrading the system. Monitors wired to small satellite antennas can be installed in schools serving the rural areas.

Satellite antennas have been manufactured in Brazil since 1984 and are now advertised on the Brazilian media. Those who can afford them will be able to enjoy programs from all over the world. The price per unit is approximately $10,000.

Teletext has also been experimental in Brazil. The São Paulo Telephone Company (Telesp) stores the information that will be open to public access. The decoder and the keyboard are domestically manufactured. Testing was initiated in 1982, and the equipment is still in experimental stages.

Microcomputers have also arrived in Brazilian industry, commerce, and educational institutions. In addition, computers for personal use are gradually becoming popular, and the domestic market is second only to North America in this hemisphere. Yet manufacturing of microcomputers is restricted to Brazilian corporations by the Política Nacional de Informática (PNI, National Policy of Information), established in 1976. This law prevents multinational corporations such as IBM and ITT from commercializing microcomputers in Brazil. At present these global corporations are intensely lobbying for change in such legislation.

With its domestic satellites and the development of technologies for satellite antennas, teletexts, and microcomputers, Brazil is making tremendous efforts to become internationally competitive in such areas. If policies encouraging indigenous technological development are continued and enhanced in the future, the field holds great financial promise.

CONCLUSION/FORECAST

The foregoing discussion indicates that broadcasting in Brazil has closely followed the U.S. commercial model. Furthermore, North American corporations have been directly involved in the process from the installation of the first transmission tower to the renting of satellite transponders. Multinational corporations have provided financial support and in turn have benefited from the commercial nature of Brazilian broadcasting. Their effect on the system may be second only to government influence.

These two forces, U.S. corporate interests and the Brazilian government, have dominated radio and television for the past six decades. Apart from the pirate stations and proposals for new legislation, there is little practical evidence that the situation will change soon. On the contrary, since 1965 the marketing orientation has prevailed over the airwaves. The creation of TV Globo, which had significant economic and technological support from Time-Life Group, consolidated this trend. Globo, followed by other networks, reproduced in Brazil the North American patterns of administration, programming, technology, content, and approach to information.

This orientation was enhanced by the military, which attempted to use the media to legitimize its authoritarian rule. The government became the number one advertiser in dollar value, and the networks the major beneficiaries of expenditures in the sector. In addition, federal funds were used to build the national microwave system and more recently to launch two communications satellites.

Since both multinational enterprises and the Brazilian government have used the media to reach massive audiences, their support to broadcasting may continue well into the future. Consequently, past tendencies toward centralization and homogenization of programs within a marketing approach may not be changed. Perhaps these trends will be considerably accelerated as both government and corporate advertising needs increase. The appearance of programs and technologies that would reflect domestic realities may then be indefinitely postponed.

Overall, it seems that Brazilian broadcasting grew as a response to the needs of international corporations and the military. These two influences do not seem to have favored the appearance of indigenous technologies reflecting the nation's socioeconomic potential and diversity. Program production is centralized in the industrial centers, and most of its broadcasting equipment has been imported from abroad.

New technologies, though, might follow a different path. The creation of the Política Nacional de Informática (PNI, National Policy of Information) was intended to protect the domestic market for the genuinely Brazilian microcomputer industry. Through this law, only Brazilian manufacturers, using indigenous technology, are entitled to commercialize their products. Although it may encourage national industry to design its own technological answers to domestic situations, it also has upset powerful international concerns and closes for them a large and attractive market.

It remains to be seen whether the information policy will survive international pressures. Multinational corporations are lobbying to convince legislators to abolish PNI. Future trends may to a large extent depend on the outcomes of this political battle. If national manufacturers, shielded by favorable legislation, are able to please an ever-demanding market, present conditions may be the beginning of the development of indigenous technologies. Yet if those protective laws are withdrawn, past tendencies will prevail.

BIBLIOGRAPHY

Almeida, Mauro. *A Comunicação de Massa no Brasil.* Belo Horizonte: Edicoes Jupiter, 1971.
Amorim, José S. D. "Comunicação e Transição no Brasil." Paper presented at the debates on New Brazilian Legislation, July 9, 1985.
———. "Televisión, Crisis Económica y Cambio Político en Brasil." *Comunicación y Cultura* (March 1985): 75–79.
Ávila, Carlos. *A Teleinvasão.* São Paulo: Cortez Editora, 1982.
Brazil. Presidência da República. *Legislação Brasileira de Comunicação Social.* Brasília: Secretaria de Imprensa e Divulgacao, 1984.
———. *Mercado Brasileiro de Comunicação.* Brasília: Secretaria de Imprensa e Divulgacao, 1983.
Cardoso, Onésimo O. "Igreja Electrônica—Os Programas Religiosos na Televisão Brasileira." *Comunicação e Sociedade* 12 (October 1984): 5–22.
Carvalho, Bernardo A. "Comunicação: Um Lobby Milionário Finge Ser Democrático." *Geraes* 42 (October 1984): 56–59.
Carvalho, Mario C. "Os Jovens Piratas do Espaço." *Critica da Informação* 6 (February 1984): 20–23.
Costa, Sérgio. "O Radio no Brasil: Da Latinha ao FM." *Comunicação* 33 (October 1984): 16–26.
"Dentel Age: TV Livre Nao Vai Ao Ar." *Folha de São Paulo* 16 (August 1985): 46.
Erbolato, Mario, and Julio C. Barbosa. *Comunicação e Cotidiano.* São Paulo: Papirus Livraria Editora, 1984.
Federico, Maria E. B. *História da Comunicação: Radio e TV no Brasil.* Petropolis: Editora Vozes Ltda., 1982.
Melo, José M. *Telemania, Anestésico Social.* São Paulo: Edicoes Loyola, 1981.
Milanesi, Luis A. *O Paraiso Via Embratel.* Rio de Janeiro: Editora Paz e Terra, 1978.
Prado, João R. *TV: Quem Vê Quem.* Rio de Janeiro: Livraria Eldorado Tijuca Ltda., 1973.
"La Vai o Brasilsat." *Revista Nacional de Telemática* 70 (February 1985): 8–25.

CANADA

Thomas L. McPhail and Brenda McPhail

HISTORY

As a nation of over 24 million people with two official languages and a land mass of almost 10 million square kilometers, Canada faces unique challenges with respect to broadcasting. These factors are complicated by its proximity to the United States, which facilitates access to foreign programming, and by its comparatively unlimited resources. In response to these elements, Canada has developed a technologically sophisticated communications system involving both public and private elements that is capable of serving over 98 percent of the nation's population.

The first private radio station intended for a mass audience was established in Montreal in 1919. It was not until a decade later, however, that the government undertook the development of a broadcasting policy in response to uniquely Canadian problems. In essence, American signals interfered with Canadian ones. Canadian programs, with less financing, did not equal the standards of U.S. features. Private broadcasters were anxious to provide service in Toronto and Montreal but were less likely to serve the less populated areas. It was decided, therefore, that Canada needed a unique solution.

The Royal Commission on Radio Broadcasting (1929), created to review the situation and determine the best way for broadcasting development to proceed, concluded that Canadians wanted Canadian broadcasting and recommended the establishment of a publicly owned national network. In response, Parliament created a national public radio service in 1932. The continued existence of private outlets was permitted, however. All stations were considered part of the single Canadian broadcasting system and all were charged with the responsibility to provide Canadian programming for their audiences.

The public network began operating two television stations in 1952. Private stations were established shortly thereafter. By 1986 the Canadian broadcasting system contained almost 2,000 public and private radio and television facilities.

Despite the technological sophistication of the system, it consistently has been confronted by three major and often conflicting themes. The first involves nationalism. Canadian broadcasting has been charged with the responsibility for fostering the national identity. This obligation places financial strains on the industry, and these economic concerns comprise the second major theme. Third, broadcasting is consistently subject to changes in the technological environment. These three challenges are interconnected, and other factors, such as the degree of American broadcast penetration and the challenge of Canada's geography, complicate them all.

A number of royal commissions, special committees, and ad hoc advisory boards have struggled to find solutions to the persistent dilemmas of Canadian broadcasting. In attempts to "Canadianize" the airwaves, governments and their regulators have instituted a "public trustee" approach and relied on Canadian content and ownership regulations to control the private sector. These decisions have imposed additional economic costs on all broadcasters, public and private alike, who must compete not only with one another for the limited advertising revenues but also with the American border stations that Canadians can access off the air or via cable technologies. Moreover, production costs are high, and many Canadian stations lack the audience base to warrant the necessary expenditures to produce high-quality shows. Finally, technological developments have also affected the Canadian broadcasting system. New innovations have increased the availability of foreign programming and further fragmented the available audience and revenues. These challenges overshadow all activity in the broadcasting arena. In short, they determine policy decisions and affect the management of individual stations.

REGULATION

The structure of Canadian broadcasting legislation and regulation traditionally has been governed by two constitutional principles. Since Canada is a parliamentary democracy, all power ultimately rests with an elected legislature that may choose to delegate its authority to appoint boards or commissions. Second, Canada is a federal nation, and therefore jurisdictional authority is divided between the central and provincial governments. Since 1982 the absolute power of Parliament and provincial legislatures has been limited by the newly enacted Canadian Charter of Rights and Freedoms. It remains to be seen what effect this far-reaching law will have on broadcasting legislation and regulation.

The first legislation controlling the medium was the federal government's Radio-Telegraph Act of 1905, which simply required the licensing of all radiotelegraph equipment. During the next two decades a number of problematic issues arose, and that legislation was recognized to be inadequate. The federal government wanted to isolate broadcasting from the partisanship of politics, prevent the chaotic misuse of the airways, control the spillover effects from the United States, and utilize broadcasting for the national advantage. It began to consider new legislation to address these concerns and in 1929 established the Royal Commission on Radio Broadcasting to investigate these issues.

In 1931, however, before the Parliament had an opportunity to act on the commission's recommendation, several of the provincial governments challenged the jurisdictional authority of the central government with respect to broadcasting in the Supreme Court. Hertzian waves and their applications were unknown to the framers of the British North American Act (1867), the legislation that divided the jurisdictional powers between the central and provincial governments. The court found several jurisdictional headings it considered broad enough to include radio communications and assigned exclusive jurisdiction to the federal Parliament. This decision was based, in part, on what the court considered to be the national role for the medium. The jurisdictional debate concerning specific aspects of broadcasting has resurfaced periodically. In the late 1960s the provincial governments specifically achieved the right to control educational broadcasting; however, other issues, including the regulation of cable television systems, are still disputed.

The Canadian Radio Broadcasting Act of 1932 declared the airwaves to be a scarce public resource and all broadcast licenses a temporary monopoly, to be operated as part of a single national system in the public interest. This "public trustee" concept has been a major theme in all subsequent legislation and regulation. The 1932 act also created the Canadian Radio Broadcasting Corporation (CRBC) and assigned it two distinct mandates. Not only was it expected to operate the national public broadcasting network, but it also was responsible for the regulation of the private stations.

Subsequently, three other independent bodies have been created by statute and assigned the authority to regulate broadcast undertakings. The "independence" of these regulatory authorities is limited. Their mandates are assigned by Parliament, and their decisions are subject to cabinet review. They report to Parliament through the responsible cabinet ministers. Over the years, ministerial responsibility for broadcasting has shifted or been shared among several departments. Since 1976, however, the federal Department of Communications has assumed the ultimate responsibility for all aspects of broadcasting, including technical, ownership, and program regulation. In addition, successive governments have established a number of investigative tribunals to review national issues, and in the late 1960s Parliament created a permanent standing committee of the House of Commons to review broadcasting matters.

In 1936 the Canadian Broadcasting Act replaced the CRBC with the more autonomous Canadian Broadcasting Corporation–Radio Canada (CBC-RC). The place of private operators in the Canadian broadcasting system was assured despite the recommendations of the earlier royal commission, which had advocated a single public network. Finally, broadcasting was redefined to include television, a known but unused medium.

The private broadcasters resented the dual role of the CBC-RC as "cop and competitor" and consistently lobbied Parliament for a separate and distinct regulator. They finally achieved their goal with the enactment of the Broadcasting Act of 1958. The legislation reaffirmed the need for a single broadcasting system "basically Canadian in content and character" and created the Board of Broadcast Governors (BBG) with the authority to regulate both the public and private sectors, thereby equalizing their positions within the Canadian broadcasting system.

The BBG dealt with a number of contentious issues during its ten-year tenure. Initially only one station had been permitted in each geographic location. The BBG allowed an additional "second" television station in certain, usually urban, locations. These stations were licensed and the first private television network was given permission to operate. The board's prime objective, however, was the Canadianization of the airwaves, and content regulations were instituted in an attempt to limit the importation of American programming and to ensure a quantitative increase in the amount of Canadian features available to audiences.

The current legislative framework for the medium is provided in the Broadcasting Act of 1968. Section 3 of this act clearly delineates broadcasting policy for Canada. Briefly stated, it declares that radio frequencies are public property; that the broadcasting system "should be effectively owned and controlled by Canadians so as to safeguard, enrich and strengthen the cultural, political, social and economic fabric of Canada"; that programming should be of a high standard and should use predominantly Canadian resources; and that all Canadians are entitled to broadcasting services in English and French. The act incorporates public and private radio, television, and cable undertakings as part of the single Canadian broadcasting system and imputes a sociocultural responsibility to all these elements.

To monitor and encourage the achievement of these lofty goals, the act created the Canadian Radio-Television and Telecommunications Commission (CRTC). The commission's mandate includes administrative regulation, the promotion of the national interest, and the advancement of the social and cultural roles of broadcasting. The CRTC is composed of five full-time appointed commissioners who comprise the executive board and ten part-time commissioners representative of the various regions of Canada. The executive committee has almost exclusive decision-making power. Part-time members must be consulted with respect to licensing decisions but cannot overturn a decision taken by the executive board. The CRTC relies on the public hearing process for information to assist in its decision making. The cabinet has the power to review CRTC decisions and issue broad policy directives. It also considers appeals of the commission's deliberations and can direct the CRTC to review these pronouncements.

The commission has addressed a number of regulatory issues. These include but are not limited to the control of content on radio and television, cable television systems, election coverage, educational television, and Canadian ownership of broadcasting undertakings. In many cases the Broadcasting Act of 1968 has not provided sufficient legislative guidance in step with the current technological environment. Recognizing this weakness, the minister of communications in 1983 announced his intention to introduce new legislation. The government wants more directive power in order that the Canadian broadcasting system can be made to respond quickly to new technological advances. New legislation has not yet been enacted, but despite the proposed changes, the objectives remain consistent: to maintain the broadcasting system as an effective vehicle of social and cultural policy; to make available to Canadians attractive Canadian features; and to foster a Canadian national identity within an ever-developing technological environment that threatens all national boundaries.

ECONOMIC STRUCTURE

The 1929 royal commission advocated the establishment of a single publicly owned broadcasting system. This recommendation was only partly realized. A public network was created, but private stations were permitted to continue operation. Eventually more and more private undertakings were licensed, so that today private radio and television stations outnumber their public counterparts. The Canadian broadcasting system, therefore, is a mixed blend of public and private elements. Although each operates with a separate and distinct goal orientation, both must function within the economic realities of the Canadian marketplace.

The CBC, or Radio Canada, as it is known in Quebec, is the public broadcaster. It functions as a federal crown corporation. Managed by a politically appointed board of directors and managing executive, the CBC operates at arm's length from the government of the day. However, it must report annually to Parliament through the minister of communications.

The corporation is a very large organization that operates a broad range of services including both English and French television networks, AM and FM radio networks, northern radio and television services in seven languages, two satellite-to-cable networks carrying the House of Commons proceedings, closed-caption services for the hearing-impaired, an international shortwave service in eleven languages, and IRIS, a teletext service. Moreover, the CBC often acts as host broadcaster for events of international interest. This vast range of duties is imposed on the CBC by its legislative mandate. The corporation is an essential instrument of Canadian cultural development, a vehicle for the expression of Canadian ideas and values.

The CBC is financed primarily by parliamentary appropriations, but some advertising time is sold on the television network. In 1983, 82 percent of CBC's total expenditures of $735.2 million was met by public funding. Since its creation, funding has been one of the most contentious problems plaguing the CBC. Some critics argue that the corporation is mismanaged and that the amount of public funding should be drastically reduced. Others want to see an end to all advertising on CBC stations, thereby increasing the amount of public funding required but reducing the CBC's dependence on the whims of advertisers. As for the corporation, it wants some stability in its funding so that long-range plans may be made in the best interests of the public.

Although the mixed system was officially recognized in the Broadcasting Act of 1958, it was not until 1968 that private ownership guidelines were legislated. The Committee on Broadcasting, a special task force established to review the Canadian situation, reported in 1965 that private broadcasters had failed to achieve the national goals set for broadcasting. Some critics believed that foreign ownership influences had inhibited the expression of Canadian ideas. The Broadcasting Act of 1968, therefore, determined that all broadcast undertakings be "effectively owned and controlled by Canadians." Effective ownership and control was later determined to be 80 percent, and foreign investment in broadcasting undertakings today remains capped at 20 percent.

Once the foreign ownership issue had been dealt with, the CRTC turned its attention to "excessive" media ownership. The commission recognized the need for large wealthy corporations to operate in the broadcasting arena but also wanted to ensure a plurality of expression involving local community input. It has enacted regulations regarding concentration of ownership and cross-ownership. Most importantly, no one owner or group of owners may control more than one media undertaking in any one geographic community. In reality, ownership and control of the electronic media remain concentrated in the hands of a few powerful corporate groups. Moreover, critics identify the typical owner as an Anglophone member of the inherited upper social class whose interests are closely aligned with those of the corporate elite in general. Therefore, they argue, broadcasters are representative of only one segment of society, and many diverse and antagonistic influences are excluded.

The private sector in Canadian broadcasting is obligated by the same economic marketplace pressures as any business enterprise. They are motivated to show a profit and have been largely successful in this.

In order to maintain levels of profitability, the broadcasters attempt to increase audience size without increasing expenditures. The best way to accomplish this is to exhibit popular foreign (American) programming that attracts large audiences and a large portion of available advertising revenues. Moreover, it is more economically efficient for broadcasters to buy foreign shows than to produce Canadian features that may or may not have equal audience appeal and advertiser support. It is in this way that advertisers control program content. Whenever broadcasting is paid for, wholly or in part, by advertisers, station managers search for programs that will attract the largest possible audiences at the least cost.

Despite the recommendation of the 1929 royal commission that no direct advertising be permitted, commercial sponsorship has become an integral part of the Canadian broadcasting system. Prices for advertising time are determined by three factors: ownership structure, local market characteristics, and audience size. Critics have consistently argued that broadcasters pay too much attention to the desires of advertisers. No regulation has been enacted in this regard. The CRTC has limited the amount of airtime that may be sold to advertisers, however. In addition, the Canadian Code of Advertising Standards establishes rules for endorsements directed at children or involving sex-role stereotyping, health concerns, consumer credit, and socially sensitive products.

The cable industry is also controlled and operated by private entrepreneurs. Many undertakings are individually owned by small independent businessmen, but 53 percent are group owned. These are responsible for 77 percent of cable revenues.

Most training for the broadcasting industry occurs in-house. A few university-based programs exist at Ryerson Institute, Toronto; Western University, London; and Carleton University, Ottawa. The province of Quebec currently is undertaking a review of training procedures for broadcasters and journalists. There is some recognition that the current situation is inadequate. A recent federally sponsored committee established to review cultural policy in Canada identified training as an important element in the creation, interpretation, and transmission of culture. It recognized the close link with education policies and objectives and acknowledged that a distinction must be made between skill training and education that tries to shape public values and interests. To date, however, the number and size of training programs has not been significantly increased.

PROGRAMMING

Since the introduction of broadcasting in Canada, programming has been controversial. In 1929 the Royal Commission on Radio Broadcasting concluded that Canadians want Canadian programming and warned that continued reception of foreign features threatened Canada's national sovereignty. Subsequent royal commissions, special committees, and task forces have reiterated these findings. The Canadian airwaves, however, continue to be monopolized by foreign, mainly American, features.

Despite early acknowledgment of the problem, it was 1959 before any attempt was made to regulate programming available through Canadian broadcast undertakings. The Board of Broadcast Governors initiated minimum Canadian program content quotas for both radio and television. These requirements met with strong negative reactions from private broadcasters. Despite the arguments of the private sector, these regulations have been strengthened.

This is not to say, however, that the regulations have been totally successful in stimulating Canadian program production. While they appear to have had that desired effect in the radio sector, television continues to be dominated by foreign fare. As outlined earlier, station managers are motivated to purchase and exhibit foreign features rather than to produce Canadian shows. Moreover, it has been possible to conform with the letter of the regulations by producing inexpensive talk and game features. By transmitting them during low-audience viewing hours both the costs and revenue losses are minimized.

New regulations for television, enacted in 1984, make this practice less advantageous. In addition to minimum content quotas, the new stipulations offer incentives to the broadcasters, including a financial assistance program conducted by the Department of Communications for the production of Canadian video programming. It remains to be seen how effective these new measures will be.

Given government policies, each sector in the Canadian broadcasting industry has developed its own programming style. Radio is primarily a news and information medium for commuters. Commercial radio stations tend to stress community identification, and programming is usually directed to one group within the community. Stations provide news, weather, and billboard-type announcements. The magazine format predominates, as information is interspersed among the playing of commercial records and local advertisements. Open-line shows are popular during non-prime-time hours. Because private radio is dependent on advertiser support and therefore "ratings," it tends to be inoffensive and noncontroversial.

Although CBC radio offers some of the same programming options as commercial stations, it is more national and comprehensive in its orientation. The aim of CBC radio is to develop a national consciousness, and its major programming focus includes public service and public affairs features. Some critics accuse the CBC of being "long-haired"; however, it is generally applauded for its high-quality offerings.

Television is most valued for its entertainment programming. Private

television, although subject to Canadian content regulation, is strongly influenced by advertisers who want large audiences during the evening prime-
time slots. For broadcasters, this translates into ready-made, high-appeal
features from the United States. To fill their Canadian content quotas, the
private operators exhibit some Canadian information and public affairs
features during prime time.

CBC television is somewhat more balanced in terms of the ratio of Canadian and American programming. Although only one-seventh commercially sponsored, CBC's prime-time schedule is dominated by commercial
sponsors. The CBC has been severely criticized for this policy, and several
suggestions have been forwarded to correct the deficiency. These range from
the abolition of any advertising on the network to shortened hours of operation. For its part, the corporation has declared its intention to voluntarily
exhibit 80 percent Canadian content. Given that each extra hour per day
of Canadian programming costs between $4 and $8 million per year, funding
remains the predominant problem in achieving this goal.

Not only is American programming available on Canadian television
stations, but Canadians have ready access to all four American networks
(NBC, CBS, ABC, and PBS) through cable systems. The cable outfits are
regulated by the CRTC and are required to give priority to local and regional
Canadian stations. Sufficient channel capacity, however, remains on most
cable systems to carry at least four American channels. Moreover, the entire
issue of CRTC control over cable operations faces challenge by some companies and provincial governments. The most contentious issue is the regulator's demand that Canadian stations be given priority. Some cable owners
are ignoring that dictum and delivering a collection of U.S. outlets to their
subscribers. The public generally supports these cable concerns because they
are delivering the programming subscribers desire, but analysts fear that
wholesale abandonment of the regulation will mean economic disaster for
Canadian broadcasters.

One of the areas in which Canadians excel is news and public affairs
programming. This expertise has developed, in part, because the costs of
producing these features are lower than the production costs for drama and
entertainment. In addition, audience response is positive, and stations are
motivated to make up their Canadian quotas with news and public affairs
features. Economic problems threaten even this sector, however. Budget
cuts have necessitated a reduction in the number of foreign correspondents,
and Canadian broadcasters are relying even more heavily on foreign (U.S.)
news sources. Even news programming, then, increasingly is dominated by
American media influences.

Historically, religious broadcasting in Canada has been very controversial.
Broadcast licenses traditionally have been denied to any group with a religious affiliation. These groups, generally fundamentalist in nature, must
purchase airtime from privately owned licensed commercial stations. Al-

though a few programs originate in Canada, most are U.S. based. Moreover, a twenty-four-hour religious programming channel is available via a U.S. satellite.

Educational broadcasting was a disputed issue in Canada until the early 1970s. Broadcasting is a federal responsibility, but education falls under the purview of the provinces. The jurisdictional debate was finally settled by a compromise that permitted each province to establish an independent authority to produce and transmit educational fare, loosely defined as programming that provides a continuity of learning opportunities. Educational television networks have been undertaken by four provinces: the Knowledge Network (British Columbia), the Alberta Educational Communications Authority (ACCESS), the Ontario Educational Communication Authority (TV Ontario), and Radio-Quebec. All produce their own features but also purchase shows from foreign sources.

Programming for children is exhibited on all the educational networks and on both public and private stations. Until 1983 the CBC also had a weekly radio show for children, but it was canceled and replaced with adult programming. In the 1984 fall schedule less than one hundred hours per week was devoted to programming specifically produced for children (other than curriculum-based educational programs) by the educational networks, the CBC-RC, and the private networks combined. This represents a decrease of about 20 percent since 1979. In addition, very little of that programming is Canadian produced. Each network may develop one show, usually a half-hour in length, for daily viewing. This balance, including animated cartoons and "Sesame Street," is purchased from foreign sources.

In sum, the record for Canadian program production in all categories is disappointing. Despite government efforts to encourage such efforts, the future appears even more bleak. Canada has failed to protect its culture from the encroachment of American values. The new technologies will not make the task easier and may, in fact, spell the demise of the Canadian broadcasting industry.

BROADCAST REFORM

Broadcasting in Canada has consistently been the subject of social, cultural, and political criticism, much of which relates to the three themes identified at the beginning of this chapter. Given the makeup of the "single system," the debate still rages with respect to public versus private ownership. Other related conflicts include CBC funding, the Americanization of Canadian television, the effects of the media on Canadian social values, and the role of government in the regulation of culture. Programming and the values and ideas that it advances appear to be at the root of these controversies.

The Canadian Broadcasting League, an amorphous collection of individuals and organizations, was created in 1930 as an ideologically oriented organization. Consistently supportive of the nationalistic objectives of the Canadian broadcasting system, the establishment and enhancement of the CBC, the development of community programming, and the emergence of nonprofit community broadcasting, it has resisted the commercialization of broadcasting, the establishment of a separate regulatory board, and the initial licensing of cable undertakings. Although it has been dissolved and revived many times throughout its history, whenever major decisions on the future direction of broadcasting are to be taken, the Canadian Broadcasting League rallies to the defense of nationalistic goals. Its major complaint is that "broadcasting in Canada and especially the relationship between programming and finance is wrong and needs reform."

In addition to the league, various federal governments have expressed concern for the way broadcasting has been developing in Canada. In response to these activities, a myriad of investigative bodies have been established to determine what Canadians want and how best to achieve it. Most recently, the Conservative government has created two committees in this regard. The first was directed to review the functioning of the CBC-RC and suggest ways in which it could be more efficiently operated. The second must review the entire spectrum of communications policy in Canada. Regardless of its specific findings, the debate on Canadian broadcasting can be expected to continue long into the future.

NEW TECHNOLOGIES

The challenge created by technological change was identified earlier as a recurring theme in Canadian broadcasting. Canada traditionally has been slow to respond to technological innovations. Rather than anticipating change and preparing to use it to further the objectives of the Canadian broadcasting system, governments have been forced to react to the changes after they have occurred. This strategy has proven to be very ineffective.

After the introduction of radio and television technologies, cable television delivery systems presented the next major challenge to Canadian policymakers. Initially, growth was rapid because the new technology provided easy access to American television signals. Moreover, with the advent of color television, cable provided clearer signals, and subscribers had come to expect better definition in their television pictures. It appears that cable has now reached its saturation point, however. Over 60 percent of Canadian households subscribe to cable services. Further penetration is unlikely, as only sparsely populated areas, where cable is not economically feasible, remain unserved. Accordingly, where available, cable remains the preferred distribution system.

Satellites also offer tremendous unrealized potential for the distribution of television signals. Canada's satellite company, Telesat Canada, operates a series of Anik satellites for domestic use. Currently, Telesat has considerable excess capacity. Although Telesat's per channel rates are comparable to those in the United States, per subscriber rates are much higher because of the small population base. At present, a number of television services are delivered via satellite, including specialized pay television, educational television, and regional channels. CANCOM, a satellite-delivered broadcasting service for Canadians living in underserved communities, is experiencing a number of difficulties. Time-zone anomalies, substantial rate differentials based on community size, reception of "free" unauthorized U.S. satellite signals, and a relatively small potential market make it difficult for CANCOM to achieve maximum penetration and thereby reduce subscriber rates to affordable levels.

Private ownership of television-receiver-only satellite dishes is permitted in Canada. This equipment, however, remains prohibitively expensive for the average Canadian. In fact, only when more powerful satellites are utilized will receiving dishes become smaller and cheaper. A problem currently exists in the use of satellite receiver units by owners or managers of large apartment or hotel complexes. These master antenna units pick up satellite signals that are then transmitted to individual units within the complex. These systems are normally used to access American satellite signals that the users perceive to be "free." Such action not only threatens the stability of the local cable outlets, it also undermines the regulatory authority, which seeks to promote the Canadian broadcasting system.

Other technological innovations that have affected Canadian broadcasting include videocassette recorders and videotext services. More than one in ten Canadian households has a VCR, and that number is still rising. Penetration of VCRs has, in fact, been faster than that of pay television services. The growth of videotext services, on the other hand, has been slower than expected. The government sponsored the Telidon system, which began in 1981, utilizing telephone, cable, television, and computer services to provide a high-quality videotext service. Despite its ability to interface with a variety of terminals, sales of Telidon have not met expectations.

In general, the new broadcasting technologies hold forth the possibility that a variety of broadcasting services will be available to Canadians. While change was encouraged initially to improve signal quality, current adjustments serve to increase viewer choice and flexibility. In effect, this exacerbates the problem of the Americanization of the broadcasting system. As more and more channels become available, many experts fear the further homogenization of the airwaves.

Of course, this is not a uniquely Canadian problem. Other nations are also aware of the increasing globalization of the communications industry. The future is not entirely bleak, however. As the number of channels increases, it will become more difficult for any one nation to produce enough programming to fill them all. The goal for Canada and other countries is to produce high-quality features capable of entertaining international audiences. Only in this way can the national production industry be saved.

CONCLUSION/FORECAST

For Canadian policymakers, the expression of Canadian ideas and values via the single Canadian broadcasting system has always been the predominant objective. The most recent policy paper of the federal Department of Communications (March 1983) emphasizes that requirement but also acknowledges the problems created by economic and technological factors. The paper attests to the reality of increased choice in the Canadian marketplace and reasserts the need for a high-quality Canadian alternative. In order to ensure that opinion, the department has initiated a program of federal incentives to help strengthen the Canadian production industry. It is hoped that this measure will provide for the exhibition of Canadian programs on Canadian television stations as well as for the sale of these features in the international marketplace.

In addition to the practical realities and problems of broadcasting in Canada, the field of communication has also been examined on a theoretical level by at least two of Canada's leading academic thinkers. Marshall McLuhan, a technological humanist, provided insights into the technical extensions of the human experience. He argued that the numbing effects of technology can be prevented by adopting attitudes of sensitivity and resourcefulness. It must be recognized that the electronic media subtly alter perceptions. Harold Innis, a technological realist, claimed that humanity is trapped within the bias of technology or communication but suggests that a balance can be achieved.

Both Innis and McLuhan recognized that the advent of instantaneous communication would lead to the globalization of values, thoughts, and perceptions. Innis, in particular, warned of the deleterious effect of American influences in Canadian society. For McLuhan, these influences are global in nature. Neither philosopher, however, foresaw the vast technological changes that were yet to affect the world and make it even smaller.

Since radio began, Canadian officials have been faced with a challenge—how to use the technology to further national goals. Those objectives have not yet been fully realized. Broadcasting respects no national boundaries. Content regulations, ownership rules, economic incentives, and other measures have all been instituted to ensure a Canadian presence on the airwaves. Only a strengthened and continuing commitment to that objective can effect any meaningful change.

BIBLIOGRAPHY

Audley, Paul. *Canada's Cultural Industries: Broadcasting, Publishing, Records, and Film.* Toronto: James Lorimer, 1983.

Canada. Committee on Broadcasting. *Report.* Ottawa: Queen's Printer, 1965.

———. Department of Communications. *Towards a New National Broadcasting Policy.* Ottawa: Minister of Supply and Services, 1983.

———. Federal Cultural Policy Review Committee. *Report.* Ottawa: Minister of Supply and Services, 1982.

———. *The Uncertain Mirror: Report of Parliament. Senate. Special Senate Committee on Mass Media.* Ottawa: Queen's Printer, 1970.

———. Royal Commission on Broadcasting. *Report.* 2 vols. Ottawa: Queen's Printer, 1957.

———. Royal Commission on Radio Broadcasting. *Report.* Ottawa: Queen's Printer, 1929.

———. Royal Commission on the National Development in the Arts, Letters, and Sciences. *Report.* Ottawa: Queen's Printer, 1951.

Ellis, David. *Evolution of the Canadian Broadcasting System: Objectives and Realities, 1928–1968.* Ottawa: Minister of Supply and Services, 1979.

Hallman, E. S., with H. Hindley. *Broadcasting in Canada.* Toronto: General Publishing Co., 1977.

Innis, Harold. *Bias of Communications.* 2nd ed. Toronto: University of Toronto Press, 1964.

———. *Empire and Communications.* Toronto: University of Toronto Press, 1950.

Irving, John A., ed. *Mass Media in Canada.* Toronto: Ryerson Press, 1962.

Jamieson, D. *The Troubled Air.* Fredericton, Brunswick: Brunswick Press, 1966.

Lyman, Peter. *Canada's Video Revolution: Pay-TV, Home Video, and Beyond.* Ottawa: Canadian Institute for Economic Policy, 1983.

McFadyen, Stuart, Colin Hoskins, and David Gillen. *Canadian Broadcasting: Market Structure and Economic Performance.* Montreal: Institute for Research on Public Policy, 1980.

McLuhan, Marshall. *Culture Is Our Business.* New York: McGraw-Hill, 1970.

———. *Gutenberg Galaxy.* Toronto: University of Toronto Press, 1962.

———, and Quentin Fiore. *The Medium Is the Message.* New York: Random, 1967.

Peers, Frank W. *The Politics of Canadian Broadcasting, 1920–1951.* Toronto: University of Toronto Press, 1969.

———. *The Public Eye: Television and the Politics of Canadian Broadcasting, 1952–1968.* Toronto: University of Toronto Press, 1979.

Prang, Margaret. "The Origins of Public Broadcasting in Canada." *Canadian Historical Review* 46 (March 1965): 1–31.

Shea, Albert A. *Broadcasting the Canadian Way.* Toronto: Harvest House, 1963.

Singer, Benjamin, ed. *Communications in Canadian Society.* Toronto: Addison-Wesley, 1983.

Weir, E. Austin. *The Struggle for National Broadcasting in Canada.* Toronto: McClelland and Stewart, 1965.

CHILE

Marvin Alisky

This nation on the geographically remote rim of the Spanish Empire pro-
claimed its independence from Spain in 1810 and, after years of battles,
achieved it in 1818. Chile's temporary constitution recognized that its Hispanic legacy had entwined cross and crown and that a republican form of
government would continue that tie. The constitution of 1833 made that
formal union permanent until the promulgation of the constitution of 1925,
which separated church and state. Anticipating the separation, both laical
and church groups busied themselves getting pioneer radio stations on the
air.

The rise and fall of the parliamentary era shaped the beginning of Chilean
broadcasting. From 1891 to 1925 a strong Congress dominated a weak
presidency, spawning a multiparty political system. Until ended by the 1925
constitution, this system encouraged nine or ten political parties each to
publish a newspaper and, after 1922, to own a radio station. Broadcasting
arose in Chile against a public life backdrop of multiparty democracy.

Daily radio broadcasting began on August 9, 1922, with the inauguration
of the first commercial transmitter as the Voz de Chile (Voice of Chile) in
Santiago. Its owners had been vying with the Ministry of Education and
with the Catholic church for the first station concession. At the time, public
sentiment in the newspapers and in Congress favored a privately owned
corporation over a government entity and a laical organization over a religious one. Chile was on the verge of legally separating church and state.
Later, during the tensions dividing the nation under Marxist President Salvador Allende during 1970 to 1973, Catholic-controlled stations articulated
domestic ideals in the face of a campaign by the government to replace

constitutional democracy with a Communist state. The incremental effort collapsed with the 1973 ouster of Allende.

After Mexico, Argentina and Brazil in 1950 ushered in television, an experimental television transmitter went on the air in Santiago in 1951. Regular television broadcasting began in 1952.

REGULATION

In 1927 when the British Broadcasting Corporation began as a noncommercial public trust, independent of partisan politics and bureaucracy even at the cabinet level, the Chilean government sent a study mission to London to confer with the Crawford Committee of the House of Commons, which had studied and drafted the BBC charter in 1926. The Chileans returned to Santiago imbued with the idea of bringing to South America a board of civic leaders representing the various interests of society—education, labor unions, business firms, and agricultural interests—paralleling the British concept. But the political unrest that had begun to pervade Chilean politics prompted Congress to veto the idea.

Instead, Chile's government decided to create a radio commission that would update and meet the needs of the growing broadcasting industry. Until then, a 1922 radio law had been the guideline for licensing and regulation, but that measure dealt more with radiotelephony messages, ship-to-shore communications at the harbors of Viña del Mar and Valparaíso, and shortwave emergency weather forecasts.

Chile participated with its neighbors for international cooperation. From November 1 to December 13, 1937, the first Inter-American Radio Conference, in Havana, found the nations of the Western Hemisphere voting to cooperate so that neighboring countries' radio frequencies and transmitting power did not interfere with each other's transmissions. Mexico, the United States, and Canada signed the North American Regional Broadcasting Agreement, which was honored until Fidel Castro ordered his Cuban government to violate it in 1985. Brazil and Argentina signed an agreement to avoid frequency and power conflicts, as did Argentina and Uruguay, guaranteeing radio harmony across the estuary of La Plata. Chile signed a treaty with Peru that mapped listening regions for northernmost Chile and southernmost Peru. But neither Chile nor Argentina chose to put in writing any binational agreement, assuming that the high peaks of the Andes Mountains would take care of most interference, given the transmitting power and the directional antennas of both shortwave and mediumwave stations.

Chile also worked for internal control. On November 22, 1944, the Reglamento de Transmisiones de Radiodifusión (Broadcasting Transmission Regulations) became the permanent ongoing legal basis for Chile's system of broadcasting. Updated periodically, this law now covers television, cable transmissions, and satellite communications.

Since radio began in 1922, Chilean governments have recognized broadcasting as a privately owned medium with commercial funding. The state, however, has from time to time engaged in broadcasting and in supporting radio and television stations licensed to universities and other entities.

During the era of Marxist President Salvador Allende's government, bureaucrats played an active role in Chilean broadcasting. From November 1970 to September 1973 Communist pressures bedeviled non-Marxist stations and networks. With only one-third of the Congress behind him and a razor-slim electoral victory of 1.4 percent plurality over two non-Marxist candidates in the 1970 election, Allende tried by nonmilitary means to communize Chile. But many radio facilities were owned by members of the reforming Christian Democratic party, known as Catholic reformers—the opposition party.

On December 27, 1970, after less than two months in office, Allende issued a decree ordering all Chilean radio outlets to play music composed by Chilean citizens 25 percent of the time and to devote an additional 15 percent of music programming to Chilean folk songs. Neither the listening public nor broadcasting managers ever accepted the decree. The national police (Carabiñeros) jailed seven radio station program directors who defied the order for two weeks. By then, the decree had engendered so much public ridicule that word went out unofficially to the minister of the interior not to enforce the music regulation. In television, Allende's Popular Unity youth group, a federation of the Communist party and the Socialist party, violently attacked the Catholic University's broadcasting station, defacing its building with obscene graffiti.

After a month of strikes by taxi drivers' and truck drivers' unions, plus a month of boycotts of retail stores, the Allende administration began to totter. On September 11, 1973, the army attacked the Presidential Palace. Pro-Allende and anti-Allende partisans fought for a few hours, and Allende was killed on a balcony waving a submachine gun that Fidel Castro had given him.

The ouster of Allende did not bring democracy back to Chile, however. Instead, a rightist regime under General Augusto Pinochet took control of the government. Before Allende's radicalization of Chilean politics, and the rightist response, Chile on the whole had enjoyed many decades of constitutional rule, elected governments, and freedom of the press.

In the period leading up to the Allende and Pinochet regimes, Chile enjoyed the fullest freedom for its radio and television outlets. Jorge Alessandri, president from 1958 to 1964, implemented the principles of liberty embodied in the National party, a unification of the longtime Conservative and Liberal parties. During the presidency of Eduardo Frei, from 1964 to 1970, the government granted full constitutional freedoms under a leader from the Christian Democratic party.

Since November 1970, however, Chile has not enjoyed a communications system free from government pressures. Allende's Marxists harassed non-Marxist and anti-Marxist broadcasters alike with tax audits, building inspections, and the like. Since Allende's rule, the Pinochet government has pressured radio and television outlets that criticize the government. Emergency decrees simply created formal censorship while the old constitution remained suspended. On March 11, 1981, a new constitution replaced the 1925 document. This new charter legitimizes military rule and has clauses that permit "state of emergency" situations that authorize formal media censorship.

ECONOMIC STRUCTURE

Chile, a long and thin land area, shaped like a thermometer, has a climate that acts accordingly. Not more than 100 miles in width, this republic stretches 2,600 miles along the South Pacific shore of South America. The farther south one goes to its tip near the Antarctic, the colder the weather. The farther north, toward the equator, the warmer. Hence the population tends to bunch in the central valleys containing the capital, Santiago, and the nearby seaports of Viña del Mar and Valparaíso.

Half of Chile's total population of 10 million lives in the metropolitan areas of Santiago and the two seaports. Consequently, broadcasting is focused on these three urban areas. Yet radio and television networks do have provincial affiliates to connect the cities of Antofagasta in the north and Concepción in the south.

Radio broadcasting has involved many other concerns. Copper mining, light industries, agriculture, and wine production have been mainstays of the Chilean economy. Each of these industries advertises heavily on the nation's airwaves.

Before the 1970s the nationwide news agency, Orbe, owned by the leaders of the Christian Democratic party, invested in small radio stations. But with the political pressure placed on Orbe by the Allende regime, the news agency divested itself of its broadcast properties. Professional sports promoters have been the major stockholders of Radio Carrera, whose programming has concentrated on soccer, tennis, horseracing, and fishing.

In the 1960s Avelino Uruzua, publisher of the humor magazine *Topaze*, popularized in Chile various programs that approached "Laugh In," "Hee Haw," and "Saturday Night Live" and focused on political satire. But under leftist and then rightist conformity, satirist producers and writers have left broadcasting. Consequently, Chilean productions of the 1980s tend to be dignified and humorless, carefully avoiding political criticism.

Broadcasting education holds several interesting contrasts. To some degree, Chile has set the standard for communications studies in South America. In 1942, for example, the Congress enacted a law recognizing a new university degree at the University of Chile in the School of Juridical and Social Sciences for attorneys specializing in regulatory law, including broadcasting. This was the first recognition in Latin America of a branch of regulatory law that emphasized the mass media in the legal curriculum.

A 1967 article in *Journalism Quarterly* declared mass-media education in Chile to be a model for Latin America. Four of the republic's eight universities then offered broadcasting and newspaper majors in professional-level schools of journalism. Of the 900 students enrolled in these areas in 1966, only 29 students completed degree requirements. Ten years later, in 1976, the number of university graduates with a media degree, which is at the master's degree level in U.S. equivalency, had increased 30 percent. Chilean universities have never been interested in offering an undergraduate degree in media education.

On the other hand, many professionals fail to support university training in communication studies. In fact, broadcast managers and program directors prefer students with general education and some skill training for six months to a year at a trade school, rather than new employees with the master's degree in broadcasting. For one thing, starting salaries would not justify hiring someone with a graduate degree at a local station, and openings tend to go to those with some local experience. For another reason, management looks with skepticism at university faculties, where the professors have not criticized the rightist government and the student organizations have been torn between leftist and rightist leaders. One network director stated: "Our universities do not graduate broadcast journalists; they graduate agitators."

PROGRAMMING

In radio, Chilean stations have been especially successful in developing morning shows with news and background commentary on matters of agriculture. Cattle and livestock ranchers and producers of domestic food crops still set aside early morning time periods to hear "ag hours" over several radio outlets. The Sociedad Nacional de Agricultura network, located in Santiago, has provincial affiliates in Valparaíso, Arica, and Los Angeles. The Magallanes Network of Santiago transmits morning farm news and features via affiliates in Antofagasta and Punta Arenas, linking the far northern and southern audiences to the central valley. The Sociedad Radiodifusoras Australes network links Radio Panamericana in Santiago with affiliates in Rancagua, Osorno, and Puerto Montt in the far south.

In Santiago the radio station Voz de Chile, owned by the Claro family, has long reflected democratic reforms of the Christian Democratic party plus some anti-Marxist views. Several Santiago, Viña del Mar, and Valparaíso radio stations draw audiences by specializing in classical, pop, rock, and jazz music.

In the realm of television drama, several Chilean producers, writers, and directors have established international reputations. In the 1960s, for example, Chilean television producer Claudio Guzmán came to Hollywood and captured top audience ratings with the hit series "I Dream of Jeannie."

In 1974 Guzmán took time from his Hollywood productions to develop a sixty-five-episode English-Spanish television series called "Villa Alegre." Each half-hour segment combined comedy situations with singing and dancing, plus dramatic presentations stressing health, nutrition, and environmental matters. The cast consisted of ten adults and eight children representative of a host of Latin American nations. The series premiered in Chile, and then recorded episodes on videocassettes aired in other South American nations as well as in California, Texas, Florida, and New York.

Television networks and their anchor stations in Santiago are all owned by universities. Channel 9 belongs to the University of Chile in Santiago, having been founded in 1959. Channel 13, the property of Catholic University of Santiago, was established in 1962. Channel 8, owned by Catholic University of Valparaíso, was created in 1959. Channel 3 is owned by the University of the North in Antofagasta.

Under Chilean law, ownership of outlets by universities does not prevent the airing of commercials. Channel 11 in Santiago, however, has a cultural format and substitutes public service announcements for advertising spots.

Channel 4 programming in some regions has been reserved for cultural and educational features by the Empresa Nacional de Telecomunicaciones (ENTEL, National Telecommunications Enterprise). ENTEL works directly with the Ministry of Education.

Programming production mirrors the population. Much of the program production for Chile originates in the greater metropolitan area of Santiago. Even features produced for the rural areas are taped there.

The government now manages a holding corporation, Televisión Nacional, which allows all programs except for news to operate as privately produced commercial shows. News features on television come from the university-operated outlets plus reports from public information producers of various government agencies. The profile is a mixture of public and private sources, with governmental control in the background. Of course, the government is ready to step in should reporting become radical or offensive.

Of the 34 television stations, plus their 91 repeaters, 23 outlets are affiliates of the National Network. The others belong to regional video networks. Inasmuch as Chile's total population of 10 million subdivides into 3 million family homes and dwellings, and there are 2.95 million television receivers in daily use, the republic has almost universal television coverage. Its video saturation holds a slight edge over the largest and most industrialized Latin American nations—Brazil, Argentina, Mexico, and Venezuela—and compares in nationwide distribution with some European countries.

Chilean broadcasting is produced in Spanish. With only a handful of Indians among its basically white and mestizo (hybrid) population, no incentive exists in Chile to broadcast in minority languages. This contrasts with its neighbors to the north, Peru and Bolivia, where sizeable segments of the populations can be found who communicate in the Quechua and Aymará languages. Like its other neighbor, Argentina, Chile has a population unified by the Spanish language.

NEW TECHNOLOGIES

Cable television so far has remained limited, being utilized to connect communities embedded in deep valleys surrounded by the Andes Mountains rising above 15,000 feet and hence otherwise cut off from direct transmissions. Satellite communication dishes can be found atop bank buildings and governmental agencies for special message transmissions.

CONCLUSION/FORECAST

Since 1970 Chile has suffered an abridgment of its heretofore constitutional democratic society. Since 1973 it has had relative stability, but at the price of media censorship.

With a population 95 percent literate and with most of its children of primary school age attending classes, Chile offers a potential for sophisticated articulation in the area of communications that many other Latin American nations lack. In fact, formal education and mass media distribution are better than in most developing nations. Chile even has a collective memory of constitutional openness for decades before 1970. Even with governmental guidance, Chilean broadcasting displays a substantial technical and production capability. As to what lies ahead, conjecture might suggest a return to a more open society.

BIBLIOGRAPHY

Alisky, Marvin, John C. Merrill, et al. *Global Journalism: A Survey of the World's Mass Media.* New York: Longman Press, 1983.

Arón, Roberto. *Anteproyecto de Legislación Radial: Facultad de Ciencias Jurídicas y Sociales de la Universidad de Chile.* Santiago: Imprenta Palma of Santiago, 1942.

Brazil. Ministério das Comunicações. *Codigo Brasileiro de Telecomunicações.* Brasilia: Dentel of Brasilia, 1980.

Chile. Dirección General de Informaciones y Cultura. *Reglamento de Transmisiones de Radiodifusión.* Santiago: Diario Oficial Press of Santiago, 1944.

Chilean Catholic Bishops, eds. *Los Medios de Difusión*. Santiago: Secretary General's Office of the Episcopate in Santiago, 1962.

Fonseca, Jaime M. *Communication Policies in Costa Rica*. Paris: UNESCO, 1977.

Ganley, Oswald H., and Gladys D. Ganley. *To Inform or to Control?* New York: McGraw-Hill, 1982.

Green, Timothy. *The Universal Eye: World Television in the Seventies*. New York: Stein and Day, 1972.

Menanteau, Dario. "Professionalism of Journalists in Santiago de Chile." *Journalism Quarterly* 44 (Winter 1967): 715–24.

Montenegro, Hernán. *TV: Comunicación o Contaminación?* Santiago: Editorial Galdoc of Santiago, 1981.

Morel, Consuelo, and Isabel Zagers. *Historia de la Radio en Chile*. Santiago: Centro de Comunicaciones Sociales de la Universidad Catolica de Chile, 1979.

Neville, Timothy, and Dietrich Berwanger. *A Handbook of TV Production in Developing Countries*. Bonn: Friedrich-Ebert, 1976.

CHINA

Dezhen Zou, Fei Wang, and Zheng Meiyun

HISTORY

Radio broadcasting first appeared in China in January 1923 when an American reporter, E. C. Osborn, installed a radio station in Shanghai. Shortly thereafter, the Chinese government authorities set up radio outlets in Harbin, Tianjin, and Beijing (formerly Peiping). The Harbin radio facility, which began operating in October 1926, was believed to be the first official radio station in China.

In the spring of 1927 the Shanghai Xinxin department store pioneered China's commercial broadcasting service. In August 1928, after the Kuomintang came to power, the Central Broadcasting Station managed by the Kuomintang government was inaugurated in Nanjing. Next came local radio outlets under the control of regional and local governments. In August 1929 the Kuomintang government issued Rules Governing Telecommunications, permitting the establishment and operation of private radio stations. This decree led to the creation of a host of privately owned educational, commercial, and religious facilities. Eventually, the number of private outlets reached fifty-five, most of which were located in Shanghai. In addition to its domestic radio networks, the Kuomintang government operated a short-wave external service, the Voice of China, in Chongqing. It went on the air in February 1939. After the downfall of the Kuomintang regime in 1949, the Central Broadcasting Station in Nanjing was moved to Taiwan.

The People's Broadcasting Service led by the Chinese Communist party started during the War of Resistance against the Japanese. In the spring of 1940 the Broadcasting Preparatory Committee headed by Zhou Enlai was established in Yanan to make preparations for installing a radio station.

On December 30, 1940, for the first time, a radio station in the service of the Communists—the Yanan Xinhua Radio Station—began its broadcasts. The station was under the supervision of the Xinhua News Agency, China's official news agency. In the spring of 1943, due to technical problems, the outlet ceased functioning until September 5, 1945. On March 20, 1947, after the Yanan evacuation, the station was renamed the Shanbei Xinhua Radio Station. It was moved to Beijing on March 25, 1949. On June 5 of the same year, the Central Broadcasting Administration (renamed the Central Broadcasting Bureau in October) was set up to oversee the nationwide broadcasting services. Since then, the broadcasting service has been independent of the Xinhua News Agency. On September 27, 1949, the Peiping Xinhua Radio Station had its name changed to the Beijing Xinhua Radio Station. On December 5 of the same year, after the founding of the People's Republic of China, it was renamed the Central People's Broadcasting Station (CPBS) and started transmitting nationwide. The Chinese People's Liberation Army stationed in the cities took over the local radio outlets managed by the Kuomintang government, keeping them on the air as well as establishing new facilities. Now there are radio outlets in every province, municipality, and autonomous region and in large cities. As to the privately owned radio stations, some were dissolved and some were merged with local outlets after a period of joint state and private ownership.

The Overseas Broadcasting Service of the People's Republic of China also started before the founding of the new regime. On September 11, 1947, the Shanbei Xinhua Radio Station began its English-language broadcasts. After moving into Beijing, the facility initiated another foreign-language program, the Japanese-language program. Following the rapid development of the overseas service, the government established a new agency, the International Broadcasting Station, separate from the home service in April 1950. In May 1978 this entity was renamed the International Broadcasting Station. The call sign of overseas broadcasting is Radio Beijing. The outlet broadcasts worldwide in thirty-eight foreign languages.

China's television service was initiated in 1958 when Peking Television began experimental broadcasts on May 1 of that year. It officially went on the air on September 2, 1958. In May 1973 it started experimental color television transmissions and since 1977 has been broadcasting color programs on two channels. On May 1, 1978, Peking Television was renamed China Central Television (CCTV), becoming the center of the nation's television network, which consists of provincial, municipal, and other district television outlets.

In May 1982 China elevated the broadcasting arrangement to ministerial level by naming it the Ministry of Radio and Television (formerly the Central Broadcasting Bureau). The ministry is in charge of the administration of the radio and television broadcasting services throughout China.

REGULATION

Radio and television broadcasting in China is organized under unified leadership with shared responsibility at different levels throughout the nation. The Ministry of Radio and Television is the highest regulatory mechanism of China's radio and television networks, which consist of radio broadcasting, television, wire services, tape recording, video recording, and phonograph recording. It authorizes allocation of frequencies and station installation and exercises direct leadership over the Central People's Broadcasting Station, Radio Beijing, and China Central Television.

The Ministry of Radio and Television is under the State Council. It reports to the council on administrative policies and technical and economic practices and follows the guidelines of the Department of Propaganda of the Communist Party Central Committee on programs. Local radio and television stations come under the direct control of the radio and television agencies of provinces, autonomous regions, or municipalities. The agency reports mainly to the local government and also to the Ministry of Radio and Television on administrative issues and technical and economic matters and follows directives from the Communist party on programs. The same is true of the relationship between regional bureaus and country bodies.

Besides offering local programs, the local outlets are required to provide the Central People's Broadcasting Station and China Central Television with features of national interest and help fulfill the assignments given by the central facilities. In so doing, they are acting as a collective reporter under the direction of the Ministry of Radio and Television. Moreover, the ministry has reporters stationed in the twenty-nine provinces, autonomous regions, and municipalities and in Chongqing, Dalian, and Hong Kong covering the areas at the request of the Central People's Broadcasting Station and Radio Beijing. They are ultimately responsible to both the Ministry of Radio and Television and the Communist party in the respective regions.

China's radio and television broadcasting is a government operation. The authorities at various levels are asked to examine the programs and see whether they are in accord with official government policies and facts. Important programs should be sent directly to the Department of Propaganda of the Communist Party Central Committee or other ministers and agencies concerned for approval, while local programs are distributed to various party committees and government officials at local levels. China's broadcasting policy focuses on educating and invigorating the people of various nationalities throughout the nation in building the socialist civilization materially, culturally, and ideologically, and on promoting friendship between the Chinese people and the people of other countries.

Although China has no broadcasting laws as of 1986 (the Committee of Education, Sciences, Literature, and Hygiene of the People's Congress has worked on a law of the press that would be applicable to broadcasting), the government has created several rules on broadcasting administration and techniques. Article 49 of the Common Program drafted in 1949 by the Chinese People's Consultative Conference stipulated that "freedom of truthful news reporting shall be safeguarded. The utilization of the press for slander, for undermining the interests of the State and the people and for provoking world war shall be prohibited. The people's broadcasting and publishing enterprises shall be developed."

During the 1950s the Press Administration (dissolved in 1952) under the Administrative Council made it a rule that the duty of broadcasting is to release news, issue official orders, and provide education and entertainment. Furthermore, article 22 of the constitution of the People's Republic of China adopted by the National People's Congress in 1982 held that "the State undertakes to develop radio and television."

In short, year after year, the departments of radio and television have never failed to abide by the documents and pronouncements issued by the Central Committee of the Communist party of China and the instructions, decisions, or notices sent out by the Department of Propaganda, the state councils, and the Ministry of Radio and Television.

ECONOMIC STRUCTURE

China's radio and television broadcasting stations at the national and local level are owned and managed by the central or local government. Apart from funds provided by the governments, income from advertising and broadcasting service is an important source of revenue, but it covers only a small portion of the total operating budget. A new policy put forward at the Eleventh National Radio and Television Working Conference is to raise funds from the public for broadcasting operations; that is, enterprises, collective economic organizations, army units, government organizations, and universities are encouraged to operate radio and television relay stations in accordance with government policies and guidelines. In addition, individuals can make donations for the setting up of small translator stations, but they are not allowed to produce programs.

Since 1983 China has established a nationwide radio and television network on four administrative levels: state, province, city, and county. The central and local broadcasting administrations share responsibilities for constructing broadcasting outlets pursuant to a unified policy and for developing planning and technical standards. The Ministry of Radio and Television is mainly responsible for overseeing service projects and some nationwide endeavors such as the launching of broadcast satellites and the central color television centers, while the local broadcasting agencies regulate the central and local broadcasting facilities and their management, including the investment of capital construction, maintenance, and personnel.

The minister of radio and television is concurrently the editor-in-chief. Subordinate to this government official are the directors of the Central People's Broadcasting Station, Radio Beijing, and China Central Television, who are in charge of programming. The chief engineer helps the minister with technical work, while the deputy ministers assist the minister in programming, technology, and administration, and the chief secretary and assistant secretary help take care of the daily office routine.

In January 1979 the China Television Service Corporation was established under the Ministry of Radio and Television and started selling advertising at home and in foreign nations. In September of the same year, with the celebration of the twentieth anniversary of China Central Television, advertisements appeared for the first time on Chinese television. In January 1980 the Central Broadcasting Station began carrying an advertising program entitled "Advertisement and Art."

In 1982, following the development of advertising in China, the State Council issued the following document: "Provisional Regulations Regarding the Management of Advertising." The guidelines stipulated that the General Administration of Industry and Commerce, with its local branches, is the regulatory body concerned with advertising in China. Accordingly, any advertising company, agency, or firm engaged in this commercial enterprise must register and obtain a license in accordance with the regulations governing the management and registration of industrial and commercial operations. In addition, the government specifically prohibited broadcast advertisements with the following content:

1. Violations of government policies, decrees, and laws
2. Disrespect to the dignity of the nation's various nationalities
3. Reactionary, obscene, ugly, and superstitious displays
4. Libelous propaganda
5. Actions counter to the government security and military regulations

To manage and operate radio and television stations, staff members are recruited mainly from other news agencies, from university and college graduating classes, and through public announcement and advertisements. The Ministry of Radio and Television places considerable importance on in-service training and organizational development activities. Since 1984 the ministry has established training classes for selected staff members.

The Beijing Broadcasting Institute is the only institution of higher learning in China that trains radio and television personnel for news programs as well as technical operations. As of 1986 the institute had a student body of more than 1,000 individuals. Since its founding in 1959, more than 4,000 specialists have graduated. They are working in radio and television stations throughout the nation. In addition, several broadcasting training schools have been created in the provinces, and preparations have begun for the establishment of two more broadcasting institutes.

PROGRAMMING

Broadcasting in China represents the interests of the socialist nation. It serves as a bridge between the Communist party and the government on the one hand and the people on the other. The programs on radio and television must reflect the wishes and demands of the people. Consequently, program policies are based upon this principle. Government policies stipulate that radio and television programming must adhere to the socialist political orientation, observe strictly the programming guidelines of the party and the government, and focus attention on the main task of unifying the people during this difficult period. In addition, China's broadcasting service is to serve the people both at home and in foreign lands. Internally, radio and television must endeavor to educate the people in patriotism and communism as well as inspire the people with enthusiasm in the building of a socialist civilization, materially and ideologically. Externally, broadcasting must highlight China's position and policies on domestic and international issues, provide truthful, varied, and vivid information about China to overseas listeners in order to help them understand China and the Chinese people, and promote friendship with the people of other countries. In these circumstances, the staff members of radio and television must be conscious of their social responsibilities, keep a close watch on social effects of programs to ensure that they are truthful, informative, and interesting, and never allow any reactionary or obscene content.

At present, there is no private programming in China. Television stations as well as television film studios managed by the government produce features in league with other organizations such as film studios and art organizations. The latter are paid for their productions and participation. The China Council for Television Play Art also purchases videotapes of foreign television programs and feature films.

Special attention is directed to news programs pursuant to instructions from the Ministry of Radio and Television. The ministry stipulates that news programs should become the core of the daily programming fare. Stress is placed upon developing an informative and timely news program that explains government policies to the people. To achieve these objectives, modern technology such as electronic news gathering (ENG) is used extensively in production and editing. Some television stations have also been equipped with mobile news vans. In addition, news programs are relayed by microwave to twenty-seven provincial capitals and municipalities except in remote areas like Wulumuqi in Xinjiang and Lhasa in Tibet, where the programs of China Central Television sometimes can be watched through experimental synchronous communications satellites. Of course, news of great immediate significance is relayed over the nation by satellite.

On April 1, 1980, China Central Television began to relay international news from VISNEWS, a British news agency, and WTN (Worldwide Television News). On January 16 and April 5, 1984, China Central Television joined Zone B and Zone A of the Asia Broadcasting Unit in news exchange, resulting in a great increase of news from Third World nations.

There are yet no regular programs on religion except for an occasional release of radio and television coverage on the activities of a religious organization. China's policy is to protect the freedom of religious belief.

Educational programs play an important part in the general programs of radio and television stations. At the beginning of 1979 China Central Television and the Ministry of Education jointly inaugurated the Television University. China Central Television broadcasts Television University features for about three hours a day in the morning to the whole nation, and there is a rebroadcast for Beijing in the afternoon. Courses include basic science, mechanical engineering, and electrical engineering as well as basic courses on technology. Television University has an enrollment of 450,000 students, not including the large number of listeners not registered in formal study. It has already graduated 160,000 full-time students and 200,000 single-course enrollments.

In 1981 the Central People's Broadcasting Station and the Chinese National Agricultural Commission jointly sponsored a Central Broadcasting School of Agriculture. It enrolled 400,000 students in the first term. In addition to these educational efforts, many stations offer language courses in English, Japanese, and French and lectures on special subjects ranging from Chinese literature to mechanical drawing.

Both the Central People's Broadcasting Station and Central Television have broadcast children's programs, of which the most popular are "Star and Touch" (for teenagers), "Little Trumpet" (for preschoolers), "Children's Life," and the cartoon "Lalin and Xiaolin." During vacation periods radio and television stations offer special programming for students.

BROADCAST REFORM

The Central Committee of the Communist party of China has issued a notice asking the various party committees and radio and television organizations at the national and local levels to strengthen and improve the work of broadcasting. China's broadcasting in the past served actually as an announcer of the Xinhua News Agency. Due to historical reasons, for a long period of time it had to depend on the Xinhua News Agency for its programs. And, of course, television could not manage without the help of film studios. Experiences have shown that in order to improve the quality of programs, both radio and television should adhere to a policy of "Walking on One's Own Feet." This policy was developed more than thirty years ago and was taken up at the Tenth National Broadcasting Working Conference in 1980. "Walking on One's Own Feet" stipulates that radio and television programs should not rely solely on newspaper and news agencies, nor should the electronic media use the latter's methods of reporting as their model. Radio and television must develop their own style and give full play to their form of operating.

In March 1983 the Eleventh National Radio and Television Working Conference expanded the policy of "Walking on One's Own Feet" into "Persisting in Walking on One's Own Feet; Carrying On One's Strong Points; Selecting the Essence in the World." This policy means that radio and television should not only focus on their specialty and superiority but also make a serious study of the experiences and strong points of many groups, including news agencies, educational organizations, and art societies, for support and program development.

In recent years, following the aforementioned policy guidelines, radio and television programs have made a distinct improvement, especially news features. The radio and television correspondents at home and abroad have sent in many news reports, produced many programs, and developed live broadcasts from around the world. In addition, the Ministry of Radio and Television has purchased a number of foreign news programs, television plays, and feature films and exchanged programs with foreign broadcasting stations as well.

Conducting criticism on radio and television is another important reform. It is stressed by many officials and viewers that praise dominates radio and television rather than criticism. Radio and television officials should handle criticism correctly, however. While offering criticism over radio and television, they must have the correct stand and explicit purposes and above all place the interests and unity of the nation and people over their own narrow interests. In addition, criticism should be helpful and solve problems. In short, criticism should strengthen the confidence of the people and the prestige of the government.

NEW TECHNOLOGIES

In 1980 the China Central Television, in cooperation with local outlets, began experimental news relay efforts from local to central television studios by microwave. Now the China Central Television station relays programs to provincial capitals and municipalities by microwave rented from the Ministry of Post and Telecommunications. The local facilities are asked to establish microwave circuits in their respective areas. By the end of 1984 the range of microwave had reached 18,485 kilometers.

On April 8, 1984, China launched its first experimental synchronous communications satellite. After traveling eight days, on April 16 it was fixed over the equator, and the next day, on April 17, China Central Television and the Central People's Broadcasting Stations successfully relayed experimental programs by satellite.

In 1985 a fiber-optic system was successfully trial-produced in China, preparing the foundation for the development of China's cable television system. In the middle of 1985 cable television networks were established in Daqing, the industrial city in northeastern China, the Jin Shan Chemical Factory in Shanghai, and the Dong Fang Chemical Factory in Beijing. Apart from these efforts, closed-circuit television systems have been created in most of the first-class hotels in China.

CONCLUSION/FORECAST

The former minister of radio and television addressed the issue of the future prospects of radio and television broadcasting in China in his speech at the Eleventh National Radio and Television Working Conference. At the end of the century, he reported, China will have a modernized radio and television network. The system will be suited to China's economic and social development and commensurate with China's international position. From the period of the Seventh Five-Year Plan (1986–90) to the end of the century, step by step, the voice of China will be heard throughout the land.

BIBLIOGRAPHY

Almanac of China's Economy, 1984. Beijing: Economics and Management Publishing House, 1985.

"Document of the Central Committee of the Communist Party." Unpublished manuscript, 1983.

Journalism Yearbook of China, 1984. Beijing: People's Daily Press, 1985.

"Report of the 10th National Radio and Television Working Conference." Unpublished manuscript, 1983.

"Report of the 11th National Radio and Television Working Conference." Unpublished manuscript, 1983.

Zhao Yuming. *A History of Broadcasting in China*. Beijing: Jilin Broadcasting Institute Press, 1983.

CUBA

John A. Lent

HISTORY

Much like other Third World nations, Cuba was introduced to broadcasting by an amateur, Luís Casas Romero, who, in 1922, operated his station 2LC. The growth of the medium was rather spectacular; by the 1930s stations had developed a technical and production capacity that allowed, in the following decade, for the export of musical and drama shows.

Havana, before the 1959 revolution, had one of the most competitive mixes of media of any city in the world—thirty-two commercial, standard-band radio stations, five television outlets, and twenty-one daily newspapers. Broadcasters were noted for their independent, controversial, and irresponsible natures, setting up stations accused of interfering with U.S. outlets, accepting bribes from and allowing their stations to be owned by government officials, and airing violent attacks against individuals in their "newspapers of the air." As a result of the latter, the government passed the world's first right-to-reply-to-radio laws. But under dictator Fulgencio Batista the authorities also instituted a strict censorship code. Cuba was among the first four Latin American nations to have television; an experimental station was opened in 1949, followed by regular telecasts in January 1950.

Throughout the 1950s, as the rebel forces of Fidel Castro campaigned in the Sierra Maestra, they realized the need for a radio transmitter to link guerrilla units, keep families apprised of the rebels' safety, and acquaint the general population with their motives. Ché Guevara, on February 24, 1958, started Radio Rebelde (7RR) for these purposes. As Batista tightened his censorship, Radio Rebelde's reputation for veracity increased, along with its audience.

Broadcasting's role in the early days of the revolution was so important that one foreign journalist said that Castro's rule was "government by television." Three to four times a week, Castro broadcast four- to six-hour speeches, informing the people of every minute action and exhorting them to support the revolution. By 1960 all radio and television stations had been expropriated by the government and incorporated into two umbrella organizations. Policies were set concerning programming, commercial time was curtailed, and the number of soap operas and foreign shows was reduced. To offset anticommunist propaganda from the United States, the government started Radio Habana Cuba in May 1961, and two years later that outlet became the fourth-largest Communist international broadcaster.

Radio and television had another growth period between 1975 and 1980, when the number of radio transmitters increased from 101 to 122 and the number of television repeaters for the two national networks more than doubled. In addition, the government introduced color television in 1977. The number of receivers increased dramatically as well—for radio, from 15.4 per 100 households in 1975 to 20 per 100 households in 1980; for television, the figures were 6.6 and 8.1 per 100 households, respectively.

As the 1980s dawned, Cuba had 54 radio stations and 3 television-originating facilities (plus 15 provincial, program-originating), all under the supervision of the Instituto Cubano de Radio y Televisión (ICRT). Of the radio outlets, 5 were national networks, 14 were provincial, and 35 were regional stations. Their total output is 900 kilowatts, reportedly capable of covering 99 percent of the island.

REGULATION

Because all mass media function as arms of the state or the Communist party for the purpose of furthering the revolution, they are regulated by the fluctuations of ideology and philosophy of the leadership. Castro, his brother Raul, and the culture minister, Armando Hart Davalos, among a few select others, have set the policies under which broadcasting operates. Their admonitions from time to time set the standard, as did the First Congress of the Communist party in 1975. A section from the platform of that congress states: "The Party shall provide systematic orientation for and attention to the instruments of the mass media and shall promote the enthusiastic and creative participation of all workers who base their opinions on the Communists ... so as to succeed in having the radio, television, written press and films carry out more and more effectively their role in the political, ideological, cultural, technical-scientific and aesthetic education of the population."

The constitution of 1976, which resulted from the First Congress, guaranteed freedom of expression, at the same time regulating the role of media, including broadcasting: "Citizens have freedom of speech and of the press in keeping with the objectives of socialist society. Material conditions for the exercise of that right are provided by the fact that the press, radio, television, movies and other organs of the mass media are state or social property and can never be private property. This assures their use at the exclusive service of the working people and the interest of society."

The First Congress, Castro himself, and others have said that media must be regulated by a fidelity to Marxism-Leninism, the interests of the working class, all-out struggle against the capitalist regimes, proletarian internationalism, and close ties to the masses and mass organizations. Earlier, in 1971 the Cuban Congress on Education and Culture set down a rather hard line on media and culture, stating that the media "are powerful instruments of ideological education whose utilization and development should not be left to spontaneity and improvisation"; that control of the media should be centralized under a "single politico-cultural leadership"; and that political and ideological conditions must be taken into consideration in staffing of the media.

Although from time to time officials ask for criticism, broadcasters know that they cannot criticize strategic goals of the revolution or Castro. As the First Congress pointed out, media criticism must "strictly observe the constructive and fraternal nature which is to be the overriding characteristic of criticism under socialism."

Thus, as this writer had delineated elsewhere, the tasks of broadcasting in Cuba are "to state and advance government policies, objectives and official positions; to report news, information and entertainment; and to mobilize and influence behavior by featuring exemplary individuals or mass organizations."

John Spicer Nichols has pointed out that censorship, in the form of written regulations, is not needed, as broadcasters are in sympathy with the revolution. Although the Department of Revolution Orientation, a division of the Central Committee of the Cuban Communist party, is described as the censorship board, this is not exactly the case. The department has some media policy-setting authority, but its duties are more operational—expressing ideological policy formulated by the Central Committee and coordinating the implementation of the policy by various media. Nichols explained that informal controls from the source subsystem, "usually in the form of the subtle process of socialization," are probably more effective. In other words, broadcasting policymakers are aligned with the goals of the revolution because 71 percent of them have "at least one significant affiliation with the Cuban power structure" as members of the ruling elite with positions in the Central Committee, Council of Ministers, Council of State, National Assembly of the People's Power, or the 26th of July Movement. Other controls come through channels (organizations such as the Union of Cuban Journalists [UPEC] or the ICRT itself), audience feedback units in stations, and the Committees for the Defense of the Revolution and the Distribution System (withholding or selectively distributing messages for the purpose of maintaining the revolutionary process).

Formally, radio and television have been under the ICRT since 1961, a dependency of the Council of Ministers and specifically of the Ministry of Communications. Despite these affiliations, ICRT enjoys considerable autonomy, even though it is headed by one of the most influential vice presidents of the Council of Ministers, José R. Fernández Alvarez.

ECONOMIC STRUCTURE

As already indicated, the broadcast media of Cuba are not privately owned, nor are there commercial facilities. Radio and television are supported by subsidies from the state or party coffers. Paid advertising is not accepted on either television or radio, although both use public service messages that stress patriotism, health, safety, cooperation, and other themes of the revolution. For example, one that this author saw on television in 1982 emphasized the presence of a good-natured, but serious, policeman, with the message "Strength lies in a popular police."

Over the years, as Cuba has suffered economic difficulties, partly due to the U.S. economic embargo and partly because of domestic setbacks (such as the overestimated sugar production campaign), broadcasting has also been adversely affected. Television was hit harder of the two media, facing problems of allocation of scarce foreign exchange to import receiving and transmitting equipment, lack of technical compatibility between the existing U.S.-built television system and those of the Soviet Union and Eastern Europe, outdated equipment kept operational by cannibalization because of the U.S. trade restrictions on replacement parts, and poorly trained technical staffs.

On the whole, Cuban television is technically modern today with mostly Soviet and Japanese equipment. But some U.S. equipment, obsolete when brought to Cuba before 1959, is still in use. The major problem for years was obtaining replacement parts, prompting one television director to remark, "Before we received our new equipment, we kept television going through the sheer ingenuity of Cuban technicians." One expert termed Cuba a "technologically isolated country committed to a technologically advanced field." But progress is being made, as Cuba spent a large amount of scarce foreign exchange to meet its First Five-Year Plan (1976–80) goal of importing half a million television sets specially made in the Soviet Union for the Cuban broadcasting system. Called "Caribe," the television sets are made in the Soviet Union and assembled in Cuba. Two types of radio receivers, "Juvenil 80" and "Ciboney," were also made in the Soviet Union for Cuban use. In the current five-year plan, Cuba is producing its own television receivers.

The complaint lingers, however, that with the allocation of foreign exchange to purchase television and other media equipment, shortages of essential consumer goods have occurred. During the period 1976–80, as the number of television receivers in homes with electricity shot up by 124 percent, the output of many basic commodities increased only slightly or actually declined. The broadcasting receivers have become affordable over the years. An eight-band radio receiver costs 80 pesos and a black-and-white television 600 pesos in an economy where the lowest-paid worker makes 100 pesos a month and the highest-paid about 500 pesos.

An important aspect of a nation's capacity to produce an economically and culturally adept broadcasting system relates to training and professionalization. The Castro government early on realized the need for training, setting up the Union of Cuban Journalists (UPEC) in 1963. Made up of 2,700 members, UPEC has sponsored courses and symposia, developed a system of volunteer journalists throughout Cuba, published periodicals and books relating to print and broadcast media, and initiated training programs for nationals of other nations. Cuba has joined the International Organization of Journalists of Prague (IOJ) in an effort to train Third World journalists, and in late 1983 the José Martí International Institute of Journalism for the training of Third World journalists was established with help from IOJ, the Latin American Federation of Journalists (FELAP), and UNESCO. The institute included modern radio equipment.

Two formal schools of journalism were started at the University of Havana and the University of Oriente in 1963 and 1969, respectively. The schools educate both Cubans and foreign students, and both young people and professional journalists and broadcasters return for degrees. The University of Havana program emphasizes liberal arts subjects in the first year, a mixture of liberal arts and writing in the second year, and theory and practice of journalism and broadcasting in the final cycle. After graduation, students are placed in positions according to where they reside and the needs of the media in that area. The central planning board of the party is responsible for the placement. An official at Radio Habana Cuba said that he usually hires graduates from Havana's school of journalism, although, he stated, there are certain individuals who do not need degrees, such as veteran journalists or recognized specialists.

One interesting scheme for the training of broadcasters resulted from the establishment of Radio Victoria de Girón (RVG) in September 1977. Developed to unite isolated rural areas, RVG was staffed by young people selected from "circles of interest." Staff selection, which starts in seventh grade, allows students six years of experience; however, they must achieve consistently satisfactory results to stay in broadcasting. Fifty-six "circles of interest" (similar to staffs) were established, one for each educational institution in the area, where students work under the direction of professional broadcasters. RVG monitors and reports on the progress of the plan in each region stimulates enthusiasm and competition between brigades in harvesting and plant care, and criticizes as an incentive to improve quality and output.

PROGRAMMING

Because radio stations are structurally organized on national, provincial, and regional levels, they provide programs that have both common and unique elements. The forty-nine provincial and regional stations, for example, cater to the needs of the smaller communities with stratification of programs, differentiating among municipal, provincial, and national levels. The smallest outlets have six to eight hours of their own features, after which they link up with the nearest provincial facility.

In the late 1970s fifteen new programs were started for national radio transmission, making 99 percent of the radio shows national productions. A partial breakdown of radio in Cuba demonstrates that 39 percent of the schedule is devoted to music; 22 percent to information; 7 percent to juvenile topics; 4.5 percent to education; 2.5 percent to children's programming; and 1 percent each to drama, history, and humor.

The five national networks attempt to serve specific programming needs. Radio Reloj, for example, is a twenty-four-hour news, information, and sports station, with a thirty-minute repetition rate. Radio Rebelde, formed in the mountains before the revolution, was mainly news and sports, with some programs of historical importance, while Radio Liberación was cultural shows and drama, including soap operas dramatizing the classics. In early 1985 Radio Rebelde and Radio Liberación merged to provide continuous broadcasts under the former's name. Another network, Radio Progreso, provides popular music, magazine shows, and some news, while Radio Musicale Nacional is mainly classical music. In October 1985 a new station, Radio Taíno, was launched to cater to the tourist trade, providing twelve hours daily, in Spanish and English, of weather and news of tourist attractions, cultural programs, and flight information. All Cuban stations combined broadcast 1,000 hours daily.

The international broadcasting outlet, Radio Habana Cuba, now airs about sixty hours of programs daily in eight languages. About one-third of the time is in Spanish, one-fourth in English, and the rest in French, Portuguese, Quechua, Creole, Arabic, and Guaraní. Music and news each make up 27 percent of the schedules, while general information makes up 40 percent. The rest of the time is announcements. Thirty-one newscasts, ranging from three to twenty minutes, as well as five commentaries daily are used on Radio Habana Cuba. The news and information are gleaned from a number of external and internal sources and interpreted by the Radio Habana Cuba departments. The station's director of information, Pedro Martínez Pérez, explained the autonomous role of the staff in selecting news and information: "We are not robots. We share a political line interpreted in a creative way. No one has to tell us exactly what to write. They don't have to come and tell us to write this or that. There is a group of journalists who participate in editorials." Radio Habana Cuba expanded its effective broadcast reach beyond the Western Hemisphere in 1979, when Radio Moscow began to relay its broadcasts through Cuba and allowed Cuba to relay its international broadcasts in French, Portuguese, Spanish, and Arabic from the Soviet Union.

The two remaining television channels broadcast 126 hours a week in 1980, 7 daily and 14 on Saturday and Sunday. Six hours of programming daily was in color. Dolores Prida, who did a content analysis in 1980, broke down the weekly program ratio in this way: news shows, which spent an unusual amount of emphasis on foreign affairs, 22.7 percent; films, 20.8 percent; children's programs, 12.48 percent; musical and variety features, 11.7 percent; sports, 10.9 percent; public service and educational spots, 6.35 percent; and soap operas, teleplays, and comedy, 5.56 percent. The most popular of the serious features have been "24 por Segundo" (24 Frames a Second), where the host describes current films, shows clips, and discusses their history and structure, and those where government officials are called upon to answer for their shortcomings. One such show is "Información Pública," which invites ministers and other bureaucrats to answer questions sent in by viewers. Also popular are cultural programs, films, and "Cocina al Minuto" (Cooking in a Minute).

Prida reported that viewers were less enthusiastic about children's shows that emphasize team spirit, sports, and the value of education. They complained that these shows were patronizing, that they talked down to the children. Many viewers also thought that there were too many newscasts and that television was generally boring.

Andre Schiffrin, writing in the *Village Voice* (April 2, 1985), described a day's television listing in Cuba as being very much like that of the United States. He spoke of the day as starting with "children's cartoons and going through the evening thriller, with a sunrise semester course on accounting thrown in. The TV professionals we talked to were quick to say that the quality of their output was very low, even the most popular shows tending to be miniseries from Latin America rather than anything resembling the better Cuban films."

Although Castro in 1980 claimed that 60 percent of television programming is locally produced, John Spicer Nichols thinks that the percentage is much lower. According to Professor Nichols, "Cheap, pre-packaged programs, such as cultural shows from East Europe, vintage movies from the United States, and documentaries from the Televisa system in Mexico are commonplace on Cuban television." Not able to fill the increasing hours of the television schedule, station personnel must rely more and more on the exchange programs, especially with Mexico, Spain, and Nicaragua.

ICRT officials have been highly defensive about television's shortcomings, often blaming them on underdevelopment. Prida mentioned what sources told this author in 1982, that there are national priorities and that Cuba cannot have a superdeveloped television system when "the rest of the country is struggling to advance economically and technicians and resources are more needed elsewhere." She came away with the impression that television lacked time, funds, and imagination, but that although Cuba does not make full use of its television potential, it is generally free from problems of other Latin American nations: programs that are largely imported and largely irrelevant and commercials that raise expectations.

Top government officials have been critical of television programming since at least 1980. In that year Raul Castro charged television with mediocrity and emphasized the need for better training, while Armando Hart Davalos, the culture minister, does not miss many opportunities to admonish television to be a cultural and educational bridge to the masses, insinuating that it has not yet achieved that stage. Yet the changes made in the mid–1980s do not reflect these criticisms. Responding to a demand for more U.S. culture, the government has allowed pirated U.S. videos to be shown on television; also, Telerebelde's hours of telecast in 1985 were extended to 3:00 A.M., probably to accommodate more entertainment rather than cultural and educational fare.

An issue broadcasters and government officials have had to cope with is the already-mentioned influx of Western culture. In 1973 pop music from the United States and Great Britain was temporarily banned from radio stations, but with Miami radio signals so available, the authorities rescinded the ruling two years later. As government officials told this author in 1982, to attempt to block out U.S. music and culture is futile with the proximity of the nations and the intercountry passenger travel. More recently, others have suggested that Cuban broadcast programming has been changed as a result of the U.S. propaganda station, Radio Martí, that is beamed to the island. More local and national public affairs shows, better news coverage, and a more lenient policy on the number and variety of U.S. movies allowed on Cuban television have resulted.

Obviously, there are aspects of programming for both radio and television that need improving. Enrique González Manet, a communications specialist, has listed that there is a need for larger public participation, more technical and scientific programs, youth debates, broader economic information, more drama based on "national actualities," better children's shows, and "further exploitation of the possibilities of orienting the population concerning the use of free-time." Also, Cuba still lacks an adequate FM service. To incorporate FM would require additional expenses and conversion or development of receiving sets capable of picking up that signal.

Usually, broadcasting for educational purposes is also listed as an area needing more improvement. Educational television dates to 1959, when a half-hour program was aired daily, initially for primary school children and later for junior high students. A 1960 study showed that teleclasses had an average audience of 200,000, two-thirds of them teachers and students; the rest were adults who had no direct link with the existing educational system. In 1961 the well-known literacy campaign was mounted using television, but radio and written materials were used as well; hundreds of thousands of adults were enrolled in these classes. Five years later, when television was reorganized, educational broadcasting was placed under the program department, and that same year a half-hour, triweekly feature focusing on increasing agricultural productivity and the "Schools to the Countryside" program were inaugurated. In the latter program, junior high school students, supported by teleclasses, went to the countryside for forty-five days to help teach the more isolated people.

In 1969, when the Ministry of Education was under great pressure to meet demands for secondary school education, television was systematically incorporated into the school program. Delegates at the First National Congress on Education and Culture in 1971 recommended more use of media in education, and part of the First National Forum on ETV in 1973 proposed that television be used to carry out pedagogical principles of the revolution.

The system of teleclasses has gradually been coordinated by teams of specialists and technical aides at the Ministry of Education and the Cuban Broadcast Institute. The ministry provides the lesson plans, teachers, monitors, and control of educational content, while CBI provides writers, directors, script people, and special equipment and trains people in technical areas. By the late 1970s, however, Jorge Wertheim reported that educational television covered only a small part of the junior high and preuniversity educational system, with twelve teleclasses of three hours duration for the training of teachers being broadcast weekly, as were four shows of two hours each for university students.

BROADCAST REFORM

As indicated earlier, Cuban broadcasting is in constant flux, reflecting social, cultural, and political criticism. The most significant reform probably relates to the attempt to make these media truly people's voices and to convert them from capitalist tendencies. To accomplish these goals, government officials have made great strides to structure broadcasting along local levels. Whereas before the revolution 80 percent of all transmissions emanated from Havana, in the 1980s 65 percent originate from the provincial level.

Participation of the people in shows is also encouraged. Arnaldo Coro Antich, a broadcast technician, cited the audience interaction possible with local stations, without the "silly talk shows of the United States." For example, he said, "Radio 1590" discusses water supply, effective use of available resources, vocational topics, and vaccination, using local artists and volunteer broadcasters. The small stations are also used as telephones, relaying messages to isolated districts.

Reforms to the system, consequently, came from the top in the form of suggestions, admonitions, and criticisms from party and government officials, and from the grass roots in the form of audience feedback through call-ins, letters, and public participation in programs.

Despite the general impression outside Cuba, there are broadcast alternatives to Cuban stations. The Cuban government does not jam outside stations, and U.S. commercial facilities (at least as far north as Philadelphia and as far west as Des Moines), the Voice of America (stationed in Antigua), and Radio Martí can be heard, as can other regional broadcasters.

NEW TECHNOLOGIES

Cuba has developed tremendously in telecommunications capacities during the first twenty-five years of the revolution. Among the many accomplishments Cuban officials are proud of is the project to put into operation one of the world's first national coaxial cable networks. With help from the Soviet Union, Cuba has built a cable network of 1,800 kilometers down the center of the island. With a potential capacity of 10,000 simultaneous channels and with a duplex channel for television transmission, the system will satisfy every kind of long-wire requirement.

Manet boasts that Cuba is the only Third World nation with a clear communication policy and total national coverage in radio, television, and the press. He also said that Cuba has had to develop its own hardware and software computer system because it could not import from the United States. Beginning in 1979, five (and later eight) data bases were set up by Cubans, with virtually no help from elsewhere, Manet added.

The nation has had outside help in other areas. Since 1974 telephone, telex, and television reception between Cuba and the Soviet Union has been possible with the use of a Soviet satellite, with a ground station at Jaruco. At first, telex was reserved for communication between a few government agencies, but now it is open to other ministries, businesses, and factories. In 1984, during National Assembly discussions on communications, it was reported that in the next five years Cuba aimed to increase the rate of communication equipment imported from socialist countries to 95 percent, thus decreasing its dependence upon capitalist markets for spare parts.

CONCLUSION/FORECAST

Cuba's development in telecommunications has been phenomenal compared to that of other Third World nations. Equally important is the fact that as the high technology has been put into place, great pains have been taken to ensure public participation in the broadcast media. Also different from efforts of other developing nations are the attempts to take the transmission out of the capital city and place it more in provincial centers; the concern to produce an indigenous product, whether it be television receivers, programs, or computers; and the belief that Cuba should help other countries in their broadcast development. Cubans have already provided aid to broadcasting at least in Angola, Grenada, and Nicaragua in the spirit of "proletarian internationalism," according to Manet. Despite the belief from some quarters that the aid comes in an ideological package, Manet said that this was not the case. Whatever the motive, Cuba's assistance in the buildup of broadcasting in Third World nations is expected to continue.

BIBLIOGRAPHY

Green, Timothy. *The Universal Eye: World Television in the Seventies.* London: The Bodley Head, 1972.

Jordan, Octavio. "Cuba's Right-of-Reply Law in Radio Broadcasting." *Journalism Quarterly* 28 (1958): 358–64.

Lent, John A. "Cuban Mass Media after 25 Years of Revolution." *Journalism Quarterly* 62 (Autumn 1985): 609–15, 704.

———. "Journalism Training in Cuba Emphasizes Politics, Ideology." *Journalism Educator* 36 (Autumn 1984): 12–15.

Manet, Enrique González. "Cultural Policy and Audiovisual Media in Cuba: A Case Study." Report prepared for Cuban National Commission for UNESCO, Center for the Study of Mass Diffusion Media. Paris: UNESCO, 1982.

Martínez Victores, Ricardo. *7RR: La Historia de Radio Rebelde.* Havana: Editorial de Ciencias Sociales, 1978.

Nichols, John Spicer. "Cuba." In *World Press Encyclopedia,* edited by George T. Kurian, 257–71. New York: Facts on File, 1982.

———. *Cuban Mass Media: Organization, Control, and Functions.* Journalism Monographs. November 1982.

———. "The Havana Hustle: A New Phase in Cuba's International Communication Activities." In *Case Studies of Mass Media in the Third World,* edited by John A. Lent. Studies in Third World Societies 10, 1980.

Otero, Rafael L. *La Información en Televisión.* Santiago: Editorial Oriente, 1980.

Phillips, R. Hart. "Cuban TV: The Fidel Show." *New York Times,* July 23, 1961.

Prida, Dolores. "Cuban TV: Worthy But Too Often Dull." *World Broadcast News* 36 (September 1980): 10–11.

Redding, Jerry. " 'Castro-ating' the Media." *Educational Broadcasting Review* 36 (June 1971): 35–42.

Vera, Ernesto. "Mass Media in Cuba." *Democratic Journalist* 11 (1979): 12–16.

XX Aniversario de Radio Habana Cuba. Havana: Editora Politica, 1982.

Wertheim, Jorge. "Educational Television in Cuba." In *Mass Media Policies in Changing Cultures,* edited by George Gerbner. New York: John Wiley, 1977.

FEDERAL REPUBLIC OF GERMANY

Wolfgang Hoffman-Riem

HISTORY

Regular radio first began in the German Reich on October 29, 1923 (a daily one-hour music program). Under the powerful influence of the Reichspost (PTT) and the electrical industry, the medium was primarily entertainment oriented. The government permitted news and public affairs programming to only a limited extent and strictly controlled both. This structure enabled the National Socialists to increasingly wield broadcasting as a tool of propaganda after 1933.

After World War II the occupying powers (the United States, Great Britain, and France) made efforts to ensure that broadcasting was free from government manipulation. Unlike the situation in the United States, however, radio was not organized on a commercial basis. A fee-financed public broadcasting system, modeled on the British Broadcasting Corporation, was created. In accordance with the nation's federal structure a number of public outlets were set up in the West German states. These broadcasters later (1950) joined together to form a kind of a network known as ARD (West German radio and television program supplier). Their activities were initially limited to radio. Television broadcasting, which was launched in Germany in 1935 but banned by the Allies immediately after the war, has existed since 1952.

A second nationwide TV broadcaster, the Zweites Deutsches Fernsehen (ZDF), was established via treaties between the states in 1963. Two external radio services also exist (Deutschlandfunk and Deutsche Welle). Private enterprises, in particular press publishers, repeatedly called for a change of laws and tried to be licensed as broadcasters. Until 1984 these attempts failed. Since then, however, a number of private organizations have been licensed. At this point a dual broadcasting system is still in the process of unfolding.

REGULATION

The German constitution (the Basic Law in 1949) specifically protected and recognized the freedom of broadcasting. This freedom guarantees the right of broadcasters and journalists to protection against government intervention. In addition, the basic legal norm required the legislature to develop a structure for the medium. In this situation the development of broadcasting has been influenced by the decisions of the federal constitutional court (Bundesverfassungsgericht). In a series of decisions, the court contended that the freedom to broadcast is not an end in itself, but serves the purpose of enabling individual and public opinion to be freely formed as well as ensuring the continuation of democracy. Consequently, legislators have set up a structure (organization and procedures) by which the freedom of radio and television is safeguarded for both broadcasters and listeners.

In addition, the court and legislators have argued that the diversity of opinion in society must be represented in programs and comprehensive coverage. The danger of an abuse of this freedom with the intention of one-sidedly exerting influence on public opinion must be avoided. According to the court, the "free play of market forces" is an inadequate safeguard in this context. The field of mass communications should not be solely entrusted to the marketplace and economic competition. Additional or at least supplementary regulations are required.

The legal regulation of broadcasting falls under the jurisdiction of eleven states. The medium is correspondingly structured along federalist lines. Until 1983 all state legislatures had opted for a system of public broadcasting oriented toward the public service philosophy of the medium. The broadcasters are state-chartered public corporations. Most of the budgetary revenue comes from statutory fees, a smaller proportion from advertising. In addition, outlets are legally autonomous. One special feature is their internal structure, which is based on the principle of pluralism. A broadcasting council, the station's most senior supervisory body, represents the interests of the general public. It is composed of a balanced representation of all important views and all political and social groups. These units have the task of electing or ratifying the election of the director general (*Intendant*), of ensuring that editorial guidelines and legal regulations are followed, and of approving the station's budget. They are also empowered to control those individuals who actually make program decisions.

This public broadcasting system is still in place. The states, however, have started enacting new media laws that permit the licensing of private facilities. The details of the various laws often differ. In all cases, however, different types of broadcasters are permitted: commercial enterprises, social groups including churches, and nonprofit organizations. Government as well as municipalities, and to a certain extent political parties, are excluded from the media. How they receive their financial revenue, whether via advertising, sponsorship, their own assets, or donations, is left up to the broadcasters. In most cases their internal structure is also left unregulated (no obligations of internal pluralism). They are, however, subject to programming regulations.

Applicants can be licensed in the individual states. Licenses are generally issued for all available transmission technologies (transmissions over the air or via cable or satellite). Accordingly, the legal requirements are the same regardless of which technologies are used. Requirements are less rigid if the program to be distributed has already been permitted elsewhere (in a different state or foreign nation) and is to be transmitted in an unabridged form via cable.

Independent commissions are responsible for licensing as well as controlling broadcasting activities. The composition of these commissions generally (not in all states) complies with the principle of internal pluralism. Each state ensures that these controlling agencies observe the law.

ECONOMIC STRUCTURE

The public broadcasters are noncommercial public service organizations. Any profits made must be channeled into broadcasting or paid over to the states rather than to private individuals. Most revenue comes from licensing fees. Fee levels are fixed by state legislatures, which try to harmonize these levels via interstate treaties. The Commission for the Determination of the Financial Needs of Broadcasting Corporations (KEF) is an advisory body that conducts surveys.

License fees are compulsory for all persons owning a radio or TV set, irrespective of whether it is actually used. Some sections of the population, the poor for example, are exempted from this fee. The license fee is divided into a radio and a television tax (amounting to DM 5.05 and DM 11.20 per month respectively in 1986, DM 1 = U.S. $0.45). The ARD broadcasters receive the revenue from the radio fee, although they must also pay an annual DM 52 million to the Deutschlandfunk. The revenue from the television license tax is split 70 percent to 30 percent between the ARD broadcasters and the ZDF.

Advertising represents a further source of revenue. The ARD public broadcasters have set up subsidiaries that sell airtime, whereas the ZDF does the selling itself. According to government regulations, commercials must not be screened on public TV after 8:00 P.M. or on Sundays and public holidays. Advertising must be made clearly distinguishable from other programs. The interruption of programs by commercials is not permissible. Total TV commercial time is limited to twenty minutes per workday. Similar regulations exist for radio spots, although these vary substantially in some cases among individual broadcasters.

In 1984 total radio license fee revenue amounted to DM 1.447 billion and total television license fee revenue to DM 2.790 billion. Of this figure, the ARD broadcasters received DM 3.400 billion and the ZDF 837 million. Net TV advertising revenue provided an additional DM 816 million, and radio advertising DM 459 million in the case of the ARD broadcasters and DM 539 million in the case of the ZDF. The cost per minute of airtime on the "Erstes Programm" of the ARD (excluding regional features) averaged DM 4,311.

It is up to private broadcasters how they are financially organized. Government regulations only require that applicants be financially and organizationally able to transmit their intended programs. Both nonprofit and commercial broadcasters can be licensed. Almost all conceivable broadcast types exist during the "take-off" phase. Foreign individuals and enterprises can also be granted a license provided that they reside or are located in the Federal Republic of Germany. There are only very limited bans on multiple and cross-ownership (regional concentration protection).

A number of media laws also give preference to so-called *Anbietergemeinschaften* (groups consisting of several parties) when issuing a broadcasting license. The members of these groups may possess highly differing organizational and financial structures such as churches, trade unions, press publishers, and mixed businesses.

The financially most powerful group of this kind in the field of TV broadcasting is SAT 1, an amalgamation of major press publishers and program production companies with the participation of the big banks. The program company Aktuell Presse Fernsehen (APF) also belongs to this group. APF was set up by 140 newspaper publishers for the sole purpose of broadcasting news and public affairs for SAT 1. The Springer-Ullstein publishing group holds 35 percent of the shares. Although SAT 1 currently only has a license for the state of Rhineland-Palatinate, it is cablecast in almost all of the states. Revenue is raised by advertising.

Due to the low degree of cable penetration, SAT 1 claimed that it could be received by fewer than 500,000 households until mid–1985. Advertising revenue was correspondingly low in 1985: DM 7.5 million. According to SAT 1, this amount covered less than 5 percent of total costs. Revenue is expected to increase, however, to DM 90 million in 1988. Information on annual expenses is vague (over DM 150 million in 1985).

Another major broadcaster is the Compagnie Luxembourgeoise de Telediffusion (CLT), which joined forces with the Bertelsmann group to control TV channel RTL plus. The license was issued in Luxembourg, and the channel is either broadcast over the air in border regions or transmitted by cable. RTL plus is less expensive to produce than SAT 1 and has higher advertising revenue (1985: DM 15 million). At present, this outlet is also unable to cover costs.

It is generally assumed that with the help of advertising income two or at most three national full-format broadcasting channels can be financed alongside public outlets. The German advertising market currently has a gross volume of roughly DM 50 billion (with a population figure of 61 million). In 1984 press publishers accounted for a net amount of DM 10.124 billion (of this figure DM 6.008 billion came from daily newspaper publishers).

The advertising regulations are not quite as strict for private broadcasters as for public concerns. As a rule, commercial spots must not exceed 20 percent of daily airtime. Programs can only be interrupted once if they are over sixty minutes long. What is more, commercials must be clearly identified as such.

Other methods of financing are also legally permissible, in particular sponsorship and pay TV. Sponsorship, however, has to be declared on the air. Pay TV is still very much in its infancy. In this field major press publishers (Bertelsmann and Springer) are cooperating with the Kirch group (ARIES GmbH)—Leo Kirch almost has a monopoly on the market as movie dealers. This group has entered into a joint venture with the Anglo-American holding concern Premiere International (participating parties include Columbia Pictures, Twentieth-Century Fox, Home Box Office, Showtime, Warner Brothers, and Thorn/EMI).

PROGRAMMING

The public broadcasters are obliged to send full-format programs—features covering all the various topic formats (especially news and public affairs, entertainment, and education). Program content must be varied and balanced. All the interests of society as a whole must be taken into account in these features, including minority interests. Program regulations provide for truthful reporting and conscientious investigation in the case of news and public affairs features, the promotion of international understanding, the observance of the population's moral and religious convictions, and compliance with general law.

There are only slight differences in the formats of radio offerings. Service shows with a great deal of music and information (especially traffic news) are the most popular. Particularly sophisticated cultural channels are also characteristic. As regards television, the ARD broadcasters share the same programming most of the day in the "Erstes Programm" and also broadcast separate "Third Programs." The ARD is also planning a channel to be transmitted via satellite and cable (Eins plus). The ZDF manages a channel that is transmitted nationally, the "Zweites Programm." Together with the

Austrian and Swiss public broadcasters the ZDF also operates a culturally oriented channel by telecommunications satellite and cable (3-SAT).

Media laws provide for reasonable and equal access opportunities for political parties (free of charge) to radio and television. Furthermore, the major churches and the Jewish religious community also have a privileged position in this respect. They are entitled to transmit their own features free of charge at certain times, programs that are included in the public broadcasting service and thus have high audience ratings. The government has no right to program access unless official announcements are to be made.

Otherwise, programming falls under the autonomy of the programming and producing departments and must, if necessary, be approved by the *Intendant* as the chief supervisory official. Public broadcasters have always tried to provide a large number of news and public affairs features as well as to screen programs for minorities. Television prime time, however, is generally reserved for shows with high ratings. In the past, ARD and ZDF have drawn up coordination arrangements to ensure a minimum of mutual agreement. These arrangements also occasionally provide for the broadcasting of sophisticated programs with a probably lower number of viewers during prime time. The current coordination arrangement may well run out in the future without substitution.

There are no program origination rules. About two-thirds of all programs are based on so-called internal productions (produced by the broadcasters themselves), and one-third are so-called external productions (including programs produced by a third party on behalf of public broadcasters). In fact, 14 percent and 24 percent respectively of all original broadcasts (excluding reruns) by the ARD and ZDF are feature films purchased externally. Over one-third of the feature films are bought from the United States. Public broadcasters, however, set aside some of their money for the promotion of German films.

Again without special legal obligations, public broadcasters screen children's programs. Following the introduction of "Sesame Street," a number of children's features were prepared concentrating on the specific educational needs of young people. Special children's offerings are also sometimes transmitted on radio. In addition, there are special educational programs, although their number has been decreasing recently.

The daily television airtime in 1984 averaged just under 9 hours and 58 minutes in the ARD's "Erstes Programm" and 11 hours and 16 minutes in the ZDF. The ratings for both channels are more or less the same (average ratings in mid–1985: ARD 86 minutes, ZDF 87 minutes, the "Third Programs" of ARD 22 minutes). On an annual average, TV sets were switched on 3 hours 3 minutes each day in 1984. Average viewing time was 2 hours 4 minutes for adults (ARD and ZDF 57 minutes apiece), and 1 hour 11 minutes for children between the ages of six and thirteen. Older people (over fifty) watched TV most: 2 hours and 36 minutes. Germans spend between 40 and 60 percent of their time between 7:30 and 10:00 P.M. watching television. Some radio outlets broadcast round the clock, whereas others have a daily schedule of up to 18 hours.

Programming regulations for private outfits vary from one state to the next. In some states, for example, broadcasters are allowed to screen one-sided programs provided that the total program range of all broadcasting is varied and balanced. Other states demand that the individual shows be varied and balanced. Broadcasters are free to choose their formats. Those that provide full-format broadcasting, however, sometimes stand a better chance of being licensed. All stations licensed in the Federal Republic of Germany are required to conduct conscientious investigations, demonstrate fairness, and observe general laws. Family viewing policy provides for youth protection by banning pornographic shows or particularly violent programs before late-night viewing begins.

Programming decisions are made autonomously by station managers. They are also free to choose how they regulate program responsibility internally. There is no obligation to broadcast special children's fare or religious/educational features. Some state laws give political parties a right to airtime during elections.

How private broadcasters actually respond to the given framework is difficult to say during the current take-off phase in this field. Both SAT 1 and RTL plus attach great importance to independent news and public affairs coverage. They include much more everyday and nonpolitical information in this format than public broadcasters and stress a more relaxed presentation of the news. Programming emphasis is on light entertainment (SAT 1, 69 percent, and RTL plus, 83 percent, compared with ARD, 49 percent, and ZDF, 47 percent). Feature films are particularly important during prime time. Internal productions account for just over 41 percent in the case of SAT 1 and about 50 percent in the case of RTL plus. The data relating to private radio outlets cannot as yet be generalized. As a result of a low degree of cable penetration (roughly 2 million households are wired and have satellite reception possibilities) it is also too early to make statements on the acceptance of private TV channels. In homes where SAT 1 can be received together with ARD and ZDF, television viewing time would seem to have been equally split among all three.

BROADCAST REFORM

In no other nation in the world has the debate during recent years over the reform of the broadcasting system been so heated as in the Federal Republic of Germany. For decades public broadcast was firmly entrenched in the awareness of the general public and in the legal and political landscape. At the same time, there was growing criticism of public radio and television. Most of this criticism was directed against the political parties that had gained influence over the executive bodies administering public broadcasting corporations and on staff appointments and programming decisions. What is more, the commitment to balanced and fair programming was increasingly used as a means of giving the big political parties an opportunity to promote their own image and to discriminate against minority parties. Finally, public outlets were criticized for being inflexible, bureaucratic, and inefficient.

The opportunity to reform this system, however, was rarely grasped. Instead, public discussion and debate focused on supplementing public broadcasting with private operators. In these circumstances, technological innovations and advancements increased the sentiment for reform. Equally important, business concerns had displayed an interest in gaining access to the electronic mass media to promote products and services. In addition, large press publishers had wanted to invest excess profits into broadcasting. Smaller press publishers shared the fear that newspapers might lose advertising contracts to commercial television. Above all, political considerations on the part of the conservative Christian Democrat parties (CDU and CSU) led to the licensing of private concerns. The conservatives felt that public broadcasting put them on the defensive and at a substantial disadvantage at election time. Private broadcasters were regarded as a more effective way of conveying the conservative political message.

A large section of the general public, especially the Social Democrats (SPD), trade unions, churches, and a number of citizens' groups opposed the introduction of private broadcasting, especially print-broadcast cross-ownership. They were able to point to the decisions of the highest court to back up their position. The courts did not rule out the possibility of private ownership, but made its introduction contingent upon tough standards and requirements. In the meantime, the states governed by the SPD decided to permit private operations. In this situation, there was a general consensus that private broadcasting could no longer be stopped and that new transmission technologies—especially satellites—would enable the distribution and relaying of programs by external broadcasters.

The parliaments of the states, however, found it extremely difficult to reach agreement on establishing guidelines for this sector. The result is a federalist compartmentalization of media laws and structures. This runs contrary to the technological possibilities of nationwide coverage and to the business interests of corporations in large markets. There have, therefore, been numerous attempts to change the legal basis of state jurisdiction. One approach is to eliminate special media laws, applying only general business law in the field. Business law falls under the jurisdiction of the federal government.

This trend in Germany is being reinforced by the efforts of the Commission of the European Communities to achieve "television without frontiers" in Europe. The aim of the commission is to enable unrestricted broadcasting in all member nations. This could result in the development of a Europe-wide marketplace.

The trend toward the introduction of commercial broadcasting can be currently observed throughout the world. The public service philosophy is generally on the retreat and will be replaced by a marketplace approach. This situation reflects the economic interests of media enterprises in a liberalized marketplace. Internationally and multinationally oriented multimedia or mixed conglomerates dominate substantial media market segments and have also gained a foothold in the Federal Republic of Germany. Deregulation of the broadcasting system is welcomed as complementary to the nonregulation of international production markets and of the sale of media software.

The growing commercialization of the medium and the gradual abandonment of its cultural orientation is faced by increasingly weak political opposition. Family organizations, churches, a number of scientists, and citizens' groups as well as a section of the SPD and the Green party are fighting against this development without being able to prevent it from taking place.

To appease this opposition, there are plans to give these groups an opportunity to voice their opinions in public access channels. In addition, certain possibilities exist in the field of community radio. The ratings and audience size of such efforts, however, are likely to be of only marginal significance.

NEW TECHNOLOGIES

Communication satellites (ECS/Intelsat) are already being used to beam down programs to individual broadcasters or cable stations. The first German direct broadcasting satellite (TV-Sat) was launched in 1987. A standby satellite will be added in 1988. It will also be possible to pick up transmissions from other satellites (the French TDF, for example) in many parts of the Federal Republic of Germany. DBS, therefore, will soon enable the reception of a large number of additional communications channels.

The Bundespost as the prime operator of telecommunications facilities, including cable, for broadcasting is currently extending its cable network. Private firms are only allowed to become cable operators in exceptional cases. The cables—generally coaxial cables—have to be wired underground, which results in relatively high costs. The number of German homes wired is also still relatively limited. At the end of 1985, 3.8 million homes out of a total of 25 million were equipped to receive cablecasting. In 1985 less than 5 percent of all households were wired up to broadband cable networks in which the programs relayed via satellite could be received. The Bundespost expects this figure to increase to approximately 12 to 14 percent in 1988.

Low-powered stations do not have a tradition in the Federal Republic of Germany. Public broadcasters generally use long-range transmitters. The search for free frequencies for low-powered stations has only just begun. Because of the geographical proximity of many nations in Europe, there is a particular scarcity of spectrum space, and almost all available wavelengths are already in use. In addition, some of the state governments are opposed to low-powered television stations, especially in cases where they are not commercially operated but run by citizens' groups. New FM radio frequencies will be available on 100 to 104 MHz after 1987 and on 104 to 108 MHz after 1995. They will be partly used for low-powered stations and partly to set up new nationwide radio chains.

CONCLUSION/FORECAST

Recent developments in German broadcasting clearly demonstrate how the interplay of technological innovation and business interests influences political policies and changes traditional structures. The vast majority of the population still adopts a positive stance toward public broadcasting, and an express desire for more private outlets is only being voiced by a minority. Nevertheless, the powerful economic and political pressure to restructure broadcasting has been successful. The business and journalistic concerns of major press publishers and a number of large companies are congruous with the political interests of the majority parties, the conservative CDU and CSU, as well as the liberal Free Democrats (FDP). Although the SPD initially tried to obstruct this development, it is now trying to shape its course. The scope for effective political influence, however, is limited. Evolving technological and economic structures make it increasingly difficult to influence broadcasting policy at state levels and even at the national level. New technologies make transborder transmissions much easier. What is more, the ramifications of business interests are generally of an international and multinational nature. In view of this general setting it is hardly surprising that the development of the broadcasting structure is characterized by three trends:

1. The internationalization of the production and the dissemination of broadcasts
2. The commercialization of program content
3. The multimedia character and multinationality of the leading companies in this marketplace

In this context national media policies are becoming more and more ineffective.

It is no coincidence that public broadcasting finds itself on the defensive. The marketplace philosophy on which plans for media expansion are based is incompatible with the public service approach. Public broadcasting finds its justification in the fact that program priorities are set according to content-related aspects and not primarily audience ratings. Competition with private outlets, however, encourages public broadcasters to devise a program policy able to prevent their commercial competitors from siphoning off viewers and listeners. If public broadcasters were to suffer substantial audience losses, state parliaments might be less willing to grant them the right to levy the license fees they need to cover costs. In anticipation of this competitive situation, public broadcasters have already started altering their programming to make sure that they have a good chance of competing with commercial outlets. This anticipatory commercialization represents a move toward quasi-private broadcasting before private broadcasting has actually arrived. Furthermore, it makes it more difficult for private broadcasters to secure an audience within a short period of time to offset costs via greater advertising revenue. Many politicians, consequently, are considering how they can help private broadcasters get off the ground. A restriction of commercial time for public stations and the transfer of a proportion of license fees to commercial outfits are just two of the possibilities being considered.

The German and European broadcasting tradition is characterized by the expectation that programming is in harmony with the social, cultural, and political values of a given society. If programs are sold on the international market or produced with the specific aim of selling products, national goals will be neglected. Public broadcasters have always bought foreign productions in the past and have tried—without a great deal of success so far—to sell their own productions internationally. Private broadcasters rely to a greater extent on buying productions on the international market or exclusively broadcast international features, as in the case of Sky Channel. It is no coincidence, therefore, that a discussion on the safeguarding of national culture and values has begun in the Federal Republic of Germany and in other European nations. Suitable safeguards have not been developed to prevent the trend toward more internationalized and commercially oriented program offerings.

Together with the possibilities of transborder communications, the creation of extended markets and the activities of multinational and international companies will probably result in an undermining of the federalist broadcasting system in the Federal Republic of Germany. The justification of federalist responsibilities in this field was based on an understanding of the medium as a cultural activity. The more broadcasting is practically and legally regarded as an economic product (as, for example, in the "green paper" on "Television without Frontiers"), the less applicable this rationale. In fact, there are signs of a renunciation of a culturally based concept and a move toward a market philosophy. In addition, the previous concept of focusing on the diversity of program content may be eliminated. In the marketplace model it is the number of broadcasters that serves as an indicator of diversity. These changes represent a radical transformation of the broadcasting system, which will probably have a considerable effect on the political structure and values in the Federal Republic of Germany.

Changes in the broadcasting system will run parallel to the expansion of telecommunications services. The Bundespost has begun extending a fiber-optic broadband network. The aim is to help modernize the economy. A large number of telecommunications services for individual and mass communication will then be possible. It is not yet clear what effect this will have on programming and viewing patterns.

Nonetheless, telecommunications services are likely to become more and more important in the population's leisure time behavior. A reduction of working hours in the foreseeable future will increase leisure time even more. Since the number of unemployed persons (currently about 10 percent of the labor force) is likely to increase, broadcasting services will also play an important role in the context of lasting unemployment. It is difficult to say how a commercially oriented broadcaster will respond to this situation in the long run. Greater emphasis will probably be placed on entertainment. Broadcasting in the Federal Republic of Germany, therefore, will probably move even further away from the concept supported by the constitutional court—that radio and television are an important medium of information and orientation in the functioning of a political democracy. Broadcasting will continue to serve as a carrier of information, but the message transmitted will have more and more entertainment value. The way in which information is presented will also be geared to its entertainment function. It remains to be seen how this will affect the task of broadcasting to disseminate information and opinions in a manner that serves the public interest.

BIBLIOGRAPHY

ARD-Jahrbuch. Hamburg: Hans-Bredow-Institut, 1985.

Bausch, Hans, ed. *Rundfunk in Deutschland*. Vol. 1–5. Hamburg: Deutscher Taschenbuchverlag, 1980.

Bismarck, Hans. *Neue Medientechnologien und grundgesetzliche Kommunikationsverfassung*. Berlin: Duncker and Humblot, 1982.

Bullinger, Martin. *Kommunikationsfreiheit im Strukturwandel der Telekommunikation*. Baden-Baden: Nomos-Verlagsgesellschaft, 1980.

Decker, Horst L., Wolfgang R. Langenbucher, and Günter Nahre. *Die Massenmedien in der postindustriellen Gesellschaft*. Gottingen: Verlag Otto Schwartz and Co., 1976.

Herrmann, Günter. *Fernsehen und Hörfunk in der Verfassung der Bundesrepublik Deutschland*. Tubingen: Verlag Mohr, 1975.

Klein, Hans-Hugo. *Die Rundfunkfreiheit*. Munich: C.H. Beck, 1978.

Lange, Bernd-Peter. *Kommerzielle Ziele und binnenpluralistische Organisation bei Rundfunkveranstaltern*. Frankfurt: Alfred Metzner Verlag, 1980.

Ratzke, Dietrich. *Handbuch der neuen Medien*. Stuttgart: Deutsche Verlagsanstalt, 1982.

Richer, Reinhart. *Privatrundfunk-Gesetze im Bundesstaat*. Frankfurt: C.H. Beck'sche Verlagsbuchhandling, 1985.
Stock, Martin. *Medienfreiheit als Funktionsgrundrecht*. Frankfurt: C.H. Beck'sche Verlagsbuchhandlung, 1985.

GREAT BRITAIN

Timothy S. Madge

HISTORY

A grasp of the history of British broadcasting is crucial for an understanding of the changes beginning to percolate into a unified and stable system in the 1980s. British broadcasting has been dominated for sixty years by the British Broadcasting Corporation. The BBC presided as a state monopoly for thirty years and still exercises the single most powerful force in British broadcasting, albeit under increasing financial, political, and social pressures.

British radio began seriously in 1920 with experimental transmissions from the Marconi Company headquarters in East Anglia. The public rapidly embraced the medium, and this popularity forced early government intervention to regulate both broadcasts and those receiving them. Because the British government was disturbed by unregulated chaos in radio in the United States, it ultimately decided to license only one organization. Late in 1922 the British Broadcasting Company monopoly started operations, after some earlier attempts at more local licensed broadcasting.

John Reith managed the company. He provided leadership instrumental in changing the organization from a private monopoly of major companies whose interest in broadcasting largely focused on creating a market for radios that they manufactured to a public corporation chartered by government to broadcast in the public interest.

The British Broadcasting Corporation emerged in January 1927. From its inception, senior staff transmitted primarily those education and information programs that they believed the public ought to have, eschewing the whims of mass public taste. Subsequently, the BBC became a symbol for the best in broadcasting worldwide.

Its source of finance was and remains the license fee—a poll tax on all households with radio receivers. This early decision to forgo any commercial base has become a major plank in the BBC's own definition of public service broadcasting.

Before World War II the BBC ran one national radio network and a regional program. In addition, the BBC had started the world's first continuous high-definition television service in 1936; this closed at the outbreak of the war, not reopening until the June 1946 victory parade in London. The war brought other changes as well. U. S. influence through the American Armed Forces Network in wartime Britain forced the BBC to introduce a "light" program of more popular music. In 1946, while reopening its prewar television service, the BBC spent limited funds to reorganize radio into the home, light, and third networks, catering to middle, low, and high "brows" respectively. Later, this decision materially affected pressure for the introduction of commercial television.

Early on, competition existed for the growing radio audience. From 1931 until World War II, and after 1946, foreign stations financed by advertising have broadcast to the United Kingdom.

After World War II advertisers and politicians in the British Conservative party eventually forced through a parliamentary bill authorizing commercial television. Apart from business pressures to allow advertising on some of Britain's home-based broadcast media, attention focused unfavorably on the BBC's monopoly. In light of Nazi Germany and Stalin's postwar incursions into East Central Europe, many expressed considerable fear over a single giant broadcasting organization and its effective ability to control and manipulate the news. These fears decisively ensured that the monopoly was broken in the relatively new area of television in 1955.

The pressure continued until the BBC's monopoly in local radio further diminished. Although commercial television had covered the nation by the early 1960s, the BBC also had continued to expand its operations. In 1964 it opened a second television network. BBC local radio stations opened after 1967 as a result of growing pressure from commercial interests to allow "competitive" radio. This demand arose in part from "pirate" radio stations that had transmitted programs to the United Kingdom from offshore locations between 1964 and 1967. These outlets had effectively demonstrated that a large young audience existed that was not served by the BBC.

By the mid–1980s commercial radio had expanded to include most urban centers (forty-eight facilities in a planned sixty-station scheme). BBC local radio had concentrated on less competitive "country" radio stations numbering around thirty. The BBC now operates four national radio outlets, having added the fourth, Radio 1, for young people in 1967 when pirate stations were suppressed. In early 1982, the Conservative government authored a "green paper" focusing on the future of the medium. Among the proposals under discussion was one to create three completely new commercial radio outlets. Community radio was also to be allowed. In general, these proposals have been welcomed.

Commercial independent television runs a single network with a regional company base. The fourth (and last) United Kingdom television network—Channel 4—opened in 1982. Pressure from commercial (independent) television companies (ITV) had grown throughout the 1970s for a service that they wished to identify as ITV 2. Eventually, in 1982 Mrs. Thatcher's government authorized the service as a complementary part of the commercial system, enjoined to reflect minority tastes.

By 1982, then, when Channel 4 opened, British broadcasting had developed into a highly structured "duopoly" in which one part mirrored the other, competing not for revenue but for audiences, using high-quality programs as bait. This highly structured and stable system, carefully added to over the past few years, has now been overtaken by events.

REGULATION

Broadcasting in the United Kingdom is primarily regulated through a royal charter for the BBC and through acts of Parliament for commercial broadcasting. The difference is important. Royal charters have a long history in the British system. They are generally permissive documents, providing a means for considerable freedom for the organization so constituted to regulate itself and to decide its purposes. Acts, on the other hand, tend to be restrictive in nature, establishing what may and may not be undertaken.

The BBC's royal charter is for fixed terms that can be extended if necessary, although no government has ever desired to make more than a few years' extension. It is now set at fifteen years and next expires in 1996. Each new royal charter has included additional requirements for the BBC; for example, to take more account of the public through various advisory bodies.

The charter does not give the BBC the right to broadcast, but it does give it critical political freedom from individual governments because it is issued by the Crown rather than the Parliament. Alterations have to go to the Privy Council, an ancient council of state of some importance. In addition, the BBC also has a "license and agreement" with the agency charged with regulating the medium, currently the Home Office. This arrangement outlines broadcasting standards; ultimately the minister may suspend a broadcast (never yet done).

In contrast, commercial broadcasting is regulated by an act that specifies the oversight of the commercial system by the Independent Broadcasting Authority, while a newly authorized Cable Authority oversees cable television. Both bodies report to the Home Office, although the Cable Authority also has a close relationship with the Department of Trade and Industry.

Its Office of Telecommunications issues the technical specifications for the cable systems.

The broadcasting acts, including the first two, called the television acts, ensure that fairly strict rules of conduct contain commercial broadcasting. The Cable Authority selects and appoints the program companies, supervises programs, controls the amount and content of advertising, and transmits the service. In addition, the appointed companies rent transmitters from the authority. To ensure compliance with its regulations, the authority employs a large staff of engineers.

Because the British system as a whole operates on a high level of consensus, the program companies through their trade associations and the advertisers through their representatives exercise considerable control over the government regulators. For example, program companies are required to submit their schedules in advance, but features are only viewed by the authority if the program companies warn about content.

The Cable Authority, which only began work in 1985, issues franchises for the newly created cable system. It has a largely permissive brief, although it is drawing up standards for advertising and violence. Because it was established during the deregulatory atmosphere of the mid–1980s, the regulatory agency lacks the same degree of formal responsibility for cable programming exercised by its counterparts. It does have a fairly specific brief on technical specifications for new cable systems to promote a nationally compatible or interactive cable network. The Cable Authority does not require schedules in advance or information regarding advertising. The system is similar to the "off-air" commercial broadcasting arrangements in that the cable firms are expected to notify the authority in advance of any major changes in output, programs, and advertising revenue.

In addition, the government uses statutory instruments to vary minor terms and conditions of broadcasting practices. Major questions, however, would be handled by a new act or an amendment to an existing act. For example, during the summer of 1985 the government authorized individual direct broadcast satellite reception on payment of an additional license fee.

Government regulation and control of frequencies for "off-air" and cable broadcasting transcend British Broadcasting Corporation, Independent Broadcasting Authority, and Cable Authority mandates. These requirements are determined between the Home Office and the Department of Trade and Industry.

Equally troublesome, Europe suffers an endemic frequency shortage. It has been estimated, for example, that 5,000 AM radio stations in Europe compete for a mere 110 AM wavelengths. The development of FM radio and UHF television has ameliorated but not solved the problem. In the United Kingdom these shortages have prevented the development of small-scale local radio, community radio, and "off-air" local television. New technologies, including multipoint distribution service (MDS) and very low-powered FM radio, have helped but have not resolved the issue.

Thus government control of frequencies remains critical. In the past, it has been used to block technological developments, especially those thought by the BBC to be inimical to its own future. With the BBC now in decline, governments have suggested that wavelengths might be taken from the BBC if needed elsewhere—as they most certainly will be if the commercial radio networks are developed.

Apart from frequency control, British broadcasting policy normally devolves to the BBC or the Independent Broadcasting Authority (the Cable Authority is too new to count). Furthermore, the House of Commons annually debates communications policy upon receipt of required reports from the BBC and the Independent Broadcasting Authority. During these sessions, governments consistently refuse to be drawn into answering questions on program policies, citing legal delegation of these issues to the industry.

From time to time, however, committees of inquiry fully examine major policy questions. Normally, the sponsoring department for broadcasting creates such committees to have a prominent chairman, last for about two years, and issue a published, lengthy report. Governments take note of these deliberations, usually legislating on some aspect, though by no means all, of the recommendations. These undertakings are now timed to coincide with the ending of the BBC's charter and with the ending of commercial television franchises. There have been six committees so far. The first four dealt specifically with the BBC and its future; the fifth and six disposed of the third and fourth television channels respectively.

Occasionally, governments also appoint various committees on technical matters and issue a growing number of short reports on topics such as direct satellite broadcasting. The "slim volumes" are used to stimulate a limited public debate over future policy options as well as to indicate how a government plans to implement changes based on consultation with interested parties.

In the current climate of deregulation these slim volumes have been used to accelerate change and to tell the public government intentions rather than to invite debate. In 1986, for example, the Peacock Committee reported on the future funding of the BBC. It recommended that the BBC take advertising to supplement its license fee income. In fact, the report has been rejected by the government, although the committee's proposal is being considered by the Conservative government.

ECONOMIC STRUCTURE

The review of the BBC finances and the Peacock recommendations lead directly into the question of the economic structure of British broadcasting.

The BBC is still the single most important entity in the system. It supervises 2 national television networks delivering 210 hours of television a week, 4 national radio networks, and 31 local radio stations, delivering 168,000 hours of programs a year. It also directs the External Service, including the World Service, but these are funded directly from the Foreign and Commonwealth Office. The BBC employs around 28,000 staff members.

The BBC's revenue comes from a fixed-term license fee payable by all households operating a television set. In 1984 there were 16 million color television licenses and 3 million black-and-white ones. Britain has 21 million households, but up to 1 million of these were thought to be evading the tax.

The BBC total income for 1983–84 was 770 million pounds. A very small proportion of this came from overseas sales of programs and publications. None derived from any form of "on-air" advertising. BBC television took 58 percent of this total; BBC radio 21 percent. The rest was spent on collecting license fees and on capital improvements.

Of the television budget for 1983–84, BBC 1 cost 22 percent (252 million pounds). Figures for BBC radio in 1984–85 totaled 220 million pounds. Of this the speech network, Radio 4, cost 45 million pounds, the classical music and drama network, Radio 3, cost 33 million pounds, the middle-of-the-road and sport network, Radio 2, cost 34 million pounds, and the popular music network, Radio 1, cost 16 million pounds. In addition, local and regional radio cost 56 million pounds. All radio expenditures are financed from the television license fee, there being no separate tax for radio.

By the mid–1970s the BBC had become used to ample revenue from the proliferation of color television licenses. Then the number of licenses reached near saturation, and in the resulting financial squeeze the corporation has had to keep returning to the government to ask for an increase in the fee (always a matter discussed by the cabinet).

Since the mid–1960s commercial television has suffered the opposite problem. When commercial television began, it was a monopoly in each franchise area. The regulatory agency, then the Independent Television Authority, devised a scheme whereby each franchised company would compete for network time (and thereby the largest advertising budget). But the smaller companies could not make sufficiently sophisticated programs in the requisite numbers to attract national audiences.

There are currently eighteen commercial concerns in the United Kingdom. Of these, Channel 4, Independent Television News, and TV-am pose special cases. The remaining organizations are all regional. Five of these (two in the biggest market, London) are network contractors providing the bulk of programs for the whole of ITV.

The remaining ten provide some network programs and deliver regional news and other features into their area. Spot advertising is limited to seven minutes an hour averaged over the day, generating effectively 100 percent of the income. Despite restrictions, ITV earned approximately 1 billion pounds in 1984–85.

The rules prohibit advertising in many half-hour programs, including certain current affairs shows and documentaries, adult education, some half-hour plays, childrens' shows, and religious features. No advertisements are allowed in schools, royal, ceremonial, or parliamentary offerings, and some other categories of current affairs and documentary offerings.

Program companies see their own advertising as a system rather than as fifteen separate units due to cross-subsidization between firms for programs. Each outfit spends most of its money on programs. Those it makes and transmits in its own area it pays for entirely. For those transmitted on the network, the cost is shared according to resources. Since a company's resources relate to the advertising revenue it earns, the amount that any firm pays to network productions is calculated on its share of the net advertising revenue after the levy earned by the entire network. The ten regional companies pay for the programs made by the central companies networked in their region according to a formula of so much per hour of share worked out between them and the "big five" each year.

Independent Television News is a company wholly owned by the program firms set up under the terms of the original television act to ensure a full and impartial news service on commercial television. TV-am only started in 1983 and operates outside the rest of the system, providing an early-morning U.S.-style breakfast show.

Channel 4, the fourth (and last) UHF terrestrial television network and a wholly owned subsidiary of the International Broadcast Authority (IBA), began in 1982. IBA provides finances through compulsory annual subscriptions paid by ITV companies. The amount taken from each company falls within a band of 14 to 18 percent of that concern's net advertising revenue. For 1985 to 1986 Channel 4 received 129.1 million pounds. The ITV companies, in exchange, receive exclusive rights to sell advertising on the channel in their region.

Commercial radio, legal in Britain since 1973 and operating in forty-eight areas, is funded from spot advertising, limited to nine minutes in any hour. Most early stations were based in large cities; more are now centered in smaller towns, and some of these outlets have been experiencing financial difficulties. One, in Leicester, declared itself bankrupt in 1985, confirming earlier fears that commercial radio might be viable only in large urban areas.

As in many other developed societies, large companies, often multinational, own commercial television and commercial radio. Television companies, in particular, have interests in many other media such as newspapers and magazines or other major leisure industries—cinema chains, hotels, restaurants, parks, and amusement halls.

Legal rules prevent foreign companies from owning outright British broadcast media, although many have some financial interest. Similar rules prevent cross-media monopolies in any one area, although a television company may have a stake in local radio stations outside its transmission area.

Strong trade union activity characterizes the mass media. In television this is particularly pronounced, having developed directly from the earlier feature film trade union activity. Endemic overstaffing has resulted.

High revenues have disguised the significance of this feature, but ITV programs may cost up to 100 percent more than those made by the BBC. For example, one hour of BBC drama cost 225,000 pounds, while ITV drama on the average was estimated to cost 400,000 pounds.

PROGRAMMING

The concept of public service broadcasting is central to all program policies. These policies are defined as follows:

1. Geographic universality—programs should be available to the whole population.
2. Universality of appeal—features should cater to all interests and tastes.
3. Minorities, especially disadvantaged minorities, should receive particular attention.
4. Broadcasting should be structured so as to encourage competition in good programming rather than competition for audience numbers.

A comparison of BBC 1 and ITV shows is as follows:

BBC	ITV
current affairs, 26.5%	current affairs, 10.5%
feature films, 18.5%	feature films, 8.5%
sports, 12%	sports, 10%
children, 6%	children, 13%
light entertainment, 6%	light entertainment, 14%
drama, 4%	drama, 23%
education, 7%	education, 8%
religion, 3%	religion, 2%
news, 6%	news, 10.5%

About a quarter of BBC television programs, including repeats, are imported, mostly from the United States. ITV is limited to a quota, negotiated with the trade unions, of 15 percent. As money has become tighter, all British television has begun to use co-production arrangements, the BBC more than ITV.

Whereas the BBC and ITV (as a network) make most of their own programs in-house, Channel 4 does not. Except for its access program, "Right to Reply," approximately one-third of its offerings originate from ITV companies, one-third from repeat or foreign sources, and one-third from small independent television or film concerns. As a result, it averages somewhat lower per hour broadcast costs than the rest of British television.

The government is given some free time, usually late at night, for public service announcements; it pays for the rest of advertising (only of course on ITV) at standard rates. Some charities also are given free airtime.

Registered political parties with a recognized standing (members in elected office) are allowed free time, strictly limited, on all television and some radio channels. Only the three main parties, Conservative, Labour, and SDP–Liberal Alliance, are given this time outside major election periods.

Radio programs are divided into both national/local types and "generic" forms nationally. Thus the BBC networks divide more or less into a speech, a classical music and drama, a middle-of-the-road (MOR) music and sport, and a popular music format. Radio 4 (speech, which includes news, current affairs, and radio drama) only transmitted 320 hours of music in 1983–84. Radio 3 (classical network) broadcast 4,941 hours.

In 1983–84 a total of 17,865 hours of music was played across the four BBC networks; there were 5,437 hours of current affairs, 1,884 hours of news, 956 hours of drama, 965 hours of sports, 599 hours of light entertainment, 410 hours of religion, and 828 hours of education broadcast on the BBC radio network.

There is no commercial network radio, although stations swap some programs and share others. Local commercial radio, known as Independent Local Radio (ILR), largely presents popular music with short news bulletins. Evening programs tend to be talk shows. BBC local radio is similar but, with its older audience, tends to be more middle-of-the-road.

Agreements with copyright societies and with the powerful Musicians' Union, which wishes to "Keep Music Live," limit all British radio in the amount of time it can play records. BBC network radio runs twenty-four hours only on Radio 2; the other three networks transmit between 6:00 A.M. and midnight. Some local commercial radio outlets broadcast twenty-four hours, but no BBC local station operates round the clock. Television starts with breakfast shows, has various breaks (including school fare) during the day, and then restarts in midafternoon through to about 12:30 P.M. All-night offerings on television are limited to special live events such as the opening of the Los Angeles Olympics.

The British Audience Research Board (BARB) evaluates audiences for the broadcasters. This body conducts daily, weekly, and quarterly surveys. The average Briton watches about twenty-three hours of television a week: BBC 1 gets 36 percent of this time; BBC 2, 10 percent; ITV, 48 percent; and Channel 4, 6 percent.

The same average Briton listens to about nine hours of radio. Of this time, 30 percent is for Radio 1; 20 percent for Radio 2; 2 percent for Radio 3; 12 percent for Radio 4; and 11 percent for BBC local and regional radio. Local commercial radio gets 23 percent of listeners, and the remaining 2 percent tunes in to pirate radio stations.

BROADCAST REFORM

Public criticism of broadcasting in the United Kingdom developed slowly but inexorably. The BBC in the first three decades was much criticized for its aloofness and remoteness from ordinary lives. But when commercial television began, it drove the BBC television market down. This led in turn to increased public criticism of all television.

In 1964 a schoolteacher, Mrs. Mary Whitehouse, founded the National Viewers and Listeners Association (NVALA), which has grown to represent part of the moral majority in Britain. It has never been established how many members NVALA has; there is no doubt, however, that it has come to express the concerns of many viewers and listeners. In short, broadcasting has too much violence, sex, and sordid programs. NVALA was instrumental, in 1984, in changing the law relating to the sale of violent (and often explicitly sexual) videotapes.

In general, however, British broadcasting is considered by many to be among the best in the world for both technical quality and programming standards. Its political neutrality is taken as given.

Culturally, since it has a very wide range of programs including many fine art ones, like opera and ballet, it is similarly well respected, both inside and outside the United Kingdom. In 1982, for example, at a ceremony in New York, British television took all five top Emmy awards.

Both the BBC and commercial broadcasting attempt to assess genuine audience concerns through a number of mechanisms of "accountability." These include public meetings, letters (all replied to), phone calls (all logged), advisory councils, access programs, and a vast range of in-depth research studies. Much is noted by broadcast managements and program makers.

Over time there has been pressure for more broadcasting. The real extent of public desire for these increases is difficult to assess. In 1986 the government allowed some community radio experiments that may test both the public's desire to listen to such stations and their willingness to organize and pay for them. The stations, allowed under special Home Office licenses, must demonstrate either a geographical or cultural community. They must, like all British broadcasting, show a high technical standard and a sound financial base. These conditions will exclude many potential "communities" but remain consistent with the state view that the airwaves are a public resource. Pressure for licensing of community radio has grown through the illegal activities of many pirate radio stations, most of which have been community based.

NEW TECHNOLOGIES

Until the 1980s British broadcasting remained a closed system, convinced that its practices and finances were the best organized in the world. A large part of the world shared that assessment. Since 1980 broadcasting has had to come to terms with three new factors and one old. British broadcasters must now take account of the European situation. New technologies are providing much wider possibilities in services, and deregulation will signal the advent of much greater competitiveness but not necessarily greater choice. Finally, the public continues to demand more media.

The Conservative governments of 1979 and 1983 have authorized the largely deregulated development of a broadband, state-of-the-art cable system designed to stimulate the information economy. To oversee this development, a new Cable Authority began work in 1985.

Cable systems have existed in the United Kingdom for fifty years. They began operations largely to overcome "off-air" reception problems. Since the 1980s, however, these organizations have been allowed to carry whatever programs they can; before, they could only carry the "off-air" broadcasts.

Cable systems pass by about 14 percent of British homes, but of these only about 8 percent are connected. Cable will grow only slowly in the United Kingdom because of the following factors:

1. Off-air reception is generally very high.
2. Television offers a wide program choice uninterrupted by many advertisements.
3. Government rules require that all cable has to be buried (an expensive undertaking deterring many would-be operators).
4. The popularization of videocassette recorders heavily undermines one of cable's main markets, feature films.

Nevertheless, where cable does exist and where the very small new pilot systems have begun, they do appear to be very popular. The industrial assessment in early 1986 indicated that cable would become an important part of future broadcasting, but not until the mid–1990s.

Cable services already rely on satellite broadcasting. In 1986 about twelve satellite channels fed directly into the United Kingdom cable systems. These included some U.S., French, and Italian services.

The British government endorsed direct broadcasts by satellites. It then secured a continuing delay, however, by insisting on a British-made satellite for this service. By the time this option became clearly untenable, other European satellites were up and running.

The government finally authorized privately owned satellite dishes in 1985, but local planning laws may prevent the public from securing this expensive item. For the foreseeable future, cable operators will continue to take most satellite services.

Videocassette recorders operate in about 30 percent of British homes. While strong copyright laws exist in the United Kingdom, there has been an unwritten agreement that home taping, providing it does not result in overt marketing of the tapes in any way, will not provide grounds for prosecution. In 1986 the government was considering whether to introduce a levy on all blank tapes (audio as well as video). This development could slow down the growth of the video market. The videodisc player has not had any noticeable effect in Britain.

CONCLUSION/FORECAST

Britain is now entering a period of turbulence in broadcasting in which the older established sections, in particular the BBC, are going to be challenged by new media, notably cable and satellites. This transformation is more noticeable in Britain because the broadcasting system has had such a long and stable history with relatively carefully planned and controlled developments. For many in the United Kingdom, the most important question in the mid–1980s was the extent to which the growth of the new media might destroy the remarkably high quality of British television programs by flooding the market with cheap imports.

BIBLIOGRAPHY

Annan, Lord. *Report of the Committee on the Future of Broadcasting*. London: HMSO Cmnd, 1977.
Briggs, Asa. *The BBC: The First 50 Years*. London: Oxford, 1985.
Burns, Tom. *The BBC: Public Institution, Private World*. London: Macmillan, 1977.
Curran, Charles. *A Seamless Robe*. London: Collins, 1979.
Curran, James, and Jean Seaton. *Power without Responsibility*. London: Fontana, 1981.
Hoggart, Richard, and J. Morgan, eds. *The Future of Broadcasting*. London: Macmillan, 1982.
Hollins, T. *Beyond Broadcasting: Into the Cable Age*. London: BFI, 1984.
Lambert, S. *Channel 4—Television with a Difference?* London: BFI, 1982.
Madge, Timothy. *Beyond the BBC: Broadcasters, Broadcasting, and the Public in the 1980's*. London: Macmillan, 1979.
Schlesinger, P. *Putting Reality Together*. London: Constable, 1978.
Sendall, Bernard. *Independent Television in Britain*. 2 vols. London: Macmillan, 1982–83.
Seymour-Ure, C. *The Political Impact of Mass Media*. London: Constable, 1974.
Smith, Anthony, *The Shadow in the Cave*. London: Unwin, 1973.

Tracey, M. *The Production of Political Television*. London: Routledge, Kegan Paul, 1978.

Tracey, M. and D. Morrison. *Whitehouse*. London: Macmillan, 1979.

Tunstall, Jeremy. *The Media Are American*. London: Constable, 1977.

———. *The Media in Britain*. London: Constable, 1983.

Wedell, E. G. *Broadcasting and Public Policy*. London: Michael Joseph, 1968.

Williams, Raymond. *Television: Technology and Cultural Form*. London: Fontana, 1974.

HUNGARY

Thomas Szendrey

HISTORY

The history of radio transmission in Hungary (Austria-Hungary until 1918) can be traced back to the activities of Tivadar Puskás, the inventor of the telephonograph, in 1893; his research first made possible what can be considered the predecessor of radio communications. He was also involved in the establishment of the company that eventually became the forerunner of Hungarian radio. Ten years later the Hungarian delegates to the First International Congress of Wireless purchased a transmitter and receiver to be used for experimental purposes; on October 13, 1914, the first radio station was placed in service just outside Budapest, and this provided communication links during World War I.

The upheavals of the war and the subsequent dismemberment of the nation, formalized by the Treaty of Trianon (1920), did not fail to have an effect, mostly negative, on the subsequent development of radio in a nation much reduced in size and subjected to the ravages of war and revolution. At any rate, in 1922 the ownership of the original Puskás venture passed to the MTI (Hungarian Telegraph Agency), and a new radio and telegraph transmitter was soon installed. Technical developments and legal issues, especially the favorable clarification of the rights of artists and others heard on the airwaves, contributed to the further development of the medium in Hungary in the early 1920s, and significant for this were the organizational activities of Ernö Szöts, the new director of the broadcasting ventures of MTI. The first experimental programs were sent on March 15, 1924; in the same year the first journal devoted to the affairs of radio also made its appearance, later to be taken over by the broadcast corporation itself. Further technical developments in 1925 resulted in the setting up of the first permanent two-kilowatt transmitter, some more experimental programs, the promulgation of a communications law (November 10, 1925), and the official commencement of Hungarian broadcasting on December 1, 1925. Within a few weeks the former corporate structure was reorganized and a new one created, now known as the Hungarian Telediffusion and Radio Corporation, headed by Miklós Kozma and authorized by the Hungarian government.

The operation of the corporation was governed by a state-issued license that in essence provided for nearly absolute government control over all aspects of the venture, but especially programming, and extended to the manufacture, distribution, and licensing even of receivers. The Ministries of Trade and Postal Services exercised the bulk of this regulation, augmented later by an interministerial committee for the oversight of programming. There were also financial provisions to assure the success of the venture for both the government and the corporation.

During the course of the early years, the radio service initiated a series of innovations, which provided the necessary impetus for the rapid expansion of subscriptions and thus the establishment of a technically progressive and financially sound operation. During the years 1926 to 1928, Hungarian radio not only increased its broadcasting capacity, but also presented a series of firsts including the first opera program, first on-the-spot transmission, first theatrical presentation, the first play written for radio, and the first broadcast from a location outside Budapest. During the latter 1920s the strength of the signal was increased to twenty kilowatts, new studios were built, and advisory councils were created for music and literary programs. All of these accomplishments contributed to the selection of Budapest as the site for the 1930 Congress of the International Radio Union.

After the organizational and technical problems were resolved, the 1930s witnessed the expansion of broadcasting in the life of the nation, best testified to by the rapid increase in the number of subscribers and the expansion of programming in terms of both scope and airtime. Consider the following: at its inception in 1925 there were 16,927 subscribers, by 1928 the number had grown to 168,553, and at the end of 1934 it stood at 340,117. In terms of social-class analysis, the majority of subscribers were merchants, craftsmen, and individuals working in the intellectual professions, totaling approximately 230,000, whereas the other social groups (mostly workers and peasants) numbered among them somewhat in excess of 100,000 radio subscribers. By comparison, in 1934 Denmark had the highest number of radio users per 1,000 population, specifically 160 per 1,000; some other figures may also be noted: Austria, 78.6; England, 144.7; Bulgaria, 1.4; Poland, 10.1; and Germany, 89. The figure for Hungary was 38.9.

Radio also developed its own programming and organizational structure. A musical advisory committee was created in 1928 under the direction of the eminent composer Ernö Dohnányi, and a literary program section was established under the leadership of the writer and essayist László Németh in 1934, soon to be followed by László Cs. Szabó, who retained this post until the closing days of World War II; this was accomplished by a reorganization of the administrative leadership in 1933. It was also in the 1930s that regular programming was introduced into the schools, commencing one of the major educational efforts that were always to remain a significant dimension of broadcasting in Hungary.

In terms of programming, broadcasters prepared wax recordings of important cultural and political events and also began a program to preserve and eventually broadcast folk music. With the coming of the war, Hungarian radio began to offer foreign-language shows and exchanged broadcasts with other nations, especially England and later the neighboring nations, ultimately even with the United States. In 1940 broadcasters introduced a series of programs for and about the military and were eventually drawn into the conflict as an important means of information and propaganda; German-language transmissions were introduced in 1942, and a retired army officer was appointed as the president of the Hungarian Radio Corporation that same year. In spite of some restrictions on its operation caused by the war effort, radio nonetheless remained on the air with only minimal interruptions and difficulties until the German occupation of the nation on March 19, 1944; soon after this the new government forbade Hungarian citizens to listen to the broadcasts of any nation with which Hungary was at war. It should be noted that at this point, in spite of the war, there were almost one million licensed radio receivers in Hungary.

As the end of the war approached and the battle lines engulfed Budapest, extensive damage was done to the building and equipment of the Hungarian broadcasting system. The radio buildings and studios were abandoned at the end of 1944, and what was left of the technical equipment was carried away or destroyed by the retreating German armies. They also blew up the Lakihegy transmission tower, at this time the tallest in Europe. With this, the radio system found itself in shambles in early 1945, to begin a process of reconstruction under difficult and trying economic and political conditions in a war-devastated country. This reconstruction involved not only the broadcasting system but the country as a whole. The former social and political system had been destroyed, and for a few years, certainly until 1948, a coalition of political parties under the guidance of the Allied Control Commission struggled to create a democratic political and social order. With the dominance of the USSR in East Central Europe generally, the Communist party eventually gained control by 1948 and transformed the nation on the Soviet model.

An institution as sensitive and fundamental to a political system as the media generally and the radio specifically was certainly the focal point of political conflict and eventually came under the direct control of the state.This was made even more evident by the fact that the radio system in

Hungary had operated under a government concession from its inception. This situation certainly did not change between 1945 and 1948, although those three years did represent a transitional phase. Complete control over the medium has been established by the Communists since 1948 and has been maintained since that time except for the few brief weeks of the 1956 revolution in Hungary.

The immediate postwar developments in the history of the Hungarian broadcasting system were closely tied to the activities of Gyula Ortutay, a former director of the folk arts section of the radio and a leading leftist-oriented cultural politician. Ortutay had been charged with the rebuilding and restructuring of the broadcast system by the Budapest National Committee on January 20, 1945. According to the terms of the armistice all means of communication were placed under the authority of the Allied Control Commission, and two months later the new Hungarian foreign minister obtained the necessary authorizations for Ortutay to proceed with the technical work needed for the restoration of broadcasting. Radio returned to the air with two small transmitters for six hours a day on May 1, 1945. It could be heard only in parts of Budapest and mostly through public speakers distributed throughout parts of the city. For a brief period the Allied Control Commission had proscribed the use of radio receivers, but that order was rapidly rescinded.

Concurrently with the restoration of broadcasting, there also took place a restructuring of the broadcast system. On June 1, 1945, a new corporate organization was established, the Hungarian Central Broadcasting Corporation; its shares were held in equal proportion by the four coalition political parties and the trade union organization. After a series of struggles among the coalition partners, as well as conflict with the former owners and licensees, the government nationalized the medium and other corporations dealing with broadcasting, information, film, and advertising. With its expanded holdings and influence, radio created its own publishing house and other ancillary enterprises, including its own philharmonic orchestra. In the same year the Lakihegy transmission tower was rebuilt, and by 1948 a 135-kilowatt station was completed. The number of radio subscribers, who had totaled only 178,000 in 1945, increased to 529,000 by 1949, or 58 per 1,000 population, thus surpassing the prewar numbers. On the occasion when this new transmitter was placed into service (December 21, 1946), Ortutay delivered a speech that not only specified the purposes of radio, but also pointed the way to the future. He emphasized that the political goal of the media was to serve a "progressive democracy," and that it had a mission in the promotion of culture and education, and he stressed the debt owed to the Soviet Union for its assistance.

The era of transition from one political system to another (1945–48) ended with the imposition of a Communist regime in 1948. Mass communications came under the direct supervision of the government, operating no longer under licenses or concessions, but controlled by the Council of Ministers through a state information office. This centralized regulation and state ownership has characterized Hungarian broadcasting since 1948.

The broadcasting system has been developed extensively since that time. By 1955 there were thirty radio studios and five regional transmitters, which at certain times of the day sent their own regional programming. The major radio stations, however, are located in Budapest and comprise Radio Kossuth, the national main service, Radio Petőfi, devoted mostly to rapid information, entertainment, and programming for interest groups, and the UHF or so-called Third Program, devoted to serious music, literature, and educational features.

By 1975 there were 2,538,000 radio subscribers, or 76 out of every 100 households. The number increased to 2,700,000 in 1980, at which time radio subscriptions were no longer required. The Central Statistical Office since then reports the number of radio sets sold in order to give some indication of the extent of listeners in the nation. Television viewing has expanded greatly since 1975; in fact, it is the most significant medium at this time.

Television was first discussed as a possibility as early as 1949, but a decision to develop it was made only in 1952. Experimental telecasting commenced in 1953, and the production of TV sets within the country was begun in 1955. A mobile transmitter became functional in 1957, studios were built in 1958, and regular transmissions commenced in 1958 to 16,000 subscribers; that number grew to 104,000 by 1960, 1.2 million by 1967, and 2.9 million by 1983. A second channel was placed in operation in 1971, and experimental color broadcasts began as early as 1969. Since that time color telecasting has vastly increased, reaching 33 percent in 1975 and expanding since then.

Since 1974 Hungarian radio and television have operated as separate organizational entities; each continues to play a vital role in the life of the nation and will continue to do so as they adopt the most recent technological changes into their own particular organizational structures and programming policies.

REGULATION

Broadcasting in Hungary, even though it began as a private venture and retained at least some characteristics of that until 1948, has always been subjected to varying degrees of government control. It was publicly owned in part until 1948 and has been totally so since that time, and that has to a great extent shaped regulatory patterns; these generally were determined by the political aspirations and values of the political system at any given time.

The law that eventually governed radio was issued on November 10,

1925, bearing the number 32.250/1925, by the Ministry of Commerce. It first stated the rights of the government to control all transmission within its airspace; any form of broadcasting required the consent of the minister of commerce. Paragraph 14 of the act further specified that a transmitter could be established only by the postal service and was to be operated within its own sphere of authority. Anyone was entitled to operate a receiver who had obtained the necessary permit for its use; the fee paid for this was to be collected by the post office as well. The act further stipulated that transmitters and receivers were permitted only for the public good, educational, or experimental purposes. The act, in effect, established a comprehensive control mechanism over the medium.

Having specified the role of the government, the state then granted a license or concession to the Hungarian Telediffusion and Radio Corporation. The post office established the transmitter and provided all of the technical equipment, but the construction of the studios and the obtaining of other related equipment and materials was to be the responsibility of the corporation. The license at first was issued for a twenty-year period, subject to automatic extensions; until it was withdrawn, no other similar licenses were to be issued. The government also specified the wavelength, and the corporation provided programming at its expense for seven hours on weekdays and eight on Sundays. Furthermore, the government required that shows be prepared a week in advance and submitted to a program committee for approval. In return for this, a percentage of the subscription fee, reaching 50 percent at the level of 400,000 subscriptions, was to be given to the corporation by the post office.

This arrangement, in effect, gave the licensee the right to exploit a monopoly situation under rather stringent government supervision, which became stricter (especially in respect to censorship of programs and restrictions on the broadcasting of certain writers and topics) as political and economic conditions gradually changed for the worse in the 1930s and 1940s. During the war years the number of additional regulations placed upon the broadcasting system increased in scope; most obvious were controls covering programming and suspension of service at certain times when the dangers of war so required.

During the 1945–48 era government supervision was exercised by the four major coalition parties, but with the obvious assistance of the Soviet delegate to the Allied Control Commission, and thus as a consequence of increased Soviet pressure, the Communists exercised an ever-increasing voice in the regulation of the mass media. Regulation of broadcasting changed after 1945 insofar as the Hungarian Telediffusion and Radio Corporation was nationalized in 1945 (one of the first large enterprises to be so) and reorganized as a corporation until even that particular organizational form was abandoned after 1948.

State ownership, in reality, involved a very direct form of government regulation, accompanied by parallel Communist party control. This became even more formalized after 1956. The Agitprop (agitation and propaganda) section, directly accountable to the Central Committee of the Hungarian Socialist Workers party (MSzMP, the official name and its abbreviation of the Communist party since 1956), exercised a controlling authority over the formal ministerial structure. In terms of supervision over the media, the Council of Ministers appoints the head of the Government Information Office, who in turn has general jurisdiction over Hungarian broadcasting; this office provides general guidelines and equipment.

More direct control over the everyday operation of radio and television, at least since 1974, is exercised by the Committee for Radio and Television. Its president is appointed by the Council of Ministers, and its membership includes the ministers of cultural affairs and education, the postmaster general, and the presidents of the radio and television systems. Its major tasks include exercising budgetary authority, offering directives for programming, facilitating technical developments, assessing the role of the media in public life, and directing the international contacts of the media. These more or less represent the contours of media regulation.

ECONOMIC STRUCTURE

Given the centralized nature of Hungarian broadcasting, one should also expect ownership to be centralized. Even though radio began as a state-controlled private enterprise and was structured on the corporate model until 1948, it was by no means ever a completely private enterprise.

The technical aspects and apparatus (excluding the studios) were established and maintained by the postal service; furthermore, a substantial portion of the subscription fees was kept by the government. Thus the broadcasting corporation was a regulated private corporation established to operate what was in essence a state monopoly. The public was further represented by the delegation of government ministers to the board of the corporation and also by the government-mandated interministerial Commission on Program Oversight. Furthermore, the interconnection was made even more evident on the level of leading personnel insofar as only politically reliable elements (until 1945 retired army officers played a prominent role) were appointed to leadership positions in the nonartistic and nontechnical areas. For example, the president of the radio corporation and the major personality in the life of radio for more than two decades, Miklós Kozma, belonged to the circle of politicians around the regent Miklós Horthy and also held a number of high offices in interwar Hungary.

On the other hand, the artists, musicians, and announcers as well as the technical and broadcasting staff were chosen almost exclusively on the basis of competence and dedication. In technical matters and development, advice was sought from the experts of foreign radio-manufacturing companies, especially English and German ones such as Standard, Ltd., and Telefunken among others.

During the war the government exercised a more direct control over broadcasting and attempted to use the radio as a sounding board for propaganda; this was never very successful because of opposition from the corporation, which saw this as cutting into its programming rights and even more directly into its ability to satisfy its subscribers, and thus into its profitability. Propaganda became dominant only for a few brief months during the waning months of the war under the German-imposed Arrow Cross government. Many of the leading radio employees did not cooperate with the Arrow Cross government officials delegated to manage the media.

At any rate, much of the broadcasting system, its equipment, its music collections, and its studios were destroyed by the war, and a difficult process of rebuilding was necessary for the technology to function again on even the most minimal level. Even though the corporate structure was retained, the ownership patterns changed insofar as the shares were divided among the four postwar coalition parties and the trade unions. Since this solution caused difficulties not only with the former owners, but also among the political parties themselves, radio became one of the first major enterprises nationalized, even though it continued to operate as a corporation until 1948.

Since that time broadcasting has been completely publicly owned and has functioned under government control; in the 1970s approximately 40 percent of the national budget earmarked for educational and cultural affairs was spent to support broadcasting. In reality, this amount supports also a research institute on mass communications, schools for training technical personnel, a publishing house, and a number of professional artistic ensembles including a symphony orchestra as well as a system of educational features.

This vast political-cultural enterprise, as a state-supported entity, serves the goals and aspirations of the government that owns and to a great extent directs it. While autonomous in some minimal respects, it is nonetheless expected to serve the information needs and cultural aspirations of the state and its political system as those have found expression in documents dealing with the cultural-educational tasks of the media generally; however, many of these are related more directly to programming concerns.

PROGRAMMING

Since Hungarian radio and subsequently television as well have always been intimately tied to the state and its dominant ideological inclinations, one would expect the programming policies and priorities to reflect those political situations and ideological commitments. This certainly has been the case, but by no means to the same extent—whether in theory or practice—at any given time. One may distinguish at least four distinct periods of programming control; while there may have been some degrees of laxness or severity in the exercise of this control, these were also generally related to the political conditions of any given era.

These four periods could be distinguished as follows: 1925–41, 1941–45, 1945–48, and since 1948. The first era was characterized by an attempt to provide information and entertainment that would reflect favorably on the values and aspirations of the essentially conservative interwar Hungarian sociopolitical system. Although there was a mechanism for the control of programming—all features had to be submitted for review and approval—an attempt was made to accommodate the wishes and desires of the radio subscribers. To this end, a number of surveys were conducted, and these provided evidence of rather conservative tastes in music, some interest in news programming, the desire to hear more dramatic presentations, and support for religious features. Quite surprisingly, there was little demand for sports programming, literary readings, language instruction, and jazz. Indeed, a 1927 survey indicated that Gypsy music and Hungarian popular songs were the most liked and jazz the least. Generally speaking, most of the surveys prior to 1944 continued to show the great desire for Gypsy and Hungarian popular music and to rate literary programs and educational features at the lower end of the scale. In spite of these surveys, the strong commitment of broadcasting to the goals of culture and education (actively encouraged by the government) prevented radio from ever being wholly placed at the service of only entertainment and the fulfillment of popular desires.

During the war years there was an attempt by the Ministry of National Defense, to place radio, as in Nazi Germany, in the direct service of war propaganda. Some concessions were made to this of necessity, but the corporation was more interested in the satisfaction, insofar as possible, of its subscribers. It was generally aware of its civic responsibilities, but there was some disagreement over the extent and nature of these. Thus a conflict of interest occurred, and the increasingly rightist and later openly pro-German governments were able to exercise some measure of control over programming. By the fall of 1944 the pro-German Arrow Cross government assumed control and turned radio into a quite direct propaganda tool until its ultimate defeat by early 1945. This defeat was accompanied by the virtual destruction of the broadcasting system.

When the first postarmistice Hungarian radio came back on the air in the early summer of 1945, programming issues were once again paramount and influenced by political considerations. The programming policies of radio in the period 1945–48 were guided by political issues. First of all an effort was made to build upon some of the programming reforms suggested by the liberal elements. Second, an attempt was made to provide more news coverage, quite understandable in an era during which events in Hungary and beyond its borders were affecting people's lives. Third, a conscious effort was made to eliminate much of the rightist and profascist (not the same by any means in the Hungarian context) individuals and their attitudes and values from the airwaves. Fourth, in the realm of music, greater emphasis was placed on folk and classical music. In addition, programming also included the introduction of Russian-language instruction as well as Russian features. In effect, the German orientation of the war years was replaced by a Soviet orientation, an obvious consequence of the outcome of World War II.

As has so often been the case in Hungarian cultural history, these developments were inevitably the consequences of political changes. After the achievement of full political power by the Communists in 1948, not only the ownership patterns (a public corporation became an organ of government), but also the programming policies fundamentally changed. Recognizing the significance of broadcasting and operating on the assumption that a state that professes to dominate everything must control mass communications, the Communists placed programming under strict party regulation. Control was especially stringent until 1956 and became so again after the revolution of 1956, which had made effective use of radio. Since 1957 there has been a consolidation in the political realm accompanied by one in the realm of programming control in the media as well. In this context, supervision over programming has remained absolute.

Programming policies were centralized by a decree of the government issued on September 18, 1974. The document stated the following:

1. Radio has the obligation of participating in the responsible propagation of the policies enunciated by the Hungarian People's Republic.

2. Broadcasting must provide rapid and accurate newscasting.

3. The medium must satisfy the desire for popular educational and cultural development on a high level.

4. Broadcasting must provide programming supportive of the creative use of leisure time.

In the estimation of the Council of Ministers, the fulfillment of these guidelines will then contribute to the informational and cultural development of the citizenry and the building of socialism. Radio also has the responsibility of presenting to the world the accomplishments of the Hungarian People's Republic and representing its political stance and public statements.

This task is divided among four programming or editorial departments as follows:

- The Department of Information has responsibilities for newscasting and educational features.
- The Department of Literary Programming includes the presentation of dramas and direct concern with aesthetic issues as well as the production of entertainment fare.
- The Department of Musical Programming is in charge of serious and popular music features and directs artistic and musical ensembles.
- The Department of Youth Programming edits all features intended for children.

There is also a coordinating division that makes decisions about the extent of particular types of programming and coordinates the work of these departments. The program orientation and policies of Hungarian television are quite similar, consisting in this case of five departments: political programming, popular education and cultural development, entertainment, youth programming, and film and coproduction.

At the present time radio stations provide 386 hours of programming per week, compared to 50 hours in 1925 and expanding to 307 hours by 1970, and television transmitters beam 91 hours per week, compared to 51 in 1970 and less than 10 at the inception of TV. Some information about the percentage of time devoted to certain types of programming may be instructive. For example, in 1982 the figures were as follows:

Radio

news, 7.2%

educational, 5.6%

cultural, 5.5%

entertainment (mostly music), 66.5%

advertising, 1.4%

other, 13.7%

Television

news, 15.2%

educational, 15.4%

cultural, 5.4%

entertainment (with films and sports), 46.5%

advertising, 3.7%

other, 13.8%

The higher percentage of news and educational programming on television may be explained by the fact that TV viewing generally demands and receives more attention than the mostly background nature of much of radio listening today; thus news and information, which are essential from the point of view of the government authorities, occupy a larger share of airtime. Considering the obvious emphasis placed upon the educational and political mission of broadcasting in Hungary, these figures reflect such concerns, and there is somewhat less entertainment programming than in most commercial broadcasting systems. Cultural politicians responsible for broadcasting often cite this as a sign of superiority when compared to programming determined or influenced only by advertising interests. Nonetheless, the Hungarian media have become more responsive to the wishes and desires of the listeners and viewers than in the 1960s and 1970s.

BROADCAST REFORM

Given the intimate connection of broadcasting and political control characteristic of the Hungarian media, programming and broadcast reform generally followed upon political change. One must, for all practical purposes, exclude the possibility of alternate broadcasting because that has been and still is legally proscribed; thus reform must of necessity operate within the system. This does not mean that the system itself has not presented alternatives, but these have not resulted in a substantial alteration of the structure of broadcasting. For example, it has been mostly because of public and political pressure that programming for nationality groups within Hungary has been instituted. Indeed, the concern with the cultural aspirations of Hungarian minorities in the neighboring states has been emphasized by numerous officials recently, and this pressure for the improvement of the cultural condition—including native-language broadcasting—is not wholly absent from the cultural-political scene in Hungary today.

Broadcasting reform within the system is mostly the consequence of the research activities of the Institute for Mass Communications, established in 1969 as a component part of Hungarian radio and television. Its function is to conduct surveys dealing with mass communications and examine the reception of programs and related issues in the light of the political and cultural situation of the country. It is concerned with the effect of current programming on the society and thus contributes to the ongoing programming policies of broadcasting outlets. It also maintains a publication program of these materials and studies, publishes Hungarian translations of the most significant theoretical and technical writings appearing in other languages, and sponsors a number of journals and reviews.

NEW TECHNOLOGIES

Concern with hegemony and the socialist character of the media has created an ambivalent, but nevertheless open, attitude and receptivity toward innovation and new technologies. Hungarian broadcasting is also concerned with the problem of a new world information order and sees its future as a part of the socialist bloc communication system.

Hungarian theoreticians analyze the new technologies in terms of their social settings and effects and recognize that modern mass communications have changed our perspectives; this is an issue that must be dealt with, since it is no longer possible to isolate the broadcasting system of any nation from the forces of technological change.

The Hungarian broadcasting system has had a tradition of adapting to new technologies evident throughout its history and exemplified by its adaptations of German and English technology during the interwar years. In more recent times Hungarian radio not only adopted stereo sound, but also carried out a series of studies dealing with the effect of this sound transmission upon the character of programming and changes in listening habits.

The ever-increasing role of television in Hungary was also accompanied by both adaptation of foreign technologies and some specific Hungarian developments. Color broadcasting has hardly become widespread, but now even newer technologies are already being adopted; however, this involves some serious problems since the electronic infrastructure of the nation is quite deficient, and thus it cannot fully and effectively make use of such new technologies as cable television, teletext, programming via satellite, and data transmission through the telephone system. Of these, the teletext has been introduced on an experimental basis, but the lack of availability of the machines and the costs involved preclude its wider use. Cable television seems to be the most promising area of future development in Hungary. Plans are under way in several cities to build large-scale antenna systems that may be developed into local-access cable systems. In fact, an experimental cable system is now functioning in the city of Pecs in southwestern Hungary.

Although there has been some discussion of the possibility of a Hungarian broadcast satellite, not much has been done. This could provide programming for the Hungarian minorities in the surrounding states, but would also open up the possibility of the reception of the programs of other nations within Hungary. This technological development would cause political problems regarding program control.

CONCLUSION/FORECAST

Even a brief survey of broadcasting in Hungary makes it quite evident that centralized control and ownership has generally characterized it; this has changed in orientation and tempo as a consequence mostly of political changes. Furthermore, the political system has until recently been able to adapt its policies to changing technologies and thus assure its continued authority. This is no longer the case, however. Centralization is breaking down as a result of technological advances on several fronts, and thus the relationship of central programming policies to individuals and small groups makes less and less sense. In short, if technology makes possible a virtual electronic Alexandria, why sustain central programming and control? This issue is of special significance for the socialist nations, which share a commitment to the centralization and control of information.

BIBLIOGRAPHY

Biró, Vera, ed. *Kulturális intézmények és szervezetek Magyarországon*. Budapest: Kossuth, 1976.

Frank, Tibor, ed. *Tanulmányok a Magyar Rádió történetéböl, 1925–1945*. Budapest: Tomegkommunikacios Kutato Intezet, 1975.

Füleki, József, and Ferenc Herczeg, eds. *Közmüvelödési kézikönyv*. Budapest: Kossuth, 1977.

Halász, Gyuka K., ed. *A 10 éves Magyar Rádió*. Budapest: M. K. Posta, 1935.

Kiss, Tivadar, ed. *Rádióévkönyv*. Budapest: Hungaria, 1949.

Lévai, Béla. *A rádió es televizió krónikája, 1945–1978*. Budapest: Tomegkommunikacios Kutato Intezet, 1980.

Lévai, Béla, ed. *Az 50 éves Magyar Rádió*. Budapest: Magyar Radio, 1975.

Magyar rádió öt esztendeje, 1925–1930. Budapest: Radioelet, 1975.

Magyar Telefonhirmondó és Rádió Részvénytársaság alapszabályai. Budapest: MTI, 1936.

Pokoly, László, ed. *Rádióra vonatkozó rendeletek gyüjteménye*. Debrecen, Nagy ny., 1937.

Rádióhallgatók lexikona. Budapest: Vajda, 1944.

Rádiórendelet. A m. kir. kereskedelemügyi miniszternek 1925. evi 32.250 számu rendelete. 1925.

Szecskö, Tamás. *Communication Policies in Hungary*. New York: UNESCO, 1979.

Szekfü, András. *A Tömegkommunikáció új útjai*. Budapest: Kossuth, 1984.

———, ed. *Public Opinion and Mass Communication*. Budapest: Hungarian Academy of Sciences, 1972.

Vass, Henrik. *Történelem és tömegkommunikáció*. Budapest: Akademiai Kiado, 1976.

Zentai, Janos. *A rádió mühelyéböl*. Budapest: Gondlat, 1975.

Additional valuable information can be found in the publications of the Tömegkommunikációs Kutató Intézet, the Institute for Research in Mass Communications.

INDIA

John A. Lent

John A. Lent

HISTORY

The British introduced radio to India in 1924 through private radio clubs. Three years later a private organization, Indian Broadcasting Company (IBC), established stations in Calcutta and Bombay. The IBC was never a financial success and went into liquidation in 1930. After efforts to resuscitate the company failed, the British decided to run the medium as an official activity under the name Indian State Broadcasting Service. After a year, in 1935, this organization was headed by Lionel Fielden of the British Broadcasting Corporation, who became the first controller of what, in 1936, became known as All Indian Radio (AIR).

Fielden has usually been credited as an effective administrator, striving to keep radio as devoid of government dependency as possible. By the 1940s, however, AIR's reputation suffered from a number of factors later listed by G. C. Awasthy: "Fielden's exit, World War II, the British ban on political and controversial broadcasts, and the denial of broadcast access to Indian National Congress leaders, however, made All Indian Radio suspect in the public's eye. The British used AIR to serve their own interests to the extent that during World War II, listeners in India had more faith in Radio Berlin than AIR." But over the years, despite its progovernment reputation, AIR introduced a number of useful programs, all with an Indian twist, including rural radio forums and divisions such as dance and song, farm and home, family planning, and youth.

Television had a late start in India, with a Delhi experimental station on the air a few hours weekly in 1959. Regular telecasts began in 1965, and the second station was set up in Bombay in 1972. Until 1976 television was under AIR; in that year the services were split into Doordarshan (pictures from afar) Television and Akashvani Radio. Television has been slow in maturing; between 1975 and 1982 only 19 percent of the population was covered. But 1982 proved to be an important year for TV, as the number of transmitters was increased from 21 to 180 (by 1984); color was introduced; a national network for simultaneous relay throughout India and a microwave linkage were put into use; and INSAT–1A, India's own built and launched satellite, was made operational. By 1984 a second television channel was developed for local viewer interest.

REGULATION

Radio and television are operated and managed by the nation's Ministry of Information and Broadcasting. As such, all sanctions and policy decisions flow from the minister, assisted and advised by a secretary and joint secretary, to the directorates general of radio and television who implement them. Each station has a director who is in charge of the program staff and, with help of the engineer, of the technical staff.

Because broadcasting is under the central government, it is subject to all the rules of various departments, financed as they are from the national treasury. Under the Indian Telegraph Acts of 1885, only the central government can establish and operate a broadcast service in India. In 1935 there was pressure to place radio under state governments; fortunately, this effort failed. Had it succeeded, broadcasting today might have as many different regulatory authorities as it has languages and dialects.

For years there have been persistent demands from political parties and other groups that broadcasting be made an autonomous corporation. Although AIR and Doordarshan are popular with the public and generally discuss public interest matters freely, the control by government is rigid, giving rise to the charge that the ruling party uses radio and television for its own ends. The autonomy demand reaches back a number of years. Nehru in 1948 favored making AIR autonomous, modeled after the BBC; he later changed his mind. His daughter, Indira Gandhi, thought autonomy a good idea when she was minister of information; later, while prime minister, she abandoned the notion, realizing that she needed the electronic media to counter political opposition.

Moreover, three special government committees recommended an autonomous body, but to no avail. The latest move, championed by the Verghese Committee, was dashed in late 1985 by Prime Minister Rajiv Gandhi, who rationalized that as long as the Indian press was irresponsible, there was no possibility of the government granting AIR and Doordarshan autonomy. The Verghese Committee was established under the brief Janata party government as a fulfillment of an election pledge aimed at the repressiveness of Indira Gandhi's emergency rule in the mid–1970s. Its recommendations stirred tremendous comment and nearly went into effect until Indira Gandhi was swept back into office. The chief proposal was that both radio and television should come under an independent, impartial, and self-regulating corporation to act as the trustee of the public interest. The body, to be called the National Broadcast Trust, was to have twelve to twenty-one members with the status of Supreme Court judges, free of government pressures. Overall, freedom from government control was to be guaranteed by the constitution.

Although Doordarshan, for example, has been strictly prohibited from using political broadcasts and speeches, election coverage, or pictures of party symbols, it still has come in for severe criticism by the opposition. The fear of government tampering with the medium has justification. Indira Gandhi certainly used the electronic media, justifying censorship at times, and claiming, "It is the duty of radio and television to project the policies of the government." During the twenty-one months of emergency she imposed on India, broadcasting became such an important arm of government that AIR was dubbed "All Indira Radio" and Doordarshan "Closed Door Darshan."

For years, even before the emergency, AIR had a reputation for being the "most officious and unmovable of the subcontinent's government agencies." Recently, there have been concerns that Rajiv Gandhi may control stations more tightly than had his mother. In late 1985 he became the first Indian prime minister to make direct suggestions on how to improve broadcasting, stating that news had to be made crisper and less dependent upon press releases; weather forecasts had to be more scientific; and programming had to reflect more of India's history and culture. At the same time, the government canceled, without giving a reason, the showing on Doordarshan of a film by Jack Anderson entitled "Rajiv's India."

Some critics have argued that government interference has been possible because broadcast and more generally communication policy has not been made clear. University lecturer Pradeep Krishnatray, for example, observed that without specific objectives AIR's growth has been determined by accidents and events, and as a result, the service has become increasingly controlled by government. He added that the red tape of bureaucracy and rigid formalism dominate broadcasting, and that various services are not coordinated with appropriate agencies, such as educational programming with the education ministry. In 1985 the minister of information and broadcasting called for a national communication policy "to strengthen the country and shape society."

AIR has had a code to deal with political coverage. According to Awasthy, the code stipulates that stations may not "broadcast criticism of friendly nations, attacks on religious communities, obscenity or defamation, attacks on political parties by name, or hostile criticism of any state or the center. Also forbidden by the code are broadcasts tending to be against maintenance of law and order or inciting to violence, those amounting to contempt of

court, aspersions against the integrity of the president, governors, or judi-
ciary, or anything showing disrespect to the constitution or advocating
change in the constitution by violence."

ECONOMIC STRUCTURE

Radio and television are owned by the government in India, and there is
little support for private broadcasting. There are groups capable of starting
stations or networks, such as business houses, some of which have newspaper chains, but the government is determined to maintain control of the
electronic media on a national level. For example, when in 1947 an Indian
Institute of Technology closed-circuit television station proposed becoming
a city outlet financed by the state and municipal monies, the central government turned down the request, stating that it violated administrative and
legislative acts.

Broadcasting is funded by receiver set licenses, sale of commercial advertising, and an annual appropriation by the central government. All revenues go into the consolidated fund of the Indian government, from which
allocations are made to AIR and Doordarshan. The director general of AIR
in 1980 told this writer that "revenue is just enough to meet our costs." At
this time AIR received Rs. 100 million annual net earnings from the commercial service and Rs. 350 million from set licenses. The annual radio
license fee is Rs. 15 (about $1.00 U.S.), and in the 1970s there were twelve
types of radio license fees with varying rates. Television set fees are Rs. 50
per year.

Although the following statistics are dated, they show the proportion of
funding that came from various sources. During 1971–72 the number of
radio receiving sets licensed was 12,772,225, yielding a total revenue of Rs.
172.7 million (about $25 million U.S.). The number of television sets li-
censed was 44,055 for a revenue of Rs. 1.1 million (about $150,000 U.S).
Total AIR income from commercials was Rs. 40 million ($5.7 million U.S.).

The AIR commercial service was started in Bombay in 1967, after much
government reluctance to introduce advertisements. What spurred the government to convert was Radio Ceylon's heavy patronization by Indian firms,
causing a loss of foreign exchange,. AIR in 1986 decided to expand commercials to more than fifty stations, allowing advertisers 5 percent of daily
airtime. This move was expected to generate a considerable amount of
revenue. Advertising from 1970 until this time had been restricted to the
special, popular entertainment network, Vividh Bharati.

In April 1984 Doordarshan began sponsorship of programs by private
companies. By June of that year there were eleven such shows, including
imports from the United States. Doordarshan began using commercials in
the early 1980s to raise revenues, and a second channel was set up in 1984
for the same reason.

For years television was secondary to radio, but in 1982 the Doordarshan budget was tripled, partly for political and technological reasons. At the time, sponsors realized the potential of television, as over 17 percent of the total advertising expenditures went to that medium. Over the next few years television advertising rates increased a number of times. Sponsorship of an imported show was Rs 2,625 per second on the national network, as against Rs 708 for locally produced features. Despite the difference, advertisers still eagerly sought sponsorship of foreign programs. The commercialization of television has resulted in the establishment of independent television producing groups to do more shows.

Standards set for advertisers follow the spirit of the programming code. Doordarshan, which uses the AIR code, does not permit the promotion of cigarettes and specifies that drugs, alcohol, or crime cannot be glorified in commercials. The AIR code states that programs and commercials cannot abridge Indian laws; offend against morality, decency, and religious laws; bring into "disrespect the rights and susceptibilities, dignity and brotherhood of all people residing in this country or bring dishonor to the sanctity of marriage and life."

Decisions concerning the expansion of broadcasting made in the 1980s have proved to be very costly for the government. Color television is a case in point. When color was started, critics pointed out that the $500 million necessary outlay was beyond India's means. Despite these claims, the state went ahead with color television, partly out of national pride (all developed nations have it) and partly to prepare for telecasts of the 1982 Asian Games in India. Initially, the government decided to import 95,000 television receiver kits (from South Korea and West Germany) for assembly in India. Then the authorities, in an effort to build up a larger color television population, cut the import levy on color sets from 320 to 190 percent and allowed 100,000 completed receivers to be imported by early December 1982. The lower levy was allowable if the sets were gifts from friends and relatives abroad. This was an extraordinary action on the part of a socialist government trying to protect its indigenous manufacturers. The purchasing binge that resulted was described by a Philadelphia newspaper correspondent: "Dealers throughout Asia actually ran out of top-line televisions. Other dealers reportedly refused to sell to anyone but Indians, who, faced with a tight deadline, were willing to pay hundreds of dollars above retail cost to get a set. Several international airlines even set up special charter flights to get the televisions back in India before the program expired December 4." The Indian government, which stopped other customs work to handle the sets, made U.S. $50 million in duty on the receivers.

These and other revenues are being pumped back into the expansion of broadcasting. In mid–1983, when the government announced its plan to increase television coverage to 70 percent of the population by the end of 1984, it put up U.S. $68 million. In 1986 the government granted AIR and

Doordarshan a combined U.S. $8.3 million over the following five years to expand coverage and modernize facilities.

More training and professional development are always favorite remedies prescribed for India's media problems. The Verghese Committee, for example, suggested that there was a "general neglect of training" and lack of skilled people at many levels. More specifically, many Doordarshan centers are run by AIR-trained people who know little about television. In cases where people are trained, they are shifted around without regard to their expertise. The committee proposed a curriculum for broadcast education and pointed out that in 1978 the only instruction was at the Staff Training School for Programs in Delhi, Hyderabad, and Shillong; the Staff Training Institute (technical) at Delhi; and the Film and Television Institute of India (FTII) at Pune. Most training, according to the committee, was of a hit-or-miss variety.

The University Grants Commission, at a 1979 workshop on media curriculum, outlined a basic broadcast journalism course, but most of the emphasis was on print media. A 1984 follow-up workshop, conducted by this author, outlined in detail a broadcast journalism curriculum applicable nationwide. Apparently, most of those recommendations were shelved or died because of bureaucratic snags.

Of institutes and universities offering training in broadcasting, the FTII is strong in technical and studio work, while the Indian Institute of Mass Communication in New Delhi, which has only one course in broadcast journalism, is heavily into the theoretical aspects of mass communications. Others are the Institute of Film Technology in Madras and the Government Polytechnic in Bangalore. Some universities, such as those at Osmania, Bangalore, and Trivandrum, among others, give rudimentary instruction in broadcasting. Although India is much better off than many Third World nations in its mass-media education, it still has not seen an increase in training proportionate to the expansion of technology.

PROGRAMMING

India must rank as one of the most difficult broadcast environments in the world. The hugeness of the land mass (seventh largest in the world, with over 600,000 villages) and population (second largest in the world, approaching 700 million), and the cultural, linguistic, and religious diversities do not allow for an easy situation. The constitution recognizes 16 languages including English, but to reach the masses, 75 percent of whom are illiterate, languages and dialects without official status must also be employed.

A recent census listed 1,952 mother tongues, and the number of government approved languages alone is 380. Complexity is the appropriate word to describe the language problem. For example, there are 17 languages, each spoken by over 500,000 people, further subdivided into 241 mother languages; and hundreds of others, plus 103 non-Indian languages spoken by over 500,000 people. Each main language recognized by the constitution has a state of its own, except for Urdu, which is the second language in two or three states. Religious variations are nearly as complex, with groups of Hindus, Muslims, Christians, Sikhs, Buddhists, Jains, and a host of others.

Each language has at least one broadcasting station, and besides the 16 recognized languages, radio also transmits in 91 dialects to gain communication with tribal communities. Traditionally, AIR's Home Service program units have included news, Vividh Bharati (light entertainment), and general culture; stations are broken down by zones representing the four major points of the compass.

In 1979 AIR averaged 1,760 hours of daily programming in all major Indian and 17 foreign languages. The emphasis then was on music, which represented 41 percent of the time, and news, 22.9 percent. News was presented in 244 separate programs in 37 Indian and foreign languages and 34 local dialects. A similar analysis of content of Doordarshan in August 1981 showed 40 percent of television was pure entertainment (feature films, film songs, interviews with film starts), 24 percent news and current affairs, 12 percent educational and informational, 7 percent agricultural and rural, and 16 percent "entertainment-masked information shows." Especially popular were Indian films, which can capture 80 percent of a potential audience. In any given week four or five Hindi films are on television. Over 85 percent of the television programming was for a general audience in 1981, 5 percent for children, 1 percent for youth, 7 percent for rural groups, and less than 1 percent for industrial workers. The programming was mainly urban oriented, despite government's wishes that television be a rural medium.

In fact, the challenge of television managers now seems to be how to get around the government's priority on education and information and produce quality shows to compete with slick imports. A recent committee, the Working Group on Software for Doordarshan, recognized in this challenge the problem that India lacked "collective national will to mobilize creative talent and to invest resources in software planning and production." The committee also criticized Doordarshan for catering to the newly rich—not the middle class or peasants—in its programs and called for more exchange shows with neighboring nations.

As television has been expanded in the 1980s, program policies have necessarily changed. More shows are needed to fill two channels, thus necessitating policies on importation of foreign programs. The introduction of national network programs in 1982 gave impetus to a policy of production of television documentaries. In recent years Doordarshan has set up program advisory committees and consultative panels involving outside specialists to come up with fresh ideas, and every production unit has hired a team of social scientists to work closely with producers on audience need assessment and programs. In an effort to keep television programming indigenous, India's first soap opera, "Hum Log," was introduced in late 1984 (and became the most popular show in India), and by 1986 efforts were made to serialize novels by Indian writers, screen epics such as "The Ramayana" and a series of Nehru's "Discovery of India," and exclusively produce telefilms. One new series, "Ek Kahani," of the 1985–86 season, portrayed sensitive stories that draw upon human emotions. At the end of each episode, the author was invited to convey his feelings about the work. There were other efforts to produce Indian situational comedies, family series in English and Hindi, drama, game shows, and detective adventures. Well-known Indian film directors were being asked to do TV films and family series.

Perhaps this reversion to indigenization of television with materials produced specifically for Doordarshan resulted because of the spate of foreign shows after 1982. A study in May to June of 1983 suggested that foreign shows made up 10.3 percent of airtime. The effect was that a veneer of westernization was covering India through mass media. Even local shows were patterned after the foreign prototypes, so that there were "curry westerns," featuring cops in India's badlands. Another broadcast investigatory committee, that of Joshi, said that Delhi Doordarshan in early 1983 had 21.1 percent foreign-film–related features.

AIR's nonnews programming is on the Vividh Bharati and General Cultural Services. The former has been basically a library service, sending dubbed programs to originating stations ten days in advance. The percentage of music on this service was 90 to 95 percent. The General Cultural Services included talks/discussions, music, plays, and features.

News presentations on both AIR and Doordarshan have been the topic of criticism for years. A 1985 study of the two services and four national newspapers reported that two-thirds of the coverage of broadcasting is official news emanating from the central government. No station gives more than 10 percent of its budget to state news; in fact, foreign news exceeds that of state coverage. The 1982 Working Group on Software for Doordarshan criticized television for not providing news and current affairs that were people oriented; instead, the body said that the news reflected ruling party viewpoints. Claiming "VIP-oriented news programs and trivial entertainment promotes complacency, and a drugged indifference to issues of social transformation," the working group suggested teamwork among news crews and concerned managements and the providing of adequate personnel and transport. The group also said that news readers were "casual artists" who looked at news scripts on the way to the makeup room, and lamented that TV news was in either English or Hindi, languages that many people do not understand.

Doordarshan had for years operated without news correspondents, depending on AIR's news division. In 1986 Doordarshan decided to completely revamp and greatly strengthen its news division by sending people for training, evaluating equipment needs, and developing, over a period of five years, a three-tier news system to cater to national, regional, and local audiences. At the same time, the network introduced a new current events show, "Janvani," which allows viewers to come to the studios to question a government minister on a controversial matter. Sixteen participants are chosen from among about 10,000 letter writers for each episode.

Programming for specialized purposes has a long history in India. In the 1950s, as already indicated, there were the developmental and educational services, including rural radio forums. In 1965 farm and home units were set up at selected stations; by 1982 fifty-nine AIR stations had these units, emphasizing agriculture and family planning programs. Since the late 1960s AIR also has had a broadcasting service for industrial workers, with twenty-five stations devoting 100 to 180 minutes per week to this group.

Educational broadcasting has been around for a long time. The emphasis on broadcasting for educational and developmental purposes, however, has been somewhat tempered in recent years. In 1986 educational radio broadcasts on a syllabus-oriented basis emanated from forty-four stations and were relayed by thirty others. On television, 45 minutes daily in eight states is devoted to education. Additionally, curriculum-oriented educational programs are televised on a regular basis from Delhi and Bombay for 160 minutes daily, and educational shows from Delhi, Srinagar, and Madras for 80 minutes. The school programs conform to the syllabus of the local schools.

Children's programming is provided on radio through the Yuva Vani unit, established in 1969. By 1981 this service was carried by twenty-three AIR outlets. It is supposed to entertain at the same time that it acts as a tool for self-development and stimulation of self-confidence. Recently, Yuva Vani has been criticized for giving youth entertainment at the expense of information needed for their growth. TV critic Amita Malik wrote in 1984 that children's television programs in India are among the world's dullest because of a lack of children's participation.

BROADCASTING REFORM

Whatever else there might be a shortage of in India, broadcasting committees and reports and their recommendations and criticisms are not among them. Broadcasting definitely receives regular critical attention. Newspapers and magazines devote regular columns and occasional editorials to it, and periodicals designed specifically for the broadcast industry abound with suggestions and complaints. To give an idea of the severity of media criticism, a *Contour* magazine article of June 29, 1980, states that Doordarshan "remains an infant with a retarded mind." *Contour* said of the large army of broadcast critics: "It is only in India that retired radio and TV personnel who until their retirement had been part and parcel of the same incompetence, re-emerge as TV critics and some of them manage to review both radio and TV."

The government, opposition parties, and media organizations often call for reforms, invariably leading to a committee to investigate the mass media. The committees looking into possible autonomy for broadcasting have been discussed; still others debated over long periods of time the credibility of broadcasting, the advisability of the introduction of color television and the expansion of television generally and software specifically.

In 1986 the credibility of Doordarshan was being attacked; Rajiv Gandhi started this criticism, claiming that televised coverage of him was a textbook example of overexposure. He said that news people seemed to want to show their loyalty by playing up government. Earlier, in 1982, the government set up a Working Group on Software for Doordarshan, which in its report recommended that

1. a national Doordarshan council be formed to advise the minister and review the stations' performance;
2. a Doordarshan Film Development Corporation be set up to provide films for television;
3. a separate training institute for television be established;
4. a new cadre of TV journalists and stringers be incorporated nationwide;
5. 15 to 20 percent of TV time be for children;
6. all commercials, except public service, be banned;
7. exploitation of the female form on TV be condemned; and
8. the over 100 low-powered transmitters be given minimum production facilities to make the medium more people oriented.

As can be seen, the recommendations reached far beyond the mandate of the committee suggested by its title.

The introduction of color television took two years of consideration, prompting the development of three committees and an open public debate. At issue were the questions of affordability (can a poor nation such as India afford to use its valuable resources on the medium?) and indigenization (can India provide the hardware/software for color television without dependence on other nations?). When the Janata government was in power in the late 1970s, the expansion of color television was given a low priority by the committee in charge. The situation changed when Indira Gandhi returned to power.

NEW TECHNOLOGIES

India, although hesitant about the introduction of black-and-white and color television, has, on the other hand, been swift in its adoption of other new technologies, especially satellite and video. In 1980 India, with Rohini 1, joined the Soviet Union, the United States, Japan, France, and China as the sixth nation to launch its own satellite on its own soil. Earlier, in 1975 and 1979, Indian satellites were built with Soviet help. After Rohini 1, an experimental geostationary communication satellite (APPLE) was sent up, as were remote sensing satellites. The first domestic satellite, INSAT–1A, was launched in 1982 for use in long-distance telephone calls, television broadcasts, remote sensing, and meteorological services. The INSAT program will, among other uses, serve the rural areas of Doordarshan and link radio and television stations throughout India. Programs are fed to INSAT in a predetermined sequence on a time-sharing schedule. One of the two television transponders is used for a national hookup and the other for a regional program on a time-sharing basis. Although INSAT–1A, designed for a seven-year life expectancy, lasted only five months, INSAT–1B (launched August 1983 at a cost of $50 million) has been more successful. The INSAT program, consisting of thirty-one earth stations, is meant to reach 70 to 75 percent of the population with television signals. Satellite technology already allowed the number of transmitters to jump from 40 to about 240 by 1986. Nearly all of those TV transmitters are hooked by the INSAT television network; the rest are fed national broadcasts by microwave. Of 91 radio stations, 86 are on the satellite network. Indian satellite pioneer Yash Pal said of this growth: "Perhaps no large country in the world has seen such a phenomenal increase in linking its inhabitants in so short a time." INSAT–1C was launched in 1986 and INSAT–2 by 1988. Development of the satellite television moves at a brisk pace despite complaints that it does not adequately serve its educational purposes because of the lack of sufficient receiver sets and of enough programming.

India was the scene of what has been described as one of the largest communications projects of all time when, in 1975, Doordarshan undertook the Satellite Instructional Television Experiment (SITE). The one-year project, which used a NASA satellite, aimed to beam developmental programs to community sets in 2,400 villages over six states with four major linguistic groups. Telecasting for four hours daily (a total of 1,500 hours), SITE promoted agricultural, family planning, and other developmental fare.

SITE evaluations went the full gamut of possibilities, from those that claimed that there were no appreciable gains in the adoption of agricultural or family planning practices to those that said that children exposed to television showed significant increases in language acquisition. Another evaluation showed that children and women learned very little from shows designed for them; K. E. Eapen summarized that while the hardware performed well, the software did not rise to expectations.

India has taken pride in its own technologies. Besides developing its own satellite system, India has also set up a microwave network, linking all major television centers and connecting places not provided with regular television complexes, and has made its own receivers for years. One hundred manufacturers produce 500,000 black-and-white receivers yearly. In the mid–1980s a Bangalore scientist was experimenting with a unique concept—using trees as natural television antennas.

Videocassette technology, although mostly imported, has swept India like a firestorm. Video clubs are nearly everywhere, and VCRs are a fixture in homes, organizations, and even long-distance buses. The potential for its expansion is almost limitless. Cable television is prevalent, especially in urban, high-rise apartments, and pay television had arrived by the 1980s. The teletext service provided by Doordarshan has not been successful, partly because of the expensive system adopted.

CONCLUSION/FORECAST

Technology has been placed in a very pivotal role in the future of Indian broadcasting. During the Seventh Five-Year Plan (1985–90), the government has set the following objectives for Doordarshan:

1. Development of studio centers in all state capitals
2. Minimum essential program production facilities for local service at all high-power transmitters
3. Ten-kilowatt transmitters with studios at all metropolitan centers for local services
4. Provision of satellite linking facilities or microwave linkages for relay of a primary service in each state
5. Manufacture of more color television receivers

An earlier prediction was that by 1990 there would be over 2 million television sets in India, 200,000 in color. But as television grew after 1982, the Department of Electronics must have thought it necessary to revise its plans, licensing 240 manufacturers to produce 8 million color TV sets by 1985. In addition, the government gave liberal concessions on the customs and excise duties for imported parts from abroad.

As for radio, the Seventh Five-Year Plan calls for the development of forty-six additional education program-production units, the expansion of FM service, and continued movement from regional broadcasting to national programming.

In conclusion, Indian broadcasting represents in a magnified way almost every known problem in the industry. The large and varied population places an unbelievable drain on the limited radio and television resources in a new developing nation such as India. Yet the fiercely independent Indians not only seem to cope with but in many cases thrive on these challenges. The result is a broadcasting system that for years has tried to maintain its self-reliance, being cautious not to become too dependent on outside forces, and has introduced innovative practices in its programming and technology.

BIBLIOGRAPHY

"Autonomy for All India Radio and Doordarshan." *Indian Journal of Communication Arts*, August 1977 and February–March 1978, 22–24.

Awasthy, G. C. *Broadcasting in India*. Bombay: Allied Publishers, 1965.

———. "India." In *Broadcasting in Asia and the Pacific*, edited by John A. Lent, 197–211. Hong Kong: Heinemann Educational Books, 1978.

Franda, Marcus. "All India Radio: Akashvani or Sarkarvani?" *American Universities Field Staff Reports* 19 (1975): 7.

———. "Television in India." *American Universities Field Staff Reports* 19 (1975): 4.

"An Indian Personality for Television: Report of the Working Group on Software for Doordarshan." *Mainstream*, April 14, 1984, 27–33; April 24, 1984, 16–23.

Krishnatray, Pradeep. "Need to Reshape All Indian Radio." *Combroad* (April–June 1984): 6–8.

Kumar, Narendra. *Educational Radio in India*. New Delhi: Arya Book Depot, 1967.

———, and Chandiram Jai. *Educational Television in India*. New Delhi: Arya Book Depot, 1967.

Lent, John A., ed. *Broadcasting in Asia and the Pacific*. Hong Kong: Heinemann Educational Books, 1978.

Masani, Mehra. *Broadcasting and the People*. New Delhi: National Book Trust, 1976.

Mody, Bella. "Lessons from the Indian Satellite Experiment." *Educational Broadcasting International* 7 (September 1978): 117–20.

Rumar, Keval J. "Media and Development: The Indian Experiment." *Communication Socialist Yearbook* (1984): 121–31.

Journals

Communicator, Indian Institute of Mass Communications. New Dehli.
Indian Journal of Communication Arts, defunct. G. C. Awasthy, New Delhi.
Indian Press, defunct. Indian and Eastern Newspaper Society, New Delhi.
Vidura, Press Institute of India, News Delhi.

ISRAEL

Dov Shinar and Akiba A. Cohen

HISTORY

Three major phases characterize the history of broadcasting in Israel. The first began in 1936 with the introduction of radio by the British mandatory authorities. "This is Jerusalem calling," announced in English, Arabic, and Hebrew, inaugurated the Palestine Broadcasting Service (PBS), founded by the mandatory officials and modeled on the British Broadcasting Corporation colonial model. With semiautonomous Hebrew and Arabic programs produced by members of these ethnic communities, the PBS developed from a subdivision in the British Post Office to an independent department of the colonial government of Palestine. Also typical of this period was the operation of radio services by the various Jewish underground movements.

In the second phase, commencing with the establishment of the State of Israel in 1948, broadcasting became part of the newly established Israeli information services, at first under the Ministry of Interior, and after a short period as a department in the prime minister's office, where it remained until 1965 under the name Kol Yisrael (The Voice of Israel). In October 1950 the cabinet established Galei Zahal, the official station of the Israeli army, to serve "the country's security needs as well as to inform, educate, and entertain the military." During this period heavy controls were exercised over the medium. The government explained them as needs arising from the tasks imposed by security constraints and by cultural, economic, and social pressures induced by the huge waves of immigrants from numerous nations and varied backgrounds.

The adoption by the Knesset (parliament) of the Broadcasting Authority Law of 1965, the introduction of instructional television in 1966, and the establishment of Israeli television in 1967 are the landmarks of the third

phase in the history of broadcasting in the nation. Representing true legislative and institutional innovation, all three events were preceded by fierce
debate in the Knesset and in the press. The law was in response to mounting
public pressure, which demanded that the management of broadcasting in
Israel be handed over by the government to a public authority.

REGULATION

Since 1965 radio and television in Israel have operated within the framework of the Israeli Broadcasting Authority (IBA), whose legal and operational charter is the Broadcasting Authority Law. The initial law, designed
to cover radio only, was amended in 1966 and in 1968 to accommodate
the needs of television. Israeli television was annexed to the authority in
1969 after it had functioned as a task force in the prime minister's office
since 1967.

According to the law, the IBA is a national service and a corporate entity.
Its five functions are as follows:

1. To broadcast educational, entertainment, and informational programs in the field
   of politics, social life, economics, culture, science, and art, with a view to reflect
   the life, struggle, creative effort, and achievements of the state
2. To promote Hebrew and the Israeli creative endeavor
3. To provide broadcasts in Arabic for the Arabic-speaking population for the
   promotion of understanding and peace with the neighboring states in accordance
   with the basic tendencies of the state
4. To provide broadcasts to Diaspora Jewry
5. To provide broadcasts to foreign countries

The specification of these functions guides the implementation of the law
and the making of policy with regard to control, management, and programming.

The formal responsibility for the execution of the law falls upon a minister
of the government (currently the minister of education and culture). Legislation, however, prevents the minister's direct involvement in the making
and execution of policy and delegates these tasks to other entities of the
authority: the Plenum, the Managing Committee, and the director general.

According to the law, the Plenum consists of thirty-one members appointed by the president of the state following the recommendation by the
government based on consultation with representatives of the Authors' Association, teachers, artists, universities, the Hebrew Language Academy,
and other public bodies. No more than four civil servants may serve on the
Plenum. Its functions include laying down the policies of the authority;
discussing reports and surveys of authority committees; issuing directives
to the Managing Committee as to the discharge of its duties; approving the

seasonal program schedule without, however, derogating from its authority to decide from time to time on specific broadcasts in all their aspects; receiving budget proposals, discussing them, and passing its recommendations to the Managing Committee; receiving from the Managing Committee and from the director general, upon its demand, reports and surveys on the ongoing work, considering these reports and surveys, and formulating conclusions; considering the annual report to be submitted to the Managing Committee and formulating its conclusions; and discussing any other matters it deems fit and formulating its conclusions.

The Managing Committee consists of seven members from the Plenum, appointed by the government, and including no more than two civil servants. Its functions are to consider and decide upon matters of the broadcasting service; to receive from the director general reports of the ongoing work of the service; to prepare the ordinary budget and development budget and submit them for government approval; to supervise the implementation of the approved budget; to submit to the Plenum an annual report of its activities and any report the Plenum may demand, and to submit to the minister any report he may request and to notify the Plenum thereof.

The director general, who is appointed by the government for a period of five years, is responsible for the implementation of policies and procedures decided upon by the higher levels.

In spite of its public nongovernmental status, the IBA is not immune to pressures by government and the Knesset. Thus, in addition to the minister in charge, the Ministry of Telecommunications is responsible for the transmission equipment; security censorship is administered by the Ministry of Defense, and the army censor applies to broadcasting as well as to the printed press; and the Ministry of Finance together with the Finance Committee of the Knesset exerts much control over the IBA's budget, mainly by approving the amount to be paid as a license fee (see under "Economic Structure").

Furthermore, the law permits different pressure groups to bear direct influence on broadcasting. Since the establishment of the IBA, the appointment of members of the Managing Committee, its major decision-making body, has officially and increasingly reflected the political spectrum including right and left wings, religious parties, coalition-opposition interests, and so forth. Such pressures have recently been illustrated by countless debates over reports on the war in Lebanon, by the discontinuation of a popular news magazine on the grounds of hurting public morale, by the now-historic controversy over broadcasting on the Sabbath, or by haphazard appointments to key positions in radio and television.

ECONOMIC STRUCTURE

As noted earlier, the IBA is an independent authority that seeks to maintain its economic independence. The 1985 budget proposal, which includes

Israeli radio and television (with the exclusion of the army radio station), amounted to roughly $49 million. The sources of the IBA's revenue were as follows:

- 70% from license fees
- 16.6% from radio advertising
- 9.0% from public service announcements and sponsorship of television programs
- 4.7% from the Jewish Agency
- 2.5% from the Ministry of Foreign Affairs
- 1.0% from miscellaneous sources

The license fee, which is levied on each household that owns at least one television receiver, is roughly $58.00 per year. It should be noted that while in the past the tax was also imposed on radio ownership, this no longer exists, as virtually every household has at least one radio receiver and one TV set. There is an extra radio license payment, however, which is imposed on radio receivers in motor vehicles and is collected at the annual vehicle test. The fee is $17.00. Moreover, the collection of the license fees from households is not total. According to the authority's commercial department, 20 percent of set owners do not bother to pay the tariff. In addition, there are various waivers given to individuals such as families of victims of Israel's wars, welfare cases of extreme hardship, and all 1,600 employees of IBA. Yet the collection apparatus, aided by a rigorous campaign of self-serving public service announcements on radio and television as well as spot checking in homes, has increased the collection rate in recent years.

The revenue from radio advertising has been on the decline over the last several years (from 25 percent of the entire budget in 1983 to its present 13 percent). This is mainly due to the expected recession as well as the introduction of sponsorship for television programs, which did not exist in previous years.

While the state treasury supported part of the IBA's budget in 1983 and 1984—8 percent in 1983 and 2 percent in 1984—this source of revenue has been totally eliminated. On the other hand, the income derived from the Jewish Agency and the Foreign Ministry is earmarked for part of the expenses of the broadcasts overseas as well as the programs in various languages for new immigrants transmitted domestically.

The 1985 expenditures were as follows:

- 11.7% for general administration
- 3.9% for development and reserve funds
- 34.5% for radio (Hebrew)
- 7.4% for radio (Arabic)

- 31.5% for television (Hebrew)
- 2.6% for television (Arabic)
- 8.4% for special activities

The special activities would include a host of events such as covering the costs of broadcasts from the 1984 Olympic Games and coverage of the 1984 elections held in Israel, as well as features to encourage early retirement of employees in order to reduce costs.

Another way of breaking down the expenditures is according to various functions. Thus 46 percent of the entire budget is allocated for salaries and fringe benefits; 39 percent goes for fixed costs and overhead expenses (payments to the Ministry of Telecommunications for the use of the transmitters, satellite fees, royalties, rental of television studios and production services, purchase of foreign programs, and various overhead charges) and changing expenses (local production); 3 percent for development; and 12 percent for repaying of debts from 1984. In the final analysis, the amount of money allocated to production of programs is relatively small compared with the money allocated to salaries and overhead.

At present, formal advertising is conducted only on radio and is limited to two of the five channels. Radio advertising began in 1960 and is administered by a private company that obtained a long-term concession from the IBA for this purpose. The policies governing advertising contents and charges, however, are approved and reviewed by the Managing Committee and director general.

Radio sponsorship is allowed for all commercial products and services, including public service announcements, with several exceptions. First, no advertising is allowed that will, in the opinion of the IBA, be unethical or in any way harmful to public safety and welfare. Thus no commercials are accepted for professional services that normally do not engage in regular promotions (including physicians, dentists, psychologists, and lawyers). Also, services that cannot provide acceptable proven standards of performance, such as astrology and matrimonial services, cannot advertise on Israeli radio. Medications and other medical and health-related apparatus can be advertised only if satisfactory medical proof is available as to their reliability and efficiency; however, little advertising for such products is actually broadcast.

No advertising is accepted that directly or indirectly contradicts any law or that might insult or offend any sector of the population, including minority groups. No advertising is allowed that contains political propaganda, that contains the names of public personalities without their expressed permission, or that includes statements that may contain libel, exaggerated claims that cannot be verified, and unreasonable price comparisons. Finally, no announcements are broadcast that begin with "Here is an important announcement" or "We interrupt our program."

No commercial can be an integral part of the program contents; rather, all commercials are presented at predetermined times, with limits set on the amount of time devoted to commercials during the program. The price paid by advertisers is calculated according to the number of expected listeners at the particular time slots.

Presently, no commercial advertising is allowed on television. For several years there have been public service announcements that initially enabled government ministries and nonprofit organizations to appeal to the public to file their tax returns on time, to conserve water and energy, to promote traffic safety, and to beware of suspicious terrorist objects. Over the years the definition of "public service" has expanded to include public organizations such as the citrus marketing board, the vegetable marketing board, the bus cooperative, the wine growers' association, and the national lottery. Announcements made by these agencies, while not specifically mentioning individual manufacturers or distributors by name, do provide information that can be considered as commercial and profit-making. In fact, the courts have received complaints from the newspapers' association, which claimed that such announcements violate the IBA's own regulations.

Also, quite recently, the IBA began to promote the notion of a TV program "sponsorship" that involves a brief announcement at the beginning and the end of various programs indicating that the program is being supported by a particular company that manufactures a specific product. This practice has also been contested in the courts. In any event, in a draft of the regulations governing sponsorship of programs, presently being discussed, it is stated that a sponsor shall not be allowed to intervene in the contents and production of the programs nor in the time and conditions of the broadcast.

There is no doubt that the age of advertising will come to Israeli television in one form or another within a relatively short period of time. Whether or not this will be done on the existing channel or on an additional channel is yet unclear and will be discussed in the section on Broadcast Reform.

The importance of training was stressed by Sir Hugh Greene, a former director general of the British Broadcasting Corporation, in a report he submitted in 1973 to the minister of education and culture, following a review of the IBA. In his report Sir Hugh states: "What seems to me to be lacking is the hard core of professionalism on which further improvement and, one hopes, further expansion can be based. Part of the answer is training and more training. . . . To save money on training, even when money is short, is false economy. . . . My first recommendation, therefore, is that the Broadcasting Authority should work out and implement a long-term training program for program staff and engineers. This is an essential pre-condition for some of my later recommendations."

Since the early years of radio in Israel, its training department has been engaged in an ongoing attempt to maintain high standards of training and professionalism. This has been a difficult task, mainly due to the constant difficult financial situation, as well as to the rapidly developing technologies that require up-to-date knowledge and facilities. In this connection, it should be noted that the facilities of both Israeli radio and television are very antiquated; they have undergone numerous additions and remodeling, but they still reside in the same quarters where radio started in 1948 and television in 1967. Moreover, when television was established, most of the personnel came from radio and were retrained for the new medium. A few were sent to France in the mid–1960s, and most of the newly established staff was trained in Israel by CBS personnel who held a contract with the IBA.

The IBA training center conducts numerous courses and training programs each year designed to teach new skills, to accommodate job changes, to introduce new technologies, and to improve the standard of broadcasting. Most of the training is done in Israel, with only a rare opportunity available for a selected number of persons to train abroad for any substantial period of time.

As an example of its activities, during 1984 the training center of the IBA conducted several courses for radio and TV news editors, for producers of radio programs, for announcers, and for reporters. In addition, minicourses were held on the collection of folklore materials and the preparation of radio youth programs, as well as computer courses for management and engineering staff. Special seminars were also held on such topics as principles of video use, documentary film production, reporting on Israel's minorities, and various office skills. Finally, lectures were given on such topics as the history of film, the Iran-Iraq war, two-dimensional art, and life on the TV series "Dallas."

In addition to the in-house training, there are several film and television departments at Israel's universities where professional training on various levels is done. Finally, Israel's Education Television Center is an important resource for training of television personnel, particularly since the center utilizes the most advanced computerized production techniques, not all of which are available at Israeli television. The center has also done considerable work in organizational development and interpersonal communication skills for staff members.

PROGRAMMING

In order to better understand the nature of broadcast programming in Israel, it is necessary to provide a brief demographic picture of the nation and its population. Israel is a small country; its size is 8,295 square miles (not including the occupied areas of the West Bank and Gaza). When it was established in 1948, there were only 600,000 Jews in the nation. Its population in January 1985 was 4,244,300 inhabitants. The majority of the population (82.7 percent) is Jewish, and the minority consists of several ethnic groups, the largest group being Muslim, and a small Christian community. The latest figures available on literacy rates indicate that among Jewish men 96 percent are literate, and among the women 89.6 percent are literate. Among the non-Jewish population the literacy rates are lower. In addition, at least 81 percent of the men and 73 percent of the women use Hebrew as their principal language. A large segment of the non-Jewish population can understand and speak Hebrew, although their principal language is Arabic. In 1984, 86.1 percent of the Jewish population lived in urban communities, and 13.9 percent of the non-Jewish population lived in urban areas.

The programming departments of Israeli radio and television operate in separate agencies; however, the annual schedules for both media must be approved by the Plenum of the broadcasting authority. In addition, the authority approves the nonmilitary programming of the army radio station.

The broadcasting authority runs Israeli radio, which operates five radio channels, four in Hebrew and one in Arabic, as well as newscasts in several other languages. All five channels operate from 6:00 A.M. until 1:00 A.M. seven days a week. One day each year, on Yom Kippur (the Day of Atonement), all broadcasting ceases. All channels broadcast in AM as well as in FM. Only the army radio station functions around the clock.

The first channel, which is free from advertising, is devoted to talk shows, classical music, drama, children's programming (two hours daily in the midafternoon), and religious features (daily readings from the Scriptures and liturgical music). The second channel, which contains advertising, is devoted to a variety of fare, including light music, current affairs, and specialty features on topics such as health, education, economics, and sports. The third channel, which also offers commercial spots, is devoted almost entirely to popular music of all varieties, Israeli and foreign (primarily in English and French, with some in Italian, Spanish, and other languages). The fourth channel, "The Voice of Music," is the only channel that transmits in FM stereo. Its major programming content is classical music as well as features about music. Arabic-language broadcasts are distributed on the fourth channel, also referred to as the Arab Broadcasting House. The content consists of music, talk shows, and current affairs. The fourth channel also presents daily news programs in various languages, including (among others) English, French, Russian, and Yiddish. The army radio outlet transmits a variety of features, some dealing with military affairs, but the majority are civilian programs such as light and popular music and discussion programs. The Arabic channel and the army station do not carry advertising.

Radio news in Hebrew is given every hour on the hour and can be heard on most of the channels, including the army station. These bulletins generally last from two to five minutes. Three hour-long programs are also produced, one at 7:00 A.M., one at 1:00 P.M., and one at 7:00 P.M.

In addition to the domestic broadcasting, Israeli radio transmits its regular second-channel features to Europe and North America on several shortwave frequencies for the benefit of Israelis who are abroad. Israeli radio also has special foreign broadcasts designed for listeners in various parts of the world (Eastern and Western Europe, South Africa, Australia, and North and South America) and also transmitted via shortwave. These programs include news bulletins and brief programs on Israeli culture and music, as well as "listeners' corners" where letters received from foreign listeners are read and discussed.

Israel's one television station is shared by three separate programming departments. All programs are presented in color, which was gradually introduced by 1982. Israel is a child-oriented society. Thus, during the morning and early afternoon hours, Sundays (a regular work day in Israel) through Fridays, the educational television system broadcasts educational and enrichment programs for the young audiences ranging from preschool children to adolescents. The educational programs that are broadcast during the school hours are used by schools at the discretion of the individual teachers. The enrichment programs are scheduled at various times throughout the day and include, among other features, the Israeli version of "Sesame Street," which is produced with the cooperation of the Childrens' Television Workshop in New York. Some of these features are designed to enhance basic reading and mathematical skills as well as the appreciation of art, science, esthetics, and music. Educational television in cooperation with the army radio station presents a daily half-hour news and interview program that began during the war in Lebanon in 1982 and continues to this very day.

Israeli television also produces a daily children's hour that begins at 5:30 P.M. This time slot generally includes at least two different programs devoted to different age groups. Some of these shows are produced in Hebrew by the youth department of Israeli television, while others are dubbed (or subtitled) versions of imported programs (mainly from the United States, including cartoons as well as drama and comedy).

At 6:30 P.M. the Arabic programming commences and lasts until 8:00 P.M. There is a daily newscast lasting thirty minutes and a variety of features on a weekly schedule. This includes entertainment as well as current affairs. On Friday evenings a feature film in Arabic is shown. The majority of the Arabic programs are produced by the Arabic shows division of Israeli television, except for the feature films, which are imported from the neighboring nations. Some of the Arabic programs are subtitled in Hebrew for the benefit of the Jewish viewers.

The Hebrew programming begins at 8:00 P.M. and generally ends about midnight. The main thirty-minute newscast is aired at 9:00 P.M., and a brief news summary is presented at the end of the evening's telecast. While the Hebrew and Arabic news departments are totally separate, including the reporters and editors, the news studio and technical staff are shared.

The weekly program schedule also includes light comedy and musical entertainment, feature films from various nations, talk shows, a documentary film, a weekly political interview program, miniseries imported from the United States and Great Britain, game shows, a religious program, a consumer-oriented program, and two weekly sports features. Israeli television also airs some of the Eurovision programs, such as the annual song festival, and some special sports telecasts (mainly soccer, tennis, and basketball). On the occasion of religious and national holidays, special features are produced. A rough estimate indicates that only about 40 percent of the programming is developed and produced in Israel. Some of these features are produced by Israeli television itself and some by several private companies.

BROADCAST REFORM

Israel is no exception to the almost classic situation whereby broadcasting, particularly television, lives under a constant barrage of criticism. The gap between the expectations that result from the broad scope and objectives of the Broadcasting Authority Law, and the limited performance ability due to serious financial, technological, and organizational constraints, seems to account for much of the existing dissatisfaction.

The major social aspects of such criticism concentrate in the area of fair representation, as required by the law. The expectation that radio and television cater equally to the Israeli variety of national, ethnic, religious, and cultural-educational as well as age- and sex-based groups has traditionally led to frustration and criticism. Examples include the debate over the discontinuation of broadcasts in certain languages (Hungarian, Persian, and Moroccan) several years ago as an outcome of financial difficulties and a decreasing audience resulting from an increase in the use of Hebrew by new immigrants; or the claims made by the militant groups among the elderly, who stress that while an entire radio outlet (the third channel) caters to the "pop" generation, and while sports broadcasting on television takes up 8 to 9 percent of the total airtime, the elderly, who comprise about 10 percent of the total population, are served specifically by one weekly half-hour program on radio and not at all on TV.

Criticism is also common on cultural grounds. In addition to the traditional complaints against the lack of depth and the superficiality typical of broadcasting around the world, there is also some locally unique criticism, such as the constant debate over religion and broadcasting. Although a Supreme Court decision ruled in 1969 in favor of television programs on Friday nights (the Sabbath eve), there is still controversy on whether there is too much or too little religious fare on radio, and particularly in TV programs. Another salient criticism is directed against what radio and television have considered as a solution to the problem of cultural representativeness: musical "hit parades" and festivals of ethnic and religious minorities (for example, the Sephardic Jewish song festival and the Hassidic song festival). A third example is the slow process of legitimization of folk music produced by composers and performers of Middle Eastern origin. After many years of merely being performed at weddings and bar mitzvahs and of being distributed with astounding economic success on audiocassette recordings in open markets and at central bus stations, this music finally made it to the prestigious radio and TV airwaves. The controversy over whether the former ban from the legitimate culture resulted from low artistic and musical standards, as argued by station managers, or from the latter's prejudiced judgment due to their own middle-class European origin, as claimed by composers, performers, and agents, represents a significant Israeli issue in which broadcasting has played a major role.

Political criticism has also found strong expression. Following the 1977 election, the extreme change in the government's identity and orientation from mild left to declared right gave intensity and velocity to an already ongoing process whereby the liberal inclinations of broadcasters were met with increasing disapproval. The reaction against the "leftist mafia," a nick-name coined for broadcasters, has been strongly felt in programming and personnel appointment policies. A popular TV satirical program was taken off the air in the late 1970s in response to harsh political criticism. The television prime-time weekly news magazine, broadcast on Friday nights, was canceled in the mid–1980s on the grounds that the Israeli people should not be exposed to "demoralizing" news on the Sabbath eve. Political con-straints, especially since the present left-right "national unity" coalition government has been in power, influence senior appointments such as the director of television, members of the Managing Committee, and its chair-person.

The convergence of such social, cultural, and political criticism has been a major source of demands for the reform of broadcasting. Additional factors have been the heterogeneity of the audience, the narrow one-channel TV framework shared by Hebrew, Arabic, and educational services, and the success enjoyed by private cable stations and by the purchase of some 300,000 video recorders (by more than one-third of the total number of households).

The importance of these demands has been well demonstrated in the inclusion of clauses to this effect in all coalition agreements that preceded the formation of the various governments since 1977. The seriousness of these demands has also been expressed in a series of high-level governmental committees, reports, and actual changes in Israeli broadcasting as well as in the constant dealing with this issue in the Knesset, in the broadcasting authority, in the press, and in academic circles.

The Kubersky Committee, named after the director general of Israel's Interior Ministry and appointed by the minister of education in 1978, analyzed the legal, sociocultural, technological, and economic aspects of the introduction of a second TV channel in Israel. In its 1979 report the committee recommended the establishment of such an outlet outside the jurisdiction of the broadcasting authority, to be funded by advertising. The committee did not, however, make specific recommendations on frameworks for implementation and governmental responsibilities.

While the broadcasting authority and the printed press expressed opposition to the recommendations, the former on the grounds of loss of control and the latter because of the expected loss of advertising revenue, the process of reform underwent additional developments. The recent Bar-Sela report, named after a deputy attorney general who headed a committee to study the problems of cable TV, specifies the conditions for licensing and operation of cable stations. The committee was established in response to the threatening proliferation of illegal cable TV stations with a good following in all parts of Israel.

The war in Lebanon between 1982 and 1985 and the still ongoing economic crisis did not allow for further actual progress, with the exception of increased political debate. Thus, in addition to the questions of whether the broadcasting authority or a new organization will be in charge of the proposed second channel, and whether this outlet or a cable network, or both, will be set up, the question of who will control and regulate additional media facilities has become relevant mainly on the political level, given the present lack of resources to implement any of the recommendations. Alluding to technical, financial, and professional considerations, the minister of education has proposed to remain in control, as proscribed by the present law, by means of using the existing facilities of the educational television station to serve as a second channel. The minister of telecommunications, on the other hand, has demanded to be given control over the second channel as stipulated in the coalition agreement with his minority party. Meanwhile, some alternative broadcasting structures have been started, such as the experiment to introduce community television in the *kibbutz* movement, where the law permits installation and transmission, in contrast with other types of profit-oriented services.

NEW TECHNOLOGIES

Since the early 1970s Israeli television has been using the services of Intelsat satellites for quick reception of foreign news via a ground station installed by the Ministry of Telecommunications. As Jordan television also uses the same source, Israel and Jordan receive the same satellite feeds and use the materials at their own discretion.

Insofar as direct broadcast satellites are concerned, two processes have been occurring. First, there is a gradual and sporadic appearance of reception dishes in various parts of Israel. Although the exact number of these dishes is not known, experts mention their proliferation especially in neighborhoods where Arabic is spoken and in locations with relatively large numbers of immigrants from the Soviet Union, suggesting that the Arabsat and a Soviet satellite are among the broadcasting sources.

The second process is the interest held by many in the theoretical possibility of launching an Israeli communication satellite. They point out that according to the International Telecommunication Union's 1979–94 program, Israel was allocated four satellite channels and "parking space" on the equator's thirteen degree west area, which is more than 2,500 miles from Israel. These experts confirm that the technological possibilities are good and expect that the broadcasting authority together with the Ministry of Telecommunications will make use of the new experimental EBU-sponsored (European Broadcast Union) satellite. Considerations of cost and channel saturation are cited as arguments against practical endeavors in this direction.

In any case, higher priority has been ascribed to "traditional" channels—broadcast or cable—than to the idea of an Israeli satellite. The dearth of channels, however, is a serious obstacle to the addition of broadcasting services. The particular geopolitical structure of the Middle East has strongly impinged on the original Israeli television plan, which called for the use of a relatively small number of VHF transmitters for a first network and other UHF transmitters for second and third networks. The channels allocated to Israel, however, by the International Telecommunications Union (ITU) plan are common outlets to Israel and her neighboring nations, so that severe potential and real disturbances have been identified, such as military communications, competing transmitters from Jordan, Syria, and Egypt, and channels occupied by civilian services. This has been one reason for the hesitation to develop a second broadcast channel and for the support received by the cable alternative. As mentioned, cable transmissions have been used in experiments with community television, but economic options and political problems still trouble supporters and opponents alike.

CONCLUSION/FORECAST

Israeli broadcasting can take credit for several achievements during the years of its existence. First, radio and television have made a decisive contribution toward the cultural integration of the various ethnic groups that compose Israel's population. The acculturation processes experienced by the huge waves of immigrants that followed the establishment of the state greatly benefited from broadcasting. Second, the democratic structure of the nation has strongly leaned on the medium for its creation, functioning, and reinforcement. Stations have indeed reflected varying views and opinions while adhering to the major principles and values of the state. Finally, Israeli broadcasting has had significant achievements as far as quality is concerned.

Numerous programs produced by instructional television and radio have been awarded international prizes, and the news and some of the series produced by television, particularly those of a historical nature, have been acclaimed in professional circles.

The history of broadcasting in Israel, however, indicates serious constraints on the development of appropriate structures and professional standards. The BBC-type structure, adopted as a model, has been deeply affected by the tendencies of centralization and political strife, which are results of the military, economic, and ideological characteristics of Israeli society. Thus, although the model persists, it has become highly politicized, reflecting more often partisan preferences and coalition-opposition dichotomies rather than the genuine interests of the public.

Examples include the tardy establishment of a public authority; the equally late decentralization of radio, which was not implemented until 1960; the heavy investment in transmission without equal efforts to improve production facilities; and the opposition to television, which caused its relatively late and unplanned introduction following the 1967 war. In fact, television was introduced for political reasons: to counterweight propaganda from Arab nations and to serve as a weapon in the then newly occupied West Bank. Further examples are the opposition to the introduction of color on the alleged grounds that the purchase of color sets would become a heavy burden on the Israeli population and the hasty retreat from this decision following the massive purchase of color sets and their utilization to watch programs from nations across the border. The prevalence of partisan preferences and coalition-opposition dichotomies in the mid–1980s causes Israel to face the danger of being subject to political pressures regarding crucial issues in the development of the broadcasting system, such as changes in its monopolistic structure, additional TV channels, cable television, the demand for the introduction of private radio, and the emerging debate over the question of direct broadcast satellites.

BIBLIOGRAPHY

Avner, Arie. "Memorandum to the Minister of Education and Culture." Unpublished manuscript, December 1984.
Feldman, Sidney. "Israel's Broadcasting Services." New York Times, March 11, 1952, sec. 2, 11.
Gotliffe, Harvey L. "Israeli General Television: A Historical Exploration of Content and Influence." Ph.D. diss., Wayne State University, 1981.
Greene, Sir Hugh. Israel Broadcasting. Report of the Israel Broadcasting Authority submitted to the Minister of Education and Culture in 1973. In Israel Broadcasting Authority, Newsletter, June 1980.
Israel. Central Bureau of Statistics. Annual Report. Jerusalem, 1984.
Katz, Elihu, and George Wedell. Broadcasting in the Third World: Promise and Performance. Cambridge, Mass.: Harvard University Press, 1977.

Kubersky, Haim, et al. "Report of the Committee on the Second Channel." Unpublished manuscript, March 1979.

Rogel, Nakdimon. "Atid Hatikshoret Be Israel." Lecture at IBA seminar, January 1982.

Shinar, Dov. "Structure and Content of Television in Israel." In *Television and Social Behavior*, vol. 1 of *Media Content and Control*, edited by G. A. Comstock and E. A. Rubinstein. Washington, D.C.: U.S. Government Printing Office, 1972.

ITALY

Roberto Grandi

HISTORY

The Italian Radio Union (URI) was designated the sole licensee for radio transmissions throughout the whole Italian territory by the government at the end of 1924. The Italian government, controlled by the Fascist party, decided to "normalize" mass communications in the years 1926 and 1927. In 1926 the government and the Fascist party succeeded in getting complete control over the most influential newspaper organizations. In 1927 the URI was replaced by the Italian Radio Audition Corporation (EIAR), which secured the license for a period of twenty-five years.

Throughout the 1930s and up to the end of World War II, the EIAR played a strategic role in the Fascist mass communications policy. At the end of World War II the Italian Radio Audition (RAI) took the EIAR's place. In 1954 the RAI broadcast the first television programs.

REGULATION

The first recognition of the legitimacy of the state broadcasting monopoly took place in 1960. In the Constitutional Court judgment no. 59 the court justified the preference for a state monopoly by the fact that "the State as monopoly-holder is placed institutionally in a more favorable position of objectivity and impartiality in overcoming the difficulties inherent in the natural limits of the medium and compliance with constitutional rule which provides the individual with the possibility of disseminating thought by all media."

In the second part of the 1960s and early 1970s a protest movement against the management of the RAI arose in Italy inside and outside the broadcasting corporation. The object of this protest was the close control exercised by the largest Italian political party, the Christian Democrats, over the RAI. The state monopoly of the RAI was increasingly viewed as a one-party monopoly by a host of organizations within Italian society.

While Italian political forces were debating media reform, the concession agreement between the government and the RAI (which had become law in 1952) was running out. In order to avoid the serious situation that would have resulted with the expiration of the broadcasting concession, the government made provisions for extending it, first by an administrative act and then by a legislative one.

The complex series of events described above resulted in judgments nos. 225 and 226 on July 10, 1974, by the Constitutional Court. In judgment no. 225 the court took the line dictated by its own judgment of 1960 and reaffirmed the validity of the state monopoly in view of the permanent scarcity of available frequencies. The court also established two basic requirements that the monopoly should meet:

- Full and objective information, characterized by broad receptivity to all ideological and cultural movements

- A legal framework allowing maximum possible access to the radio and television media

In judgment no. 226 the court ruled on the constitutionality of the state monopoly over cable television. The judges ruled that theoretically there are no obstacles arising from the limitation on available channels. In practice, a serious risk of monopoly or oligopoly exists in the case of television because of the expense of establishing a network covering a vast part of the national territory. Accordingly, "The same reasons which render the state monopoly of hertzian broadcasting legitimate also justify state exclusivity over similar services." But the court came to a different conclusion "with regard to the installation and operation of cable radio and television networks with a limited operating area." The tribunal stated that local installations of limited scope are compatible with a separate state network of national scope.

Nine months after the Constitutional Court's judgments nos. 225 and 226, the New Regulations Governing Radio and Television Broadcasting became law with act no. 103 in April 1975. The main characteristics of the new structure of the RAI are as follows:

- Confirmation of the state's prerogative on radio and television broadcasting on the national scene and of broadcasting by wire, cable, or any other means, since they are an essential public service of preeminent national interest.

- Management of the television monopoly by a public corporation; a parliamentary commission of forty members runs the service.

- Participatory control of the service by the regional councils by reformation of the internal structure of the corporation in the interest of complete decentralization.

- Access to the means of broadcasting is granted to political, cultural, religious, economic, and social groups of relevant social interest; consequently, the congressional corporation shall set aside, for suitable broadcasters, time amounting to not less than 5 percent of total television program hours and not less than 3 percent of total radio program hours.

- Distribution of the corporation's administrative council of twenty members as follows: six members elected by the shareholders' assembly (in fact, the RAI is part of the Institute for Industrial Reconstruction, a public group that has jurisdiction over activities such as banking, utilities, telecommunications, electronics, transportation, construction, and other industries), ten members elected by a majority of three-fifths of the parliamentary commission, and four members selected from candidates put forward by the regional councils.

- Permission for advertising within the limits drawn up by the parliamentary commission; its total duration may not exceed 5 percent of radio and television airtime.

- Restriction of cable television to a single-channel local network system (this is a departure from the Constitutional Court's judgment no. 226).

- Establishment of a third regional television channel, which started to broadcast in 1979.

Beginning with the implementation of the radio and television reform law, several private radio and television stations started operations. To wire a town for cable can be economically feasible if it is possible to cable by multichannel coaxial cable or fiber optics. In this case the cable may carry many television channels and other services. However, Italy advocated the possibility of utilizing only one single-channel local cable television system to complement the more economic hertzian television system. Consequently, there are no cable television systems presently operating in Italy.

In spite of this, in the second half of the 1970s local progressive organizations, social and cultural groups, and professional associations as well as economic and political conservative forces hoping to increase their role in private enterprise came to operate private radio and television stations. At the beginning of 1976, 500 local radio stations were operating in Italy. One year later there were over 360 private television facilities and over 3,000 private radio outlets.

In this new situation, large and powerful economic groups were launching massive attacks on the media market, trying to control various cultural and advertising corporations. The most influential "independent" newspapers and weekly magazines played a supporting propaganda role in favor of local commercial broadcasting. This effort could be considered in direct competition with the interests of their own advertising revenues. Nonetheless, the Italian newspapers, instead of opposing the increase of commercial television outlets, actually were hoping to enter this new market with the establishment of their own local facilities. As might be expected, the commercial television station boom increased the amount of the advertising market from 475 billion Italian lire in 1976 to the present 3,700 billion.

On July 28, 1976, the Constitutional Court judgment no. 202 declared against the legitimacy of the public monopoly of local radio and television transmissions when they do not exceed "local limits and do not interfere technically with essential public service." The motivations of the "liberation" of local broadcasting are as follows:

- The Constitutional Court decided that on the basis of both present technological knowledge and practical activity of several local broadcasting stations, it is realistic to rule against the concept of the scarcity of television and radio channels available at the local level.
- Reservation to the state of local hertzian broadcasting lacks a constitutional legitimacy because of the availability of channels and because the cost to establish and to operate a local station is not so expensive as to involve the risk of oligopoly.
- If the danger of creating monopoly or oligopoly does not exist in local broadcasting, there is no reason to delegate the service to the state.

With this ruling, the court developed guidelines to be followed by the Parliament in establishing comprehensive broadcasting legislation for Italian radio and television. But the Parliament has not yet acted in developing regulatory standards as requested by the court. For this reason, the private broadcasting system is still in limbo.

In December 1984 the Italian government approved a decree in anticipation of a comprehensive law governing the entire broadcasting system— a law Italians are still waiting for Parliament to enact. The main points of the decree (no. 807) are as follows:

- Official recognition of the Italian broadcasting system as a mixed private and public entity
- Permission for private television networks to broadcast the same prerecorded programs over the whole national territory
- Production of 25 percent (40 percent from July 1986) of the total feature films and TV series broadcast in one of the European Economic Community nations
- Restriction of commercials broadcast by the private television stations to 16 percent of total weekly time and 20 percent of each hour.

ECONOMIC STRUCTURE

Since 1974 a steady growth of local broadcasting stations has taken place through two distinct phases. An anarchic and wild increase of local privately owned radio and television stations occurred from 1974 to 1978. The features of this period included a very low level of professionalism, an interesting level of local creativity and public access in a number of local facilities, and a very high percentage of film and music broadcast by local television outlets.

The second phase, from 1979 until the present, has been dominated by a trend toward centralization and concentration of the broadcasting system. Advertising investments have shifted noticeably away from the newspaper and magazine sector toward television. In fact, commercials for the entire radio and television sector increased from 25 percent in 1975 to 53 percent of all advertising expenditures in 1985. During the same ten-year period, the percentage of newspaper sponsorship declined from 30 to 21 percent and the percentage of magazine endorsements from 31 to 20 percent. Although overall advertising investments in Italy are still low in comparison to other industrialized nations, observers expect continued expansion over the next five years.

Revenues for public television come from both promotions (about 35 percent of total revenues; the parliamentary commission decides this amount each year) and licensing fees. On the other hand, private television depends almost entirely on proceeds from commercials.

As of 1986 the television market consisted of some 600 private facilities that are beaming signals, but only about 100 of these can be considered strong. Roughly 250 stations are considered precarious because their survival depends exclusively on subsidies. In essence, they are likely to be absorbed by stronger outlets or disappear entirely. Another 250 are designated as weak in that their survival depends on local advertising plus subsidies. The remaining 100 strong facilities transmit regularly with stable program schedules, can boast a well-defined audience, and operate under the umbrella of one or another of the major networks.

Two businessmen serve important roles in the private television market. Selvio Berlusconi is the chief stockholder of the three most important private networks, Canale 5, Italia 1, and Rete 4, while Callisto Tanzi, head of the Parmalat dairy conglomerate, is the chief stockholder of the fourth private network, Euro TV.

The private broadcasters (mainly Berlusconi's networks) have continued to cut into RAI's audience share so that as of 1986 the public sector accounted for about 45 percent to 50 percent and the private sector for the rest. The RAI's first channel continues to be the most watched, immediately followed by Canale 5. Italia 1 surpasses RAI's second channel and Rete 4. The rest of the television audience (about 11 percent of the total) watches Euro TV, RAI's third channel, and the local television outlets. Breakdown of audience viewing shares into public and private percentages varies considerably according to the day, the hour, and even the season. As an example, the average daily breakdowns of audience viewing shares in two periods (from November 25 to December 22, 1984, and from April 28 to May 25, 1985) were the following:

November–December	*April–May*
RAI 1, 30.4%	RAI 1, 23.4%
C 5, 24.8%	C 5, 28.7%
RAI 2, 12.8%	RAI 2, 12.2%
I 1, 10.8%	I 1, 13.1%
Rete 4, 7.2%	Rete 4, 10.6%
E TV, 4.6%	E TV, 3.7%
RAI 3, 2.3%	RAI 3, 2.0%

As in the case of commercial television, since the Constitutional Court ruling of 1976 private radio broadcasters have proliferated dramatically. Listeners are almost equally divided between the public stations run by the RAI and thousands of local private broadcasters.

PROGRAMMING

At the beginning of the 1980s the big question was how and why the private television stations had managed in such a short time to attract such a following. Some of the reasons are as follows:

- The private commercial television stations have adopted a program model that includes a heavy dose of entertainment.
- Several well-known entertainers have been lured away from the public broadcasters by the private outlets.
- The private facilities have begun to compete directly by offering programs of high technical quality.

In 1986 RAI started a counteroffensive designed to regain its leadership role and a larger share of the viewing public. First, RAI has increased the number of entertainment programs, especially feature-length films, variety shows, miniseries, and talk shows. Second, and equally important, RAI has endeavored to better organize newscasts and other news coverage, including sports on a national level. In this area RAI does not face direct competition since Parliament has failed to approve a bill allowing private outlets to transmit live features on a national basis. Finally, RAI is planning the production of high-quality technically solid television series. Not only could these compete with the programs offered by the commercial stations, but they could also be aimed at a larger European audience via satellite or cable distribution. To successfully undertake this innovation, however, RAI will have to overhaul its present model of television production.

While it is difficult to offer a definitive assessment of the breakdown of television programs by genre, the following overview is fairly accurate:

- Feature-length films account for between 20 and 30 percent in Berlusconi's three networks and for between 10 and 18 percent on RAI's three channels.
- Television series (mainly from the United States) account for between 25 and 35 percent in Berlusconi's networks and between 15 and 20 percent in RAI's outlets.
- Variety and talk shows account for between 10 and 15 percent on Berlusconi's facilities and between 20 and 30 percent on RAI's channels.
- Ten percent of Berlusconi's networks' time is devoted to soap operas, mainly from the United States.
- Cartoons account for between 5 and 10 percent of airtime on Berlusconi's networks and between 2 and 5 percent on RAI's outlets.
- Eight percent of the RAI's television airtime is focused on cultural programs, news, documentaries, and sports.

RAI and Berlusconi are actually able to get almost 90 percent of the total television viewers with similar offerings, especially at prime time. In the last three years RAI's schedule has become more commercially oriented, while Berlusconi's operation has become more alert to self-production than before.

In addition, both RAI (as a public outlet) and Berlusconi (as a private operation) are actually ready to play an important role in the development of the European broadcasting system. In these circumstances, RAI's European projects are as follows:

- An increasing involvement in coproductions with both public and private corporations
- The direct broadcast of Italian-speaking programs into foreign nations (RAI is actually managing Channel 31 in New York City)
- An agreement with the West German Television network ZDF, the French A 2, English Channel 4, and Swiss and Austrian public television for the production of television series
- A multilanguage channel broadcast by the DBS Olympus, beginning at the end of the 1980s.

Not to be outdone, Berlusconi's European projects are as follows:

- Berlusconi and Seydoux have obtained a television license for the first French private channel, La Cinq.
- Berlusconi is aiming to become a stockholder of the most important European private networks thanks to his expertise in the private television marketplace.
- Berlusconi purchased the film studio, Roma, situated near Madrid, as the first sign of his involvement in the Spanish film and television market.

The Italian radio market trend is experiencing a less global process of concentration than the television arena. Both the local commercial radio outlets (which are supposed to be aimed solely at maximizing both audience and profits) and the so-called alternative radios (which aim to give an opportunity to speak to those who lack programs) are in a process of centralization. As regards a generic breakdown of radio programs, the following generalizations are in order:

- Only a few local commercial radio stations broadcast news and talk shows.
- A decreasing number of news and information programs are sent by the alternative radio outlets.
- Local private radio stations transmit an increasing percentage of music features.

BROADCAST REFORM

A real broadcast reform movement took place in the 1970s. The Constitutional Court rulings and the New Regulations Governing Radio and Television Broadcasting were, in part, answers to that movement. But since the Constitutional Court decisions of 1976, Italians have waited in vain for the legislature to develop a national policy regulating the mixed public and private system.

In the interim, the debate over a national broadcasting policy has ranged over a host of issues including but not limited to programming policies, advertising and commercialization, audience research techniques, news coverage, consideration of a public service philosophy, and collaboration with European nations. In reality, however, the demand for access, accountability, and public participation are not major factors in the current discussions.

NEW TECHNOLOGIES

Traditionally, Italy has lagged behind the most industrialized European countries in electronics and telecommunications. In spite of the lag, the following are the most interesting initiatives in Italy:

- RAI started its own teletext service, called Televideo, in 1985.
- The SIP (the national public concessionaire for the operation of both local and national telephone service) has started a view-data experimental service, called Videotel.
- RAI began experimental service on the Direct Broadcasting L-Sat satellite Olympus in 1987; in fact, Italy received the exclusive use of one of the two channels for DBS broadcast.
- RAI will start experimental television service on DBS as part of the Sarit project in 1989.

- RAI is participating in a series of broadcasts by the Orbital Test Satellite belonging to the European Postal Administration.
- Italcable (the national public concessionaire for the operation of international telephone service) is planning to lay an underwater trans-Atlantic fiber-optic cable to provide a television hookup with the United States.

CONCLUSION/FORECAST

The Italian broadcasting policy of the eighties is directed toward a consolidation of the mixed public and private broadcasting system based on the duopoly at the national level. In fact, the national public broadcasting corporation, RAI, will share its national audience and national advertising investments with Berlusconi's network. At the same time, hundreds of private local television stations will share both the audience not covered by RAI and Berlusconi's networks (no more than 15 percent of the total television audience) with regional and local sponsors. One of the consequences of competition between RAI and Berlusconi is the increase of entertainment programs (especially in prime time) and a decline in cultural and educational offerings as well as the disappearance of any public service philosophy.

But the broadcasting policy of the last part of the eighties and of the nineties, thanks to the DBS, has to be considered on a European level. Many experts predict that European broadcasting DBS policy will be financed almost completely by advertisers. In 1983 sixteen European commercial advertising interests were only 25 percent bigger than United States concerns and a little larger than Japanese advertisers. A European advertising trade association forecasts a 2 to 3 percent increase in advertising in the four strongest advertising nations (United Kingdom, West Germany, France, and Italy) between 1985 and 1989 alone. Moreover, the same study predicts the following breakdown of advertising by television in 1989:

Italy, 42%
England, 31%
France, 22%
West Germany, 12%

During the same period, satellites carrying between 90 and 200 DBS channels will be at the disposal of European public and private broadcasters. Of course, the future use of these DBS European outlets will depend on the relationships among the number of channels technically available, the cost of programs, the typologies of target audiences reachable by each single channel, and the amount of advertising investments ready to finance commercials on these outlets.

In contrast with this very optimistic opinion forecasting tens of DBS channels broadcasting shows and commercials to European nations at the beginning of the 1990s, it is possible to offer a different scenario. While it will be feasible to establish European channels offering specialized features including music, sports, and film, it will be much more difficult to develop outlets with a program format addressed directly to all Europeans, mainly because of the following:

- There are not sufficient products that can be advertised in the same way all over Europe.
- Planning of numerous television campaigns can also cause some corporations dissatisfaction with the television campaigns.
- European habits and television consumptions are not the same in the various nations.
- Strong competition will cause a scarcity of high-quality programs.

In short, the European broadcasting panorama of the 1990s will be characterized by a technological proliferation of channels available coupled with difficulty in fitting all of them with financial resources and programs.

BIBLIOGRAPHY

Agostini, Angelo, and Barbara Fenati. *Abstracts in Italian and English of a Few Research Studies.* Torino: ERI, 1985.
Balassone, Stefano, and Angelo Guglielmi. *RAI-TV: L'autarchia impossibile.* Roma: Editori Riuniti, 1983.
Bartolomei, Alessandra, and Paola Bernabei. *L'emittenza privata in Italia dal 1956 a oggi.* Torino: ERI, 1983.
Bechelloni, Giovanni. *L'immaginario quotidiano.* Torino: ERI, 1984.
Bruzzone, Mariagrazia. *Piccolo grande schermo.* Bari: Dedalo, 1984.
Cesareo, Giovanni. *La televisione sprecata.* Milano: Feltrinelli, 1974.
Faenza, Roberto, ed. *Senza chiedere il permesso.* Milano: Feltrinelli, 1973.
Grandi, Roberto. "Western European Broadcasting in Transition." *Journal of Communication* 28 (Summer 1978): 75–78.
Grandi, Roberto, and Giuseppe Richeri. *Le televisioni in Europa.* Milano: Feltrinelli, 1976.
Grossi, Giorgio. *La RAI sotto analisi.* Torino: ERI, 1984.
Hutter, Paolo. *Piccole antenne crescono.* Roma: Savelli, 1978.
Iseppi, Franco, and Giuseppe Richeri, eds. *Il decentramento radiotelevisivo in Europa.* Milano: Angeli, 1980.
Monteleone, Franco. *Storia della RAI dagli alleati alla DC, 1944–1954.* Bari: Laterza, 1979.
Papa, Antonio. *Storia politica della radio in Italia.* 2 vols. Roma: Guida, 1978.
Pinto, Francesco. *Il modello televisivo.* Milano: Feltrinelli, 1980.
Richeri, Giuseppe, ed. *Il video negli anni 80.* Bari: De Donato, 1981.
Siliato, Francesco. *L'antenna dei padroni.* Milano: Mazzotta, 1977.
Vacca, Giuseppe. *L'informazione negli anni ottanta.* Roma, Editori Riuniti, 1984.

JAPAN

Kenji Kitatani

HISTORY

Japan has a dual broadcasting structure, that is, a commercial and a public system. The commercial system now earns approximately $4 billion from television and $578 million from radio billings annually. There are 102 commercial outlets transmitting signals via 5,883 relay stations, and 59 radio corporations broadcasting via 245 transmitters. The public broadcaster, NHK (Nippon Hoso Kyokai), is the world's wealthiest public broadcasting system. The $1.4 billion budget operates two television networks (general and educational) and three radio networks (general AM, educational AM, and FM). The television networks have 6,791 transmitting stations, of which 53 are production centers with studio facilities.

Although the potential of broadcasting was recognized as early as 1915, it was not until March 22, 1925, that radio first came to Japan. Great debates went on in the Ministry of Communications as to what form the medium should take. Since the ministry was already deeply involved in constructing costly telephone and telegraph projects, it did not want to assume responsibility for developing broadcasting. Thus the ministry adopted plans for a nonprofit and noncommercial broadcast system in the form of a state public utility corporation. This corporation was placed under the control of the Ministry of Communications and funded by listeners' fees paid directly to the corporation.

By 1926 three radio stations were established in Tokyo, Nagoya, and Osaka through the ministry's support, and on August 6, 1926, these three stations were merged into a single broadcast entity, Nippon Hoso Kyokai (Japan Broadcasting System) or NHK, the sole broadcast authority in Japan. Between 1930 and 1945, as Japan moved toward militaristic rule, NHK

became a propaganda weapon of the government under the control of the
Ministry of Communications, and when Japan lost the war in 1945, NHK
was placed under the control of the General Headquarters of Allied Forces.
In 1950 a new broadcast law was enacted by the postwar government's
Ministry of Posts and Telecommunications. NHK was dissolved, and a new
corporation with the same name was established under these new regulations, which prohibited intervention in NHK programming by the government, political parties, or other authorities. The corporation was to be
managed and supported by the public alone. In February 1953 NHK introduced regular television service and in 1960 began operating two radio
networks and two television networks, both general and educational. Since
then NHK has become one of the largest public broadcasting systems in
the world.

The Broadcast Law of 1950 contained a significant provision: commercial
broadcasting was to be permitted for the first time, allowing for the use of
advertising. During the initial period of commercial broadcasting, especially
television broadcasting, the influence of national newspapers was clearly
dominant. Matsutaro Shoriki, publisher and president of the powerful Yomiuri Newspaper, founded commercial television broadcasting in Japan. He
was able to gain the support of two other national newspapers—Asahi and
Mainichi—and on that basis persuaded the business and political leaders
to allow commercial operations in 1953.

When Shoriki's television facility, Nippon Television Network (NTV),
began its broadcasts, the growth of commercial television depended on not
only the number of home television sets, which were only about 3,000 in
1953, but on the actual number of viewers. NTV set up 220 open-air
television sets in Tokyo, and huge crowds of people gathered in front of
these sets. Such open-air sets were in use until around 1960, when the
majority of Japanese began to own home receivers.

The Tokyo Olympic Games in 1964 brought significant changes in Japanese television broadcasting. For the first time, the coverage of events was
dominated by television rather than radio or print media. In response to
the public demand for live relay of the games, NHK increased its relay
stations to 252, and 48 commercial television corporations also opened 259
relay transmitters covering more than 90 percent of Japanese households.

During the 1960s television became the most influential mass medium in
Japan. The audience had grown tremendously, along with the increase of
both television broadcasters and receiving sets. During the decade the number of broadcasters grew from 43 to 81 companies among the private sector
alone, and the number of sets increased from 3 million in 1960 to 22 million
in 1970.

Not only did the television broadcasting industry grow, but the advertising
expenditures for TV increased from $10 million to $968 million between
1960 and 1970. Thus the telecasters kept expanding the airtime to answer

both sponsors' and viewers' demands. All the private telecasters were broad-casting an average of sixteen hours a day, and NHK was transmitting eighteen hours a day in both network services by 1970. Easy access to television was provided by the construction of new transmitters that allowed coverage of virtually all of Japan.

After the rapid increase in expenditures and technical progress of the 1960s, Japanese television at the beginning of the 1980s, especially the private sector, entered an era of retrenchment and outspoken criticism con-cerning social and political issues. Because of the rapid growth and social change of the 1960s, the Japanese audience was not aware of television's function and its status as an influential medium. In the 1970s, however, it became evident that some members of the audience were aware of televi-sion's social, political, and cultural influence. The audience realized that it should have a right to demand what it wanted to see on television.

As in the United States, sex and violence became controversial issues for the private telecasters during the 1970s. It was easy for station managers to win the ratings war by providing such fare, and the amount of sex and violence kept increasing in the early 1970s. Nudity became popular among the late-night private television shows, and several prime-time programs even included scenes that showed female nude bodies as the programs' attraction. Moreover, several soap operas in the afternoon time period began to show many violent sexual scenes and were gaining more than a 20 percent share of the ratings.

A significant number of complaints and criticisms were finally made to the National Association of Broadcasters of Japan (JNAB) for action. In August 1972 the JNAB General Assembly expressed a concern that the society might reject the broadcasters' programming on an ethical basis and suspect that they were incapable of self-control. In 1975 JNAB issued new standards that regulated sex and violence on its television programs. In addition the new guidelines limited advertising to less than 18 percent of the total broadcast hour and included a provision prohibiting exaggerated advertising claims.

After 1975 it seemed that the JNAB's new program standards were ef-fective, and a large number of controversial programs, especially sex-ori-ented features, faded from the private television programming schedule, except for one or two late-night shows that are still on the air.

REGULATION

In 1945 Japan's capitulation to the Allied Powers ended the wartime government monopoly of broadcasting. Japanese mass communications were controlled by the General Headquarters of Allied Forces for several years, and NHK was no exception.

In 1947 the postwar government issued a new constitution that established the legal basis for broadcasting. Article 21 stated, "Freedom of assembly and association as well as speech, press and all other forms of expression are guaranteed. No censorship shall be maintained, nor shall the secrecy of any means of communication be violated."

On June 1, 1949, the communication ministry was abolished, and a new Ministry of Posts and Telecommunications was created. A subordinate Radio Regulatory Agency patterned after the Federal Communications Commission of the United States was established to regulate, supervise, and enforce instructions for all broadcasting activities.

In December 1949 the Radio Regulatory Agency submitted the outline of the broadcast law to the General Headquarters of Allied Forces, which controlled all decisions of the Japanese National Diet, requesting the Diet to establish three bills to control radio-wave activities: the Broadcast Law, the Radio Law, and the Radio Regulatory Commission Establishment Law. At a December cabinet meeting the three bills were approved, and after a few minor revisions the laws went into effect on June 1, 1950.

The salient points of the three new statutes were as follows:

- The Radio Law, which contains 9 chapters and 166 articles, was designed to serve the public interest by guaranteeing fair and efficient utilization of radio waves by regulating the licensing of wireless stations and personnel.
- The Radio Regulatory Commission Establishment Law set up the format of the Radio Regulatory Commission as an administrative organization to supervise structure and clarify the commission's authority and operation.
- The Broadcast Law regulated the actual operation of both private broadcasters and the NHK in Japan.

Among the three laws, the Broadcast Law is the most significant because of its importance to private broadcasting. As mentioned, the law contains two basic provisions: (1) NHK was dissolved and a new corporation of the same name was established that did not permit participation by the government, political parties, or other authorities in NHK programming; the corporation was managed and supported by the general public. (2) Private broadcasting was to be permitted for the first time. Thus the law permitted the use of advertising by private broadcasters in Japan. Under article 5–13 of the law, the private broadcasters were allowed to commercialize broadcasting. The article states: "In case a private broadcast enterpriser charges an advertisement broadcasting, it shall announce in the broadcast that the broadcasting is an advertisement broadcasting."

The Broadcast Law guarantees two basic operational rights to all broadcasters: freedom of expression and freedom of programming. Freedom of expression is granted by article 1–2. This section explains that the law is issued to assure freedom of expression through the impartiality, integrity, and autonomy of the medium. Under article 3 the freedom of programming is also guaranteed. The article states, "Broadcast programming shall never be interfered with or regulated by any person excepting the case where he does so upon the powers provided for by law."

As private broadcasting, especially television, became popular, the 1950 Broadcast Law was forced to adapt to the new demands of both broadcasters and viewers. In 1957 the Ministry of Posts and Telecommunications started to develop a frequency-allocation plan for television stations throughout Japan. Before 1957 there was no specific frequency-allocation plan, and all the television licenses were given to the stations by the ministry on a temporary basis. There was strong pressure, however, from applicants interested in operating television outlets.

In June 1957 the ministry announced its First Channel Plan, authorizing private television broadcasters to exist on a prefectural basis and NHK to establish its television outlets throughout the nation, allocating a total of eleven VHF channels for each viewing area. As a result of this scheme, thirty-six private television licenses and seven NHK television licenses were issued in October 1957. In addition to the above plan, the ministry issued governmental guidelines that had some effect upon private broadcasters.

By the late 1950s each television station was broadcasting programs according to its own code of practice. This created a need for the telecommunications ministry to construct some kind of general television programming standard. In March 1959 the ministry amended the Broadcast Law of 1950 and forced both private telecasters and NHK to keep "balance" in the broadcast day among the cultural, news, entertainment, and educational programming hours. The amendment also required both NHK and private telecasters to establish program councils that would maintain acceptable programming standards.

According to article 51, which was added to the 1950 Broadcast Law, private outfits were required to operate a self-regulatory broadcast program consultative organization that was given the authority to keep the broadcasters' programming acceptable to the general public. The article suggests that the organization members shall be nominated by the broadcaster from among experienced persons who reside in the appropriate district of the station's service area.

In addition, one important prohibition for the private operators were added to the Broadcast Law by this amendment. In order to protect the independence of private telecasters, the provision prohibited contracts for exclusive programs supplied to the private operator from any single source. In effect, this amendment actually prohibited the existence of private network corporations in Japan. Article 52–3, entitled "Limitations of Arrangements Relating to Supply of Broadcast Programs," effectively prevented the formation of large, centralized network corporate structures and distinguished the Japanese broadcast industry from American broadcasting, which is dependent in many ways upon such legally sanctioned network structures.

In sum, the following arrangements characterize broadcast regulation in Japan:

1. Commercial broadcasting provided an alternative to the established, previously government-owned NHK.
2. Commercial broadcasting was authorized to serve local audiences rather than national audiences as an alternative to NHK, which is centralized.
3. Centralized tendencies of commercial broadcasting are controlled by the law in terms of capital and programming.
4. Commercial broadcasting is also protected from the other media's control by the government guidelines, and is expected to be and remain independent.

ECONOMIC STRUCTURE

According to the Broadcast Law of 1950, NHK is required to broadcast for the public welfare in such a manner that it may be received all over Japan. As noted previously, to satisfy this requirement, NHK operates a massive number of stations and transmitters.

These activities are financed by receivers' fees that are paid directly to NHK by some 26 million households having television sets. The Broadcast Law stipulates that "any person who is equipped with receiving equipment capable of receiving the broadcasting provided by the corporations shall conclude a contract with the corporation with regard to reception of its broadcasting." What makes NHK different from other public broadcasting systems such as the BBC and the Swiss SRG is that fees are paid directly to the corporation rather than to the government for disbursement to its broadcast operation. The current fee is about $4.00 per month for those with color television sets and $2.50 for those with black-and-white receivers. The tax can be paid at the local post office, deducted from one's bank account, or collected at one's front door every two months. Although the Broadcast Law requires the government to approve NHK's budget and inspect its account annually, NHK seems to maintain complete control over the disbursement of its funds.

As a business, Japanese private television is extremely successful. As previously mentioned, in 1984 the industry earned approximately $4 billion from television advertising. In 1983, 34.6 percent of Japanese advertising was used on television, while newspapers and radio attracted only 30.1 and 5.1 percent each. Commercial telecasters have established a voluntary limit of 18 percent of the total broadcast time to schedule commercials. The airtime is sold in two ways, either as program sponsorship or as commercials within existing programming.

The cost of television advertising varies in each market. The highest rate is in the Tokyo market, where a thirty-second spot costs at least $5,000. The rate system is similar to the U.S. system, and rates, as in the United

States, are based upon the size of the audience available at different times during the broadcast day. The majority of Japanese commercial television corporations earn substantial profits, except for several small independent UHF stations that have not yet become established in their markets.

The large number of commercial and public television stations provides the average Japanese citizen with easy access to great quantities of television programming. In 1984 NHK's two networks each operated eighteen hours a day, while private stations transmitted between eighteen and twenty-two hours a day. In major cities there are at least four private television channels and two public channels available for viewers. Thus the accessibility to broad television service in Japan is extremely good, at least in urban areas.

In 1984 there were 32 million television sets in Japan for a population of 125 million. This number of receivers was the second largest in the world, after the United States. The statistics indicate that one out of four Japanese owns a TV and over 99 percent of the total Japanese households have sets.

The popularity of television is very high in Japan, as evidenced by the number of hours the average Japanese spends in front of a set. A recent study on viewing habits revealed that Japanese spend about three hours a day watching programs. This exposure is higher than the hours that the Japanese spend for radio and print media. The Japanese use radio and print media less than thirty minutes a day. Indeed, the consumption of television programming is greater than that of all other media at the present time.

As mentioned, NHK operates two networks, the general and the educational television services. The general television service broadcasts eighteen hours a day from 6:00 A.M. to 12 midnight and carries news, sports, cultural programs, and entertainment fare. The service carries cultural features on about one-third of its schedule each day. News accounts for about 30 percent, entertainment for 25 percent, and educational features for 12 percent of its daily schedule. The shows are all broadcast in color. Except for about two hours of local news and public affairs, all the programs originate in Tokyo.

NHK's educational service is the world's most comprehensive educational television system. The service provides many kinds of education to all types of viewers. For example, there are several hours of cultural programs designed specifically for housewives. NHK offers these educational programs in color eighteen hours a day. In terms of production, the programs are all made by Tokyo Broadcast Center. Locally produced features are limited to occasional sports education programs such as "Swimming Class" and "Skiing Class," which are transmitted from leisure resorts.

In contrast to NHK's "high-culture" general service, the commercial telecasters present entertainment television to the public. In fact, about 50 percent of total airtime in 1984 was devoted to entertainment features. The content of prime-time programming is usually historical or modern drama, music shows, crime drama, or situation comedies. Magazine shows targeted to housewives dominate the late-morning, noon, and late-afternoon periods. Soap operas are aired during the early afternoon. In the late-night programming schedule there are several adult-oriented programs that often introduce erotic themes. The typical network-affiliated station depends heavily upon the Tokyo outlet for programming, carrying its features about fourteen hours a day, and produces only local public affairs shows and news programs at the station. For afternoon scheduling, when network programs are not available for several hours, these stations usually air syndicated programs of their own choice. Approximately 96 percent of commercial broadcasting programs are produced in Japan, and only a limited number of television shows are imported from the United States and Europe.

The Broadcast Law prohibits the existence of any network corporation that controls the programming of more than one television station. One of the basic purposes of this statute was to prevent multimedia control by a single corporation. According to the Ministry of Posts and Telecommunication's "Basic Outlines Regarding the Licensing of Private Broadcasting," there are two licensing principles: (1) to prohibit a single person from owning or operating more than one television station in order to preserve the broadcast opportunities for public ownership and operation of broadcast stations, and (2) to avoid the threat of multimedia domination on the part of programming monopolies by supervising television licensing.

Despite these policies, there are four television and three radio commercial networks operating in Japan. Initially, these chains were formed primarily to exchange news and coproduce their national news programs. Thus they all use the word "news" in their appellations, yet they all exchange a wide variety of programs, mostly produced by their "key" outlets situated in Tokyo.

In spite of governmental regulation, then, how have commercial television stations been able to operate in Japan? The basic answer can be divided into four subsidiary parts:

1. Since each commercial station is restricted to serving only one or two prefectures in accordance with the broadcast law, each station's news-gathering capability is quite limited. In order to provide nationwide coverage of news, it is necessary to exchange news with other broadcasting outlets.

2. The cost of program production is high, and it is financially difficult for local stations to produce many features. By pooling production or funding for the common programs with other facilities, the cost of program production can be decreased.

3. Many advertising sponsors want to buy national spots, and it is more efficient to establish network programs to meet the sponsors' needs.

4. The majority of television performers reside in Tokyo, and it is difficult for the stations outside of Tokyo to book their appearances.

There are five private television networks operating in Japan: Nippon News Network (NTV as its key station), Japan News Network (TBS as its key station), All-Nippon News Network (TV Asahi as its key outlet), Fuji Network System (Fuji Telecasting as its key facility), and TV Tokyo Network (TV Tokyo as its key station). Not only are there contrasts in programming between NHK and private outlets, but there are also dramatic differences among the private networks themselves.

Among the five networks, Nippon News Network (NNN) has a tradition of commercially successful, highly rated programming and has been one of the leading chains in the past ten years. NNN's strength lies in sports and entertainment. It was the first to introduce nudity and other sexually oriented features and is reputed to be the "wild network." One of the reasons for this phenomenon is that the president of NTV, Yosoji Kobayashi, has developed many original and successful programming forms during his period of management. The revenue raised by such efforts has assured the network's strong position among the other concerns. Since NNN affiliates are all partly owned by the Yomiuri Newspaper, many executive and news editorial positions are occupied by retired Yomiuri Newspaper employees and others on leave from the newspaper. Under the lifetime employment system, which operates in all major corporations in Japan, this is not unusual. Even at the Nippon Television Network, which has operated independently for thirty years, the key positions of administration and news are still dominated by the parent company. By implementing this personnel policy, the Yomiuri Newspaper continues to hold a successful media conglomerate. In the view of broadcast journalists, however, Nippon Television Network's inability to dictate its own editorial policies and administration is extremely frustrating.

Japan News Network (JNN) is the oldest and most prestigious network in Japan and has many station affiliates that originated as radio stations. This radio-television cross-ownership characteristic may be traced to JNN's key outlet, TBS. Initially, TBS was a radio station, Radio Tokyo, and had ties with many commercial radio facilities before television began. Thus many radio stations that later cross-owned television concerns became the major affiliates of JNN. The revenue of this chain is the highest among the five; however, the profit per employee is the lowest. The large number of employees, especially in radio, is the major cause of this situation, and JNN affiliates can be expected to decrease the size of their labor force in the near future.

JNN is also the most independent organization in Japanese broadcast journalism. Although the majority of its twenty-five affiliates are partially owned by Mainichi and other regional and local newspapers, its key station, Tokyo Broadcasting System, has come to be considered as the commercial counterpart of NHK in its news operation. The evolutionary power of this station could be the result of a decline in percentage of ownership by the newspaper groups. A major factor in the change of corporate investment during the 1960s and 1970s was the imposition of heavy requirements concerning the updating of equipment. To generate the capital required for the conversion, stations sold shares to the public. As a result of new offerings and stock splits, total stock of the original newspaper corporation remained fairly constant in numbers, but declined in percentage of ownership. In the case of Tokyo Broadcasting System, Mainichi Newspaper's stockholding rate dropped from 8.16 percent in 1970 to 0.81 percent in 1977. It was a common experience for Japanese viewers to watch news programs that were produced by newspapers' television news departments during the 1950s and 1960s. Even now, all but JNN mention over the air the connection between the television news programs and the newspapers.

Fuji Network, which consists of the Fuji News Network division and the Fuji Network System division, has twenty-six affiliates and is led by Fuji Telecasting in Tokyo. The network is parented by Sankei Newspapers, and the personnel transactions are similar to those of NNN. Fuji's strategy has been to provide young adult-oriented entertainment and show business-oriented news operations. Its comparatively small number of employees is a strong point for the future.

All-Nippon News Network has twenty affiliates sharing the Asahi Newspaper tie. The key outlet is TV Asahi in Tokyo. It also has a strong affiliate, Asahi Broadcasting Company in Osaka, and the prime-time programming is mostly shared by the two facilities. As their names clearly indicate, the domination of Asahi Newspaper is seen throughout the chain.

TV Tokyo Network has only four affiliates. Except for its key outlet in Tokyo, all are recently licensed UHF stations, and the audience share is significantly smaller than that of other networks. The chain is financed by the nation's strongest financial paper, *Nihon Keizai Shinbun*, and is eager to expand to other markets for future growth.

An examination of recent television programming suggests that the development can be divided into three periods: the pioneering, competitive, and stabilization stages. During the 1950s, the "pioneering decade," both the broadcasters and audience were not certain of what kind of programming would be suitable for Japanese television. Besides this uncertainty, two major barriers existed: the antitelevision movement of the movie industry and the technical difficulties of television production. As a result, programming was dependent on many live sports and imported features that did not require too much development of television production skills.

During the "competitive decade" of the 1960s, both the variety and quality of television programs showed significant progress. The increased size of the audience resulted in more funds for both network and private broadcasters. They were able to furnish more equipment and personnel for their programming, and more features were produced by the telecasters themselves. While the industry was expanding, competition was also increasing in intensity. Higher program ratings meant more money for the private concerns, and the competition increased throughout the decade.

Then the 1970s, the "stabilizing decade," began. Increased rating competition among the television broadcasters, especially private outlets, resulted in the programming of many sex- and violence-oriented features. The programs were criticized by the audience, which could now evaluate the television programming. After consideration by the industry, it seems that the competition was restrained by self-regulation, and the programming of television entered a more stable era.

NEW TECHNOLOGIES

Japan has been a leading nation in telecommunications technologies. The Japanese were the first among the Western broadcasters to introduce multiplex television sound in the late 1970s. In both network and commercial broadcasting channels, the majority of imported feature films and news programs are now transmitted bilingually with two audio channels (Japanese and English, French, or German), and sports events and music programs are broadcast with stereophonic audio.

In April 1978 the first experimental direct broadcasting satellite (DBS) was launched by the Japanese Space Development Agency, and in January 1984 the first operational DBS was launched. NHK has been transmitting special television programming for the remote islands where terrestrial signals could not reach before. The third DBS is expected to be launched soon, and the satellite will likely carry not only NHK signals but also commercial broadcast channels.

Between 1983 and 1985 both NHK and commercial broadcasters began introducing teletext service. The network service is primarily a subtitle service for people with hearing difficulties. The commercial outlets, however, will carry news, weather information, and other information with advertising. The Japanese teletext system is called a "pattern" system, which sends letters in the form of dot patterns, and is different from the "code" systems, which are widely adopted in the United States and Europe.

Since 1953 cable television has been widely used in Japan as a means for community reception in remote areas. In 1985 there were 34,000 such cable systems serving 3.7 million homes. Recently, however, cable television has been perceived as the most effective means of telecommunications due to its multichannel video and audio capacity. Two-way fiber-optic systems are considered to provide such revenue services as home shopping, home security, and home banking, in addition to pay TV and carriage of off-air signals. Railway companies, broadcasters, department store chains, and others are eager to secure construction and operation licenses, and by the end of 1990 cable subscribers are expected to exceed 10 million homes.

In addition, the nation's monopolistic common carrier, Nippon Telegraph and Telephone Corporation, and the Ministry of International Trade and Industry have been experimenting for a wider use of cable technology through the Hi-OVIS (Highly Interactive Optical Video Information System). At this point, however, it is reported to be difficult to operate two-way traffic and create consumer demand to make the system economically feasible.

In November 1984 Nippon Telegraph and Telephone Corporation established another new medium service—CAPTAIN videotext. The two-way interactive information system sends character and pattern information to home television sets via telephone lines. Some information pages are provided free of charge to the users, and others require payment for the use of information in addition to the line usage fee.

NHK's Technical Research Laboratories have developed their own high-definition television system (HDTV) with 1,125 scanning lines and are eager to have the system adopted as a universal standard.

None of these new technologies, however, developed as a result of consumer demand—rather, they were developed for the technological innovations and commercial opportunities. Thus it is interesting to observe the Japanese situation, where these new media technologies are introduced to the already media-rich population.

CONCLUSION/FORECAST

The previous discussion of the Japanese broadcast industry suggests the following positive aspects:

1. Japanese broadcasters have a strong commitment to the public.
2. Both the public and the commercial financing of the media are highly successful.
3. The programs distributed by the industry have a strong influence on the society.

There are, however, several negative contentions that should be mentioned:

1. Due to the lifetime employment and collective decision-making system characteristic of Japan, journalists and producers often choose to complement but not to push their individual news angles or program themes.
2. The programming of commercial broadcasters still often offers excessive sex and violence to attract higher ratings.

In short, the Japanese broadcasting industry, like its business counterparts, is highly successful, while the thematic quality of programming is often sacrificed for the stability and financial success of the commercial broadcasting corporations.

Although there are a number of new media technologies that are expected to compete with the existing structure and take away the traditional television viewers, it should not be difficult for the broadcasters to sustain their dominant position. Both NHK and commercial broadcasters have more than thirty years of program production experience and the ability to produce almost fifteen hours of fresh features a day on each channel. As long as they maintain the capabilities to provide news, information, and entertainment, no new media technology can threaten this matured industry.

BIBLIOGRAPHY

Dentsu Inc. *Nihon no Kokokuhi*. Tokyo: Dentsu, Inc., 1984.
Fujitake, A. "Trends in the Studies of Television in Japan." *Studies in Broadcasting* (March 1977). Tokyo: NHK.
Japan. Ministry of Posts and Telecommunications. "Report on the Present State of Communications in Japan." Tokyo: *The Japan Times*, 1984.
————. National Association of Commercial Broadcasters. *Nippon Hoso Nenkan '84*. Tokyo: Koken Press, 1984.
Murofushi, Takanobu. *Teribi to Shoriki*. Tokyo: Kodansha, 1984.
NHK. *Fifty Years of Japanese Broadcasting*. Tokyo: NHK, 1976.
NHK Hosogaku *Jyosetsu*. Tokyo: NHK, 1970.
NHK Radio and Television Culture Institute. *The History of Broadcasting in Japan*. Tokyo: NHK, 1967.
Nozaki, Shigeru, et al. *Hoso Gyokai*. Tokyo: Kyoikusha, 1976.
Uchikawa, Y. "Process of Establishment of the New Systems of Broadcasting in Post-War Japan." *Studies in Broadcasting* (March 1964). Tokyo: NHK.

KENYA

L. John Martin

HISTORY

While Kenya, like most of the rest of Africa, moved from tribalism to nationhood, the need for a mass medium to create a bond among the people and to help them develop as a nation became evident. A nation with Kenya's oral tradition naturally took to radio as the primary means of mass communications. Radio was not new to Kenya. Next to South Africa, which introduced broadcasting in 1924, Kenya is said to have been one of the pioneers in African communications with a radio station dating back to 1926, a mere four years after the British Broadcasting Company began operating in Great Britain. In July 1927 the British colonial government signed an agreement with the British East African Broadcasting Company, and in August 1928 Kenya became the first British colonial territory to have a regular public broadcasting service.

Of course, the programs were all in English, and Kenya radio had very few African listeners at that time. In September 1931 this agreement was replaced by another with Imperial and International Communications Limited. IIC, which in 1934 became Cable and Wireless Limited, signed a twenty-five-year contract with the colonial government to provide the technical equipment and to be responsible for programming in English. In exchange, it was given a monopoly on the colony's international telegraphic traffic. In 1939, at the beginning of World War II, Cable and Wireless Limited added Asian languages to its domestic programming, while the colonial Department of Information rented transmitter time from the company to provide afternoon programs in Swahili, Kikuyu, Kikamba, Nandi, Luo, Luhya, Kipsigis, and Arabic. The broadcasts were from Nairobi, Changamwe, Nyeri, and Kisumu and were called the African Broadcasting Service. After the war the British Forces Broadcasting Service began to provide entertainment and BBC relays in English for British troops stationed in Kenya as well as including several programs for African troops in the British army.

Two years before the Cable and Wireless Limited's contract was to expire, the colonial government appointed a commission to make recommendations about the future of broadcasting in Kenya. At the same time, it extended the contract for two years. On the recommendation of the 1954 commission and with the help of a colonial development and welfare grant, the Kenya Broadcasting Service was established in 1959.

That same year a commission on television was appointed under the chairmanship of Commander J. C. R. Proud "to expand and report on the advantages and disadvantages of a television service for Kenya." It was to recommend ways of operating such a service and what its relationship should be to radio. The commission thought that the advantages of introducing television outweighed the disadvantages if it was well planned and placed under the control of a single authority. In 1961, by ordinance in Council number 24, the Kenya Broadcasting Corporation was created with responsibility for both radio and television. By October 1962 a television transmitter and studios had been built, and television was officially inaugurated in 1963.

REGULATION

On December 12, 1963, Kenya became independent, and the following year on July 1 it nationalized the Kenya Broadcasting Corporation under Nationalization Law number 12, renaming it the Voice of Kenya. Between 1959 and 1961, as the Kenya Broadcasting Service, it had been controlled by a board of governors comprising four Europeans, two Asians, and two Africans. For the next three years it was operated as the Kenya Broadcasting Corporation under contract by a private consortium of East African, British, Canadian, and American entrepreneurs. Its balanced governing board consisted of nine members, with equal representation from government, the contractors, and the general public. Knowing that Kenya would soon become independent, the colonial government was anxious to give the new nation an autonomous voice patterned after the BBC.

The newly independent African state, however, had important uses for broadcasting and was not about to place it in the hands of a foreign-controlled private company. Consequently, the new government placed the Voice of Kenya (VOK) under the Ministry of Information, Broadcasting, and Tourism (which later became the Ministry of Information and Broadcasting) as a public service organization charged with providing information, education, and entertainment to the people of Kenya. Another branch of the ministry controls the Kenya News Agency (KNA), the primary objective of which is to serve the VOK. Under this arrangement, VOK does not have a news-gathering staff but depends on wire services and KNA for both its domestic and foreign news. KNA, in turn, gets its foreign news by subscribing to Reuters, Agence France Presse, UPI, and TASS.

Kenya has been a republic since December 1964, when it withdrew from membership in the Commonwealth. At that time Jomo Kenyatta, leader of the Kenya African National Union (KANU), became its first president. With the assassination in 1969 of Tom Mboya, who belonged to the Luo tribe and was minister of economic planning and development and secretary general of KANU, civil unrest followed. This resulted in the banning of the opposition party, Kenya People's Union. When President Kenyatta died in 1978, Vice President Daniel arap Moi was endorsed by KANU and became the chief executive. Following civil unrest and criticism of government policies, the unicameral National Assembly officially declared Kenya a one-party state in June 1982.

Since then, there has been an attempted coup and some subsequent unrest and violence. At such times, the government exerts pressure on the privately owned print media to avoid criticizing leaders and their policies. The government also imposes a so-called "third-country rule" under which nothing unfavorable may be disseminated about any nation with which Kenya maintains friendly relations.

Since broadcasting in Kenya is a government monopoly, and everyone on the Voice of Kenya staff is a civil servant, care is exercised in the reporting of sensitive news on radio and television. Thus, when Mboya was assassinated, the Voice of Kenya did not report the news at first for fear of fomenting violence. Many Luos interpreted this silence as a conspiracy within the Kikuyu-dominated government, which everyone is fully aware controls all broadcasting in Kenya through the Ministry of Information and Broadcasting. Kenyans have been told that the ministry provides policy guidance "on all matters related to sensitive political issues."

Sydney Head described how radio handled the news of the death of President Kenyatta—the first experience Kenya had of power changing hands. Government House phoned the news to the station director, James Kangwana, who immediately convened an emergency meeting of his staff. "The responsibility of handling the delicate assignment gave us a frightening sense of power," Kangwana said. He went on to observe that "we were probably more concerned with the implications of the truth than with the truth itself."

The broadcasting services are headed by a director, under whom are a controller of programs (radio) and a controller of programs (television). The radio operations consist of two nationwide networks and some local vernacular radio facilities. The two networks are the national service, which broadcasts in Swahili (the official language), and the general service in English. In addition, the vernacular services comprise the central service,

which broadcasts in Kikuyu, Kikamba, Kimeru, and Hindustani: the western
service, which has features in Kuria, Kisii, Kalenjin, Teso, Luhya, and Luo;
and the northeastern and coastal service, with programs in Somali, Turkana,
Rendille, and Boran. There is a head of general service and a head of national
and vernacular services. There are also heads of radio operations and of
eastern services, which includes Nairobi. There is only one television network in Kenya, and its programming is 65 percent in English and 35 percent
in Swahili. It is managed by a head of television productions and head of
television operations, both of whom report to the controller of programs
(television).

Also a part of the Voice of Kenya is the Kenya Institute of Mass Communication (KIMC), a mass communications school for both VOK staff
and public information officers. KIMC was a priority project of the ministry
when the government nationalized broadcasting. It saw immediately that
unless it produced its own technicians, it would have to continue to depend
on British, American, and other foreign staff. Besides engineers, the school
trains radio and television producers (since 1969), information specialists
(since 1970), and film producers (since 1975). KIMC is headed by a principal, who is a government employee as are all other employees of the VOK.
Students get a monthly allowance of 750 shillings (about $50), of which
320 shillings are withheld for board. Upon graduation, students must serve
a minimum of three years in a government position at a starting salary
ranging from about $1,200 to just over $2,000, depending on their assignment.

Additional training in broadcast journalism leading to a two-year degree
is offered by the School of Journalism at the University of Nairobi, which
is a state-supported institution. In 1968 the Ministry of Education asked
UNESCO for assistance in creating a journalism school at the university,
which it did in 1970. Funds were provided by UNESCO, Norway, Denmark,
and Austria.

ECONOMIC STRUCTURE

With an annual per capita income of just over $300, and a population
of over 20 million, increasing at an annual rate of 4.1 percent (the fastest
growth rate in the world), Kenya is not in a position to do any fancy
broadcasting. Even if it were, only 41 percent of the population can afford
to own a radio receiver. Television set ownership is largely limited to the
major cities of Nairobi (population 1.3 million) and Mombasa (population
460,000).

Until World War II there was not even much point in broadcasting in
the vernacular languages. Anyone who could afford a radio receiver was
either a European or understood English. Programs in Hindi and Arabic to
the relatively large and well-to-do Indian and Arab business community

followed later. In 1949 a simple and cheap radio receiver, often referred to as the "saucepan special," was manufactured, and it rapidly opened up the nation to the medium. It was supplanted by the transistor radio a few years later, making radio ownership commonplace in Kenya.

The same, of course, cannot be said for television. According to a 1985 study by the Kenyan Central Bureau of Statistics, there were 2.7 million radio sets and 119,000 television receivers registered in the nation that year. Counting nonregistered sets, another source estimated 2.8 million radios and 140,000 television sets in 1984. By 1986 ownership of radio sets had probably reached 3.5 million and television set ownership had gone up to 246,000. Of some 14,000 television sets in Kenya in 1968, 11,000 were said to have been owned by Europeans and Asians, and 500 were community sets. TV is still owned mainly by wealthy, urban Kenyans and by expatriates.

Because of the limited set ownership, television is not a viable commercial enterprise. A UNESCO report in 1977 called television in Africa "an elitist medium that has nothing to do with reaching the people, the masses." The 1954 commission had termed television "economically impracticable in Kenya." But the 1959 commission was of a different mind and recommended introducing television soon, greatly overestimating potential revenues from advertising.

During the brief period that broadcasting was being operated by a four-nation commercial consortium, revenues came from advertising, receiver license fees, and a government subvention. The fact that the corporation was losing money right from the start and had to call on the government to bail it out (to the tune of close to one million dollars in its final year) was certainly not the only reason why broadcasting was nationalized by the government, but it may well have speeded up the takeover.

For the next five years the ministry continued to derive its budget from receiver license fees—20 shillings (about $1.35 at the 1986 exchange rate) annually for radio and 60 shillings (about $4) for television—commercial advertising revenues, and the treasury. But, like other nations, it soon found the collection of annual license fees from set owners burdensome and haphazard. Starting in 1970, taxes for both radio and television receivers were abolished in favor of a one-time permit for the life of the set collected at the time of purchase of the set. This fee is in addition to the 50 percent import duty paid on receivers.

Both radio and television accept commercials. The content, length, and placement of spots, however, is determined by a committee. Promotional endorsements are reviewed for appropriateness and good taste by the VOK censorship committee, representing the Ministries of Information and Broadcasting, Education, Culture and Social Services, and Home Affairs. Commercials must have been produced in Kenya using Kenyan talent. In addition to commercials, radio and television programs themselves may be sponsored by business interests. Advertisers, mostly foreign corporations, cover most of the recurrent expenses of radio but only 25 percent of television operations.

PROGRAMMING

About half of the population in Kenya own radio receivers and nearly half claim to listen to radio practically every day. Of these listeners, more than 60 percent say that they listen in Swahili, as against only 16 percent who claim to listen in English. This is even fewer than the 20 percent who say they listen in Kikuyu. Fewer than 10 percent listen in each of the other vernacular languages and in Hindustani.

Not surprisingly, therefore, more than half of a national sample in a recent study by a local market research firm said that they listened to the national service, which broadcasts on seven medium wavelengths and two shortwave frequencies. Only 3 percent said that they listened to any of the nine medium and two short wavelengths on which the general service is transmitted in English. On the other hand, 7 percent said that they tuned in three vernacular languages and Hindustani on the one mediumwave and two shortwave transmitters. All these transmissions are out of the Nairobi studios of the Voice of Kenya. The western service in six vernacular languages broadcasts from studios in Kisumu and has a 6 percent listenership rating. The northeastern and coastal service has only two shortwave transmitters with studios in Mombasa. Its listenership to four vernacular languages is less than 1 percent. In addition, both the national service and the general service programs are broadcast on FM out of Nairobi.

On a typical day the national service starts its broadcast day at 6:00 A.M. with a lesson from the Koran. In 1984 Muslims were allotted 8.5 hours a week of radio time. Since more than 60 percent of the population of Kenya is Christian—almost 40 percent Protestant and the rest Catholic—Christian churches, through the National Council of Churches in Kenya (NCCK), were given 24 hours a week of radio time. The NCCK and the Catholic mission, through a joint broadcasting committee, arrange for nightly nondenominational epilogues and live transmissions of Sunday church services.

The reading of the Koran in the morning is followed by a couple of hours of "Greetings of the Day," with a break for a fifteen-minute news program. During the course of the day there are six more fifteen-minute newscasts and an hour's goodnight greetings at the end of the day at 11:00 P.M. or midnight. Most of the remaining programs are educational, dealing with home life, child rearing, health, and farm life. Interspersed are fifteen-minute to one-hour musical interludes throughout the day. On Saturdays there are one or two sports roundups.

The general service is very similar, except that there is a hiatus from 9:30 A.M. until noon and again at 2:15 until 4:00 P.M. There are as many news programs as on the national service but more music. The western, central, and northeastern/coastal services go off the air for longer periods. Programs of music and talk shows last between thirty minutes and one hour and thirty minutes in each of their various vernacular services. This shortchanges about 40 percent of the population that does not understand English or Swahili, but as Sydney Head has pointed out, when a nation must accommodate each of several languages, it cannot fully serve any of its language groups. Incidentally, all news is first written in English, then translated into Swahili and the vernaculars.

Kenya has had educational broadcasting since independence, when the Ministry of Education assigned an education officer to the Kenya Broadcasting Corporation. A thousand radio sets were issued to primary schools, and daily half-hour programs in English language for the primary schools and in English literature for the secondary schools began to be broadcast in May 1964. The programs were almost all obtained from the BBC. In 1965 the Schools' Broadcasting Service, as it was called, was transferred from what had become the Voice of Kenya to the Ministry of Education. A BBC producer was lent to the ministry, and he produced a series entitled the "Beginning of Science."

In 1966 a team of Canadian educators assisted the Kenya Institute of Education in the preparation of radio courses coupled with correspondence instruction in teacher education. The teacher shortage had forced Kenya to use radio broadcasts and correspondence study to speed up the training of educators.

In 1967 the first Kenyans were appointed as producers in the Schools' Broadcasting Service, and programs in the sciences, English, and Swahili were added or expanded. By 1970 the service was providing five hours of daily programs and had added mathematics as well as history, geography, and literature for secondary schools. The features were based on course materials developed by the Kenya Institute of Education. In July 1976 the Schools' Broadcasting Service was renamed the Educational Media Service because it had been decided to include broadcasts for out-of-school audiences. This was done on the recommendation of UNESCO and with the support of the World Bank. A visual section was added at about the same time, and Educational Media Service was made a department of the Kenya Institute of Education in the Ministry of Education. In 1983 Kenyatta University College was directed by the president of Kenya to offer an external degree via radio and to investigate the possible use of television as well.

One of Kenya's out-of-school educational projects on radio is known as the Homa Bay project, which broadcasts for two hours daily in Dholuo, a vernacular spoken in southwestern Kenya near Lake Victoria. The programs are locally produced. In addition, national service programs are rebroadcast to the area in Swahili. The project, which is supported by UNESCO and some European foundations, has also provided subsidized radio receivers for the poor farmers who live in the area.

Only 3 percent of the public own television sets, mainly in town and among the better educated. Yet 26 percent of the public claimed to have watched television in the previous year, according to a recent survey conducted by a local market research firm. Of the viewers, 6 percent had seen television at a community center and 11 percent in a friend's home. Another 9 percent had seen it in a variety of places.

Television is broadcast in English and Swahili on Channel 4 out of Nairobi and, since 1970, on Channel 6 out of Mombasa. Reception is limited to about a one-hundred-mile radius around each of these two cities. It is also picked up at Timboroa and retransmitted on Channel 2 for the western part of Kenya.

Television programming starts at 5:30 P.M. on weekdays and at 4:30 P.M. on Saturdays and Sundays. There are two fifteen-minute news programs at 7:15 P.M. in Swahili and at 10:00 P.M. in English. Sign-off is at about 11:15 P.M. or later, especially on weekends.

The news programs are by far the most popular in Kenya, both on radio and television. In a 1980 survey 73 percent of Kenyan radio listeners said that they liked the news programs best, followed by 29 percent who favored the talk shows. Next were greetings, pop music, and religious programs, followed by 12 percent who liked the commercials best. Rural and urban Africans differed little, but Asians and Europeans placed music of all kinds—pop, light, and classical—immediately after the news programs.

Except for the 22 percent who said they had no particular favorite program on television, the news was preferred by the largest proportion (18 percent), followed by wrestling (11 percent). German soccer and sports were each favored by 4 percent; all other programs were picked by no more than 1 or 2 percent.

Very little time on radio is given to foreign coverage. In a 1983 study Dr. Joseph Mbindyo, director of the University of Nairobi's School of Journalism, found that the English-language general service devoted only 4 percent of its time to foreign coverage during the month of November. Most of this was in the news programs, 31 percent of which dealt with foreign news. A third of the foreign news on radio concerned international organizations such as the United Nations, and another 21 percent was about African nations.

On the other hand, 59 percent of VOK's television airtime contained foreign content. Of the news programs, 56 percent concerned foreign nations—22 percent of it being about African countries and 14 percent concerning international organizations. About a third of the foreign news dealt with the developed nations of the West. Almost all foreign news on television is taken from VISNEWS, a British news agency.

In 1963, 90 percent of the programs were imported from abroad. Twenty years later, in 1983, the proportion of imports had dropped to 59 percent, about the African average. In 1970 Kenya's Ministry of Information and

Broadcasting had decided that at least 70 percent of its programs would be locally produced, and in the mid–1970s it even announced that it would go completely local in its programming. But the inexorable demands of the studio that is on the air six or seven hours a day are hard to satisfy when both talent and money are in short supply, and VOK has had to accept much slower progress toward self-sufficiency.

The United States provides most of the imports (close to one-half) followed by Britain (nearly one-third). West Germany is next with about 9 percent, followed by occasional imports from international organizations such as the United Nations and the International Red Cross, Australia, France, Brazil, Yugoslavia, Holland, Canada, and Ghana, among others. Popular programs from the United States have been "Dallas," the "Jeffersons," "Roots," "Flintstone Frolics," and the "Little Rascals." Imports from Britain and other nations have frequently been of sports events and educational programs. Soccer is especially popular.

BROADCAST REFORM

The government of Kenya estimated in 1977 that 64 percent of the rural population over the age of fifteen was not attending school and could not read or write in any language. While the situation has improved in the past decade, radio still has an important role to perform in contributing to national development. A 1985 study by Dr. Mbindyo indicated that 86 percent of the public considered radio to be the best source of information for welfare improvement, as against only 17 percent who believed that television could be used for such purposes.

Three things are normally emphasized by Kenyans in talking about broadcast reform. First and foremost is the need for material equipment to help Kenya build up its communications infrastructure. Without modern equipment Kenya cannot hope to speed up its reforms, its leaders say, and they look to the United Nations and to affluent Western nations to provide assistance. Second, Kenya must become more self-sufficient in program production. It cannot continue to depend on the industrialized nations for information gathering, processing, and distribution. Yet Kenya, like most other African nations, must rely on the West even for news about neighboring states. Not only national pride but its aim to use media for national development requires a Kenyan perspective in its mass communications. This is especially urgent in television, but is generally true of all media. As publisher Hilary Ngweno put it: "If I could have a reporter in London or Washington, I would want him to be a Kenyan with a Kenyan perspective and aiming at a Kenyan audience."

Third, both journalists and communication scholars speak of the need for a campaign to educate the public about the critical importance of press freedom. The African Council on Communication Education, an organization comprising thirty schools of journalism and private members from all over Africa, recommended that "in order to create an atmosphere in which journalists can discharge their responsibility to society effectively the constitutional guarantees for freedom of the press should be strengthened, and that the establishment of institutional frameworks like press commissions should be encouraged, to provide protection for journalists and guarantee them a certain measure of security of tenure."

There has been no movement for the introduction of private broadcasting facilities in Kenya, nor is it likely that the present government would look favorably upon such a venture. As it is, Kenya is one of the few nations in sub-Saharan Africa that continues to have privately owned print media. And except for difficulty of access to government information, there are few complaints. More foreign correspondents are based in Nairobi than anywhere else in Africa because, as one American journalist put it, "the weather is nice, communications are good and the government leaves us alone."

NEW TECHNOLOGIES

Kenya is constantly testing new transmitters, especially in the shortwave band. According to the 1986 *World Radio TV Handbook*, new 250-kilowatt transmitters were being tested on 4,840, 4,980, 6,050, 7,220, 7,225, 9,665, 9,725, and 11,765 kilohertz at different times of the day. Since the distances that must be covered are great and 95 percent of radio sets in use can receive shortwave, this will enable the Voice of Kenya to blanket the entire nation. While 97 percent of sets can receive mediumwave and 6 percent can receive FM, the locations of transmitters on these wavelengths make for poor reception in some parts of the country.

Of the 3 percent of homes with television, it is estimated that 15 percent are color sets. Many of these sets are used more for home viewing of videotapes than for television reception. In 1979 there were 35,000 VCRs in Kenya, and this number had risen to 75,000 by 1981. At that time sets cost around $680. Moreover, at least one hundred videocassette libraries in Nairobi and Mombasa had sprung up. The easy availability of uncensored video movies has had a major negative effect on movie attendance, especially in the two big Nairobi Asian cinemas. Kenya has strict film censorship laws.

Slow but steady progress is being made in replacing old black-and-white cameras with color TV. In 1985 there was only one color TV van in Nairobi, but others are being added. Nairobi, Mazeras for the coastal areas including Mombasa, Timboroa for western Kenya, and Nyeri and Meru for the central areas have all recently acquired ten-kilowatt color transmitters. The Nyeri and Meru transmitters are not yet operational, but the others are. Mombasa has a complete production studio, enabling it to originate programs and to share them with Nairobi over a post office microwave link. All, however, still use 16mm film that must be sent to Nairobi for processing, editing, and eventual transmission. Television producers and technicians are being posted in all provinces of Kenya so that developments in the rural areas may be covered on television.

Kenya has no cable network at present, and there are no plans to install one. Kenya is serviced by Intelsat, although it uses the services sparingly because of the cost. Thus, although VISNEWS has a daily satellite news package for television, Kenya prefers to rely on its airmail service. Most of the news provided by the agency tends, therefore, to be outdated by the time it is received and ends up being used in the weekly magazine rather than on the daily news shows.

CONCLUSION/FORECAST

A number of factors combine to make radio the most important communication medium in Kenya, and these factors will probably continue to prevail well into the twenty-first century. National development and cohesion, considered primary goals not only in Kenya but in all sub-Saharan African nations outside of South Africa, cannot be attained without mass communications. If the aim is to march together, there must be a common drummer.

Print media cannot supply the bonding material for at least four reasons. First, the literacy rate is too low to support reliable, comprehensive, authoritative newspapers and magazines. It takes a "critical mass" of newspaper and magazine sales to provide the economic base for excellence. Second, while Swahili is the official language and English is a nearly official language that is taught in all the schools, several other languages are spoken exclusively by fairly large segments of the population. These are tribal groups that must be reached for national cohesion. This multiplicity of languages adds to the cost and the ineffectiveness of printed communications. The language problem, of course, increases the cost of broadcasting as well. But listeners in the vernacular languages do not have to be literate in them.

Third, print media also suffer from the lack of adequate transportation facilities. Broadcasting, especially via shortwave, can cover vast territories. The necessary roads and carriers do not exist for transporting print media. Forth, while radios are relatively expensive, they are a one-time investment that more than 40 percent of the population has been able to afford. After that, the only expense is an occasional battery—which admittedly must seem major to many, although most parts of the nation now have access to relatively cheap electricity. As an added attraction, radio provides a lot of entertainment as well as education. On the other hand, print media are an unaffordable, continuing expense. Only 11 percent of the population purchased daily newspapers and only 16 percent had ever read a magazine, according to a 1980 national survey.

The literacy rate will, of course, rise in the years to come. Since January 1980 primary education has been free in Kenya. Yet in the following year only 72 percent of eligible children were in school, and this was mainly in the few urban areas. In the northeastern province, for example, only 4 percent were receiving education. With rising literacy, the multilanguage problem will be reduced, since children will be taught both Swahili and English in the classroom. But the economy is not likely to show marked improvement in the next twenty years, especially in view of the rapid population growth. This will militate against the development of an economically healthy print media or the rapid growth of transportation facilities. For the same reason, television as a mass communications medium is not in the cards for Kenya in the foreseeable future.

Will Kenya improve its broadcast fare in the coming years? There is no doubt that there has been much progress. Next to Nigeria, Kenya has better training facilities than any other sub-Saharan African nation apart from South Africa. It has put much effort and money into improving the product and reducing its dependence on foreign imports. One cannot help but admire it for its perseverance. Naturally, "improvement" is an idiosyncratic measure. One should probably ask whether listeners/viewers will like the programs better, and the answer to that is "some may." But generally people like what they are used to. Will they then get more from the programs in terms of education and entertainment? Undoubtedly, since one of the benefits of training and experience is that one learns to do a more effective job more economically.

What can Kenya do to improve its broadcasting hardware? Along with most other African nations, it must put greater effort into maintenance, both in the manufacture of spare parts and in the training of maintenance technicians. Kenya's desire to modernize is very laudable, but a country can emphasize modernization beyond its capacity to benefit from the latest technology. Before investing in high technology, Kenya must be sure that it can afford it, that the probable continuing demand for the hardware is high enough to warrant the investment, that communicators are trained in its use and, along with the audience, will benefit from its use, and, probably most importantly, that there is a concurrent budget line for training programs in maintaining the hardware.

BIBLIOGRAPHY

Akenga, Jamen. "Voice of Kenya—Past and Present." *Combroad* (September 1982): 28–35.
Alisky, Marvin, John C. Merrill, et al. "Africa." In *Global Journalism: A Survey of the World's Mass Media*. New York: Longman Press, 1983.
Barty-King, Hugh. *Girdle Round the Earth: Story of Cable and Wireless*. London: W. Heinemann, 1979.

Commonwealth Broadcasting Association. *Handbook, 1985/1986*. London: Commonwealth Broadcasting Association, 1985.

Hachten, William A. *Muffled Drums*. Ames: Iowa State University Press, 1971.

Head, Sydney W., ed. *Broadcasting in Africa: A Continental Survey of Radio and Television*. Philadelphia: Temple University Press, 1974.

———. *World Broadcasting Systems: A Comparative Analysis*. Belmont, Cal.: Wadsworth, 1985.

Katz, Elihu, and George Wedell. *Broadcasting in the Third World: Promise and Performance*. Cambridge: Harvard University Press, 1977.

Mwaura, Peter. *Communication Policies in Kenya*. Paris: UNESCO, 1980.

Mytton, Graham. *Mass Communication in Africa*. Denver: Arnold, 1983.

Ngoda, Harold. "Development of Educational Broadcasting in Kenya." *Combroad* (March 1984): 7–11.

Stauffer, John, Richard Frost, and William Rybolt. "Recall and Comprehension of Radio News in Kenya." *Journalism Quarterly* (Winter 1980): 612–17.

U.S. Information Agency. *Country Data Papers: Africa*. Washington, D.C.: U.S. Government Printing Office, 1986.

Wedell, George. *Making Broadcasting Useful: The Development of Radio and Television in Africa in the 1980s*. Manchester, Eng.: Manchester University Press, 1986.

Wilcox, Dennis L. "Kenya." In *World Press Encyclopedia*, edited by George Kurian. New York: Facts on File, 1982, 569–77.

———. *Mass Media in Black Africa: Philosophy and Control*. New York: Praeger, 1975.

KOREA

Jim Richstad and In-hwan Oh

HISTORY

Broadcasting in Korea started on February 12, 1927, when the nation's first radio signals were sent from the capital city of Seoul. Korea was at that time under Japanese colonial rule.

Korea was liberated from the Japanese domination in 1945 but soon found its territory divided into two parts, with the northern half, the Democratic People's Republic of Korea, coming under Communist rule. Since then, North Korea has remained firmly in the Communist media pattern and is largely closed to most of the outside world, with limited development in broadcasting. (Broadcasting in North Korea will be examined in a separate section.) In 1948 the Republic of Korea was established in the southern half of the nation, and the radio broadcasting network named KBS (Korean Broadcasting Station) was placed under government supervision. The government-run KBS became a public corporation in 1973 with the promulgation of the Korean Broadcasting System Law.

The first privately owned radio, the missionary CBS (Christian Broadcasting System), went on the air in December 1954. Pusan MBC (Munhwa Broadcasting Corporation) became the first commercial radio station when it transmitted on April 15, 1959, followed by MBC in Seoul in late 1961. These were followed by two other commercial radio stations, DBS (Dong-A Ilbo Broadcasting System) and TBC (Tong-yang Broadcasting Company).

In television, KBS started broadcasting in December 1961. TBC and MBC joined KBS in television in December 1964 and August 1969, respectively. Color broadcasting started in December 1980, using the NTSC-M system.

A dramatic rearrangement of the broadcasting companies in Korea took place in December 1980, when the Korean Broadcasting Association adopted a resolution to merge five commercial companies into the public network of KBS under a government ruling to make broadcasting a publicly owned medium for the nation. As of September 1985 there were two TV networks (KBS and MBC) and three radio networks (KBS, MBC, and CBS) in Korea.

The reorganization of the Korean mass media structure was undertaken as a response to public criticism of commercialism and sensationalism on television, the government said. Critics replied that the television programs were designed more for the urban well-to-do than the less affluent members of society, and this had the potential of being damaging.

Under the reorganization, the then commercial television TBC was taken over by the then public corporation KBS. The commercial network MBC was turned into an organization of a public nature when KBS became MBC's largest shareholder.

The radio networks were also consolidated, with KBS absorbing two newspaper-owned commercial stations, TBC and DBS. MBC-Radio, like MBC-TV, cut its tie with a newspaper and remained as a separate entity, with KBS as its major holding company. The religious station CBS was prohibited from broadcasting news and commercials.

Similar consolidations occurred in the press and news agencies, with seven daily newspapers eliminated and the two major general news agencies reorganized into the Yonhap News Agency. In the restructuring, three newspaper organizations lost their broadcasting services—Dong-A Ilbo lost its DBS radio service, Joon-ang Ilbo lost its TBC radio and television services, and Kyunghyang Shinmoon lost control of MBC.

REGULATION

The Korean Broadcasting Commission (KBC) is the governing body of broadcasting in Korea. Established in March 1981 under the Basic Press Law, the commission is entrusted with the mission of deciding basic media policies for the nation.

The commission consists of nine members appointed by the president of the republic for three-year terms. Three of the commissioners are the nominees of the speaker of the National Assembly, and three others are nominated by the chief justice. Government officials (those in the teaching and legal professions are not included) and those in broadcasting and related businesses are not eligible. The chairperson and the vice chairperson are elected from among the members. The Basic Press Law stipulates that the commission members shall be subject to no external direction in performing their duties.

The commission is responsible for the operation and programming of broadcasting, advertisements on radio and television, the operation of the

Broadcasting Deliberations Committee, basic policies of broadcasting at the request of the minister of culture and information (the government), major public service projects to be financed by the Korea Broadcasting Advertising Corporation, and relations between broadcasting networks and matters related to joint projects and cooperation.

The commission makes an annual report to the assembly on its activities. The agency's operation fund is provided by the Korea Broadcasting Advertising Corporation from the latter's public service fund. When necessary, the commission may get a subsidy from the government.

The Korean Broadcasting Deliberations Committee (KBDC) is the main self-regulatory body of broadcasting in the nation. The committee was set up on March 1981 under the Basic Press Law after the Korean Broadcasting Ethics Committee was dissolved. The KBDC is composed of nine to fifteen members elected by the General Council, which consists of the heads of all broadcasting stations in Korea. The committee members include a representative of the KBS, one representative for all the other broadcasting stations, and seven to thirteen persons representing educational, religious, and cultural circles. Election of the committee members and revisions of major rules must be approved by the minister of culture and information.

When any program is found to be out of compliance with KBDC guidelines, the committee can take punitive actions against the broadcasting station involved by giving a warning or seeking clarification, correction, retraction, or apology. The panel can also ask the stations to take disciplinary actions against those employees involved in the program under scrutiny. In case a station fails to follow the directives of the body, the minister of culture and public information orders the station to comply.

Broadcasting in Korea is considered a public service, and there is a significant and pervasive amount of governmental influence and control. The president of the republic, for example, appoints the members of the Korean Broadcasting Commission, which is the governing body of broadcasting. In addition, government control of broadcasting and other forms of mass communications in Korea was dramatically enhanced under the sweeping changes incorporated in the Basic Press Law in 1981.

The Press Arbitration Commission, composed of officials appointed by the government, is a case in point. This body was set up in March 1981 to impartially resolve disputes arising from alleged infringement by both the print and broadcasting media upon individual rights. If a dispute is reconciled, the agreement has the same effect as that of a court ruling. No application for a correction of media report can be filed with the court without going through this entity.

Overall national policy on broadcasting sets three broad guidelines:

1. To help achieve the national goals for a more democratic, more egalitarian, and more affluent nation

2. To help attain a peaceful reunification of the country
3. To further enhance the public nature of broadcasting

Broadcasting stations are required to secure a license from the Ministry of Posts and Telecommunications after being recommended by the minister of culture and public information.

The Basic Press Law, which is the basic document for regulations and decrees related to the mass media, includes the following provisions affecting broadcasting:

Article 29 (Freedom of Broadcasting Programming). Unless otherwise specified in this law or any other laws, no one may regulate or interfere with the work of drawing up broadcasting programs.
Article 30 (Autonomy of Broadcasting Management). Autonomous management of a broadcasting network shall be guaranteed and the supervision of a broadcasting network by the state shall be limited to such matters as are stipulated in law.
Article 31 (Public Mission of Broadcasting). Broadcasting shall respect the ethical and emotional sentiments of the people and serve to spread social justice, promote the fundamental civil rights and increase good will among nations.

The legal structure of broadcasting in Korea establishes the following boundaries:

1. Only a juridical person can operate a broadcasting station.
2. No one may operate mass-media enterprises of more than one description among newspapers, news services, and broadcasting. (A newspaper owner, for example, cannot own a news service and a broadcasting station.)
3. Affiliated enterprises shall not jointly own more than one-half of the stocks and shares of more than two mass-media enterprises among newspapers, news services, and broadcasting stations, with an exception for special juridical persons established by law. (Even a business tycoon running many companies, for example, cannot operate more than one mass-media organization.)
4. Mass-media enterprises shall not receive financial contributions from any foreign person, government, or organization under the pretext of a donation, grant-in-aid, or the like. Exceptions shall be made for contributions from foreign educational, sports, religious, charitable, or similar organizations devoted to international friendship. Commercial advertisements placed by foreign persons or organizations also can be considered an exception to the provision.
5. An individual person or a profit-making organization shall not hold more than 49 percent of the shares or assets of a broadcasting enterprise.

ECONOMIC STRUCTURE

There are three Korean broadcasting networks: the Korean Broadcasting System (KBS), the Munhwa Broadcasting Corporation (MBC), and the

Christian Broadcasting System (CBS). There are also two overseas evangelical radio stations whose main purpose is to bring the Gospel to the Communist countries in Asia: the Far East Broadcasting Company (FEBC) and the Asia Broadcasting Station. One foreign network, the American Forces Korea Network (AFKN), is in operation, mainly for the American soldiers stationed in Korea under the Korean-U.S. defense treaty.

KBS, a corporation set up with investment from the government, operates 3 television channels (KBS-TV 1, KBS-TV 2, and KBS-TV 3) and 6 radio channels (Radio 1, Radio 2, Radio Seoul, FM 1, FM 2, and Educational Radio). KBS has 24 local stations and 518 relaying and transmission facilities across the nation, hooked to the central station in Seoul, to reach virtually all parts of the country. KBS also runs an overseas radio, Radio Korea.

Government stipulations require that the president of KBS be appointed by the president of the country. The minister of culture and public information appoints board members and auditors. In addition, KBS is required by law to set 10 percent or more of its weekly fare for news and commentary and 40 percent or more of the broadcast hours for educational programs. Within this framework efforts are being made to uphold the principles of programming freedom, management autonomy, and public interest as specified in the Basic Press Law.

KBS revenue comes from television license fees and radio and television advertising. The licensee fee system changed in July 1986 from "fee per set" to "fee per household." There is now a tax of $2.75 (U.S.) per month per household, regardless of how many color television sets are in the home. Fees for black-and-white sets were discontinued. The revenue generated was $148 million (U.S.) from TV license fees and $161 million (U.S.) from advertising.

MBC was a privately owned commercial network up to the end of 1980. The private nature of the organization changed drastically to that of a public broadcaster when the portion of shares held by private citizens was turned over to KBS. Thus KBS has a strong interest in MBC. MBC-Seoul has 19 local affiliate stations linked to the key facility in Seoul through 76 relaying and transmission outlets. In addition, MBC operates one television channel, one AM radio channel, and one FM outlet. In early 1986 the MBC-TV network covered 87 percent of Korea and MBC-FM covered 86 percent. With 70 more transmission stations scheduled to be put in operation, MBC intends to cover more than 90 percent of the nation. MBC receives its revenue from radio and television advertising fees, which amounted to $104 million (U.S.) in 1984. One-fifth of the funds are spent for public service projects initiated by MBC.

The Christian Broadcasting System is a missionary radio network with its key station in Seoul and four local outlets dispersed in the nation. CBS is a juridical foundation whose board members consist of delegates sent by the major Protestant denominations and other social dignitaries selected by the board of directors. The major source of revenue is from donations plus a subsidy from the government.

The FEBC and the Asia Broadcasting Station are juridical foundations with eleven board members each. The two radio stations are under a joint operation. Board directors for both stations consist of two types of persons: Protestant ministers and influential Christian businessmen. The FEBC and the Asia Broadcasting Station are supported financially by the Far East Broadcasting Company, an evangelical foundation.

The Korean Broadcasting Advertising Corporation (KOBACO) is the exclusive sales agent of advertising for all of the broadcasting media in Korea. KOBACO's revenue comes from the commission fee paid by the broadcasting stations for sales service of all the advertisers. KOBACO provides financial support for various programs that fall into the broad fields of mass communication and art and culture. In addition, it funds such features as domestic and overseas training for mass communication professionals. By the end of 1983 KOBACO in its first three years had generated 56.8 billion Korean won ($71 million U.S.). The organization's activities are under the supervision of the minister of culture and information.

The advertising industry in South Korea is second only to Japan's in Asia, but its performance is hampered by the practice of in-house sponsorship and government regulation. One Korean observer notes that "advertising has always been regarded as a necessary evil, rather than a useful marketing tool." Advertising is regulated by law in terms of hours and numbers of commercials to be aired. Major regulations include are following:

1. Advertising is prohibited from taking more than 8 percent of the total hours of transmission.
2. Two blocs of commercials are allowed per hour, with each bloc consisting of up to three commercials and ninety seconds in the case of television and four blocs of commercials and eighty seconds for radio.
3. Identification or business cards are allowed up to six per hour, ten seconds each at the time of station identification and program announcement.

All orders for broadcast advertising are handled through KOBACO. Orders are placed either directly to KOBACO or through advertising agencies. As of September 1985 seven advertising agencies were recognized as bona fide companies in the case of television advertising, receiving commissions for their services through KOBACO. The unrecognized advertising agencies are not paid commissions. Broadcasting stations pay 20 percent commissions to KOBACO for television advertisements placed; KOBACO takes 13 percent and the remaining 7 percent is paid to the agency. In radio commercials, seven advertising agencies are recognized. The outfits are paid 8 percent commissions for radio commercials they place through KOBACO, with the remaining 12 percent commission being taken by KOBACO. For television and radio advertisements placed through unrecognized agencies or directly by advertisers, the 20 percent commissions go to KOBACO.

Commercial messages are carried by radio and television stations in a bloc system, by program sponsorship, and by the use of spots. KBS-TV 1 adopted the bloc system prevailing in some Western European nations and has two blocs on weekdays, four blocs on Saturdays, and six blocs on Sundays, each bloc not exceeding five minutes. KBS-TV 2 and MBC-TV accept both program sponsorship and spots. KBS-Radio 1, Radio 2, and Radio Seoul, and MBC's Radio and FM accept commercial messages in program sponsorship and spots. KBS-FM 1 and 2 air no commercials.

As of September 1985 there were nineteen universities and colleges that had communication or journalism departments. Of these, nine offered master's degree programs, and eight of the nine offered doctoral programs. In addition, a professional graduate school of communication offered its master's program mostly for those already working on newspapers and in broadcasting. Several other professional graduate schools offered master's programs for communication majors along with other academic concentrations.

Almost all educational institutions have their own wired broadcasting facilities on a small scale, mostly radio outlets, for practice and campus broadcasting. Students interested in the media join clubs, and some of them, whose academic areas include humanities, social sciences, and natural sciences, pass the employment examinations.

Training programs for broadcasters also are organized by the networks and the press institute. KBS, for example, provides midcareer training courses for all employees at least once every five years and special offerings for those in art work, engineering, and other sections.

PROGRAMMING

Programming comes under the Basic Press Law rules, which stipulate that features shall be programmed in a balanced manner among the fields of politics, economy, society, and culture, and there shall be a proper balance and harmony among the various kinds of programs (article 41, Programming for Broadcast). Under the Implementation Decree of the law, 10 percent or more of the weekly broadcasting hours are to be for news reporting, 40 percent or more for general education, and 20 percent or more for entertainment (article 29, Criteria of Programming). The minister of culture and public information in 1984 called on Korean broadcasters to promote the "great cohesion of the nation" and encouraged them to promote the "integration and reaffirmation of the identity of Koreans."

In this regard, programming trends in the second half of the 1980s focus on Korean culture, history, and learning from other nations. The two major broadcasting networks have gone to considerable efforts to draw out traditional culture in various aspects of life and produce features to assist the people to realize who they really are and to enhance their sense of self-identity. Korean history has been reinterpreted from a Korean perspective in various offerings to correct the distorted interpretations made by the Japanese before 1945 from their colonialist perspective. The third major trend is to use documentaries to show the Korean people what can be learned from successes in other countries so that Korea can survive in a competitive world. These programs cover management, technology, and foreign trade.

Under the regulatory guidelines, KBS sets its program policies for fuller news coverage, more features for family viewing, and strengthening of offerings for major audience segments. Other policies are for more forum programs to gain better audience feedback. A special effort is being undertaken to familiarize the people with sports in preparation for the 1988 Summer Olympic Games.

KBS eloquently demonstrated how powerful, how influential, and how useful a television network could be through its campaign for family reunion. It is estimated that during the Korean War over 10 million people became separated from loved ones. The reunion campaign started on June 30, 1983, and was initially intended as a three-hour special but soon developed into a telethon. Millions of Koreans watched the program hour after hour and day after day, with tears in their eyes, so moved were they whenever a family reunion took place after almost thirty years of separation. The televised campaign ended on November 14, 1984. In recognition of the success, KBS was named "Ad Honorem" Gold Mercury International for the Campaign for the Reunion of War-separated Families.

Television programming includes game shows, music programs, and drama. MBC is the leader in dramas, but KBS surpasses MBC in content in most other program areas because of its more advanced facilities. Dramas are the favorite type of feature. In fact, MBC's "Love and Truth" maintained a 60 percent average rating, which is double the average rating for a dramatic series. The program went contrary to most dramatic programs by focusing on the well-to-do instead of the usual working-class themes.

All television and radio programs are planned, organized, and produced by broadcasting station personnel, except for one ten-minute television program for the armed forces, which is broadcast once a week by KBS-TV and MBC-TV, and seven fifty-five–minute radio programs for the military, aired seven days a week by KBS-Radio I and MBC-Radio. These features were produced by an agency within the Defense Ministry.

KBS-TV 1 (VHF) places strong emphasis on information and education, and KBS-TV 2 (VHF) primarily serves regional communities with information and entertainment. KBS-TV 3 (UHF) is an educational service for students at all levels and the general public, with programs designed to supplement school curricula and provide lifelong learning. The three television services together are on the air an average of 44 hours daily.

KBS-Radio 1 (AM) provides general service for 22 hours daily. Its programming ration is 25.6 percent for news and commentary, 58.3 percent for educational programs, and 16.1 percent for entertainment. Radio 2 (AM) goes on the air for 22 hours daily with an emphasis on entertainment for youth. Its program ratio is 14.8 percent for news and commentary, 43.6 percent for educational programs, and 41.6 percent for entertainment. Radio Seoul (AM) provides news-oriented features for listeners in the capital city and suburbs. Its ratio is 49 percent for education, 36.1 percent for news and commentary, and 14.9 percent for entertainment.

Radio Korea serves overseas audiences with programs in eleven languages on sixteen shortwave frequencies, for an aggregate total of 106.5 hours a week. The languages used are Korean, Russian, Portuguese, and Spanish. The areas served are Southeast Asia, the Middle East, Africa, Europe, North America, the Asian mainland, and Oceania.

In late 1985 the total weekly broadcasting time for the MBC-TV was 89 hours, of which its local affiliates took 10.3 percent for their own features. News programming was 18.96 percent of the weekly airtime, cultural programs 57.3 percent, and entertainment programs 23.74 percent.

The MBC-AM radio airs 54 hours per week, devoting 51.2 percent of its airtime to cultural programs, 32.4 percent to entertainment, and 16.4 percent to news and commentary. The MBC-FM radio airs 147 hours per week, with 56.5 percent of its broadcast time devoted to cultural programs and 43.5 percent to entertainment.

Up to the end of 1980 CBS transmitted evangelical programs, news and commentaries, cultural and educational fare, music, and entertainment. At that time CBS operated under a limited commercial license granted by the government, permitting sponsors for no more than 30 percent of the program hours. But with the rearrangement of the broadcasting system in late 1980, CBS stopped all news programs and commercials, confining programs to religion and music. As of September 1985 CBS transmitted 21 hours a day, devoting 71.5 percent of its airtime to evangelical programs, 19 percent to music programs, and 9.5 percent to general education. Its listening area includes most of South Korea and parts of North Korea and Manchuria.

The Far East Broadcasting Company (FEBC) and the Asia Broadcasting Station are missionary radio stations whose aim is to bring the Gospel to the regions of such Asian Communist countries as Russia, China, and North Korea. The FEBC broadcasts 18.5 hours a day in four languages—Russian, Chinese, English, and Korean. The Asia Broadcasting Station goes on the air 10.5 hours daily in five languages, including the four mentioned above plus Japanese.

As the nation's economy expands and the broadcasting networks become more secure financially, there is a growing tendency in television reporting toward more extensive, more in-depth, and more well thought-out coverage appropriate to the medium. International developments are being covered more fully in both news and feature formats as they affect Korea. Against the backdrop of rising social problems in the process of industrialization, television has started focusing attention on these issues.

KBS-TV 1 and MBC-TV both air their forty-five-minute news programs at 9:00 P.M. KBS-TV 1 has a fifty-five-minute news program at 7:00 A.M. When TV 1 and TV 2 are combined, KBS airs five- and ten-minute news bulletins almost every hour. The same situation prevails at MBC. The proportion of news programs weekly is 25.9 percent for KBS-TV 1, 3.3 percent for TV 2, 4.5 percent for TV 3, and 19 percent for MBC-TV. The main radio programs are at 8:00 A.M., 12 noon, and 7:00 and 9:00 P.M. KBS-Radio 1 assigns 23.2 percent of its weekly airtime to news, Radio 2 14.9 percent, Radio Seoul 38.4 percent, and MBC-Radio 16 percent.

Children's programs enjoy regular coverage over the networks. KBS-TV 2 and MBC-TV air a program for preschool children early on weekday mornings, and TV 1 and TV 2 and MBC-TV transmit programs for elementary school children early on weekday evenings consisting of drama, film, and cartoon series, domestically produced and imported.

KBS-Radio 1 has almost an hour of programs for children early weekday evenings, including news, dramas, and other features. KBS-Radio FM 1 has a thirty-minute music feature for children each day early in the evening. MBC's AM Radio has a thirty-minute program early in the evening, Monday through Saturday.

Educational Radio (UHF) airs general education, language, and correspondence courses appropriate for high school and college students. Its programming ratio is 62.7 percent for adult education programs, 28.2 percent for school features, and 7 percent for general cultural fare. The total daily broadcast time for language instruction (English, French, German, Chinese, Spanish, and Japanese) is four hours. Radio correspondence courses for college students are aired seven hours a day from Monday through Saturday and nine hours on Sunday.

BROADCAST REFORM

The nation's opposition forces and activist students claim that broadcasting has favored the ruling power and urge that the medium must fight for greater freedom from government control. In an ongoing controversy, television is singled out by the opposition parties and groups for its progovernment leanings in politics-related coverage. In a recent political campaign opposition party leaders claimed that both networks denied them access during the election. Also during the campaign the president of KBS was charged in a lawsuit filed by the opposition party leaders with using KBS in support of the ruling party. Shortly thereafter, the president of KBS was appointed as minister of culture and information. Consequently, in political reporting television remains under strong criticism from the opposition parties and groups for its progovernment slant.

In addition to political criticism and charges of favoritism, there is growing concern over programming. In fact, there is a continuing controversy over the influence of television on young adults. According to some Korean scholars, television could incline youths toward the cultural goals of Korea and away from criminal activities, while others say that since the medium is a major agent of socialization, it could lead to deviant behavior.

In this regard, the government has become an active agent of reform. It instituted a clean-up campaign by banning 172 periodicals it described as "lewd" and causing "social decay and juvenile delinquency." At the same time, the government ordered an end to broadcasting of "decadent" programs, leading to the elimination of soap operas, comedies, and song-and-dance features on television.

Finally, there has been mounting criticism against advertising liquor and medicine on television. In response, the two television networks run the liquor commercials late in the evening.

NEW TECHNOLOGIES

Korea has moved on many fronts to upgrade broadcast technologies over the past several years, with special emphasis for coverage of the 1988 Summer Olympic Games. The Seoul Olympic Radio and Television Organization was formed for the 1986 Asia Games and the 1988 Olympics, and an estimated 149.1 billion won was expected to be spent on Olympics-related communication, including broadcast relay facilities, post offices, and other services.

In preparation for the Olympics a number of developments have already taken place. In 1980 the NTSC-M color system replaced the old monochrome one, and MBC in 1982 opened a news broadcasting center with four color studios, including one that seats 650 people. KBS installed fifty Pye TVT television transmitters and also purchased a microwave distribution network. Plans were under way to offer an advanced television system to viewers in Seoul during the Olympics, with hotel reservation information, downtown traffic conditions, weather, and Olympic schedules. Mobile earth stations were also under consideration as well as electronic mail, video conferencing, videotext, and teletext systems.

As of September 1986 three earth stations were in operation, connecting Korea with the rest of the world through the Intelsat satellites over the Pacific, Indian, and Atlantic Oceans. Discussions and studies have been ongoing for several years about a domestic Korean satellite in a stationary orbit. The Korea Industrial Development Institute recommended a satellite by the 1988 games instead of continuing improvement of ground communications. In 1984 the president suggested a launch date for the mid–1990s and concentration on existing technologies until then.

During the discussion over satellite communications, other technological developments proceeded apace. For example, television's multichannel sound system (stereo system or one speaker for the Korean language, another for a different language) was adopted by the government. In addition, VCRs continue to sell well. By the end of 1985 an estimated one million households will have their own VCRs. This is expected to affect patterns of television viewing, which, in turn, will affect patterns of broadcast programming.

BROADCASTING IN NORTH KOREA

Information about broadcasting in North Korea is difficult to obtain and confirm, as well as often years out of date. There is no certainty, but it seems likely that broadcasting is on a limited scale, although there is a vigorous external broadcasting service in Radio Pyongyang, the main radio broadcasting station in North Korea. Radio Pyongyang has a formal format of revolutionary music and news.

Broadcasting is an integral part of the government, as in most Communist nations, and is designed to indoctrinate the masses with the party's belief. The Central Broadcasting Committee of the State Administration Council, which is under the control of the cabinet, oversees the medium. Administration is also shared by the North Korean Workers' party. Broadcasting is further divided along provincial and county lines, where different committees control each division.

At the end of 1981 Radio Pyongyang broadcast in eight languages (Korean, Japanese, English, French, Russian, Spanish, Arabic, and Kuoyo) for an aggregate of 590 hours. North Korea operates the sixth-leading external broadcast service in the world in terms of airtime. The "Voice of the Revolutionary Party for Reunification" broadcasts Korean affairs for more than 65 hours a week. Its main aim is to unify the divided nation under the Marxist-Leninist theory of government.

North Korea operated seven mediumwave and twelve shortwave transmitters as of 1982. Programs are broadcast through loudspeakers into factories and large open areas in North Korean towns. Moreover, a beginning television network is in operation, but there is little information on it.

CONCLUSION/FORECAST

In 1986 a bill was introduced in the National Assembly in South Korea to allow private persons to set up and operate CATV systems. This would provide more diversified television channels for the general public. The government plan calls for a start of CATV operation before the 1988 Summer Olympic Games.

There is also a strong prospect that outside commercial producers will be allowed to make some programs such as drama for broadcasting, instead of having the networks produce all their programs. This policy shift, if it comes, is likely before the Olympics, and can be seen as an easing of government control on mass communications.

Another important development is likely to be an increasing emphasis on the information function of broadcasting, with a de-emphasis on the entertainment function. One of the challenges facing those engaged in broadcasting is how to make programs of an educational nature entertaining as well.

BIBLIOGRAPHY

An, Tai Sung. *North Korea: A Political Handbook.* Wilmington, Del.: Scholarly Resources, 1983.

Browne, Donald R. *International Radio Broadcasting: The Limits of the Limitless Medium.* New York: Praeger, 1982.

Hahn, Bae-ho. *Communication Policies in the Republic of Korea.* Paris: UNESCO, 1978.

Head, Sydney. *World Broadcasting Systems: A Comparative Analysis.* Belmont, Cal.: Wadsworth, 1985.

Korea. Broadcasting Commission. *KBC KBDC.* Seoul: KBC, 1985.

Korean Press Institute. *Korean Press Annual, 1985* (in Korean). Seoul: Korean Press Institute, 1985.

Kurian, George T., ed. *World Press Encyclopedia.* New York: Facts on File, 1982.

Lent, John A., ed. *Broadcasting in Asia and the Pacific.* Philadelphia: Temple University Press, 1978.

Martin, L. John, and Anju Grover Chaudhay, eds. *Comparative Mass Media Systems.* New York: Longmans, 1983.

Munhwa Broadcasting Corporation. *Munhwa Broadcasting Corporation Yearbook, 1985* (in Korean). Seoul: Munhwa Broadcasting Corporation, 1985.

"South Korea Press." *Far Eastern Economic Review*, August 22, 1985, 23–30.

Additional information may be found in issues of *Asian Broadcasting, Asian Survey*, and *Korea News Review*.

MEXICO

Marvin Alisky

HISTORY

Daily radio broadcasting came to Mexico over six decades ago. In 1917, Constantino de Tárnava of Monterrey and a handful of other Mexican engineers in northern Mexico established the republic's first amateur radio stations. By 1919 radio hobbyists Juan Buchanan and Jorge Peredo in Mexico City were operating their radio transmitters four or five nights a week, despite the continued fighting of the Mexican Revolution during 1910 to 1920.

The distinction between radiotelephony and radio broadcasting should be noted. Radiotelephony, which preceded broadcasting, had its beginning when governmental and amateur experimenters launched point-to-point communications with other operators, without mass audience involvement in the transmissions. That is to say, sounds were transmitted through the air from transmitter to receivers, constituting telephone conversations without telephone lines.

Broadcasting really began when stations started to plan regularly scheduled programs that would entertain or inform large numbers of people at the same time, albeit the early audiences for commercial radio in Mexico totaled only 500 to 1,000 listeners at any given hour. In essence, person-to-person transmissions gave way to broadcasting to mass audiences.

On October 9, 1921, Tárnava in Monterrey launched station TND 24-A, which he converted from an amateur experimental station into commercial radio outlet CYO in November 1923. Another pioneer radio station, CYB, today called XEB, in Mexico City became the second commercial facility to go on the air seven days a week. XEH and XEB brought daily broadcasting to Mexico. (When an international conference in Madrid in

1931 created standardized call letters among most nations of the world, Mexican outlets all began to identify themselves with the letters beginning with XE, and CYO became XEH.)

By late 1922 Mexican listeners were also able to tune in Spanish-language programs from powerful Cuban and Puerto Rican transmitters. In fact, in newspaper advertisements in Mexico City, retail stores were citing the early growth of daily commercial radio service in various Latin American republics. These advertisements also pushed sales of receivers inside Mexico by reminding readers that if they did not have receivers that could pick up shortwave broadcasts from South America, they could purchase low-priced sets to pick up standard-band programs from the neighboring United States, especially the programs from the clear-channel 50,000-watt stations in California, Texas, Louisiana, Florida, Illinois, Ohio, Kansas, and New York.

From March to June 1923 broadcasters in Mexico exerted considerable pressure on federal officials to license stations. Finally, the president of the republic, Alvaro Obregón, ordered the secretary of communications to formally license broadcasters, resulting in the first license for a commercial station to be issued to El Bueno Tono cigarette company to operate XEB. Shortly thereafter, other outlets were licensed by the government.

Television came to Mexico in 1950. On August 31 XHTV Channel 4 in Mexico City aired the first telecast in Latin America. The next morning Channel 4 aired the annual state of the union address of Mexican president Miguel Alemán. Given the positioning of receivers in various public locations, these initial efforts reached an audience estimated at around 200,000 viewers.

REGULATION

Mexico's fundamental legal basis for licensing and regulating broadcasting springs from the Federal Law of Radio and Television (LFRT, Ley Federal de la Radio y la Televisión) of 1960, as amended in 1969, 1975, 1978, and 1985. Article 4 of the LFRT proclaims: "Radio and Television constitute an activity of public interest; therefore, the State must protect the activity and will be obligated to be vigilant towards the required social function compliance." Article 5 of the LFRT provides four specific guidelines for broadcasters:

1. Affirm respect for moral principles, human dignity, and family relationships.
2. Prevent negative disturbances for the harmonious development of children and youth.
3. Contribute to the raising of the cultural level of the people, conserving national characteristics, customs of the nation, and traditions and exalting the values of Mexican nationality.

4. Fortify democratic convictions, national unity, and international friendship and cooperation.

Officers of the Inter-American Broadcasters Association in recent years have stated that they consider the fundamental goals of this Mexican law regulating broadcasting to be the most idealistic preamble of any communications law in the Western Hemisphere.

In addition, the law further stipulates that only Mexican citizens who can prove financial solvency may apply for a license for a commercial station. Moreover, only legally recognized educational institutions or government units may apply for a cultural outlet.

Licenses for radio and television stations are issued for periods of five years, with renewals invariably automatic. Since 1934 not one broadcasting license has been permanently revoked, though several outlets have been suspended from broadcasting for brief periods of time for violating operating regulations. Unofficially, some corporate owners have been pressured into selling their facilities to new broadcasters. For example, in 1942 radio station XEG in Monterrey continued to sell airtime for daily news commentaries by a spokesman for Nazi Germany after the Mexican government had declared war on the Axis. In these circumstances, the minister of internal affairs jailed the commentator for subversion and forced the sale of the station to new owners.

Not surprisingly, the Internal Affairs Ministry has played an active role in regulating broadcast content. For example, during the 1964 municipal political campaign in the state of Yucatán, a scheduled radio speech by an opposition candidate was ordered canceled by the government in Mexico City. In 1966 in Morelia, capital of the state of Michoacán, five radio stations aired detailed reports of student riots despite warnings from federal officials that publicizing disturbances violated the law. Consequently, these stations had to suspend operations and pay a fine.

In 1969 state involvement in program content was formally recognized by an amendment to the LFRT directing the government to convene a special commission to determine the best utilization of public service messages from the authorities that all radio and television stations must transmit. Composed of representatives from the ministers of *gobernacion*, finance and public credit, public education, health and welfare, and communications and transportation, the commission can demand up to 12.5 percent of all airtime from broadcasting stations and networks throughout Mexico. This airtime, calculated in pesos at the standard rates for advertisers, is considered payment in lieu of taxes for broadcasters added on to the normal corporate and income taxes.

In practice, the government does not ask any network or station for the full 12.5 percent of its airtime; there is no need to do so. Commercial news programs usually include any important announcements the government wants circulated plus features supportive of major policies. For example, radio and television have consistently produced and broadcast programs encouraging mass support for the government's policies on slowing down Mexico's population explosion. These features, including soap operas, talk shows, and spot announcements, can be heard throughout the broadcast day across Mexico.

ECONOMIC STRUCTURE

Many broadcasting stations and networks in Mexico are privately owned, but the state operates its own facilities as well. In addition, the state produces radio and television programs for airing on private commercial outlets.

From the 1920s to the 1950s noncommercial outlets were few in number. On July 18, 1924, the Ministry of Public Education received its authorization to open its studios in the ministry's building, and on November 29, 1924, educational station CZE went on the air. It changed its call letters to XFX in 1928, and to XEDP plus a shortwave counterpart, XEXA, in 1937. By the 1940s the National University's station, XEUN, a 5,000-watt outlet, plus shortwave duplicator XEYU, served Mexico City and its environs. In addition, for brief periods of time throughout these years the Ministries of Defense, the Navy, and Agriculture each maintained a radio station.

From 1938 to 1942 the dominant political party, now called the Institutional Revolutionary party (PRI or Partido Revolucionario Institucional) managed station XEFO, which was technically licensed to the president's press department. By 1953 several state and municipal governments had experimented with operating radio outlets.

In the late 1970s the federal government funded television and radio stations for several universities and directly operated a nationwide television network. In addition, the government directly produced taped radio series for distribution over commercial outlets. In 1981 the corporation Televisa, the holding company for Mexico's four commercial television networks— Channels 2, 4, 5, and 8—negotiated with the government to turn the Channel 8 network into a cultural chain, shift it to a Channel 9 network, and let the new entity carry all the public service announcements and government programs.

In April 1985 the LFRT was amended, creating a public noncommercial holding company paralleling Televisa, to be called Imevisión. As a result of this action, the republic has all educational, cultural, governmental, and any other noncommercial television administered by Imevisión. The new concern has four nationwide government networks: Channels 7, 11, 13, and 22. In addition to the commercial and government broadcasters, in the major metropolitan areas of Mexico five cable networks supply programs from the United States (ABC, CBS, NBC, PBS, and Movie Channel), and one Mexican cable company, Cine, airs motion pictures produced in Mexico, Spain, and Argentina as well as films from Brazil, Italy, and France with a sound track dubbed into Spanish.

In contrast to government broadcasters and noncommercial concerns, wealthy Mexican entrepreneurs have been central to privately owned broadcasting stations and networks in Mexico. Emilio Azcárraga, Sr., inaugurated radio station XEW on September 18, 1930. Shortly thereafter, he built Mexico's first nationwide network by connecting this Mexico City outlet to provincial affiliates plus powerful repeater transmitters and shortwave duplicators. The XEW network became and has remained the most popular source of radio programming not only for the republic of Mexico but also for many listeners in northern Guatemala and the Spanish-speaking areas along the U.S. borderlands.

Azcárraga's older brothers had launched CYL, one of Mexico's first radio stations, in 1923. Luís and Raúl Azcárraga were the owners of the pioneer chain of retail stores selling receivers in Mexico, La Casa del Radio. After Emilio died, his oldest son, Emilio, Jr., and investors in a large family-controlled corporation continued to be involved not only with XEW but also with the Televisa Corporation. In an interview in 1952 Emilio, Sr., stressed that broadcast advertising had helped lift Mexico's economy out of the doldrums of the economic depression of the 1930s by stimulating retail sales for Mexican-made products. In the 1970s administrators of the Azcárraga organization expressed the same enthusiasm for television advertising.

Azcárraga production entities expanded news and musical programs on the XEW network while developing daily serialized dramas or soap operas on their other pioneer radio network affiliated with XEQ in Mexico City. By the 1950s rival radio networks, RPM or Radio Programas de México and RCN or Radio Cadena Nacional, were concentrating on soap operas. In the 1970s Mexican television began to expand its video serialized dramas at the same pace it had with radio in the period 1935 to 1960. Interestingly enough, during the 1970s and 1980s Mexican radio has become highly specialized, with FM outlets providing rock, popular, and country music and AM facilities concentrating on folk music, sports, news, and talk shows.

Financier E. Guillermo Salas, noted for his work with the Anglo-Mexican Cultural Institutes, for which Queen Elizabeth bestowed on him knightly honors in London, from the 1950s to the 1970s pushed Radio Mil (Radio One Thousand) into a multistation complex in Mexico City. Since there are no restrictions regarding station ownership or market concentration in Mexico, Salas acquired a host of outlets in the Mexico City metropolitan area. Focusing on specific program areas such as jazz or folk music, his stations dominate the market.

In 1950 Rómulo O'Farrill, Sr., chief stockholder in the corporation that publishes the Mexico City daily newspaper *Novedades* and its English-language affiliate the *News*, established Mexico's first television station, XHTV Channel 4. Like the Azcárraga family of broadcasting investors, the O'Farrill family has been involved in the automobile business as well as various trade and professional magazines. In 1951 electrical engineer and electronics researcher Guillermo González Camarena established the third television station in Mexico, Channel 5, after Emilio Azcárraga, Sr., had put XEW-TV on the air as the second outlet.

On January 8, 1973, the government devised a holding corporation, Televisa, with an umbrella ownership of commercial Channels 2, 4, 5 and their respective nationwide networks, plus Channel 8, whose ownership was private with the government a minority stockholder. Thus since 1973 the rival Azcárraga and O'Farrill families have found themselves associated in the umbrella corporation Televisa.

One other factor affecting the economic structure of broadcasting in Mexico is unionism. In Mexico the government requires both labor and management to be organized industrywide. On January 30, 1986, the Union of Radio and Television Employees, the industrywide trade union representing both the performing and technical employees of the Mexican broadcasting industry, signed an agreement with its employers, the station and network managements represented collectively through their mandatory membership in the National Chamber of Radio and Television Broadcasters. The 1986 agreement recognized that Mexico has been suffering a rate of 50 to 60 percent inflation in recent years. In the 1986 contract, a historic document in the Mexican broadcasting industry, the union for the first time agreed to a pay increase less than anticipated inflationary increases. The alternative might have been large-scale layoffs among broadcast employees.

Training has kept pace with other developments in Mexican broadcasting. As early as 1952 the National University of Mexico began offering a degree in journalism. Heretofore, a few schools had offered training for newspaper work at a vocational high school level. In addition, a few university-level courses are available in other educational institutions in Mexico City and in seven provincial cities at universities, institutes, and trade schools.

According to the union of broadcast employees, a majority of television technical personnel handling cameras, control panels, lighting, and other basic elements of production have at least a twelfth-grade education, and a sizeable minority of them have at least two years of university training.

Broadcast journalists in Mexico still tend to enter radio and television work after apprenticing on the staff of a newspaper or magazine. Writers of drama and continuity range across a spectrum of training and experience from previous work in advertising agencies to menial positions in motion picture studios.

PROGRAMMING

As has been noted previously, as television grew bigger, traditional radio fare tended to shift more to music or formats of specialization, with some stations being the voice of sports or jazz or rock music or soap operas. In television, however, variety of programs has remained a mainstay. Each station and network tries to reach various groups with diversified program formats.

Beginning in 1976, the government's Radio and Television Cinema Bureau has produced various children's program series and furnished them to commercial television networks. The bureau has also provided sports reports, book-review panels, weekly dramas, home economics shows, medical and health programs, documentary series on Mexican history, and a host of science features.

Still offered are television and radio programs originating in the 1940s teaching adult literacy. Since 1971 every radio station in Mexico has devoted a thirty-minute program to teaching literacy to adults who dropped out of primary school or who never attended school. The Mexican Radio Institute coordinates contributions of the Ministry of Public Education, the Radio and Television Cinema Bureau, and the programming staff of Imevisión networks. The latter staffers are involved because some radio literacy programs are adapted for noncommercial television networks.

Mexico is the only non-Communist republic in Latin America prohibiting religious programming. Communist Cuba and Marxist Sandinista Nicaragua do not allow religious themes in broadcasting because of Marxist opposition to organized religion. But Mexico presents a special case.

While 90 percent of the population is formally affiliated with the Roman Catholic church, in practice one Mexican in three never attends church, not even for such pivotal events as weddings, funerals, or Christmas or Easter services. A projected image of bishops and archbishops as enemies of democracy began during the struggle for independence from Spain. It was reinforced during the monarchy of Archduke Maximilian, whose government was imposed on Mexico by the force of a French army of occupation but supported by the Catholic church. During the thirty-five-year dictatorship of Porfirio Díaz, the church once again received special privileges, putting the hierarchy for the third time at odds with the public in general. The Mexican Revolution began in 1910 and fighting ended in 1920, but continuing social reforms were designated by capitalizing the word "Revolution" to indicate an ongoing set of reform policies. One of those, strict separation of church and state, reflects itself in the Mexican law by forbidding priests and nuns to appear in public in clerical garb and to broadcast even innocuous statements on radio or television. In fact, only the visit of Pope John Paul II brought Catholic pageantry to prime-time television as a world-class news event.

Politically, every facet of the spectrum from Communist left to Fascist right has been covered in news reports periodically. As for formal campaigns for office, individual candidates cannot purchase or receive free airtime. Instead, the government allots blocs of time to the eight political parties certified to be on the ballot for federal, state, and municipal offices. Preceding each general election, the government matches parties, two or four at a time, for panels or roundtables or with half-hour programs allowing each party spokesperson a few minutes on radio and television.

Broadcasting fails to develop programs for all groups in Mexican society, however. Mexico's minority of Indians who understand only Náhuatl (Aztec), Maya, Zapotec, Mixtec, Yaqui, Tarascan, and Tarahumara languages total 3 million out of a 1986 population estimated at 80 million. In other words, these Indians linguistically constitute only 3.7 percent of the total citizenry, though racially Mexico remains basically a mestizo (Spanish-Indian) or hybrid society. Mexicans of pure European origin make up no more than 15 percent of the total population, and approximately 10 million of the mestizos are ethnically Indian but Spanish speaking. Still, 3 million citizens are almost completely shut off from broadcasting, which is basically aired in Spanish. The Public Education Ministry, in cooperation with the National Indigenist Institute, furnishes only twenty-seven hours of radio programming weekly in three languages (Náhuatl, Maya, and Zapotec) disseminated over regional radio networks in the states of Yucatán, Oaxaca, Chiapas, Puebla, and Morelos. As for television, no regular programs are broadcast in any Indian language, though special features and miniseries of four to six programs of a basic educational nature have been aired from time to time.

NEW TECHNOLOGIES

Antenas parabolicas or satellite communications dishes are multiplying rapidly in Mexico's metropolitan regions. The largest private corporation supplying the rooftop receivers of microwave, fiber-optic, and other advanced transmissions is Orbicom, Inc. This company assists customers, whether businesses or individuals, to arrange credit through the Banco de Comercio, the Banco Nacional de México, American Express, or Diners Club de Mexico. The Ministry of Communications and Transportation facilitates issuing permits for satellite dishes through a special office.

As noted earlier, cable networks in Mexico carry mostly programs from the United States, though one channel does air primarily old Mexican pictures originally produced to be shown in movie theaters.

CONCLUSION/FORECAST

Unlike any other Latin American republic, Mexico has a geographical position that invites both domestic and foreign competition involving the wealthiest broadcasting nation in the world, the United States. Along the 1,900-mile U.S.-Mexican border, Spanish-language radio stations from California and Arizona to New Mexico and Texas compete vigorously with radio stations inside the Mexican portion of the borderland. As for television, in Mexican border cities such as Tijuana, Mexicali, Nogales, Ciudad Juárez, Laredo, and Matamoros, Mexicans watch more U.S. programming than ever before. The U.S. programming comes from full-time Spanish-language television stations in Los Angeles and San Antonio, affiliates of the Spanish International Network (SIN). Affiliates in Phoenix and El Paso also add to the newer competitive factor of across-the-border viewing.

In Mexico the foreign competition centers very little in political pressures from rivals, albeit the Soviet Union maintains a daily barrage of shortwave programming beamed into Mexico; rather, the listening surveys indicate that Mexican listeners and viewers will turn their dials to what they like if the local offerings do not attract them. Competition is vibrant throughout the republic.

At the technical level, production standards in Mexican television during the past thirty years have steadily improved and now compare favorably with those found in nations with economies more developed than that of Mexico. Similarly, Mexican radio can boast of some of the best and worst radio production, similar to what a scholar might find when researching broadcasting systems in many other nations with the same gross national product.

What lies ahead for Mexican broadcasting? Mexico has entered a difficult period in its national life as a huge foreign debt, high annual inflation rates, and political corruption undermine the decades-old stability of the republic. In these circumstances, broadcasting can help ameliorate the challenge to political stability.

BIBLIOGRAPHY

Alisky, Marvin. "Early Mexican Broadcasting." *Hispanic American Historical Review* 34 (November 1954): 513–26.
————. *Latin American Media: Guidance and Censorship*. Ames: Iowa State University Press, 1981.
Alisky, Marvin, John C. Merrill, et al. *Global Journalism: A Survey of the World's Mass Media*. New York: Longmans, 1983.
Cremoux, Raúl. *La Televisión y el Alumno de Secundaria del Distrito Federal*. Mexico City: Centro de Estudios Educativos de Mexico, 1968.
De Noriega, Luis Antonio, and Frances Leach. *Broadcasting in Mexico*. Boston: Routledge and Kegan Paul, 1979.
Eoff, Pamela. "Television in Mexico." Master's thesis, University of Texas at Austin, 1978.
Esquivel Puerto, Emilio. *Anecdotario de Radio y Televisión*. Mexico City: Delgado Valero, 1970.

Lewels, Francisco J., Jr. *The Uses of the Media by the Chicano Movement.* New York: Praeger, 1974.

Mejía Prieto, Jorge. *Historia de la Radio y la Televisión en México.* Mexico City: Editores Asociados de Mexico, 1972.

Pierce, Robert N. *Keeping the Flame: Media and Government in Latin America.* New York: Hastings House, 1979.

Viya, Miko. *La Televisión y Yo.* Mexico City: Costa-Amic de Mexico, 1970.

NIGERIA

Joseph Kinner

HISTORY

Nineteen thirty-two was an eventful year in Nigerian history, for it was then that Nigeria began to tap the potentialities of modern mass communications. On December 19, 1932, the British Broadcasting Corporation launched the world's first regularly scheduled shortwave program service. This Empire Service from Daventry was intended to develop political, cultural, and economic links between Britain and the English-speaking peoples. When Lagos was selected as one of the overseas monitoring stations of the British Broadcasting Corporation, Nigeria became one of the first broadcasting-conscious African nations.

Next, the Posts and Telegraphs Department began to pipe programs rebroadcast by the BBC Empire Service to loudspeakers in subscribers' homes. This was known as the Radio Distribution Service (RDS). The inauguration of this service in Lagos on December 1, 1935, marked an important point in the history of radio broadcasting in Nigeria.

Further expansion of the service to other parts of the nation depended primarily on the financial resources of the government. A station was established in Ibadan in 1939. World War II slowed down progress, but expansion picked up again just before the end of the conflict. In 1944 another outlet opened in Kano. By 1950 stations operated in Enugu, Abeokuta, Zaria, Jos, Kaduna, Ijebu-Ode, Port Harcourt, and Calabar. In the early 1950s the government established additional stations in the urban areas of Warri, Katsina, Onitsha, Sokoto, and Maiduguri.

Radio broadcasting reached a new level of administrative and professional development with the creation of the Nigerian Broadcasting Service (NBS) in 1951. Although the NBS was part of the Department of Information, which held responsibility for writing and producing its news features, the NBS enjoyed a measure of autonomy. It organized its own administrative structure, hired its own staff, and produced its own programs. It also assumed control of all the provincial radio stations in various parts of the country.

During this time the NBS created three administrative divisions—the western, eastern, and northern regions. In each area the NBS created regional broadcasting facilities. The provincial broadcasting houses then came under the supervision of the appropriate regional unit of the NBS. The NBS in Lagos coordinated the functions of the regional outlets.

On April 1, 1957, the NBS became a corporation. The new entity, the Nigerian Broadcasting Corporation (NBC), provided a national program and a regional program in each region. Regional stations consolidated radio distribution services within their respective areas. Programs were transmitted in the major languages of the region, and the national program of the NBC was broadcast in English and the three main languages of the nation—Hausa, Ibo, and Yoruba.

In television, the Western Nigerian Television (WNTV) started broadcasting in October 1959. It was the first television station in Nigeria, and indeed in the whole of Africa.

Soon after Nigeria became independent from Great Britain on October 1, 1960, a second regional television station, the Eastern Nigerian Television (ENTV), went on the air. It was followed the next year by the northern region's own TV station (RKTV), broadcasting from Kaduna. Within two years of self-rule, all three Nigerian regions had their own television facilities, owned and controlled by the regional governments.

During the years of Nigerian independence, however, the nation's political, social, and economic structures have undergone remarkable change. These changes have had profound effects upon the broadcasting industry.

With the advent of military rule in 1966 and the subsequent creation of twelve states from the former three regions of Nigeria in 1967 there came a tremendous desire to expand broadcasting facilities in every state. The establishment of stations gathered momentum until 1976, when seven additional states were created in the nation. Efforts were then made to provide NBC outlets in all of the nineteen states. By 1978 this was achieved. It was at this point, however, that the government undertook a reorganization of broadcasting.

The military decree no. 24 of 1977 established the Nigerian Television Authority (NTA) as the only body in Nigeria empowered to undertake television broadcasting. All ten existing state-owned TV stations were immediately taken over by this agency. By government decree no. 8, February 1979, all state-owned radio stations were handed over to the respective state governments, and the Federal Radio Corporation of Nigeria (FRCN) was created.

During the civilian government (1979–83) the number and influence of state-owned stations increased tremendously. The federal government, however, found its own presence in the states diminishing, and in 1981 the FRCN returned to the nineteen states on mediumwave to re-establish its presence. This resulted in confusion throughout the broadcast industry. When the military assumed control at the end of 1983, it undertook a review of broadcasting. As a result of these deliberations, some stations were merged together and federal facilities were once again returned to the states.

As of 1986 the structure of the FRCN was based on a zoning of the nation, with headquarters at Ibadan, Kaduna, Enugu and the director general's office in Lagos coming together to form one directorate. The FRCN maintains a dynamic external service, Voice of Nigeria (VON), and broadcasts domestic programs in twelve Nigerian languages, while national features are provided in English as well. Each of the nineteen states has its own radio station; Radio Abuja, which commenced operation on the occasion of the twentieth anniversary of Nigeria's independence on October 1, 1980, continues to transmit from the territory of Abuja.

In 1986 Nigeria also had thirty-four television stations. Twenty-two of them were owned and controlled by the federal government's NTA and broadcast on VHF, while the remaining twelve were owned and controlled by individual state governments and broadcast on UHF.

REGULATION

Broadcasting in Nigeria is regulated at federal and state levels through government broadcast policies, employment, and funding as well as by broadcast and press laws. Other factors—economic, social, political, and cultural—limit access to the media and thereby constitute a form of control. To begin with, it is important to understand the administrative arrangement of broadcasting, both at the federal and state levels, for it is this structure that constitutes the human mechanism for regulating the system.

The Federal Radio Corporation of Nigeria (FRCN) is administered by the government through a board of directors. The board is responsible to the minister of information, under whose office the corporation is grouped with some other departments. The extent of government involvement is absolute because both the board and the chief executive (director general) are appointed by the minister.

The director general's office and headquarters have undergone reorganization with the creation of a new post of director of headquarters administration. Functioning from the office of the director general, this directorate looks after corporate affairs ranging from personnel matters to international relations on behalf of the director general. The director general, of course, makes the final decisions.

State-owned broadcasting stations in the country are headed by a general manager and operate through their boards of directors and boards of governors. The boards are appointed by governments. Members of these units interpret government policies the way they understand them.

Government policy on broadcasting is in the form of a statement of provisions, guidelines, and objectives. These act as a guiding light for those who plan news, features, and public entertainment programs. In the case of radio broadcasting, the policies are guided by the following objectives:

1. The provision of efficient broadcasting services to the entire people of the Federation of Nigeria based on national objectives and aspirations and to external audiences in accordance with Nigeria's foreign policy

2. The provision of professional and comprehensive coverage of Nigerian culture, the promotion of cultural growth through research, and the dissemination of the results of such research studies for the benefit of the public

3. The positive contribution to the development of the Nigerian society and the promotion of national unity by ensuring a balanced presentation of views from all parts of the country

4. To ensure the prompt delivery of accurate information to the people

5. To provide opportunities for the free, enlightened, and responsible discussion of important issues and to enhance useful two-way contact between the public and those in authority

6. The provision of special broadcasting services in the field of education and in all other areas where the national policy calls for special attention

7. To promote orderly and meaningful development of broadcasting in the nation through technical improvements, adequate staff training and development, and staff exchange with other nations

8. To promote research into various aspects of the communications media and their effects on the Nigerian society

9. To make every Nigerian feel proud of being Nigerian

Legislation of radio broadcasting comes through parliamentary procedure by legislative acts in times of civil governance or by decree during the military regime through the highest ruling body, the Armed Forces Ruling Council.

Radio broadcasting is structured and operated in accordance with necessary legal guidelines flexible enough to be adapted to changing times and circumstances. But professional service is without prejudice to any race, creed, or region. All the known safeguards against infringement of human rights are obeyed to the letter.

Similar to radio, the Nigerian Television Authority (NTA), the body responsible for operating the twenty-two federal government–owned stations, is headed by a director general (DG). The DG along with other members of the NTA governing board are appointed by the federal minister of information after prior consultations with the head of state. The authority derives its powers from decree no. 24 of 1977, which also puts it under the jurisdiction of the minister.

The NTA governing board is made up of persons with requisite experience in mass media, education, management, engineering, arts, and culture. There must also be a representative of the federal Ministry of Information on the board as well as one person representing women's organizations in Nigeria. As its name implies, the board governs the operations of all the stations in the network in accordance with the minister's directives and in concurrence with federal government broadcast policies and Nigeria's broadcast and press laws. There is a measured amount of autonomy, however, enjoyed by individual NTA stations.

Each of the outlets is headed by a general manager (GM) appointed by the authority. In the day-to-day running of the station, the GM is assisted by his management staff. Decisions based on the initiatives of the GM and his managers are allowed only within the confines of what the authority permits. For example, the NTA has determined that no more than 30 percent of all programs on any NTA station at any time may be foreign produced. It is left to the discretion of the GM to decide whether to broadcast 10, 20, 25, or 30 percent foreign programs.

For television and radio broadcasting, the federal Ministry of Communications regulates the issuance of transmitters and broadcast licenses. Although the 1979 constitution (parts of which have been suspended) allows individuals to operate TV or radio stations, no concern has yet been granted a license. In addition, no TV station is presently equipped with a transmitter powerful enough to broadcast to more than parts of five states at a time.

Like the NTA stations, state television outlets have to apply for a broadcast license from the federal government's Ministry of Communications, the same office that decides the strength of transmitters to be issued. Each of the twelve state-owned stations in Nigeria has an administrative structure similar to that of the federal government–owned NTA facilities. They are each headed by a general manager who is appointed by the state governor after consultation with the state's commissioner for information.

Each of the state stations has a board of directors similar to the NTA governing board. They are under the state Ministry of Information, Social Development, Youth, Sports, and Culture. The state commissioner for information and his permanent secretary supervise the operation of state facilities. These outlets are subject to the same broadcast and press laws of the land. In general, the degree of autonomy that state facilities might enjoy in their day-to-day affairs varies from station to station according to what freedom individual state governments allow. All flexibility is subject to the commissioner and the governor's magnanimity.

According to the statement of government objectives, the aim of television broadcasting is to promote the cultural, social, political, economic, and technological uplifting of the Nigerian people. Thus programs are designed, produced, or bought to fit in with the authorities' perception of these goals. While this statement of policy may seem lax and open to flexible interpretation, practitioners in reality exhibit a strong sense of self-censorship.

Providing more definite control and subject to stricter enforcement are the press and broadcast laws as well as the Nigerian television broadcasting and advertising code. These include the laws of libel, contempt of court, obscenity, and sedition. Others are the copyright laws and the Official Secrets Act.

The television code emphasizes the objectivity, impartiality, and balance in programming. It seeks to uphold moral values, social ideals, and legal decorum. The code forbids violence and cruelty on TV and favors high professional broadcast standards.

In addition, there are several codes meant to regulate the kind of advertisements that can be broadcast on television. In essence these rules are designed to protect young children and other susceptible individuals against misleading, dishonest, immoral, and superstitious advertisements.

One final, perhaps inadvertent regulation on television in Nigeria is the prohibitive cost of television sets. Because of government fiscal policy, which regards television as a luxury good and therefore attracting a high excise duty, the price of a black-and-white receiver is about twice the per capita annual income of the country, and that of a color set, about five times. This, as should be expected, has seriously limited the growth of sets and therefore access to television programming.

From the foregoing, it is clear that while government is not directly involved in daily station operations, it has a strong hold on the mechanisms that regulate the media. Indeed, government officials actually own broadcasting, appoint chief executives, formulate policy, and to a large extent fund broadcasting. Despite increasing demand for private participation in Nigerian broadcasting, the industry has remained in government control and will probably remain so for some time to come.

ECONOMIC STRUCTURE

All television and radio broadcasting stations are owned by the state or federal governments. The FRCN depends entirely on government subvention for its operations since by decree the FRCN is not to undertake commercial broadcasting. (The FRCN operated a commercial service before the national government encouraged the state stations to be exclusively involved in advertising. There has been a proposal before the corporation to re-establish its commercial service.) On the other hand, while all state government−owned radio stations in the country obtain a greater percentage of their finances from their respective governments, they also get additional revenue from commercial advertisements. Television stations are financed largely by state and federal subventions and partly by revenues from commercial advertising.

Although the governments of the federation have a strong voice in the running of the medium, the provisions, guidelines, and objectives establishing the FRCN indicate, among other things, that impartiality is preserved in that body in respect to matters of political or industrial controversy or current public policy debates.

The management structure allows for a central board of management with the director general as the chairperson, supported by zonal directors and the director of technical services. The headquarters, under the director general's office, is headed by a director while the entity formed by grouping Lagos, Ibadan, Enugu, and Kaduna zones has a director.

In 1987 the economic downswing resulting from plunging oil prices put a tremendous strain on broadcasting. It caused not only significant staff reductions, but a severe parts shortage as well. Since the government's biggest revenue earner is petroleum (90 percent of Nigeria's export revenue is derived from oil), the government has had no choice but to reduce expenditures in all areas, including broadcasting. Aside from reducing staff and budgets, broadcasters have focused on an unprecedented commercial advertising drive to offset falling oil prices. In short, there is renewed interest in advertising.

The FRCN operates a training school in Lagos for program-related matters as well as a technical and engineering training facility at Sogunle. Students from all over Nigeria—indeed from many parts of Africa—attend these schools. Graduates serve in broadcasting institutions throughout the nation. In addition to these efforts, several colleges and universities have departments of mass communications and journalism. Most of these offer advanced degrees or diploma courses. The NTA also operates a television college in Jos for news and production staff.

PROGRAMMING

In a general sense, there is a similarity in the programming policy of all broadcasting stations in Nigeria. As much as they can, broadcasters try to create or acquire programs that fit government policies.

Programs on television fall into three broad categories: public enlightenment, entertainment, and news and current affairs. In terms of program type, by far the most important section is public enlightenment. This includes all children's features and religious and educational programs. Also included here would be all women's programs. Most of the entertainment shows are musicals, comedies, and dramas. Others in this group would be operas and full-length TV films. The news and current affairs efforts encompass national and international news, sports, and documentaries.

While there are more program types within the public enlightenment section, the airtime allocated to these features comes in third behind entertainment and news and current affairs. While this may vary slightly from station to station, the percentage distribution is as follows: entertainment, 48 percent; news and current affairs, 36 percent; and public enlightenment, 16 percent. Sometimes the line that separates news and current affairs from public enlightenment features becomes so blurred that it is hard to distinguish between the categories.

In a typical week, every TV station will provide between thirty minutes and two hours of free airtime to the government for public affairs broadcasts. These features are classified as public enlightenment programs.

Electronic coverage of news on the national network is quite impressive, although the same cannot be said of coverage on the state facilities. Foreign news is monitored from the British Broadcasting Corporation, the Voice of America, and other international services as well as through subscriptions to Reuters, Associated Press, and the national News Agency of Nigeria (NAN).

It is important to note that independent private producers have emerged in Nigerian broadcasting. This is perhaps inevitable because of the difficulty in meeting the 70 percent production quota set by the government. In recent times, shortages of personnel, lack of spare parts for equipment, and the general dearth of funds to develop features have created the independent producer. The independent producer is funded by companies that sponsor such programs.

In a nation as large and diverse as Nigeria, the challenges posed at all levels of broadcasting are indeed great. The FRCN and the state-owned stations are responding to the challenge admirably, however, by airing programs in many of the indigenous languages spoken in the country. The FRCN broadcasts in twelve languages—Edo, Efik, Fulfulde, Hausa, Igala, Igbo, Izon, Kanuri, Nupe, Tiv, Urhobo, and Yoruba—to ensure that at least 85 percent of the population is covered by programs. The national program reflects the views and values of the Nigerian people and is designed to express the Nigerian personality through broadcasting. In addition, the government uses the broadcast media as a national forum to address vital issues. The current "War Against Indiscipline" (WAI) is a case in point. Appropriate jingles and slogans have been produced and broadcast; radio talk shows and discussions, drama sketches, and even religious features carry information to help the Nigerian people change their attitudes generally. This effort to inculcate the ideals of nationhood is yielding good results.

Programming also provides comprehensive and professional coverage of the indigenous culture. State-owned radio stations are in fact required to broadcast in local languages spoken in the states in which they operate. These facilities carry programs and news offerings in an average of forty-five Nigerian languages. Program materials include traditional music, news and current affairs, and talk shows.

Another key dimension of programming is the promotion of cultural growth through research. The results of research studies are propagated. As indicated in the objectives of broadcasting, the overriding theme is expected to reflect the federal character of the population and the nature of the society in programming to ensure accuracy, objectivity, and constructiveness.

Apart from domestic broadcasts, there is the Voice of Nigeria (VON), the external service of the FRCN. The first external service of Radio Nigeria was fully established in 1962. Today VON broadcasts to many parts of Europe, the Far East, East Africa, and other overseas nations in six languages—English, French, Hausa, Swahili, German, and Arabic. The objective of this unit is to project the culture and traditions of the Nigerian people.

BROADCAST REFORM

Broadcasting in Nigeria has seen many changes within its comparatively short span of existence. In an attempt at overall cohesiveness and to bring continuity to the broadcasting industry, many critics advocate a national policy on the media. They correctly point out that broadcasting is a dynamic rather than static process and requires financial support and planning to cope with worldwide technological developments. Those who advocate a national policy also argue for the creation of a national control agency for the industry. This body would regulate broadcast operations, establish standards, and monitor performance.

The most vocal reformers are calling for private ownership of the media. composed of academicians, practitioners, and entrepreneurs as well as some government employees, this group continues to advocate private enterprise.

NEW TECHNOLOGIES

Because of the oil crisis and a shortage of funds, not enough quality programs are being produced locally. While it is cheaper to buy quality foreign programs, the government policy does not allow TV stations to exceed the 30 percent limit. In these circumstances, for many of those who can afford it, the videocassette has become a substitute for television. In fact, the VCR trade has become big business in Nigeria. Rather than establish an independent program outfit, it seems more lucrative to create a video duplicating service. In such a situation of high demand, copyright enforcement is not just hard, it is almost futile. The high cost of VCR machines, however, has made this endeavor an elitist substitute for television.

In Nigeria, cable television is not presently being considered by the government and will not be for the foreseeable future. The nation, however, does enjoy satellite communications links with the rest of the world. The

Nigerian Telecommunications Corporation (NITEL) under the minister of communications was able to beam the Los Angeles Olympics in 1984 and the World Cup from Mexico in 1986 via satellite.

CONCLUSION/FORECAST

Broadcasting began in Nigeria in the early 1930s in response to a rapidly changing society, increasingly urban and industrial, to a political system in which there was increasing dissatisfaction with British colonial rule, and to altered perceptions of that society and its political and colonial government. As broadcasting developed in the urban areas in the 1940s and in the regions during the 1950s, its progress and programs reflected more the indigenous cultures and desires of Nigerians. By the time Nigeria became independent from Britain in 1960, Nigerians were in control of virtually all professional and administrative positions of broadcasting. With the appointment of Victor Badejo as director general in 1963 the Nigerianization of broadcasting was complete.

While there have been several changes in the nation's political, social, and economic structures since independence, government officials and professionals within the media have maintained a strong emphasis on educational and public programming in the local and regional areas as well as within the states and at the national level. In a country the size of Nigeria (356,700 square miles), with an estimated population of 100 million and great diversity of cultures and geography, this has not always been easy. The task of producing and disseminating programs in as many indigenous languages as possible has been and continues to be a great challenge to those in broadcasting.

As Nigeria plans for the future, those in government and in the communications industry look forward to domestic and external broadcasting playing an increasingly important role in the development of the nation. Financial resources will have to be made available or generated to assist in the continued growth and achievements of broadcasting, but given the support of the government and the high degree of professionalism in the industry, the future looks very bright.

In the present economic situation of Nigeria, the government is not likely to add to the existing number of television stations. Neither is the government likely to allow private ownership of the media in the near future. In view of the need to raise additional revenues, however, there is a possibility that the authorities will allow commercial broadcasting to return to the national network. In addition, it seems likely that as it becomes more difficult to produce local programs, more independent production companies may be seen providing fare for Nigerian television. In any event, the absence of a national broadcasting policy continues to hamper developments.

BIBLIOGRAPHY

Broadcasting Corporation of Oyo State. *BCOS Cadence for 1985: Data Analysis.* Ibadan: BCOS, 1985.

Chalmers, Tom. *Our Broadcasting Service.* Lagos: Crownbird Series, 1953.

Fasoro, Remingius. "Nigerian Television and International Relations, 1959–1979." Master's thesis, University of Ibadan, 1980.

Head, Sydney, ed. *Broadcasting in Africa: A Continental Survey of Radio and Television.* Philadelphia: Temple University Press, 1974.

Ikime, Obaro, ed. *20th Anniversary History of WNTV.* Ibadan: Heinemann, 1979.

Kinner, Joseph. "The Study of the Origins, Development and Role of Radio Broadcasting in Southern Nigeria, 1923–1951." Ph.D. diss., University of California, Los Angeles, 1979.

Ladele, Olu, et al. *History of the Nigerian Broadcasting Corporation.* Ibadan: Ibadan University Press, 1979.

Mackay, Ian. *Broadcasting in Nigeria.* Ibadan: Ibadan University Press, 1964.

Milton, E. C. *A Survey of the Technical Development of the Nigerian Broadcasting Service.* Lagos: NBS, 1955.

Mytton, Graham. *Mass Communication in Africa.* London: Edward Arnold Publishers, 1983.

Nigerian Yearbook. Lagos: Times Press, 1986.

Stein, Jay W. *Mass Media, Education, and a Better Society.* Chicago: Nelson Hall, 1979.

Uzodinma, Ifeyinwa B., ed. *NTA Handbook, 1981.* Lagos: Corporate Affairs Division, NTA, 1982.

PERU

Marvin Alisky

HISTORY

By 1922 daily radio broadcasting had become available in South America from Brazil and Argentina in 1920, to Chile and Venezuela in 1922. By then, Peruvians in Lima with shortwave receivers were tuning in nightly to these neighboring republics and to a few powerful transmitters from the United States.

In Lima, Peru's President Augusto B. Leguia ordered his minister of defense to inaugurate a shortwave radio station so that the army and the national police could communicate with those patrolling ports on the Pacific coast in the southern part of the republic. Aside from radiotelephony messages, the transmitter could then broadcast to a larger audience of fishermen and mining engineers the latest weather bulletins from meteorological stations. Thus on July 28, 1921, the centennial of the date in 1821 when Peru declared its independence from Spain, two radio transmitters went on the air, one in Lima and one in the provincial city of Ilo in southern Peru.

These two stations of Radio Nacional, today the name of the nationwide government network, by 1923 were supplementing bulletins about the weather with reports about agriculture and mining, but with little in the way of entertainment, except for brief periods of transmission of music followed by periods of silence. The two transmitters were on the air not more than four hours a day, from 5:00 to 6:00 A.M. and from 6:00 to 9:00 P.M.

On June 20, 1925, commercial radio station OAX in Lima started daily broadcasting in Peru to a mass audience. The inaugural program featured music, the poetry of Ricardo Palma, and a speech by the president of the republic.

In 1935 the state contracted with the Marconi Company to create the government's own radio network, Radio Nacional, adding to the two original part-time shortwave outlets several mediumwave or standard-band (AM) stations. Also in 1935 the government itself first attempted to produce full radio programs of fifteen-minute and half-hour formats.

Television developed much more slowly in Peru than elsewhere in South America. Introduced in 1958, it has been operated by government-owned stations or by stations with 51 percent government equity. From almost the very beginning, government ownership and control have characterized the medium.

REGULATION

In November 1971 the military government of President Juan Velasco by presidential decree, Law 19020, issued a new law of telecommunications. It permitted the government to expropriate 51 percent of all privately owned television stations and 25 percent of all privately owned radio outlets. This action was a case of overkill on the part of a government determined to control the media. The Locke audience survey in Peru from 1958 to 1971 had periodically shown that listeners were tuned more to the news programs of the government's Radio Nacional network. A 25 percent stock ownership leverage was simply unnecessary.

Similarly, the government had owned Channel 7 and its provincial network ever since video came to Peru in January 1958 when that Lima channel was launched atop the Ministry of Education building. Later, four commercial channels with corresponding networks went on the air. But in 1971, at the time of the government purchases, television news commentators were not employees of the stations but rather under contract to the sponsors of their programs. Ironically, most of those sponsors of news programs were government corporations. Again, the bureaucrats already had the mechanisms for influence and guidance of TV news without the posturing of quasi-expropriation.

After Conservative President Fernando Belaúnde was freely elected for a five-year term in 1980, his civilian administration, sympathetic to the private sector, unraveled the military era's socialism by decree. In 1985, Liberal Civilian Alan Garcia was elected president for the 1985 to 1990 term and continued the policy of his predecessor to keep government from interfering with Peruvian broadcasting. Accordingly, the current telecommunications law established a bureau within the Communications Ministry empowered to issue licenses to private companies. The national government retains control of the pioneer station in Peru, Channel 7 in Lima. Carlos Ausejo since 1984 has been chairman of the station's board of directors, chosen by the president of Peru from among subcabinet-level administrators from the Ministries of Communications, Interior, Finance, and Defense.

ECONOMIC STRUCTURE

The aforementioned Channel 7, like the other Lima television stations, anchors a network of provincial affiliates and a few satellite repeater transmitters, the latter originating not even a station-break identification but simply boosting the signal over the Andes Mountains to rural communities. (In the following paragraphs, discussion of the ownership of Lima's commercial TV stations indicates ownership also of each channel's small string of provincial affiliates.) With the greater Lima metropolitan area containing 5 million people in a republic whose total population is slightly under 20 million, Peru demographically must be considered for broadcasting purposes as a republic of a dozen cities plus a dozen towns strategic for their ocean port or lake front or mountain pass locations. Arequipa, the second-largest city in Peru, with half a million people, illustrates the concept that despite a total land area of 450,000 square miles (the size of Alaska or twice the size of Texas), demographically Peru is really big Lima, Arequipa, and ten other cities.

In Lima, Channel 2 is owned by a corporation headed by Bernardo Batiensky, Remigio Morales, son of Peruvian President Francisco Morales (in office 1975–80), and Luís Vargas Homes. Some 15 percent of its stock is also owned by the Televisa Corporation of Mexico. Channel 4 is owned by six partners, headed by Nicanor González, Mauricio Arbulu, and A. Umbert as company officers and senior partners. Channel 5 is owned and operated by Genaro, Héctor, and Manuel Delgado Parker. The three Delgado Parker relatives incorporated as a family enterprise. Channel 9 is owned and operated by a corporation whose principal stockholders and officials are Carlos Tizón Pacheco, Fernando Barco Saravia, and Julio Vera Gutiérrez.

The government has issued a permit for a licensed transmitter for Channel 11, formerly reserved as a cultural or educational channel, but now scheduled to become a commercial facility owned by Augusto Belmont. Channel 13 is owned jointly by the privately funded University of Lima and West German investors, along with principal Peruvian stockholders José Leon Barandarán and Guido Ventura. Channel 27 is Peru's only UHF outlet, serving only the Lima metropolitan area with subscription cable service, programming motion pictures.

PROGRAMMING

As noted earlier, the government's Radio Nacional has the largest radio audience for news. Privately owned radio stations in Lima that feature popular, folk, rock, and jazz music draw the largest audiences for entertainment. These are outlets "Radio Central," "Radio Miraflores," "Radio Excelsior," and "Radio Cronica." "Radio Inca" and "Radio Central" continue to air various soap operas, though some of the daily serialized dramas formerly aired on radio from the 1940s through the 1970s have been either transformed into video soap operas or phased out.

Television programming is a mixture of taped programs in Spanish from Mexico and Argentina and popular series from the United States with the sound track dubbed into Spanish. Some vintage series live on as reruns in Peru. These include the Three Stooges films, which get recycled in Lima year after year. Laurel and Hardy films, with Spanish-dialogue sound tracks, also live on in rerun after rerun in Peru.

Sports programs, ranging from special documentaries produced by Peruvians to sports features from abroad, get prime-time preference during certain times of the year. For example, when soccer championships at regional, national, and worldwide levels approach, weeknight programs appear in addition to Sunday afternoon live broadcasts of soccer matches that go on year-round. Not only on Sunday afternoons, but weeknights in prime time, any channel that happens to air a soccer match captures a big share of the receivers tuned in at that hour.

On late afternoons and Saturdays, children's video features center on cartoon shows and shows about animals. More than half of all programs on Peruvian television stations and networks are foreign in origin, including shows from the United States and Britain with Spanish-language dialogue dubbed onto sound tracks, and Spanish-language programs from Mexico, Argentina, and Spain and one series each from Venezuela and from Colombia.

In recent seasons, the program "Musica para la Juventud" (Music for Youth) has been very popular. This PBS-TV series of the New York Philharmonic's Young People's Concerts directed by Leonard Bernstein from 1973 to 1980 was furnished to Channel 13 by the U.S. Information Agency as a gesture of goodwill from the U.S. government to the Peruvian people.

In the early afternoon all the Lima channels tend to fill up airtime with reruns of U.S. series of several years ago, such as "Cannon," "The Flintstones," "The Partridge Family," and the 1959–63 series "The Untouchables." This latter series, based on the adventures of Eliot Ness, has run every other year since 1973 on one of the Lima channels.

In 1983 a public opinion survey asked a cross section of viewers of Channel 5 what musical series they would like most to see again. A large number responded Fred Astaire. Presumably that meant the musical films he had been in over a long period of time. But the station's management located in Hollywood the few specials he had produced specifically for TV and instead aired those as "The Fred Astaire Theater."

Any animal show gets a large children's audience in the late afternoon. The ancient "Rin Tin Tin" series still gets recycled in Peru, along with "The Little Rascals" and Laurel and Hardy films.

BROADCAST REFORM

With no censorship or government guidance since the return of the civilian control in 1980, Peru generally does enjoy political criticism on the air. In June 1984, however, when Channel 4 aired its regular Sunday-night popular show "Horizonte," censorship erupted. This investigative series is produced by César Hildebrandt. On the Wednesday before the June 3, 1984, program, Hildebrandt informed the minister of the interior that he had twelve minutes of interviews implicating national police with drug traffic criminals. The interior minister heads the national police called Civil Guards and Peruvian Investigative Police (PIP in Spanish). During the Sunday-night program, at 9:20 P.M., with ten minutes to go in the half-hour documentary, the screen went black. A moment later a routine feature on Peruvian humorists filled in. It had been taken from the film archives just before show time. The next morning the show's producer told this author that the interior minister had ordered that change just before airtime. In fairness to the Peruvian government, this writer has not found another glaring example of censorship since mid–1984.

The Law of Telecommunications (Ley de Telecomunicaciones) enacted in August 1980 stands as the current basic broadcasting law. It allows provincial affiliates in remote cities without sufficient local advertising resources to simply carry most of the Lima-originated programs of a network, provided that the local outlets do offer their own local news. The prime example of this situation is the TV facility located in Iquitos, the city in northeastern Peru in the heart of the Amazon jungle on the Amazon River flowing westward from Brazil. This local outlet is linked to Channel 4 in Lima and carries only programs from Lima except for two nightly local newscasts.

The cabinet-level minister of transportation and communications has a vice minister for radio and television, who supervises the licensing of stations and the periodic checking of network operations to see that laws are respected. The 1979 constitution provides for that ministry to maintain a national system of social communications. A subcabinet administrator heads that agency, to ensure that every station airs some cultural or educational program sometime during the week. The requirement can be met by one half-hour feature aired at any hour the program director desires.

CONCLUSION/FORECAST

Peruvian broadcasting, given the level of development of the republic, compares favorably with other nations with a $17.1 billion gross national product. Peru's large foreign debt of $13.4 billion totals approximately four-fifths of its GNP, putting this republic in the middle range of developing nations. Of those Latin American, African, and Asian countries with a similar GNP and similar debt obligations, some one dozen nations, none has a broadcasting system any more extensive than that of Peru, and most do not even approach Peru in the number of TV stations on the air.

Although 40 percent of all Peruvians speak some Indian dialect, usually Quechua or Aymara, less than 30 percent of the total population is non-Spanish-speaking monolingual. The weakness in the Peruvian broadcasting system remains the small number of radio programs aired in Quechua, the largest of the Indian language groups.

BIBLIOGRAPHY

Alisky, Marvin. "Broadcasting in Peru." *Journal of Broadcasting* 3 (Spring 1959): 118–27.

――――. "Government Press Relations in Peru." *Journalism Quarterly* 53 (Winter 1976): 661–65.

――――. *Historical Dictionary of Peru.* Metuchen, N.J.: Scarecrow Press, 1979.

――――. *Latin American Media: Guidance and Censorship.* Ames: Iowa State University Press, 1981.

――――. *Peruvian Political Perspective.* 2d ed. Tempe: Arizona State University Center for Latin American Studies, 1975.

Einaudi, Luigi R. *Revolution from Within: Military Rule in Peru since 1968.* Santa Monica, Calif.: Rand Corporation, 1971.

Palmer, David Scott. *Revolution from Above: Peru, 1968–1972.* Ithaca, N.Y.: Cornell University Latin American Studies, 1972.

Werlich, David P. *Peru: A Short History.* Carbondale: Southern Illinois University Press, 1978.

SAUDI ARABIA

W. Leonard Lee

HISTORY

It is perhaps a truism, but nevertheless valid, to qualify the broadcasting system of each nation of the world as being a mirror of the society it represents. In this regard communications scholars have categorized nations according to prescribed formulas that cover a rather broad spectrum. Unfortunately, this practice does not always aid the student of international broadcasting in coming to grips with the cultural norms implicit in the more traditional societies. Therefore, they can become barriers to understanding. In many instances, these cultural norms have a direct effect upon the development and maintenance of broadcasting systems, and this is especially true when Saudi Arabia is the nation being examined.

The Kingdom of Saudi Arabia is a monarchical state whose system of governance is directly related to family lineage. The effectiveness of its governance depends, however, upon how the reigning monarch incorporates the Sharia (Islamic Law) into the infrastructure of the society. Integral to this infrastructure is the role of broadcasting, which, when used judiciously, becomes the cement that binds the society together. Such is the intent of the broadcasting philosophy that is prevalent in the Kingdom of Saudi Arabia.

It is also important to note that in a nation that for centuries has been a verbal society relying upon interpersonal relationships for message transference, the advent of broadcasting became a significant phenomenon that affected all levels of society. How this phenomenon is being integrated into Saudi society is a study in effective leadership, diplomacy, and persuasion.

Inherent in Saudi society is the unquestioning obedience to the rule of

Islam, which is a permeating factor for the totality of life. The religion of Islam is not separated from government rule, societal standards, or jurisprudence. In fact, it is the touchstone of Saudi reality. Saudi Arabia is not only the birthplace of the Prophet of Islam but also the heart of Islamic Holy Tradition. As keeper of the Holy Places of Islam, Saudi Arabia is the fulcrum for the pilgrimage of the faithful, an obligation for each believer at least once in a lifetime. Therefore, it is not only besieged by thousands of Muslims each year, but its governance is kept under constant scrutiny by the *ulama*, Islam's religious leaders. Into this religious glass house are thrust the trappings of what are considered to be the miracles of a modern society, not the least of which is the age of telecommunications.

Although modern electronic technology has the propensity to cover large distances and thus create the image of geographical homogeneity, it is obvious that transmissions are wasted if there are no people available to receive signals. Therefore, it is important to note that geography is an important element in the development of radio and television services in Saudi Arabia. The most recent population estimates identify Saudi Arabia as having approximately 9 million people living within its borders. These people live in an area estimated to be about 2,331,000 square kilometers, which can be roughly equated in the United States to the size of the area east of the Mississippi River.

Comparisons lose their validity, however, when one realizes that of the large expanse of Saudi Arabian terrain about 98 percent is considered desert. Until a few years ago most of the people were considered to be nomadic or seminomadic. Spurred by the leadership of the late King Faisal (1964–75), rapid economic growth and urbanization have increased, with approximately 95 percent of the population becoming settled. As of 1986 it was estimated that some cities and oases have densities of 770 people per square kilometer. Urbanization is an important factor when it comes to television saturation, especially in Saudi Arabia, where, at least in its early days, television programs were geared toward select rather than mass audiences.

The founding father of what is considered to be modern Saudi Arabia was King Abd Al Aziz (1902–53), who literally wrested the nation from rival factions and united the region into what is now the Kingdom of Saudi Arabia. It was his diplomacy and stature that minimized the interfamily rivalries as the sons of the royal lineage vied for positions of power in the government. Ruling by decree, he began to consolidate the nation. With the discovery of oil in the 1930s, he had the economic power to make changes which have gradually transformed the country. During the early years the populace was almost totally illiterate. Therefore, King Abd Al Aziz recognized the potential of radio to reach the people and, in so doing, effect a consensus. It was not until 1949, in the face of bitter disapproval from religious leaders, that he was able to establish the nation's first local broadcasting station, located in Mecca. He supported his decree with the insistence that readings from the Koran be regularly broadcast, allaying further criticism. The final argument that seemed to have stemmed the flow of opposition was the statement: "Can anything be bad which transmits the Word of God?"

While it was undoubtedly King Abd Al Aziz who set the tenor for Saudi Arabia's utilization of the electronic media as a consolidating and an informational force, it was his son King Faisal who established the governmental machinery that allowed these media to come of age. King Saud (1953–64), Faisal's elder brother, in 1953 issued a decree establishing the first mass-media regulatory agency, the General Directorate of Broadcasting, Printing, and Publishing. At that time, however, Faisal was the crown prince and prime minister, and it was generally understood that this decree had his imprinting on it. In 1963 a cabinet-level office was established to replace this agency that became the Ministry of Information. It is this ministry that has supervised the development of broadcasting in Saudi Arabia.

REGULATORY STRUCTURE

As indicated previously, the Kingdom of Saudi Arabia is structured to allow the nation to be governed in a monarchical manner. The power is from the monarch, who is advised by the Inner Council of Ministers, usually princes of the royal family. This power is then advocated by decrees for the governance of the affairs of state.

The Ministry of Information, one of the ministries of major importance to the state, and most particularly to broadcasting and print media, has responsibilities for both internal and external operations. These responsibilities are viewed in a prescriptive form since the governmental incentive is to mold the society around a Koranic base. Such a prescription, however, while tilted toward the authoritarian model, can only be viewed in the context of the Arab Renaissance. This renaissance is a concerted effort generated by enlightened leadership to bridge the cultural gap that exists between the East and West by the transformation of a Bedouin society into a modern Islamic state. This state, partly because of its enormous oil wealth, is able to step boldly into the international arena while transfiguring its own nationhood with the robes of modern technology. Thus within two years after the issuance of the decree (1962) establishing the Ministry of Information, plans for the creation of a television network were developed. Furthermore, the ministry plans to streamline the flow of information, including the formation of the Saudi Press Agency, which has become the primary source of news in the nation.

The function of the Ministry of Information is perhaps less qualifiable than students of the responsibility model would consider appropriate, but it is a mission that integrates the reality of the emerging nation with its traditional past. This task is best articulated by Dr. Mohammed Abdou

Yamani. In a foreword to a ministry publication he indicates that the commitment of the ministry is to devote the latest methods of communications dissemination developed by the human mind to the promotion of the truth. It is the intention of the government that this message be disseminated among the Saudi people as well as to others of the world because "the word of the Truth is our message." The fact remains that the interpretation of truth in the Kingdom of Saudi Arabia is not isolated from cultural and religious norms; therefore, the role of the ministry is one of consolidation and enlightenment, a role that is not unlike that played by some of its Western European counterparts. This role, of course, is in sharp contrast to the American model, which is driven by a desire to keep the government under surveillance while engaging the public as a business enterprise.

The distribution of authority within the ministry is divided into two distinct divisions: administrative affairs and information affairs. A deputy minister heads each of these areas. Two assistant deputies, one of whom has the responsibility for engineering while the other covers personnel, finances, and supplies, serve the division of administrative affairs.

General policy is, of course, determined initially through decrees and then filtered through each organizational structure. Within the division of administrative affairs, however, one agency is a support mechanism (administration) while the other provides the effective administration of the engineering networks and the development of feasibility studies. These studies focus on the increasingly important role telecommunications is playing in Saudi Arabia.

The parallel structure of the media side of the ministry's organizational chart reveals a more complicated arrangement, indicating the complex nature of administering the informational resources of an independent nation. Three assistant deputy ministers and a director general of the Saudi News Agency serve the deputy minister. The director general carries the same organizational weight as the assistant deputy positions without the corresponding title. This organizational arrangement is a nuance of some import because, as will be indicated, the other directors general report directly to their corresponding assistant deputies. It can be inferred that such a distinction makes the position of the news agency unique. The three assistant deputy ministers supervise overseas information, internal information, and radio and television affairs. Further division of responsibilities reveals that a director general of press reports to the assistant deputy minister for overseas information. A director general of publications reports to the assistant deputy minister for internal information, while three director general positions serve the assistant deputy minister for radio and television affairs. These positions cover the areas of technical affairs, production and programs, and broadcasting service.

The media services function of the ministry is integral to the integrity of the image being advocated by the nation. Obviously, the kingdom, under the present governmental structure, continues to advocate its traditional Islamic philosophy for the governance of the Saudi society. At the same time, it is responding to the nuances of an increasingly better educated populace that requires from the government greater access to sophisticated technology in order to effect a more acceptable lifestyle. The ministry is continuing to respond to these implicit and explicit parameters as reflected in the establishment of modern information centers in Riyadh and Jedda with branch offices in Medina, Dammam, and Al-Kassim.

The overseas information processing serves two functions: (1) to introduce the government and its policies to the world through the print media, films, slides, and audiotapes; and (2) to dispense the necessary information to the Islamic faithful, who, in turn, seek to fulfill the religious obligation of embarking upon a pilgrimage to the Holy Places during the season of the Hajj. This latter activity is a considerable undertaking, when literally thousands of pilgrims besiege the Holy Shrines to take part in a prescriptive ritual that is regimented, time consuming, and fatiguing. As the host, Saudi Arabia takes its obligations very seriously; to do otherwise would be a gross neglect of a sacred duty. Thus the government structure responds to this informational intensity by seeing that the ministry is given enough resources to respond to the informational needs of the pilgrims who reside throughout the large expanse of the Islamic world.

The fulcrum of these activities, which govern the dissemination of information in the Kingdom of Saudi Arabia, focuses upon the role played by the Ministry of Information. That role assumes continued emphasis upon developing a sophisticated, telecommunications-oriented society. The extent of that sophistication is reflected most clearly in the emphasis given to the establishment of internal, regional, and international communications networks—networks that belie the stereotype of an emerging Third World nation.

On the international scene the nation is a member of the International Telecommunications Union (ITU), the European Broadcasting Union (EBU), the Asian Pacific Broadcasting Union (ABU), the Arab States Broadcasting Union (ASBU), the Islamic States Broadcasting Organization (ISBO), and the Broadcasting Organization of Non-Aligned Countries (BONAC). The nation is active in developing and maintaining its relationships with contiguous states of the region. The Gulf States play an important role in the development of informational sources within the kingdom, and the ministry is therefore active in maintaining communication links with them. As part of these activities Saudi Arabia participates actively in Gulf Vision, the Arabian Gulf States Joint Programs Production Institution, the Gulf States Information Documentation Center, and the Gulf Center for Coordination of Radio and Television Training.

ECONOMIC STRUCTURE/PROGRAMMING

The early years of broadcasting in Saudi Arabia can be categorized as the political winds of change. During the 1930s King Abd Al Aziz was in theprocess of consolidating a nation that he wrested from the tribal norm of the Bedouin Arab. This new country of great expanse needed his aura to hold the government together. He recognized that radio possessed the potential for keeping his expanded family in contact with each other. Overcoming the objections of the powerful *ulama*, he established a modest broadcasting system that by the late 1940s had branched out from its primary Koranic readings mode into the beginnings of indigenous programming. This, unfortunately, was restricted in its outreach and coverage to the Western Province because of limited airtime, while other nations, notably the British Broadcasting Corporation, were broadcasting regularly into the country.

Under the direction of Faisal, who was later to become the crown prince and king, the establishment of a governmental office to consolidate broadcasting interests was started. During the 1950s, when the nation lacked the enormous wealth engendered by the oil boom, the emphasis given to the development of a broadcasting system was politically astute. Such an action is made more understandable by the fact that the "Voice of the Arabs" from Cairo lay siege to the monarchical rule of the Saudis during the presidency of Gamal Abdel Nasser. This rhetorical battering spurred the Saudis into creating their own airwaves response, which then became a tournament of ideologies that even today harbors some sting. This is not to say that the only motivation for the establishment of broadcasting was dictated by the changing political climate in the region. Saudi Arabia advocates that its central thrust is to be the "keeper of the Islamic observance" and, in that spirit, has extended its shortwave coverage of the Islamic world to include programming in Urdu and Indonesian languages as well as features in Swahili and Persian. Later, programming in Bimbarra and even Korean has been added.

The war of 1967 provided a unifying factor in the war of words between Egypt and Saudi Arabia. At this time both of these leaders engaged in a cooperative dialogue. Such a positive outcome can be attributed not only to creative leadership and a common enemy, but also to the communications links developed in radio and television.

For radio, the 1960s can be described as the establishing period, the 1970s as the age of expansion, and the 1980s as the consolidation period. Statistical information indicates a considerable growth in the number of receivers from 950,000 in the middle 1970s to over 3 million in the middle 1980s. This represents an increase of over 200 percent in ten years. For the American consumer, this might not appear dramatic; but for a nation that was ostensibly newly consolidated within this century and that subscribes to a religious tradition that attempts to protect its traditional sanctities from unacceptable foreign intrusion (including initially the advent of radio and television), these statistics speak volumes.

As of 1986 the Ministry of Information was exerting considerable effort to program broadcasting according to a prescribed philosophical base. This base is translated into various "services" that in themselves reflect a specific emphasis. This type of format resembles the British Broadcasting Corporation model, which in its early broadcast development divided its service into two distinct parts—the Home Service and the Light Program. The Home Service was considered "high-brow," emphasizing cultural programming of an intellectual nature, while the Light Program offered more entertainment fare. Since the Saudi radio system has been strongly influenced by the British model, the nation has opted to organize its broadcast service into distinct modules. These modules are arranged as follows: the General Program, the Second Program, the Directed Program, the Voice of Islam, and the Holy Koran Broadcasting.

The General Program, since October 1982, has been broadcast daily from Riyadh with a broadcast day of 20.5 hours ranging from 5:30 A.M. until 2:00 A.M. the following morning. Using a 2,000-kilowatt transmitter broadcasting on a medium wavelength, the signal reaches most of the Arabic-speaking nations in the region. Generally, the program categories consist of religion, culture, folklore, drama, information, education, and health. The religious component of the General Program has been filled in the past by a feature with the signature of the Voice of Islam. This voice is predicated upon the Islamic *da'wa* (literally call), a call for the attention of the faithful. Islamic scholars and teachers interpret the tenets of Islam to the listeners to persuade the public against any scurrilous ideas that may be foreign to traditional views. These discussions are generally interspersed with news bulletins about the Islamic world.

The Second Program, like its counterpart, is broadcast solely from Riyadh on a medium wavelength generated by another 2,000-kilowatt transmitter. It covers the same area as its counterpart, but its broadcast day is 18 hours long, beginning at 6:00 A.M. and ending at midnight. Programming centers around offerings with popular appeal, entertainment, drama, culture, and science. General-appeal features are aired from 6:00 A.M. to 6:00 P.M., with the last portion of the broadcast day devoted to "high-brow" culture and scientific programs. This portion of the day is reserved for a more specialized audience.

Initially, the Holy Koran broadcasts were originated in Mecca, a city shrouded in Islamic history, tradition, and religious ritual. Since Riyadh has become the "information center" of the nation, the Holy Koran service is provided solely from Mecca. The program transmits for a broadcast day of 18 hours, from 6:00 A.M. until midnight. As the title of the service suggests, its main function is to send Koranic readings and recitals, absorbing 75 percent of the airtime. The remaining time deals with commentary on Koranic verses, the Prophet's traditions, and interviews with religious leaders.

The Directed Program is primarily an external service transmitting programs to other than Arabic-speaking nations. Its aim is to establish Saudi Arabia as the center of Islamic thought and tradition. Integrated with this theme is the role that the nation plays throughout the Islamic world as an arbiter of justice. In all, twenty-three language segments are broadcast, representing approximately twelve different languages, including English and French. The programming is coordinated in Riyadh and is transmitted via shortwave about 20 hours a day. Thus the message of the nation is continually being espoused via a multiplicity of frequencies to a diversified audience and at considerable expense.

Radio broadcasting in Saudi Arabia has reached a peak of sophistication that is perhaps rivaled only by the industrial nations of the East and West. The nation boasts 4 transmitting locations, 37 programming centers, and 6 broadcasting entities that use 12 languages and are on the air for 24 hours daily. Radio is playing its vital part in the transformation of a desert nation into a telecommunications giant.

Although radio development in Saudi Arabia had an obviously earlier history than television, their developmental progress is remarkably similar. It was King Abd Al Aziz who recognized the power of radio in helping to consolidate the nation, but it was his son Faisal, as crown prince and prime minister, who nurtured it through the building stages so that it could reach its maturity after his tragic death. Likewise, it was Faisal who built the foundation of the presently burgeoning television network that crisscrosses the nation of just 9 million residents. In 1962, at the height of the political impasse between Egypt and Saudi Arabia, Faisal, to dispel the overt and covert opposition by the *ulama* against the invasion of the electronic media into the heart of the nation, stipulated that the government aimed to utilize this means of "innocent entertainment" to enhance the moral and traditional framework of the Sharia (Islamic Law), the Koran, and the Sunna (the Prophet's Traditions). He further indicated that it was prudent to allow this medium to be used as an educational, informational, cultural, and recreational tool within the parameters of moral obedience to Islamic law and tradition. Predicated upon this pronouncement, the wheels of government were set in motion for the establishment of two television stations, one in Riyadh and one in Jedda, which were completed in 1965.

Prior to this time, a portion of Saudi Arabia had been exposed to television originating in its land from a station located in Dhahran. This principality was the primary base for oil production and management and housed a horde of Americans bent on making their fortunes in the oil industry. A U.S. Air Force contingent was also stationed in this "little America." In 1957, under the direction of this contingent, television became a part of the entertainment cycle of the compound. The television signal was often weak, with sound received via an FM radio and a fare that was usually droll. It was television, however, and it was seen and heard by many in the region. Eight years after the U.S. Air Force had begun its broadcasts, Saudi television was broadcasting its own programs in its own language.

To be sure, governmental leaders viewed television as much more than "innocent entertainment." Its complexity demanded the commitment of dedicated individuals and extraordinary finances to create a network system to reach all areas of the nation. The ideal of being able to communicate with all of the people via this medium was a major consideration in establishing a television network that could be used as an educational tool for health, literacy, and classroom support. The nation was beginning to experience greater geographical coordination as a result of new roads, improved telephone and telex system, and better domestic airline service. It was reasoned by government leaders that television, just like radio, could be used to encourage nation building.

The inauguration of the stations in Riyadh and Jedda ushered in the initial phase of the network development. These were complemented by additional facilities in Medina (1967), Al-Kassim (1968), and Dammam (1969). The sixth addition, completed in 1977, is located in the mountainous region of Abha and serves the province with two transmitters located on the mountain of Nahran. In spite of these efforts to saturate the nation with television signals, the nature of the terrain still thwarted government officials. The signals that originated from Abha were relayed to cover the Southern Province. The Western Province was fed by relay signals originating in Medina and Taif, while the Northern Province because of the terrain was serviced with mobile transmission units. Approximately thirty-three television transmission centers, distributed throughout the nation, are served by microwave. These facilities, in conjunction with three small centers hooked to the Riyadh and Jedda stations via coaxial cable and the fleet of mobile stations, when fully functioning are purported to cover 90 percent of the nation.

While this networking was being developed with the main centers of signal disbursement originating from the Riyadh and Jedda studios, other production operations were being constructed. One such studio was in Taif, the summer residence of the king and thus the seat of government during the summer months. A studio in this city has obvious political as well as cultural importance. Two other studios were also built in Mecca, a city of major significance in Islamic history. One studio was established to cover the events surrounding the activities associated with the Holy Mosque, including prayer rituals, and the other to be used as an informational center for pilgrims during the season of the Hajj. Mecca was also a site for the development of a microwave system that linked the Holy Shrines back to the Mecca studio for pertinent coverage of the religious rituals integral to the season of the Hajj. This same microwave system also links the Mecca studio with the Intercontinental Hotel located in the city, which is used as a site for major conferences, thus facilitating television coverage of these events.

It was reasoned that while this networking was fulfilling a primary engineering need, the blueprint would be enhanced with satellite technology. In 1978 arrangements were made to utilize the capabilities of Intelsat, orbiting over the Indian Ocean, to serve as a relay link and to complement the television ground network. With the Riyadh station serving as a central distribution point, nine ground stations were commissioned to extend the network, this time from outer space. Under this structure Riyadh sends its signal via microwave to a ground station that is routed through the satellite to other ground facilities and rerouted via microwave to the fixed and mobile transmitting outlets for final distribution to the home receivers. Such an achievement in such a comparatively short period speaks for the government's determination to expend resources to forge media connections with all of the nation.

Networking is necessary for signal transference, but receivers are indispensable for reception. Accordingly, it is important to note that television, unlike radio, requires that viewers purchase expensive sets in order to view programs. The expense, of course, is further increased if the choice is color. According to information available, there were approximately 3 million television receivers in use as of 1983, which equates approximately to 250 sets per 1,000 population. If one can extrapolate from these figures, it can be inferred that in 1986 there were 3.5 million receivers in use. Such an equation would mean that less than 40 percent of the population was capable of receiving a signal in spite of the sophisticated network signal coverage developed by the government. Such figures can, of course, be misleading; but if there is some accuracy in them, it would seem that the government has to make more receivers available to the public if the goal is to have access to programming. Unfortunately, gathering such statistical information is difficult at best. Because the total funding for broadcasting is allocated by the government, which does not collect a license fee and does not permit advertising, there is little or no motivation to engage in audience research as done in other nations.

Nevertheless, programming that is being aired on a regular basis amounted in 1984 to over seventy-five hours per week. Such programming has local origination, regional origination from other Arabic-speaking nations, primarily Egypt, Lebanon, and Jordan, and foreign origination from such countries as the United States, Great Britain, and France. In these circumstances, there are strict rules governing the acceptability of programming, so censorship is practiced assiduously. Such conduct raises the ire of democratic nations, where freedom of speech is always an issue. For the present, in Saudi Arabia adherence to conservative interpretations of Islamic tradition is the rule that translates into television censorship.

In 1981 recorded data from independent sources showed that the populace was treated to 3,000 program hours. This programming was broken down into five categories: information (14.5 percent), education (6.3 percent), religion (12.5 percent), entertainment (39.5 percent), and other (20.8 percent). This data indicated a strong emphasis upon entertainment as program policy, with other features next (including sports), with information and religion having almost equal time, and education in last place. Information reported by government publications states that the program distribution comprised seven categories: religion and culture (25 percent), variety and musical (12 percent), foreign films and series (8 percent), local and Arabic drama (15 percent), sports (10 percent), children (15 percent), and news and information (15 percent). This data is probably more reflective of the intended achievement of the television service. In an analysis of this data the religion and culture category assumes a primary role, followed closely by drama and news and information. Children's programming has the same percentage as the drama and news categories. This reflects the attention given to the new generation of Saudi nationals. Variety programs along with sports and foreign fare rate last.

There is a concerted effort to engage local and regional talent in the development of indigenous program production. More citizens than ever are engaged in the educational process at all levels, and the future holds promise for a cadre of media writers who would service the needs of studios and the expanded television service. Until this happens, the Saudi television service will continue to gather material where it can—material that is conditioned by the stringency of the Islamic code.

Broadcasting approximately seventy-five hours a week, Saudi television serves a broad spectrum of the needs of the nation. Cable and microwave networks interface with satellite ground stations through fixed and mobile relay stations to reach audiences in sophisticated cities and developing villages. The programming fare ranges from live broadcasts of the prayer rites in the sacred cities of Medina or Mecca, news about the Arab world, school programs, family dramas, and sports to foreign films. All of this has been built on the vision of King Faisal, who saw potential in the "innocent use" of an entertainment media.

NEW TECHNOLOGIES

While the use of a satellite to reach its population is not new to the government of Saudi Arabia, the potential for regional as well as internal communication links via Arabsat is a recent phenomenon for the region. Both Kuwait and Saudi Arabia were the gentle prodders in helping to make this become a reality, with Saudi Arabia being the major shareholder in the Arab Satellite Communication Organization and the provider for the main telemetry tracking and command station. One satellite is launched and two more are planned. The current satellite will allow for some 1,700 telephone lines and 7 television channels.

Some observers credit the telecommunications development as the nation's most significant achievement. In early 1978 there were but a few public telephones. Since the latter part of 1978 the availability of lines has increased from 200,000 to over 1.5 million. In 1986 there were in excess of 4,000 public telephones available in both towns and villages, with a projected goal of having over 2.5 million lines available by the end of the decade. The telephone system is computerized, thus making it easier for a citizen to place an international call than for a European to place a call from a major city to some of the smaller villages in the countryside.

The first telex was installed in 1974, and now there are over 14,000 subscribers placing more than a million messages a month. In addition, coaxial cable links have been established with Bahrain and Kuwait, with another cable being run over the recently constructed causeway physically linking Saudi Arabia with Bahrain. The causeway link is almost as notable to the Gulf Arab as the channel link is to the British and French.

Finally, microwave communications are being extended that interface with Bahrain and Qatar in the Persian Gulf area, North Yemen on the western border, and Jordan and Syria on the northern border.

CONCLUSION/FORECAST

The development of communications in Saudi Arabia is not restricted to the integration of the electronic media and telecommunications into the new patterns of life for this traditional society. The outdated stereotypical Arab image depicted by the Lawrence of Arabia saga has been replaced by a modern city dweller who is as much at home in a sophisticated urban environment as any European or American. The difference is dictated by the style and substance of a religious base that determines the structure of these societies. In ways of development, Saudi Arabia takes the form of a Western nation—paved roads in abundance, with over 60,000 kilometers completed, a rail service that carries over 140 million passengers in operation, an international airline service with an excess of 22 million passengers per year, and seaports unloading 32 million tons of cargo each year. In addition, over 1,200 hospitals and health centers have 17,000 beds available with sophisticated services and a host of health care professionals. All of this, and more, exists in a nation that at the turn of the century was considered to be the land of the nomad, a barren desert wasteland.

The eighties and beyond for the nation pose a time of consolidation with operating budgets in the billions of dollars—the present budget is fifty times greater than the budget of the seventies. The litany of development is long and the sophistication of the modernization process is remarkable. Continuing progress is structured around a society struggling to remain traditional as it opens its borders to the rest of the world. With the religious and political ferment that surrounds the region, this will be no easy challenge.

BIBLIOGRAPHY

Bailey, Robert. "Telecommunications: Saudi Arabia Leads the Middle East Market." *Middle East Economic Digest* 29 (November 1983): 1–14.

Boyd, Douglas A. *Broadcasting in the Arab World.* Philadelphia: Temple University Press, 1982.

Clements, Frank. *Saudi Arabia.* Santa Barbara, Calif.: Clio Press, 1979.

Nyrop, Richard, et al. *Area Handbook for Saudi Arabia.* 3d ed. Washington, D.C.: U.S. Department of State, 1977.

O'Sullivan, Edmond. "Radio and Television: Early Days and Growth." Riyadh: Ministry of Information Publication, Gulf Centre for Documentation and Communication, 1984.

———. "Saudi Arabia." Background Notes. Washington, D.C.: U.S. Department of State. 1983.

———. "Saudi Arabia: Completing the Quiet Revolution." *Middle East Economic Digest* 29 (June 1983): 33–34.

———. "Telecommunications in the Middle East: Entering the Satellite Age." *Middle East* 101 (March 1983): 103–4.

United Nations. *United Nations Statistical Yearbook.* 9: 1–27. New York: U.N. Publishing Service, 1983.

Williamson, John. "Middle East Telecommunications." *Middle East Economic Digest* 29 (October 1983): 1–28.

Young, Arthur N. *Saudi Arabia: The Making of a Financial Giant.* New York: New York University Press, 1983.

SOVIET UNION

Thomas F. Remington

HISTORY

Although the Russian scientist A. S. Popov demonstrated wireless radio at around the same time as Marconi, the development of broadcasting in Russia owed its greatest impetus to World War I and the Bolshevik Revolution of October 1917. Lenin's party regarded radio as an effective means of mass propaganda that could be particularly useful in reaching the illiterate population as well as serving to spread the revolutionary message to the rest of the world. Encouraged by the Soviet government, the medium developed quickly. By 1928 there were sixty-five transmitting and receiving stations in Soviet Russia and the national republics (some of the latter broadcasting in the native languages), and several million listeners. Stalin's forced draft industrialization program further contributed to the spread of radio, particularly through the installation of wired reception points in public places.

On the eve of World War II the nation had 5.8 million wired points and another 1.1 million receivers. Radio received a tremendous impetus from the war despite the destruction of nearly half of all broadcast facilities in the early stages of the German invasion. By the end of the war both foreign and domestic broadcasting had increased in volume to greater than prewar levels. Although by 1947 there were over one hundred stations around the country, the broadcast network was highly centralized in the war's aftermath: local facilities operated essentially as adjuncts of Central Radio, transmitting little locally produced programming. Local broadcasting, however, developed rapidly in the late fifties and early sixties, a boom period for television as well. By the mid–1960s Central Radio transmitted seven programs, and there were nearly 300 receivers per 1,000 population. Since 1967 wired radio reception has also accelerated its growth, particularly to serve rural areas as well as to ensure that large cities have access to multiple programs.

Experimental television broadcasting started in Russia in the 1920s, and regular transmissions to hobbyists began in the 1930s. The dependence of early TV on a spinning mechanical (Nipkow) disk held back television, however, and only in 1939 did regular broadcasting begin on a limited basis in Moscow and Leningrad. Development was effectively halted during the war, but in the postwar reconstruction period an ambitious plan for television was implemented. During the 1950s and 1960s television enjoyed its greatest expansion: nearly 130 cities built TV studios, while Central Television in Moscow added three programs. In the same period the number of sets in use increased rapidly, from 4,000 in 1950 to 50 million by 1973. Color broadcasting began in the 1960s using modified SECAM standards (Séquence Couleur à Mémoire—French color TV system).

A push to centralize program content and ensure uniform technical and political quality became evident in the 1960s. Concomitant was the effort to expand the reach of central television to all parts of the nation through satellite transmission as well as cable links. The first communications satellite for television (beginning the Molnia series) went up in 1965 to serve the Soviet Far East and was received by the Orbita system of ground stations. Today twelve Molnia satellites at any given time orbit elliptically over the earth, transmitting Moscow's First Program, as well as telephone and other signals, to ninety earth stations, primarily in Siberia, the Far East, and the Far North. These have been supplemented by geostationary satellites of the Gorizont, Raduga, and Ekran series, which also serve the Orbita ground receivers and, increasingly, smaller community dish antennas as well as the Soviet-bloc Intersputnik organization and direct links to Soviet allies such as Cuba. As coverage of the Soviet population slowly advances beyond its present 90 percent, the trend of development is toward increasingly high-powered satellite transmitters broadcasting Moscow-based programming to even smaller dish receivers serving towns, settlements, and even apartment buildings. With 240 million able to watch Moscow's First Program and almost 127 million now within reach of the Second Program, the USSR has advanced far toward the goal of total coverage of the nation with the programming of central television.

REGULATION

For both radio and television, decisions about appropriate technologies, program content, the balance of central and local broadcasting, the pace of production of receiving equipment, and other major issues have been made by the Communist party of the Soviet Union and have reflected the varying political needs and impulses of different periods. The broadcast media, even more than the print media, have been essentially free of commercial and competitive pressures, although maximizing audience penetration remains a central objective, and the inevitable competition between television and other news, arts, and entertainment media has economic as well as political and cultural ramifications. Finally, radio and television programming across the nation is highly centralized and dominated by the productions of the central studios in Moscow.

The USSR State Committee of Radio and Television Broadcasting stands at the apex of a pyramid of parallel state committees in the fifteen union republics of which the USSR is composed that in turn direct equivalent committees attached to provincial governments throughout the nation. All local broadcast committees, in keeping with the Soviet principle of "dual subordination," are answerable both to the local government and to the superior radio and television committee. These government bodies provide funding, guidance, and support for broadcast and reception facilities, but political decisions involving programming lie in the power of the respective branch of the Communist party.

Through its agitation/propaganda departments at every level, the party monitors the ideological content of all publicly disseminated information in the country and instructs media organizations on general themes and issues to be emphasized. At the summit of the party hierarchy stands the Department of Propaganda of the CPSU Central Committee, normally overseen by a senior party secretary, which exercises close supervision over all the mass media. Another very important means by which the party ensures adherence to its policies by broadcasters is the control it exercises over appointments to politically sensitive positions. A good political record is essential to advancement in broadcasting as in other careers. A third line of control is the secretive censorship bureaucracy, known as Glavlit, which reviews and approves the content of all material to be aired.

Although propaganda of Marxist-Leninist doctrine is but one of the goals radio and television serve, they, like all forms of mass communications, are treated as instruments for molding the consciousness of the Soviet population, especially for groups, such as those living in remote villages, who are poorly reached by other elements of the mass propaganda system. "The basic direction of television broadcasting," according to the *Great Soviet Encyclopedia* in a formulation that also applies to radio, "is the all-round illumination of the practical activity of the Soviet people in realizing the production and social program laid out by the 26th Congress of the CPSU, implementing the decisions of the November 1982 and June 1983 plenums of the Central Committee of the CPSU." While the propagandistic mission that broadcasting serves does not exclude programs of an artistic, educational, or entertainment character, it does require adherence to certain political and cultural standards while seeking constant improvement in technical capabilities. This has tended to keep programming highly centralized. In 1970, for example, the party stepped in to reverse a trend toward the establishment of new program channels that could not be served by programming of acceptable quality. Similarly, the party has pressed to make radio and television an intrument of unification of the widely dispersed and multinational population by ensuring the transmission of central programming to all parts of the nation.

The relationship between centrally and locally produced programming has varied with time. During World War II Central Radio restricted its broadcasts to one program, which carried, together with other material, the dispatches of the Sovinformburo, founded in 1941. Sovinform material, the daily editorial in *Pravda* (the central party newspaper), and radio news programs were mandatory for all radio stations throughout the nation. After the war local radio stations continued to broadcast a mixture of locally produced programming and the transmission from Central Radio. The accelerated installation of wired radio transmission in the late 1960s and early 1970s aimed not only at increasing the penetration of radio into rural areas, but also at ensuring that major Soviet cities would offer three programs: the all-union channel (First Program), the all-news channel Mayak (to be discussed later), and a channel for local programming. In this way scarcely any community is out of the reach of centrally produced programming.

A comparable evolution toward centralization of broadcasting is apparent in the case of television. Not only did the government link individual metropolitan stations with Moscow using cable relays and satellites, but it elevated Moscow Television into the major source of programming for the nation as a whole. Although Central Television, formerly Moscow Television, airs some matter produced by a national republic or other local studio, its own productions are the predominant source of programming. Moscow First Program became an all-union program by a party decree of 1962. Second Program, which previously broadcast primarily to European Russia, became an all-union program by a party decree of 1982 and is carried by satellite to many parts of the country. Future plans call for ensuring that all areas of the nation receive both offerings, as well as for converting Moscow's Third Program, which carries educational and scientific material, into a third all-union channel. A fourth program in many regions allows viewers to watch locally produced television, including productions in their native languages.

The high level of penetration of virtually all regions of the nation by multiple channels of Central Radio and Central Television attests to the determination and ability of the party leadership to centralize control over the mass media. In addition to the goal of political integration through ideological uniformity, however, centralization of broadcasting also fosters fluency in comprehension of the Russian language among non-Russians, since the programs of Central Radio and Central Television are in Russian.

Another goal that radio and television serve is to support Soviet foreign policy through broadcasting beyond Soviet borders. For example, Radio Moscow broadcasts in seventy-seven languages an average of 260 hours a day. Specialized Soviet-operated transmitters beam programs such as the National Voice of Iran, which is based in Baku, to select target nations. An important function of the satellites is to serve the Soviet-bloc Intersputnik organization, the Eastern bloc's rival to Intelsat, which currently numbers fourteen members. Through ground stations in countries friendly to or allied with the Soviet Union, programming originating in the Soviet Union and other bloc nations is received and retransmitted at low cost. Since all traffic is routed through Moscow, only direct links with the Soviet Union are possible. The Eastern bloc's Intervision Network, operated by the Prague-based Organization for International Radio and Television, produces news and program material for Soviet allies through feeds from member states.

The rapid evolution of specialized training for broadcast journalists reflects the rapid pace of development of the broadcast media themselves. As is the case with Soviet journalistic education generally, broadcast journalists receive their training at a variety of institutions, including over thirty institutions of higher education, some of which have faculties or divisions of journalism, as well as scholarly institutes, conservatories, and party schools. Between 1972 and 1977 some 1,133 individuals graduated with specialized training in broadcast journalism. The most prestigious institution turning out broadcast journalists is the journalism faculty of Moscow University, which in 1958 created the first *kafedra*, or chair, in broadcast journalism in the nation. In its first quarter-century of existence, this *kafedra* turned out some 2,000 graduates, 80 to 90 graduates each year from its five-year program. Students receive a good deal of practical experience in addition to courses in history, theory, and other subjects; they have fully equipped radio and television studios to work on, and from their first year they work at producing news broadcasts sent out by cable to the entire journalism faculty. Talks by media personnel and summer internships in broadcast organizations round out the practical side of their training. Once employed in a media organization, most print and broadcast journalists join the Journalists' Union, which embraces nearly 100,000 editors, writers, broadcasters, photographers, and other working media personnel. The union sponsors various kinds of continuing education for journalists, as well as providing them with certain material benefits.

At the same time, however, all journalists, broadcast journalists included, must be kept conscious of their role as frontline troops in the global ideological struggle. Political education, therefore, is an integral part of a journalist's schooling and continues throughout his or her active career. The party-sponsored adult political education system, currently enrolling some 60 million people, offers journalists basic political instruction and courses tailored to the specific activity of various categories of media personnel. In addition, the union offers evening, weekend, correspondence, and other types of professional and political refresher courses to journalists on a regular basis in each city and province.

Political education is differentiated by the nature of journalists' jobs and their level of responsibility. For example, for heads of provincial radio and television committees, the party school since 1974 has offered month-long courses at which high-ranking officials and specialists lecture. For broadcast and print journalists, the party organization of republics and provinces runs ongoing seminars that meet one day a month. Such courses are nominally voluntary, but most journalists are party members and are accordingly expected to attend.

Finally, it is the responsibility of the party organization in each jurisdiction to which a media organization is attached to inform and instruct the editors of current party policy, indicating what stories should be covered, what themes and issues should be highlighted, and how particular subjects should be treated. Regular briefings and press conferences are held in many localities, and at the central level it is customary for the Department of Propaganda of the Central Committee to convene heads of the central media organizations after major party meetings or decisions to instruct them on how the media should assist in the implementation of policy. Through the professional and political training journalists receive and through regular consultations between the party's ideological managers and the media, the party works to realize its aim of making the media an integral part of the party apparatus.

PROGRAMMING

The high degree of centralization of programming on Soviet radio and television through nationwide saturation of all-union programs emanating from Moscow facilitates considerable differentiation of programming by target audience. The introduction of second all-union programs on Central Radio and Central Television also eases the task of reaching as many major segments of the population as possible with features specifically tailored to their occupational or vocational interests. Material of a social and political nature (news, comment, feature stories on production achievements, interviews with officials or leading workers, documentaries, and similar matter) occupies a prominent position in the programming of both radio and television.

As of 1975, for example, news and other sociopolitical material occupied approximately 23 percent of airtime on the First Program of Central Television. A larger share (38 percent) was taken up with the arts, and another 16 percent with other cultural and educational shows. Popular science and shows for classroom use, at 8 percent of the total, are the next largest category. Only about 5 percent of airtime was devoted to sports programming, since other channels were used much more heavily for sports coverage. Ideological aspects aside, then, one might compare it to American public television programming. First Program of Central Radio is similar in that it concentrates on political and social programming (including political education, press reviews, and international affairs) together with arts and features. Over time, the share of airtime given over to news and other political material has declined somewhat on both radio and television. In 1940, 60 percent of the content of Central Radio broadcasts was sociopolitical, of which the largest share was news. Similarly, news broadcasts, which took up almost 20 percent of the airtime of Central Television's First Program in 1966, fell to 8 percent by the mid–1970s. This came about largely because of the introduction of the major news program on Soviet television, "Vremia" (Time), in 1968. At about the same time, other sociopolitical material fell from about 20 percent in 1966 to about 15 percent by the mid–1970s as programming of other kinds expanded.

Each feature of Central Radio and Central Television is given a certain distinctive profile in the overall structure of programming, although they overlap to some degree. On Central Radio, for example, Fourth Program is largely devoted to music, although the daily average is under ten hours of broadcasting. Third Program focuses on the arts as well as educational material. In 1964 a party resolution directed Central Radio to introduce a twenty-four-hour program, called "Mayak" (Lighthouse), devoted to news interspersed with classical and popular music. Five- to seven-minute segments of news and comment are selected and repeated at half-hour intervals in a manner comparable to "all-news" radio stations in the United States. The unusual format of "Mayak" was intended to appeal to the new generation of listeners of portable radios.

On Central Television the two all-union channels, First and Second programs, both broadcast on average about thirteen to fourteen hours a day, but on somewhat different schedules and offering somewhat different mixtures of programming. Whereas First Program offers a larger menu of concerts, operas, ballets, and dramas, Second Program broadcasts a larger number of sports events. In addition, Second Program uses the prime evening viewing hours to show the more popular shows from First Program. Daytime hours on Second Program are used for educational and popular science material (since the nation does not yet have an all-union program specifically for such features) as well as for local productions. In western regions of the Soviet Union, Moscow-produced Third and Fourth Programs are also seen. Third Program (aired seven hours a day) concentrates on scholastic and popular science shows (which may subsequently be rebroadcast on First or Second Program to all-union audiences), while Fourth Program (broadcasting six hours a day) carries cultural, political, and social material.

The major television news production, "Vremia," established in 1968, is the principal national daily roundup of domestic and international news.

Designed as a Soviet counterpart to the professionally produced news productions of Western television networks, it uses regular anchorpersons who appear in the picture with recorded film images. Many of the news items are selected for inclusion in other shows such as "Musical Evenings for Youth" and "Acquaintance with Opera."

Several shows acquaint viewers with life in diverse parts of the Soviet Union, stressing the multinational variety of the Soviet population and the harmonious, brotherly relations among ethnic groups that are said to characterize it. These include "Our Address Is the Soviet Union," "Songs Far and Near," and "The People's Creativity." Still other programs deal with foreign cultural life, including "The Creativity of Peoples of the World" and "The Screen Gathers Friends."

Film series are the single most popular television genre. For example, documentaries on Soviet history including a fifty-part series on events of the last fifty years have been produced, as well as a twenty-part series on World War II (the latter was intended for international viewing). A film production company affiliated with central television called Ekran (Screen) annually creates over one hundred documentary films for television. In addition, it produces numerous feature films and film series, many of them based on domestic and foreign literary works.

Science-oriented programs are also popular. The single most popular program on Soviet television is a show called "In the World of Animals," which explores the lives of exotic species of wildlife. Other programs in the popular science or educational category include "The Film Travel Club," "Man, Earth, Health," and "Science Today."

Still other programs are aimed at parents, book lovers, chess players, and gardeners. Specialized programs are intended to assist teachers, high school graduates preparing for university entrance exams, students in evening and correspondence courses, and professionals interested in continuing education in fields such as medicine and management.

Centralization of resources in the studios of Moscow Central Television and Central Radio makes possible the extensive differentiation of programming that the party regards as essential for maximizing the full potential of broadcasting on the public. It also permits the differentiation of roles in the mass-media system between the broadcast media and books, film, magazines, newspapers, and the oral propaganda network.

From the standpoint of the party authorities, the very appeal of Soviet television has generated new challenges. As Soviet research (much of it discussed by Ellen Mickiewicz in her book, *Media and the Russian Public*) has demonstrated, television has had a substantial though not always direct effect on public media habits. Television has become as ubiquitous in Soviet society as in any democratic society of the West, and television viewing is nearly universal, although quantity and tastes in viewing vary widely. Television has reduced the audience for movies and other artistic media and has forced the latter to turn out products with lower and more commercially successful standards. Television also seems to have reduced the time spent in visiting with friends and neighbors. The flexibility and popularity of the medium have allowed television to usurp some of the roles previously played by other media of communication. The effort to use television as an instrument for molding the active "new Soviet person" may suffer by virtue of its very popularity as a form of relaxation and passive recreation.

FEEDBACK FROM THE AUDIENCE

Organized popular movements aimed at challenging the present structure of broadcasting or programming in the media are incompatible with the party monopoly on political life. On the other hand, popular response to radio and television, as to other mass media, is a welcome and important part of the Soviet communications system. The habit of writing letters to the authorities, to public figures, and to media organizations is deeply ingrained in Soviet life. Central Television received nearly 1.7 million letters in 1983, Central Radio over 600,000. Correspondence from listeners often provides the basis for interview and other programs, and some programs on both radio and television are built around live telephone calls from listeners, who can address questions directly to prominent officials or scholars in the studio. These formats have proven highly popular and effective since they combine the spontaneity of live broadcasting with the authority of an official's response.

In addition to the substantial volume of spontaneous reaction to the broadcasts of radio and television, media authorities make wide use of audience surveys to determine likes and dislikes on the part of the viewing public. Survey data (1977) from one city on time use, for example, revealed that 83 percent regularly viewed television and 81 percent listened to radio, higher proportions than those for newspaper and book reading, concert and play going, or attending the local club. Surveys have also uncovered the regular audience for particular programs: films and the newscast "Vremia," at about a 50 percent share of the television audience, attract the highest proportions of regular viewers. Moreover, "Vremia" and the program "In the World of Animals" enjoy the highest ratios of favorable to unfavorable ratings (61.6 percent rate "Vremia" highly, 6.6 percent not highly; the figures are 64.7 percent versus 6 percent in the case of "In the World of Animals").

Audience response, as gauged by letters and surveys, does help guide programming decisions. In some cases, sizeable groups make incompatible demands. For example, urban workers generally prefer not to have new films shown after the conclusion of "Vremia" (around 9:35 P.M.), whereas that is the preferred time for rural residents. The prime viewing time slot, from 7:00 to 11:00 P.M., gives rise to many conflicting preferences. One solution is to divide programming between First and Second programs. For the almost half of First Program viewers who cannot yet receive Second Program, however, this is unsatisfactory. Viewer preferences also influence decisions on what shows to repeat. Programming decisions are not made strictly or exclusively on the basis of viewers' preferences, of course. Final decisions are made by the government's radio and television broadcasting committee and may be overridden or modified in accordance with the decisions of the party Central Committee apparatus. Major considerations in programming are, as indicated, maximizing penetration of the population overall, maximizing impact through differentiation of audiences, maintaining high political, technical, and cultural standards, and ensuring that radio and television play their part in the ideological formation of the society.

NEW TECHNOLOGIES

The aim of expanding the reach and variety of centrally produced programming, which, as noted above, is the driving force in the rapid development of Soviet television, lies behind the development of new generations of satellite transmitters and ground receiving stations. The newest generation of communications satellite used for television is the Ekran series, which is distinctive in the satellites' high power output (they use a 200-watt transponder) and the resulting small size and low expense of the receiving equipment needed. This means that small communities or mobile work crews can pull in central television. By 1983 some 2,100 small antennas in the Ekran system had been mounted. Future plans call for development of a new frequency band for television satellite broadcasting that will permit still higher power transmission and smaller antennas. Soon so many light, powerful, and mobile dish antennas will be in use in the nation that even though reception of all Soviet signals requires a signal converter, the threat of direct reception of foreign television signals may become a reality. Against this possibility the Soviet Union sought as early as 1972 to persuade the United Nations to adopt a convention requiring prior consent by states to the reception of television signals from foreign countries (and even stipulating that in case of violation, the offending satellite could be destroyed by the injured government). A modified version of this proposal was adopted in the form of a nonbinding resolution in 1982. Considering the scale of Soviet jamming of foreign radio broadcasts and the immense appeal of television, it is clear that direct access by a large proportion of the Soviet population to Western television broadcasts would be treated by the Soviet authorities with the utmost seriousness. Even where Soviet citizens already can watch Western television (for example, nearly half a million Estonians can receive and understand Finnish broadcasts), Soviet ideological authorities respond with intensive counterpropaganda.

A similar dilemma has already arisen with videocassette recordings. The spread of videocassette recorders, often obtained through black-market channels, has created a market for illegally imported Western cassette recordings of uncensored material. Nevertheless, Soviet authorities envision harnessing this technology as well for domestic purposes by establishing domestic production of VCRs and tapes. It is likely, however, that as with other goods, some demand will remain unmet and will lead to illegal circulation of Western imports.

Finally, Soviet writers also envision the introduction of cable television, although how it will be used has not yet been decided. The late head of the *kafedra* of broadcast journalism of the Moscow University journalism faculty, Professor Enver Bagirov, wrote enthusiastically in 1984 of the perspectives that cable television offered for live interaction between broadcaster and audience. Some live call-in shows are already aired, as noted, on radio and television. Whether interactive cable television will be widely developed is a matter for speculation.

CONCLUSION/FORECAST

It is notable that Soviet authorities have not refrained from developing any new technology in radio and television out of fear of its political consequences. Rather, in each case, development has been guided by the general objectives of maximizing the penetration and impact of the medium. The same objectives are likely to govern future development by extending the reach of television into the most remote regions of the nation and abroad through satellite broadcasting and by increasing the appeal of television with the spread of color broadcasting and color sets and the continued differentiation of programming by means of the new cassette and cable technologies. Although local programming is likely to increase, it is unlikely to displace the dominant role of central programs emanating from Moscow. Above all, as long as the rule of the CPSU remains intact, radio and television will be treated as important means of upholding party power and policies.

BIBLIOGRAPHY

Conquest, Robert. *The Politics of Ideas in the U.S.S.R.* New York: Praeger, 1967.

Egorov, V. V. *Televidenie i zritel.* Moscow: Mysl, 1977.

Gurevich, P. S., and V. N. Ruzhnikov. *Sovetskoe radioveshchanie: stranitsy istorii.* Moscow: Iskusstvo, 1976.

Hollander, Gayle Durham. *Soviet Political Indoctrination.* New York: Praeger, 1972.

Hopkins, Mark. *Mass Media in the Soviet Union.* New York: Pegasus, 1970.

Inkeles, Alex. *Public Opinion in Soviet Russia: A Study in Mass Persuasion.* Cambridge: Harvard University Press, 1958.

Iurovskii, A. *Televidenie—poiski i resheniia: ocherki istorii i teorii sovetskoi televizionnoi zhurnalistiki.* Moscow: Iskusstvo, 1975.

Lendvai, Paul. *The Bureaucracy of Truth: How Communist Governments Manage the News*. Boulder, Colo.: Westview Press, 1981.

Mickiewicz, Ellen Propper. *Media and the Russian Public*. New York: Praeger, 1981.

Roth, Paul. *Die kommandierte öffentliche Meinung: Sowjetische Medienpolitik*. Stuttgart: Seewald Verlag, 1982.

———. *Sow-Inform: Nachrichtenwesen und Informationspolitik der Sowjetunion*. Dusseldorf: Droste Verlag, 1980.

Shanor, Donald. *Behind the Lines: The Private War against Soviet Censorship*. New York: St. Martin's Press, 1985.

SWEDEN

Timothy C. Tomlinson

HISTORY

As was the case in most other nations, radio amateurs were responsible for the early experiments and developments of broadcasting in Sweden. After this brief period of "private" radio, however, formal structure was brought to broadcasting in the country when the government established AB Radiotjänst in 1925 as the organization to manage all radio activities. Private radio continued to exist for a time, but such operations were eventually absorbed by the monopoly structure that was enacted by the government. The new organization was independent of the government while at the same time receiving its operating revenues from it.

In order to ensure its independence, AB Radiotjänst was set up as a nonprofit public corporation with no shares held by the government. Instead, the corporation was owned by companies in the radio industry, the press, and the Swedish News Agency. All power over programming decisions was the responsibility of the broadcasting organization, while the government was directly responsible only for the physical transmission of the radio signals and all facilities through its telecommunications administration. Ostensibly, the state had no direct control over the organization and operation of broadcasting, but the government did establish guidelines for program production, content, and financing. The original agreement gave the broadcast organization sole responsibility for program content, but the government expected the agency to be reliable, objective, and neutral in its programming. At best it was a delicate balance between the ideas of perceived philosophical independence and indirect state control. This dual approach to broadcast regulation has continued to persist throughout the history of broadcasting in Sweden.

The broadcast services provided by AB Radiotjänst began with the operation of one radio channel that was the only outlet for nearly thirty years before Sweden's Parliament agreed to allow a second channel in the mid–1950s. Just a few years after the creation of a second radio channel, the possibility of developing a television service became real. Subsequently, in the late 1950s Parliament passed legislation establishing television as a public enterprise that would be managed through the existing broadcast organization. Also at that time, as the responsibilities of the organization were expanded to include television, its name was changed to Sveriges Radio AB (Swedish Broadcasting Corporation). At this stage in its history, the corporation assumed responsibility for production and programming of radio and television.

The period of the 1960s proved to be important as Sveriges Radio continued to expand its operations. In 1964 the organization added a third radio channel featuring more entertainment-oriented programming. This action was a direct response to pirate broadcasters operating off the coast of Sweden. Not surprisingly, the third radio channel is the most popular outlet in Sweden. In 1969, after expanding radio service, the corporation created a second television channel. Since then, color television has been implemented as well.

Unlike many other European nations, Sweden was able to remain neutral during the two world wars that have taken place since the inception of communications. This fact has helped the nation to escape some of the basic changes brought about by these conflicts. This is perhaps one reason why broadcasting in Sweden has remained quite consistent in both its structure and its underlying philosophy since its inception in the early 1920s. Another reason may be the fact that the nation has enjoyed relative stability in its political leadership for much of this century. The Social Democrats held control of the Swedish government for forty-five years prior to 1976. They lost control in 1976 to a nonsocialist coalition, but have since regained their majority position. Because of these factors, changes have not been rapid or massive in Sweden's broadcasting system.

REGULATION

The regulatory structure of Sweden's broadcasting system remained essentially intact until the 1950s when the government responded to the introduction of television. In 1966, however, three important bills were passed that brought about further revision and reform in Swedish broadcasting. The legislative actions included the Radio Act, the Broadcast Liability Act, and an Enabling Agreement between the broadcasting company and the government. The first two legislative acts are still in force as primary policy documents. The Enabling Agreement was changed in 1979 to reflect the structural change that took place in Sveriges Radio.

The Radio Act contained many of the basic elements that shaped the structure of broadcasting, but it also established some important program content guidelines as well. Through it, the Swedish Broadcasting Corporation (SBC) has been given the "sole and exclusive" right to determine the programs to be broadcast. An added section stipulated, however, that the right must be exercised "impartially and objectively." The act also explicitly prohibited any form of prior censorship—especially on the part of the government. Furthermore, the act established the Radio Council as the official body to ensure that there have been no violations of the Radio Act or the Enabling Agreement.

The Broadcasting Liability Act was enacted to align the broadcasters with the press in regard to liability. Essentially, it provides broadcasters with the same protection as the press concerning immunity from liability except in obvious cases of libel. As with the press, only one person associated with a program can be liable—usually the program supervisor.

Two important notions have emerged out of the legislation that organized broadcasting in Sweden. Each act and any subsequent revisions have promoted the idea that the activities of broadcasting should be carried out with impartiality and objectivity. These are seen as basic requirements for the SBC, since it is a public service organization. In addition, the Radio Act stipulated that the programs must satisfy a broad range of public tastes and must be presented in "suitable form." Just what these phrases mean in terms of actual program content is quite difficult to determine. It is clear, however, that the idea of impartiality does not apply to features that would threaten the national political structure. The SBC is also bound by rules to uphold the fundamental concepts associated with a political democracy such as freedom of speech and freedom of assembly. Another guideline states that programming must reflect an overall balance between various perspectives and interests. The implication is that this requirement need not be met within each individual program; rather, it might be met over a period of time.

While the Radio Act and the Broadcasting Liability Act represent important pieces of legislation, the Enabling Agreement established between the SBC and the government is the basic regulatory document regarding the fundamental structure of broadcasting in Sweden. This agreement grants SBC the "sole and exclusive" right to transmit broadcast programs in Sweden. It also sets forth the relationship between the SBC and the telecommunications administration, which operates the physical transmission facilities. Furthermore, the agreement outlines the organization of the SBC, basic programming policies, and the company's financial structure.

One of the most important sections of the agreement concerns the structure of the board of governors of the SBC. When the current agreement was revised in 1979, it changed the size and responsibilities of the board. The composition of the board is important even though, according to the law, it is not to have any direct influence on programming decisions. At

various times, however, it has encouraged certain types of prosocial programs and actually prohibited others that may have been supportive of
negative values.

Even though the board of governors has occasionally exerted direct influence on program decisions, the only body that is authorized to respond
to and investigate possible program violations is the Radio Council. The
council has eight members and is entirely independent of the SBC (its members are appointed by the government). Since prior censorship is explicitly
forbidden by law, the council can only act on complaints about shows that
have already been aired. It may also investigate programs on its own ini-
tiative, even if no public complaints have been filed. The council has the
authority to investigate and raise objections to specific features if they are
found in violation of the Radio Act or other broadcast legislation. The
council itself has no punitive powers, but it can report to the government
and make recommendations for disciplinary action. In the event the violations are of a serious nature, the government can invalidate the Enabling
Agreement with the SBC through parliamentary action.

The matter of freedom in program content has historically been a sensitive
issue in Sweden. Freedom from government influence is to be upheld, but
it is also seen as important that various rights and interests be protected.
In addition to the general guidelines concerning program content in the
Radio Act, there are also some specific content proscriptions. While the act
is vehement in its rejection of prior censorship, it proposes that the SBC
needs to create programs in such diverse areas as religion, music, drama,
art, literature, and science. Also, it must meet the needs of the minority
communities as much as possible. Since the revisions in 1979, even more
explicit content stipulations have been added. Program producers are now
required to minimize the presence of violence, alcohol, and swearing in their
productions. Sexual content, which is quite controversial in many other
nations, seems to be of lesser concern to the Swedish audiences and producers than the other issues.

ECONOMIC STRUCTURE

The Swedish Broadcasting Corporation is a limited, public corporation.
Its ownership pattern was established with the formation of the original AB
Radiotjänst. The radio industry, press, and Swedish News Agency each held
one-third of the shares of the organization. Those percentages were changed
during the reorganization in the 1950s so that the press held 40 percent,
trade and industry interests 20 percent, and "popular movement" groups
such as labor unions, consumer protection groups, adult education associations, temperance agencies, and churches held the remaining 40 percent
of the shares. As of 1986 the ownership stood at 20 percent for industry
and commerce, 20 percent for the press, and 60 percent for the "popular

movement" groups. This trend represents the government's interest in allowing the general public a greater voice in the functioning of the broadcasting system. After all, since the SBC is a nonprofit organization, its shares have no monetary value. Being a shareholder is essentially just a way of having representation on the board of governors.

The SBC, as a nonprofit agency, generates little income on its own. Advertising has never been allowed in the Swedish broadcasting system, and that stance has remained firm over the years. Its operational budget is appropriated by the government through the collection of special receiver license fees from owners of television sets. Parliament sets the amount of the license tax every year and has given the responsibility for its collection to the Swedish Telecommunications Administration. The payments collected go into a special broadcasting fund from which Parliament makes its annual allocation to the SBC. The government is not obliged to distribute the total amount collected to the SBC's operational budget and generally does not since the Telecommunications Administration's funding also comes from the collection of the tax. In addition, the National Board of Building and Planning, which is responsible for the construction and maintenance of radio and television production facilities, receives an allocation out of the license fee. The only parts of the national and regional broadcasting operations that are not funded by license fees are the Swedish Educational Broadcasting Company and Radio Sweden International, which operates external services for the government. Both of these agencies are financed through regular taxes.

In addition to the license fees, it should be noted that the SBC does gain a small amount of revenue from the international sale and distribution of selected radio and television programs. It also has a small record company. The income from these operations, however, has little effect on the total budget needs of the corporation.

Fees were formerly charged for radio receivers as well as television sets, but now only households with televisions have to pay the license tax. The current license fee is Kr 576 for black-and-white sets ($82), and Kr 736 for color sets ($105). There are approximately 3.2 million licenses issued, about 2.8 million of them for color sets.

The distribution of the money to broadcast operations changed in 1979 when a major reorganization of the SBC took place. In an effort to decentralize power in the broadcasting structure, Parliament voted to break up the SBC into several subsidiary companies. The Swedish Broadcasting Company became the parent company with the four following subsidiaries: Swedish Radio Company, Swedish Television Company, Swedish Local Radio Company, and the Swedish Educational Broadcasting Company. The parent outfit is primarily responsible for overseeing the long-range planning and development of the group of companies, but it also handles distribution of finances to the subsidiaries. Roughly 50 percent of the money goes to the television company, while the national radio services receive 20 percent and local radio 10 percent. The parent company itself gets only about 1 percent of the total broadcasting budget.

Each of the companies operating under the umbrella of the SBC has its own particular type of corporate structure. When the government decided to reorganize the SBC in 1979, it was attempting to loosen the grip of the monopoly somewhat in order to provide each area of broadcasting more autonomy. Previously, there had been one board of governors for the entire broadcasting system. With the reorganization, however, each subsidiary company has its own board. The board of the parent outfit now consists of fifteen members—the director general and fourteen others. The government appoints seven of those members (including the chairperson), five are representatives of the shareholders, and two come from the ranks of the employees. The boards of each of the subsidiaries also have fifteen members, and all but two on each committee are appointed by the SBC's board.

The responsibilities of each company are fairly well defined, and each produces programming for distribution on both national and regional levels. The Swedish Radio Company, or Sveriges Riksradio AB (RR), programs and operates the three national radio channels, has its own symphony orchestra, and manages Radio Sweden International, among other responsibilities. The Swedish Television Company (SVT) manages two television channels, SVT1 and SVT2, which contain regional broadcasts as well as the standard national programs. The Swedish Local Radio Company (LRAB) oversees the operation of twenty-four local radio stations throughout Sweden. This service is actually more accurately a regional service than local because the twenty-four areas roughly coincide with county boundaries. Finally, the Swedish Educational Broadcasting Company (UR) is responsible for producing educational programs for both radio and television that are aired over the networks of the other three subsidiaries.

PROGRAMMING

As in most nations that are organized under a "paternal" orientation to broadcasting, the programs seen in Sweden represent a wide variety of types and appeals and are not necessarily concerned with garnering the largest audience possible. This eclectic approach to programming is demonstrated at all levels of broadcasting and is reflective of the philosophy that guided the structuring of the SBC and its operations.

Programming in radio takes place on four different levels: internationally with the services of Radio Sweden, nationally through RR, regionally through LRAB, and locally through *närradio*, or neighborhood radio.

As an external broadcasting service, Radio Sweden International has a dual purpose. It is intended as an information source for Swedes living in other nations as well as a general source of information about Nordic life for the rest of the world. Radio Sweden is on the air seven days a week for twenty-two hours. It broadcasts news, commentaries, and some entertainment in thirty-minute blocks in seven languages throughout the day. In addition to Swedish-language broadcasts, English, French, German, Spanish, Portuguese, and Russian programs are offered. These broadcasts are primarily informational since Radio Sweden is under the jurisdiction of RR and is designed to be independent of the state.

National radio programming is produced by the Swedish Radio Company and is disseminated through three networks or channels: P1, P2, and P3. Each channel has a different format, and there is rarely much duplication of program types. P1 is mostly news and other types of talk shows of cultural or informational interest. This channel is programmed almost entirely by RR and broadcasts for about eighteen hours a day during the week and sixteen hours a day on weekends. P2, unlike P1, is programmed by the Swedish Educational Broadcasting Company as well as RR and is on the air the same amount of time as P1. Typical fare includes classical or serious music, stock reports, educational shows, and broadcasts in minority languages such as Finnish and Sami. The third channel, P3, is jointly programmed by RR and the Swedish Local Radio Company. Nationally, the format is primarily light music and entertainment, and P3 is the only broadcast service in Sweden that is available twenty-four hours a day. The twenty-four regional radio stations operated by the LRAB can preempt P3's national programming for a total of three hours per day Monday through Friday and for one hour on Saturday and Sunday. These preemptions are commonly regional news items, cultural affairs, minority-language programs, and sports coverage.

Of the three radio channels, the vast majority of the total listening audience is tuned to P3 at any given time. Approximately 70 to 75 percent of all listeners are tuned to P3, while 25 percent are listening to P1 and 1 to 2 percent are tuned to P2. This is indicative of the popularity of the light music and entertainment programming and the regional radio segments found on P3. It is important to note that even though a type of program is popular, it may not receive a great deal of airtime. Conversely, even though a show may not have a large audience, it may still be a significant part of the broadcast schedule. This is demonstrative of the SBC's policies regarding programming in the perceived best interests of the audience even when such programming may not be popular.

Given the national structure of radio in Sweden, it is not surprising that program production is heavily concentrated in Stockholm, with about 70 percent of all production taking place there. The other 30 percent is carried out in ten regional centers throughout the nation. In 1986 there were several efforts undertaken to place more production outside of Stockholm. These attempts at decentralizing production are aimed at creating greater diversity and more regional autonomy.

One major development toward this end was the formation of the LRAB. The twenty-four stations that operate under the company's leadership are fairly autonomous. Each is expected to reflect the distinct cultural, social, and political flavor of its region. The general programming guidelines put forth in the agreement between the company and the government stipulate that the stations are to foster communication between the people and their elected officials as well as promote more informed participation in the democratic process. They are also to support the cultural and artistic communities in their respective regions.

The public reception of the LRAB's stations has been significant. Their segments are among the most listened to of all the programming on P3. This popularity led to an experiment in 1985 where three local stations were given transmitters of their own and the opportunity to broadcast for greater periods of time during each day. The experiment was considered very successful and subsequently led to pressure for the addition of a fourth radio network that would be devoted entirely to the LRAB. This matter has been proposed to Parliament for legislative action.

There is another form of radio in Sweden that, unlike the others, is not connected in any way with SBC or its subsidiaries. It is called *närradio*, or neighborhood radio, and it is truly a local or community service. *Närradio* started on an experimental basis in 1979 after Parliament had previously authorized a three-year trial period for such broadcasting. These are low-power stations with very limited range, and virtually any group willing to commit itself to transmit on a regular basis for at least one year can have airtime. In addition, the groups must defray all production and transmission costs themselves. The groups must also be noncommercial and must have a purpose other than just to broadcast. Charitable organizations, religious groups, community action agencies, labor unions, and political parties commonly claim airtime. *Närradio* broadcasts are not bound by the same regulations as the SBC's operations, and therefore content need not attempt to be balanced or objective. The organizations that take to the air are free to strongly promote their particular points of view. But even though there are fewer content restrictions, advertising is still not allowed. Groups are free to solicit donations, however, to cover their costs.

Närradio is an important development because it signals a strong move away from the long-standing monopoly and centralized nature of broadcasting in Sweden. The Social Democrats were opposed to the original experiment, which was authorized during the moderate/conservative coalition's brief term in office. Interestingly enough, after coming back into power, the Social Democrats extended the trial period of *närradio* for another three years. After six years of the experiment, the government (again the Social Democratic majority) decided in July 1985 to make it permanent.

Television programming and production is the responsibility of the Swedish Television Company (SVT). It operates two channels, SVT1 and SVT2, which are national in coverage. Unlike the national radio services, which have fairly different program formats, the two television services carry many of the same types of shows. Although there is no competition between the two in the same way there would be in a commercial system, each is certainly conscious of the popularity and type of program offered by the other channel during most time periods. If there is a difference between them, it is in the amount of each type of program that they air. SVT1 tends to carry a little more religious and cultural fare, news, and sports, and significantly more minority-language programming. SVT2, on the other hand, often has more current affairs, films, and light entertainment. Apart from educational features for school children that are aired some mornings and afternoons on weekdays, SVT1 broadcasts for six hours each afternoon and evening Monday through Friday, and on weekends the channel operates between eleven and twelve hours each day. SVT2 is on the air five hours daily Monday through Friday and about ten hours per day on weekends.

Whereas all three radio channels are programmed by RR, the two television outlets are responsible for determining their own features. But like the radio services, television must present a wide variety of program types without constant regard for popularity. News must be offered in a balanced and straightforward manner, and there is to be suitable material available in minority languages such as Finnish, Greek, Turkish, and Serbo-Croatian. In addition, programming for children is a high priority on the broadcast schedule. Also, any entertainment shows are subject to approval regarding violent content. All of these guidelines, then, serve to shape the content and structure of the television schedule.

One of the problems faced by most small countries is producing enough television offerings to fill up available space on existing channels. Though SVT has an active production branch, it is not able to produce enough material to program both television outlets completely. Therefore, imported shows are a vital part of the program schedule. SVT produces about 55 percent of the programs aired in a year, but the rest come from independent Swedish producers, from other nations in the European Broadcasting Union, or by purchase from such major producers as the United States and Great Britain.

Nearly 50 percent of all imported programming comes from the United States and Great Britain, 20 percent originates from Finland, France, and West Germany, and the rest comes from Western and Eastern Europe as well as South America, Africa, and Australia. Programs from the United States fare quite well, with many of them showing on the prime evening time slots. Such popular shows as "Hill Street Blues" and "Magnum P.I." were broadcast during the very best time slots.

Both SVT1 and SVT2 produce about thirteen hours of original programs each week. The bulk of this production work involves news and current affairs and children's features. They also produce a fair amount of light entertainment and cultural shows. In addition to this, SVT operates six regional television production centers that produce regional news broadcasts that are carried over the two SVT channels and cumulatively produce twelve hours of coverage per week.

Of the 55 percent of the total program schedule that SVT produces, many of the features are coproductions with companies from Sweden and often other nations. Dramatic productions and films for television are commonly produced in partnership with various other companies. SVT has often collaborated with the film industry either through the Svensk Film Company or the Swedish Film Institute. Such efforts have resulted in a wide variety of programs from Ingmar Bergman's "Scenes from a Marriage" to opera and children's features. Miniseries have also been developed, such as the Kr 35 million production of "August Strindberg—A Life." This seven-hour, six-episode series was the most expensive production ever undertaken by Swedish television. But aside from collaboration with the Swedish film industry, SVT has also worked with other European nations. SVT2 and the Finnish national broadcasting organization, YLE, jointly developed a comedy series called "Next Door Neighbors," a story about a Finnish and Swedish family living together in a Stockholm suburb. Such efforts benefit all involved by lowering production costs and ensuring greater distribution.

In recent years there has been increasing sentiment for greater decentralization of television production. The majority of the programs seen reflect either an international viewpoint or an urban perspective from Stockholm. Accordingly, regional television production has been receiving more attention and emphasis. There has also been an investigation into the possibility of creating local television in a fashion similar to that of *närradio*. Because of the expense, however, local television has been slower to develop.

BROADCAST REFORM

As in virtually any broadcast system, criticism comes from many sectors of the society. Sweden is no exception. There have been numerous government committees investigating structure and the future of radio and television. Social critics have lamented the fact that there is so much foreign-language programming on the air. Others have complained that programming is too limited and generally not entertaining enough. Still others have foreseen the strong competition the SBC faces from cable and satellite operators.

But while all of these criticisms contribute to the shaping of the broadcast structure, political forces remain the most influential bodies with regard to broadcast policy. The major reorganization of broadcast operations that took place in 1978–79 was largely the result of a shift in political power from the Social Democrats to a nonsocialist coalition. During that time, not only was the SBC reorganized, but non-SBC broadcasting was allowed under the experimental *närradio* concept. When the Social Democrats returned to power, they upheld the changes because of strong public support for them. This kind of political scuffling has gone on for some time, as the Social Democrats have long upheld the notion of a paternalistic broadcasting system while more conservative parties have sought basic changes in the system.

One of the more persistent and potent promoters of broadcast reform is the Conservative party. It has long pushed for advertiser-supported broadcasting in Sweden. The party has introduced motions to Parliament calling for commercial radio and television services. The party's thinking is that such a system would be "free" to viewers, would provide a responsiveness to competition and viewers' preferences, and allow the nation to compete with international cable and satellite concerns.

But even aside from such radical restructuring of the broadcast system as proposed by the Conservative party, there have been other more modest suggestions. The SBC itself has been pushing for the addition of a pay television service, which it sees as an additional potential source of revenue for the company. Even though the Parliament has rejected SBC's requests, it is investigating the possibility of a national pay television system that would be totally independent of the existing company. Others are calling for a third television channel that would be commercially supported as a supplement to the current outlet.

NEW TECHNOLOGIES

While other nations have begun implementing cable television and satellite broadcasting, Sweden has been hesitant to explore these means of transmission and is now lagging behind much of Europe. Most of the reluctance, of course, stems from the possible detrimental effects these technologies might have on the existing structure with the influx of foreign programming—much of which would be entertainment oriented and commercially supported. The government has been careful to guard the monopoly granted to the SBC and has not been anxious to expand programming choices beyond what the SBC can offer.

With this kind of prevailing attitude, it is not surprising that cable television exists only on a very limited basis in the nation at the present time. As of 1986 only about 100,000 homes were wired for cable. In 1986, however, Parliament passed legislation allowing cable television transmissions throughout the nation. Permits will be granted to anyone with a cable network (one per locality). As with other television operations in Sweden, no advertisements or sponsored programs will be permitted. But even if cable begins to spread, it is unlikely that it would ever be available to the entire nation because of the sparse population in northern Sweden.

Satellite broadcasting, on the other hand, could ensure programming for all regions, and that may be one reason why the nation has moved in that direction. In the late 1970s Sweden, Norway, Denmark, and Finland agreed to collaborate on a satellite project called Nordsat. The system was to make the television channels in each country available to the other nations in the project. Eventually, Denmark dropped out of the agreement, and it was abandoned. The idea of satellite television was later revived, and Sweden, Norway, and Finland are now committed to an effort called Tele-X. There will be two television channels that will transmit an assortment of programs from each nation.

Although Sweden has lagged behind in cable and satellite technologies, the nation implemented teletext services very successfully. Originally intended as a service for the hearing-impaired, teletext has had a much wider acceptance. The service transmits subtitles to programs, news items, and general information. Approximately 6 percent of all televisions have been equipped to receive this service.

Another technology that has developed rapidly is videocassette recordings. There are 3.2 million television households in Sweden, and over 650,000 of them own videocassette recorders. The video industry grossed over Kr 400 million in 1986.

CONCLUSION/FORECAST

Broadcasting in Sweden has remained quite stable over its history, with few major changes. Beginning with the change in political power, however, some important concepts began to take shape that may have started a series of transformations that may result in drastic restructuring of the broadcasting system. The questions of advertiser-supported broadcasting, pay television, cable legislation, and satellite development are all issues that are being debated in both social and political circles. Regardless of which political party gains power, these concerns must be dealt with, and significant changes are likely to occur.

Sweden's broadcasting system had been relatively unaffected by outside broadcasting forces until the advent of satellite distribution of programs, which is very difficult to control or limit. In the face of such outside programming competition, the issues concerning technological developments that the Swedish government has avoided must now be addressed. Whether or not the proposed changes are desirable socially or politically, they are now inevitable.

BIBLIOGRAPHY

Berg, Ulf. *Foreign Fare on Swedish Television*. Stockholm: Sveriges Radio, 1978.
Browne, Donald. "Alternatives for Local and Regional Radio: Three Nordic Solutions." *Journal of Communication* 34 (1984): 36–55.
Dahlgren, Peter. "Television in the Socialization Process: Structures and Programming of the Swedish Broadcasting Corporation." In *Television and Social*

Behavior, vol. 1 of *Media Content and Control*, edited by G. A. Comstock and E. A. Rubinstein. Washington, D.C.: U.S. Government Printing Office, 1972.

Gustafsson, Karl Erik. "Media Structure and Policy in Sweden in the Early 1980's." In *Current Sweden*, published by the Swedish Institute, no. 301. Stockholm: Swedish Institute, 1983.

Hedebro, Göran. "Communication Policy in Sweden: An Experiment in State Intervention." In *Communication Policy in Developed Countries*, edited by Patricia Edgar and Syed A. Rahim. London: Kegan Paul International, 1983.

Hultén, Olof. *Mass Media and State Support in Sweden*. 2d rev. ed. Stockholm: Swedish Institute, 1984.

———. "Scandinavia: Nordic Collaboration." *Intermedia* 14 (1986): 32–34.

Hultén, Olof, and Ivar Ivre. "Sweden: Small but Foreboding Changes." *Journal of Communication* 28 (1978): 96–105.

Ivre, Ivar. "Conflict and Resolution in Sweden." In *Mass Media Policies in Changing Cultures*, edited by George Gerbner. New York: John Wiley, 1977.

Landstrom, Sven Åke, Head, International Relations, Swedish Radio Company. Interview with author, Stockholm, Sweden, July 15, 1984.

Ortmark, Åke. "Sweden: Freedom's Boundaries." In *Television and Political Life*, edited by Anthony Smith. New York: St. Martin's, 1979.

Paulu, Burton. *Radio and Television Broadcasting on the European Continent*. Minneapolis: University of Minnesota Press, 1967.

Ploman, Edward W. *Broadcasting in Sweden*. London: Routledge and Kegan Paul, 1976.

Soderstrom, Herbert. "Broadcasting in Sweden." In *Broadcasting around the World*, edited by William E. McCavitt. Blue Ridge Summit: TAB, 1981.

Svard, Stig. "Sweden Re-regulates Its Media Mix." *Intermedia* 10 (1982): 27–28.

The Audience and Program Research Department of Sveriges Radio publishes a number of its studies in English. These are available to interested individuals.

UNITED STATES

C. Joseph Pusateri

HISTORY

Wireless communication in the United States was the product of the cross-fertilization of a score or more inventors and a succession of "firsts" of one kind or another. Among those Americans who can claim a share of pioneering honors in the prehistory of broadcasting was Nathan B. Stubblefield, who may have transmitted the human voice as early as 1892 in a Murray, Kentucky, demonstration; Reginald A. Fessenden, who certainly broadcast an impromptu program from Brant Rock, Massachusetts, in 1906; and Lee De Forest, part inventor and part radio missionary, who broadcast from the Eiffel Tower in 1908 and put Enrico Caruso and the Metropolitan Opera on the air in 1910. Such progress led David Sarnoff, a young executive with the Marconi Wireless Telegraph Company of America, a subsidiary of the British corporation, to draft a company memorandum in 1916 suggesting a "Radio Music Box" that would bring music into the home by wireless. The proposal, though it pointed the way to the future, elicited no immediate response.

Full-fledged broadcasting made its debut in the years following World War I. Historians of broadcasting have never ceased disputing which station among a half-dozen contenders can rightly regard itself as the nation's oldest. Among those contenders are KQW in San Jose, California (now KCBS), Detroit's WWJ, and WHA in Madison, Wisconsin. But most Americans still associate the birth of broadcasting with Westinghouse Electric's establishment of KDKA in Pittsburgh in November 1920. The origins of KDKA lay in the experimental radio activities of Westinghouse engineer Frank Conrad. When Conrad's amateur broadcasts from a transmitter in his garage workshop (including the playing of phonograph records) began to attract local attention, vice president H. P. Davis of Westinghouse sensed a potential market for receiving sets built by his company. A broadcasting station would supply the necessary programming that the public could then hear on Westinghouse sets.

As a result, on the evening of November 2, 1920, from a shack on the roof of a factory building at Westinghouse's East Pittsburgh plant, KDKA first went on the air. It broadcast to a local audience of probably no more than a few hundred listeners the voting results in the presidential election between Warren G. Harding and James M. Cox. Today, sixty-seven years later, KDKA is still the flagship property in the Westinghouse group of stations.

In the months following KDKA's first broadcast, radio became a public passion in the United States. By the end of 1922 there were already almost 600 licensed stations and an estimated 400,000 receiving sets in use. Commercial or toll broadcasting developed rapidly, with the first sponsor message being carried by station WEAF (New York City) in August 1922. Another significant development in the early history of the electronic mass media was the founding of networks or "chains" of stations. In 1926 the National Broadcasting Company (originally jointly owned by the Radio Corporation of America, General Electric, and Westinghouse) came into being, and its long-time rival-to-be, the Columbia Broadcasting System, appeared just a year later.

Interestingly enough, while radio broadcasting was still in its infancy, work had already begun on finding a viable television system. Early attempts at developing a mechanical approach to transmitting and receiving a visual image were eventually superseded by an all-electronic system devised principally by Vladimir K. Zworykin of RCA and by Phil Farnsworth, who worked independently of any large corporation. By 1938 David Sarnoff of RCA pronounced home television technically feasible, and a year later NBC began telecasts from the New York World's Fair.

World War II, however, delayed the further growth of television as a mass-entertainment medium so that it was not until the late 1940s that its impact finally began to be felt. Not until 1951, for instance, did television operators show their first collective profit, earning $41.6 million as compared to a loss of $9.2 million the year before. Three years later, in 1954, with over 400 TV stations on the air, with two-thirds of American homes owning at least one television set, and with NBC beginning regular network telecasts of programs in color, the advertising revenues taken in by the television industry surpassed those of radio for the first time. Television had clearly reached maturity.

In sum, broadcasting in America is both a process and a business. As a process, it can be defined as radio, television, and cable communication intended for reception by the public at large. The words and pictures of the process are supplied by some 10,000 radio and 1,200 television stations along with 6,600 cable systems operating today in the United States that together provide the principal leisure-time activity for the American people. But broadcasting is also one of the nation's preeminent businesses. In 1983, for example, commercial broadcasting had total advertising revenues of approximately $21.3 billion. Hence broadcasting has been since its inception an increasingly vital force in American society.

REGULATION

The regulation of radio and television broadcasting has always been regarded as a federal matter in which state and local governments were to play little role. Only with the emergence of the cable industry did the states and especially individual municipalities begin to exercise any major regulatory authority in the field of mass media.

The federal regulation of radio communication predates the broadcasting era, since it originated with the Wireless Ship Act of 1910 and the Radio Act of 1912. The latter was the first general law for governmental control of radio. It vested the power to license both stations and operators in the Department of Commerce and Labor (then a single entity). With the emergence of broadcasting in the twenties, though, the need for legislation to deal with an entirely new environment became apparent. The result was the passage by Congress of the Radio Act of 1927.

The statute established a five-member Federal Radio Commission (FRC) that could issue station licenses, allocate frequency bands to different types of radio services, and assign individual stations to designated frequencies with specifically authorized watts of power. It spent much of its seven-year existence trying to devise an equitable accommodation of some 700 different stations within the broadcast band in the face of constant protests from owners, politicians, and various citizens' groups about discrimination against their often-contradictory interests. When Franklin Roosevelt moved into the White House in 1933, he appointed an interdepartmental committee to study the role of the nine government agencies involved with various forms of electronic communication. In late 1933 the committee recommended to the president the formation of a single body that would be both an expanded FRC and the regulator of all interstate and foreign telephone and telegraph systems in the United States.

Taking its cue from the committee's recommendation, Congress passed and Roosevelt signed the Communications Act of 1934 creating the present Federal Communications Commission (FCC). Several of the provisions of the law were borrowed from the earlier 1927 Radio Act. The FCC began operating in July 1934 as an independent federal agency headed by seven (now five) presidentially appointed commissioners.

A major responsibility of the FCC is the regulation of broadcasting. That takes three main forms:

1. The allocation of space in the radio frequency spectrum to broadcast and non-broadcast services.

2. The assignment of stations in each service to specific frequencies and owners within their appropriate bands in such a manner as to avoid interference with other stations on the same or adjacent frequencies.

3. The regulation of existing stations to see that they are operating in accordance with FCC rules and the provisions of their authorizations. At the time of periodic license renewal, the FCC supposedly reviews the station's record to determine if it is indeed operating in the public interest.

It is a basic principle in the philosophy behind broadcast regulation in the United States that the airwaves belong to the public and that broadcasters, who occupy particular segments of the electromagnetic spectrum, do not own those portions. They have no permanent property rights; rather, they are trustees for the public. In a real sense, therefore, broadcasting is a business similar to a public utility. In the words of a 1966 federal court decision: "A broadcaster seeks and is granted the free and exclusive use of a limited and valuable part of the public domain; when he accepts that franchise it is burdened by enforceable public obligations. A newspaper can be operated at the whim or caprice of its owners; a broadcast station cannot." Both the 1927 Radio Act and the 1934 Communications Act require broadcasters to serve "the public interest, convenience, and necessity." By law, each station license contains a statement that the licensee has no right to continue to operate the facility beyond the term stated in the license. The maximum term of a license for a television station today is five years and for a radio station seven years.

The FCC is forbidden by section 326 of the Communications Act from censoring program content. Review, evaluation, and perhaps sanctions by the FCC after the fact, however, as opposed to prior restraint, have not been interpreted as a violation of First Amendment rights. Penalties for violation of FCC rules range in stringency from mere reprimands to fines of as much as $10,000, short-term probationary license renewals, or ultimately, denial of renewal altogether. The latter penalty has been relatively rarely applied by the commission.

The American system of broadcasting is thus anchored in private enterprise, but a central principle of its operation has been the requirement of social responsibility. Nevertheless, during the past decade a considerable momentum has developed toward what is being called "deregulation." While the movement began during the term of President Carter, it accelerated with the coming of the Reagan administration in 1981. A major proponent of deregulation is Mark Fowler, the former chair of the FCC. In articles and speeches he has questioned some of the most basic assumptions underlying the Communications Act, including the public nature of spectrum frequencies. He has suggested that they no longer be considered a public resource, but instead that broadcasters be granted property rights to the frequencies they use. Hence they would be able to buy, sell, and program their property as they chose without having to seek permission or subject themselves to scrutiny by the FCC.

Deregulation has eliminated a number of lesser regulations, especially for operators of radio stations. A good deal of what broadcasters refer to as regulatory "underbrush" has been cleared away, reducing needless paperwork requirements for record keeping and reporting. But Fowler has not been successful in securing congressional approval of his more extreme views on the substitution of a pure marketplace philosophy for the public interest standard reflected in the Communications Act, and it does not appear likely that he will be any more successful in the immediate future.

ECONOMIC STRUCTURE

The owner of a broadcast station may be one person, a partnership, or a group of persons operating as a corporation. Any of those three types whose role or chief business is one broadcast property is a single owner. A group owner has two or more stations in different cities.

There is an FCC prohibition on the ownership by the same individual or entity of two stations of the same type (AM, FM, or TV) in the same community or in nearby communities where signal coverage considerably overlaps. This is known as the "duopoly" rule. But the rule does not prohibit a licensee from owning stations of different services in the same community (over 75 percent of all FM stations are owned by the licensees of AM stations in the same city). The FCC, however, is enforcing a "one-to-market" rule designed to reduce the number of such combinations. The rule forbids a new licensee from acquiring both a radio and a television station in the same city. Furthermore, another FCC rule on cross-ownership prohibits television stations from being co-owned with cable systems in the same market.

Group ownership of broadcasting properties has become a major characteristic of the industry today. By 1982, for instance, 83 percent of all TV stations in the fifty largest market areas in the United States were group owned. All three of the national television networks (NBC, CBS, and ABC) are group owners of a significant number of radio and television stations. These properties are known as a network's O and O (owned and operated) stations, and they are generally located in the country's major economic markets. Nonnetwork group owners also include some large-scale organizations. Among the best known are Capital Cities Communications (which has acquired ABC), Metromedia, and Westinghouse Broadcasting (also known as Group W), the pioneer in the development of the non-network group operation.

Radio and television networks play an important role in American broadcasting. They provide an advertiser a nationwide or regional interconnected chain of stations for the delivery of commercial messages, and they supply an affiliated station a stream of programming that it could not produce itself. In addition to the major national networks, there are over a hundred smaller networks that share programs within a geographical region or have some other common orientation such as programming in a foreign language or for a specific religious denomination. Sometimes broadcasting entrepreneurs will paste together an ad hoc network of stations simply for the showing of a particular program or series of programs.

But it is with the national full-service networks that the public most identifies. The economic link between a network and an affiliated station is the affiliation contract, a document that by law is renewable every two years. In exchange for the use of a station's on-the-air time (the term is "clearance"), the affiliate receives a payment or network compensation, the size of which varies according to differences in the affiliate's market size, ratings, and other factors. Actually, a station measures the value of its affiliation with a network not in terms of compensation so much as the larger audiences that national programs attract. An affiliate expects to and does earn substantial revenues by selling its own time to advertisers anxious to reach those audiences built by network programming.

Television is much more of a network-dominated medium than radio. In the latter case network programming has been reduced in most instances to little more than a news and feature service since blockbuster entertainment shows deserted radio more than thirty years ago and fled to television. Of the 777 total commercial television stations operating in the United States in 1982, 80 percent were affiliates of one of the networks. The three major networks were relatively evenly balanced in their numbers of affiliates, with NBC having 215, ABC 206, and CBS 200 in 1982. Since that date ABC has increased its affiliate share slightly, mainly at the expense of NBC, but the exact numbers are continually fluctuating as some stations switch allegiances.

PROGRAMMING

Successful programming is vital to a commercial radio or television property since it spells the difference between profit and loss. Unpopular programming results in few listeners or viewers, an insufficient number of advertisers buying airtime at low prices, and sooner or later, economic oblivion. It is essential that programming be tailored to the nature of the medium itself, whether radio or television.

In the case of radio, for instance, the audience tends to tune in and out at various times of the day as opposed to listening for extended periods. The implication is clear: programming has to be constructed so that a listener can tune in at regular times and not feel that he or she has missed anything significant. Segments, therefore, are brief packages of music, news, talk, and features, generally no more than a few minutes long. If you just missed the sports results, stay tuned because they will be broadcast again very shortly.

Moreover, most radio stations, whether AM or FM (and the latter now draw the larger audiences) usually specialize in a particular kind of programming. The various kinds are referred to as "formats," and there has come to be a bewildering variety in recent years. In the music category they range from "Top 40" stations that play only a tight list of contemporary hit records targeted to appeal to teenage listeners to "easy listening" outlets that play lush orchestral recordings that would be most appealing to an affluent audience. Other format categories besides music include all-news operations, all- or mostly telephone talk stations, and MOR (middle-of-the-road) radio that usually consists of a mixture of program approaches. The larger and more cosmopolitan the market area, the more variations one will find in formats and formulas.

Unlike radio, television requires a sit-down audience that is usually prepared to devote a sizeable block of time to viewing what the schedule offers. When television programming is discussed, a distinction must be made between the schedule content of network-affiliated stations and that of nonnetwork or independent ("indies," as they are called in the trade) stations. Affiliated stations are supplied with about one hundred hours of programs each week by their respective networks, or about 70 percent of the affiliate's airtime. Ironically, daytime programming is actually more profitable for the networks because of the heavy production cost of the prime-time shows and their high-salaried stars.

Although it forms only a relatively minor portion of television programming, broadcast journalism has been of considerable importance for at least two reasons. First, for an increasing percentage of Americans, news on television is their principal source of information about the world in which they live. Recent surveys indicate that the number of those who rely on TV as virtually their sole hard news source may be as high as two-thirds of the population. Second, for the networks especially, quality news programming imparts considerable prestige to a broadcast organization, masking somewhat the contradictory depressing quality level of much of the prime-time entertainment the same company might offer its mass audience. In effect, carrying on the journalistic tradition of Edward R. Murrow can presumably help rebut the continuing charge that network programming is indeed the same "vast wasteland" an FCC chairman saw over twenty years ago. The networks, therefore, maintain large and elaborate news divisions with reporters stationed all over the world, and they engage in a fierce competition to score journalistic scoops.

The most publicized aspect of this competition, though, is the constant ratings race between each network's early-evening half-hour news program. The competition becomes very personalized because it often appears to be simply a popularity contest between the "anchors" or chief national re-porters/commentators of the different programs.

For independent stations, the program schedule is dominated by syndi-cated shows. These are of two types, off-network and first-run. Off-network shows are those that first appeared on network schedules and then, when their runs were complete, were resold to independent stations for showing again. Some former network programs such as "I Love Lucy" have been shown and reshown again and again on independent stations. First-run pro-grams, of course, are specifically packaged by imaginative syndicators and producers for sale to independents without any previous network showing. This form of programming has become increasingly evident the last few years as the number of independent stations has increased. It is most often a game or talk show, though some dramatic programs have lately been produced for first-run syndication. With skillful selection and sufficient capital, an inde-pendent can today air those programs, off-network or first-run, that will al-low it to achieve a very respectable rating in the local competition with established affiliated stations. More and more, independents in the 1980s are impressive money-making enterprises.

BROADCAST REFORM

Traditionally, any movement to reform broadcasting in the United States usually was drawn from those individuals or groups who favored the further extension of public regulatory authority either by statute or by administra-tive oversight. That traditional reform movement has not disappeared. Cit-izens' groups still respond to such ongoing concerns as the level of violence in TV programs, the increasing sexual explicitness seen on the home screen, and the quality of shows aimed at children, and they call for action on all those fronts and more.

During recent years new campaigns also have been launched. One of the most ardent has been spearheaded by the citizens' organization MADD, Mothers Against Drunk Driving. It and its allied groups have been seeking an FCC ban on the advertising of some beverages, namely beer and wine, on television. In effect, the campaign is intended to bring about the same sort of prohibition as when cigarette advertising was banned from the air-waves in 1971. Whether MADD will secure a corresponding elimination of alcohol commercials remains to be seen.

In today's more conservative political climate, however, the most dramatic effort at broadcast reform is coming from the Right and not the Left. The deregulation movement, already discussed, if carried further than the point it has already reached, has the potential for being the most radical reform of the American broadcasting system yet seen. The marketplace philosophy espoused by the Reagan administration envisions the removal of much of the long-established responsibility government had assumed for monitoring the conduct of the broadcasting industry.

A significant victory that the deregulators achieved in the Congress was the enactment in late 1984 of a cable communications bill. It frees cable system operators in the United States from a great deal of the control that local municipalities were formerly able to exert over those businesses through the franchising process. Basically, cable operators are now able to set their own rates for the services they offer the public without having to seek prior approval from a city government. There is no doubt that the exponents of deregulation view the Cable Communications Policy Act of 1984 as one of the first in a series of actions they hope will spell a new era in the relations between private enterprise and public authority in America.

The history of public broadcasting in the United States can be divided into two distinct periods. In the first, prior to 1967, noncommercial radio and television was primarily educational. As a matter of fact, the establishment of educational stations went back to the very earliest days of broadcasting in the 1920s when a number of universities and colleges received licenses. After 1967, though, educational broadcasting was expanded to include cultural, informational, and frankly entertainment programming designed to appeal to a much wider audience.

The year 1967 marked the dividing line because it saw the passage of the Public Broadcasting Act, which established the Corporation for Public Broadcasting funded by congressional appropriations and private contributions. The corporation, in turn, created the Public Broadcasting Service, whose primary function was and is to distribute television programs to its affiliated or member stations, thus representing a fourth (but nonprofit) national network. In 1970 the corporation launched National Public Radio to produce and distribute radio programming for its member stations. In addition, of course, individual stations do produce, air, and even distribute at times their own local shows and thus do not rely simply on what is received from PBS and NPR.

There has been a growing audience for public broadcasting. One recent survey has indicated that about 55 percent of those households with television sets watch a PBS station at least once a week. What they see is an imposing menu of high-quality programming such as "Sesame Street," public television's most celebrated series, the "MacNeil/Lehrer Report" in the news field, and the long-running "Masterpiece Theatre" drama showcase for British productions. Not everything on a public station approaches the excellence of the programs just mentioned, but there is no doubt that the overall quality level of what is being offered has been steadily rising.

Problems remain, however, for noncommercial broadcasting, and they usually center on the issue of funding. Governmental support is always uncertain, especially in periods of changing political ideologies. In the last decade, for instance, conservatives have accused public radio and television of being dominated by a liberal bias, and as a result right-of-center politicians are often less than enthusiastic in their readiness to provide generous governmental financial support. To a considerable extent, noncommercial broadcasters have had to rely on repetitive pleas for contributions from private citizens and corporations. At times it may seem to viewers of public television that the number of on-the-air appeals for contributions exceeds commercial minutes on for-profit stations. Nevertheless, the noncommercial system offers the public alternative programming that more often than not is a refreshing escape from beer advertisements, car chases, and unfunny situation comedies.

NEW TECHNOLOGIES

The last decade has spawned a string of new technologies that seem to pose future challenges to traditional broadcasting. Some of these technologies, such as cable television, actually began development much earlier, but it was during the seventies and early eighties that they came to real prominence.

Cable television is a nonbroadcast distribution system consisting of wires and associated equipment designed to carry TV signals. The first cable system was put into service in Astoria, Oregon, in 1949. At that time and during its formative years it was known as community antenna television (CATV), and it was intended to provide rural communities with broadcast signals picked up by a master antenna. Later, cable operators realized that large cities offered a lucrative potential cable market also since the systems could give subscribers more and better signals than they might otherwise receive.

According to November 1984 data, about 44 percent of all TV homes were wired for cable service. Industry prognosticators have estimated that by 1990 well over 60 percent of the nation's homes will be using cable. With the passage of the Cable Communications Policy Act, cable's future may be even brighter.

Other relatively new technologies affecting the telecommunications industry include the use of satellites. They provide programmers and common carriers with a reasonably inexpensive method of transmitting their signals nationally. While the first commercial satellite was put into the sky in 1965, the real rush for satellite video transmission began ten years later when Time Inc.'s Home Box Office subsidiary began distributing its premium cable TV programming by means of an RCA-owned "bird."

Also to be mentioned in the category of new technologies is low-powered television (LPTV), a service authorized by the FCC in 1982 to add as many as 4,000 additional stations to the full-power ones presently operating. Low-power licensees operate on unassigned channels but with limited power so that they do not interfere with primary stations. They are also free from many of the regulatory requirements that full-power facilities must respect. The FCC, however, has been slow to approve many LPTV licenses, which are now being awarded by lottery, a new approach to identifying first-time licensees. Whether LPTV stations will ever make the television marketplace more competitive than before is doubtful, since most of these operations will almost inevitably hold little attraction for advertisers and thus have minimal earnings potential.

Among the other technologies of the present and future that can be cited are MDS (multipoint distribution service), a means of transmitting video, text, or data by omnidirectional microwave signals to subscribers equipped with special antennas; HDTV (high-definition television and stereo sound); and teletext, a one-way electronic publishing service that can be transmitted over a standard television channel and received by the viewer with a special decoder, authorized by the FCC for TV station and cable system use in 1983.

In general, the newest media have so far failed to gain a collective foothold that would allow them to begin displacing conventional broadcasters and cablecasters from their established places in electronic communications. It is not that there has been anything intrinsically wrong with these futuristic technologies. It is just that conventional broadcasting and cable were there first and established ingrained public habits. Scores of companies have already lost millions investing in the new technologies, and they have learned belatedly to be careful when attempting to ride a new wave of the future.

CONCLUSION/FORECAST

It is likely, therefore, that broadcasting as we know it will not change its essential form during the remainder of this century. A minority of the nation's population will utilize the special and innovative services that some of the new technologies offer, but most Americans will continue to rely on the conventional radio and television they enjoy (or at least tolerate) today. Hence the changes we are most liable to see in the next fifteen years will be sharply circumscribed by the system already in place.

For example, network television is not likely to disappear in the 1990s. The major networks' share of the viewing audience will certainly decline somewhat. That trend exists now because of the impact of cable and of video recorders capable of playing programs bought or rented at a nearby store. Nevertheless, most experts agree that television networks should remain an efficient means of distributing entertainment programming.

We may see more networks, particularly since the FCC has recently decided to allow group owners to hold more licenses than in the past—twelve instead of seven in any broadcast service—and those organizations by growing even larger could become more formidable competitors of NBC, CBS, and ABC. But even the emergence of new networks assembled by affluent group owners would not alter the basics of what has come to be regarded as the American system of broadcasting. That system is well established and capable of a great deal of accommodation to new developments, whether they be technological or entrepreneurial. The waves of the future may wash over the system, but they are not going to sweep it away.

BIBLIOGRAPHY

Barnouw, Erik. *A History of Broadcasting in the United States.* 3 vols. New York: Oxford University Press, 1966–70.

Brown, Les. *Les Brown's Encyclopedia of Television.* New York: Zoetrope, 1982.

Cole, Barry, and Mel Oettinger. *Reluctant Regulators: The FCC and the Broadcast Audience.* Reading, Penna.: Addison-Wesley, 1978.

Dunning, John. *Tune in Yesterday: The Ultimate Encyclopedia of Old Time Radio, 1925–1976.* Reading, Penna.: Addison-Wesley, 1978.

Ellmore, R. Terry. *Broadcasting Law and Regulation.* Blue Ridge Summit: TAB, 1982.

Gitlin, Todd. *Inside Prime Time.* New York: Pantheon, 1983.

Greenfield, Jeff. *Television: The First Fifty Years.* 2d ed. New York: Crescent, 1981.

Head, Sydney W., with Christopher H. Sterling. *Broadcasting in America.* Boston: Houghton Mifflin, 1982.

Heighton, Elizabeth J., and Don R. Cunningham. *Advertising in the Broadcast and Cable Media.* 2d ed. Belmont, Calif.: Wadsworth, 1984.

Kahn, Frank J., ed. *Documents of American Broadcasting.* 3d ed. Englewood Cliffs, N.J.: Prentice-Hall, 1978.

Krasnow, Erwin G., et al., *The Politics of Broadcast Regulation.* 3d ed. New York: St. Martin's, 1982.

Rice, Ronald E., and Associates. *The New Media.* New York: Sage, 1984.

Rosen, Philip T. *The Modern Stentors: Radio Broadcasters and the Federal Government, 1920–1934.* Westport, Conn.: Greenwood Press, 1980.

Sterling, Christopher H., and John M. Kittross. *Stay Tuned: A Concise History of American Broadcasting.* Belmont, Calif.: Wadsworth, 1978.

Udelson, Joseph H. *The Great Television Race: A History of the American Television Industry, 1925–1941.* University: University of Alabama Press, 1982.

Williams, Frederick. *The Communications Revolution.* New York: Sage, 1982.

INDEX

ABC (Australian Broadcasting Corporation/Commission), 1–4, 6–8, 9, 10, 11

ABEPEC (Brazilian Association for the Teaching and Research of Communication), 43

AB Radiotjänst, 269, 270, 272

ABT (Australian Broadcasting Tribunal), 3–7, 9–11

ABU (Asian Pacific Broadcasting Union), 247

Advertising: across national borders, 31–32, 52, 55, 73, 101; banned, 142; by government, 45, 113, 238; catalyst for reform, 17, 137, 279; impact on careers, 36; inclusion in national systems, 25, 52, 109, 136, 151, 165, 174, 191, 230; influence on programming, 8, 40, 100–101; introduction of, 35, 137, 174, 176; Kobaco, 206–7; limitations on, 18, 19, 27–28, 73, 111, 137, 151, 230; newspaper competition, 23, 32, 98, 167, 178; prohibited, 25, 82, 252, 273; revenues, 19, 40, 39, 72, 94–95, 110, 150, 174, 285; standards for, 4, 73, 151; television versus radio, 37, 137, 150, 178, 284; time restrictions on, 7, 19, 38, 93–95, 166, 206

AFTS (Australian Film and Training School), 7

AIR (All India Radio), 133–42

Akashvani Radio, 134

Al Aziz, Abd, 244, 245, 250

All-Nippon News Network, 181–82

Arabic-language broadcasts: Africa, 187, 190, 233; Asia, 212; Middle East, 147–48, 150, 154–55, 157–58; Saudi Arabia, 243–54; South America, 84

Arabsat, 159, 253

ARD (West German radio and television program supplier), 31, 91, 92, 93–97

Asahi Newspaper, 174, 181–82

ASBU (Arab States Broadcasting Union), 247

A 2, 31, 169

Audience research, 96, 113–14, 120, 127, 140, 168, 192, 265–66

AUSSAT, 11

Australia, 1–12, 154, 195, 277; ABC, 1–4, 6, 8, 9, 10, 11; ABT, 3–7, 9–11; Australian Broadcasting Control Board, 5; economic structure, 5–8; history, 1–2; programming, 8–10; reform, 10–11; regulation, 2–5; Special Broadcasting Service, 1–2; sta-

ABOUT THE EDITOR AND THE CONTRIBUTORS

PHILIP T. ROSEN, Associate Professor of History and Director of Continuing Education at the University of Alaska, Anchorage, formerly served as the Dean of Erie Metropolitan College at Gannon University. Prior to that, he was an exchange scholar in the Philippines, Colombia, and Australia. He received his Ph.D. in history from Wayne State University, where he studied under Forrest McDonald. His area of specialty is modern American history. He is the author of *The Modern Stentors: Radio Broadcasters and the Federal Government, 1920–1934* (Greenwood Press, 1980), nominated for the National Historical Prize, and a contributor to *In Peace and War: Interpretations of American Naval History, 1775–1984* (Greenwood Press, 1984) and *American Business History: Case Studies*. In addition, he has published numerous scholarly articles. He has also participated on panels hosted by the American Studies Association, the Pacific Branch of the American Historical Association, the Smithsonian Institution, the U.S. Naval Academy, and the Society of the History of Technology. Currently, he is completing a manuscript on Herbert Hoover for publication by the Hoover Presidential Library Association.

MARVIN ALISKY is Professor of Political Science at Arizona State University, Tempe. Prior to that, he was an NBC news correspondent in Latin America. He has written a host of articles for scholarly journals as well as for the popular press. In addition, he has authored and coauthored several books on Latin America, including *Latin American Media*, *Global Journalism*, and *Uruguay: A Contemporary Survey*.

AKIBA A. COHEN is a Senior Lecturer at the Communications Institute and Director of the Center for the Study of Communications in Israel at the Hebrew University of Jerusalem. He is the coauthor of *Almost Midnight: Reforming the Late Night News* and the author of a forthcoming book, *The Television News Interview*. He has contributed articles to several scholarly journals, including the *Journal of Communication*, the *Journal of Broadcasting*, and the *Journalism Quarterly*.

DIRK DE GROOFF is a Research Assistant at the Center for Communication Sciences at the Catholic University of Leuven. He was formerly the Project Leader at Mediatel, a "new media" study group of the Belgian Association of Daily Newspaper Publishers. He has written several books on telematics.

G. FAUCONNIER is a Professor at the Center for Communication Sciences at the Catholic University of Leuven. He teaches such subjects as mass communication, communication theory, and advertising theory. He has written many books in these areas and has also carried out a number of research projects for Belgian and international organizations.

ROBERTO GRANDI is an Associate Professor of Mass Communication at the University of Bologna. In 1978 he was a visiting scholar at the Annenberg School of Communications at the University of Pennsylvania. He is author of *Comunicazioni di Massa: Radio e televisione negli Stati Uniti*, coauthor of *Nuove forme del potere, Radio e televisione, Le televisione in Europa*, and editor of *I segni di Caino*. He is a contributing editor to the *Journal of Communication*.

WOLFGANG HOFFMAN-RIEM is the Director of the Hans-Bredow-Institute for Radio and Television Broadcasting. He is the author of a host of scholarly publications on constitutional law, media law and policy, and tax law and economic regulations. In addition, he has been a visiting scholar at the Stanford Law School and the Harvard Law School.

JOSEPH KINNER is a member of the History Department at Gallaudet University. His present research interests center on the history of broadcasting in Nigeria. In 1986 he was awarded a Fulbright Fellowship to conduct research in Nigeria.

KENJI KITATANI is an Assistant Professor of Telecommunications at Indiana University. He has coauthored several books on American and Western European media economics and policy. In addition, his articles appear frequently in the Japanese press.

W. LEONARD LEE is the Chair of the Communications Department at California State University, Dominguez Hills. His principal research interest is broadcasting systems in the Middle East. He has published several articles in scholarly journals.

JOHN A. LENT is a Professor of Communications at Temple University. He is the author of a host of books and articles on the mass media in the Third World.

KURT LUGER is an Assistant Professor in the Department of Communications at Salzburg University. Interested in mass media, youth culture, and communications, he has authored several articles.

TIMOTHY S. MADGE is a Visiting Fellow at the City University, London. In addition, he is editor of the *Young Guardian* and the author of *Beyond the BBC*. He is also a well-known journalist and serves as a communications consultant.

L. JOHN MARTIN is a Professor and Director of Graduate Studies in the College of Journalism at the University of Maryland. Prior to that, he was a research administrator in the United States Information Agency. He has written a host of articles and books including *International Propaganda*, and has edited *Comparative Mass Media Systems* and *Propaganda in International Affairs*. In addition, he is editor in charge of international journalism for the *Journalism Quarterly* and was for eleven years editor of the *International Communication Bulletin*.

BRENDA McPHAIL is a Research Associate with the Graduate Program in Communications Studies at the University of Calgary. Her research interests are in the area of broadcasting and public policy. In addition, she is currently doing research for the Canadian Federal Government's Broadcasting Task Force. She is also the coauthor of *TELECOM 2000: Canada's Telecommunications Future*.

THOMAS L. McPHAIL is Professor of Communications and Director of the Graduate Program in Communications Studies at the University of Calgary. He is also a consultant to the Federal Department of Communications on its Telecommunications Policy Review. He is the author of *Electronic Colonialism: The Future of Broadcasting and Communication* and coauthor of *TELECOM 2000: Canada's Telecommunications Future*.

ZHENG MEIYUN is a Researcher at the Institute of Journalism of the Chinese Academy of Social Sciences. She has published several articles in the field of broadcasting and has coedited a book entitled *Selection of Laws of Journalism of Foreign Countries*.

IN-HWAN OH is a Professor of Mass Communications at Yonsei University. He earned a doctorate in sociology from the University of Hawaii while on a scholarship from the East-West Center.

OMAR SOUKI OLIVEIRA is an Assistant Professor in Communications Studies at Niagara University. His principal research has been on the Brazilian broadcasting system, and he has written several articles on this subject.

C. JOSEPH PUSATERI is Dean of the College of Arts and Sciences and Professor of History at the University of San Diego. He is the author of *Big Business in America: Attack and Defense*; *Enterprise in Radio: WWL and the Business of Broadcasting in America*; and *A History of American Business*. He is presently completing a manuscript on the history of broadcasting at Westinghouse.

THOMAS F. REMINGTON is Associate Professor of Political Science at Emory University, where he served as the first director of the Soviet and East European Studies Program. He is the author of *Building Socialism in Bolshevik Russia: Ideology and Industrial Organization, 1917–1921*. In addition, he has written a host of articles on Soviet mass communications. He is presently at work on a manuscript on Soviet party management of ideology and communications.

JIM RICHSTAD is Professor of Communications at the University of Oklahoma. He has published numerous articles on international broadcasting. In addition, he has authored *New Perspectives in International Communications*, and is the coeditor of *Evolving Perspectives on the Right to Communicate*.

JEFFREY M. RUSHTON is Deputy Federal Director of the Federation of Australian Broadcasters. He also serves on the Council of the Australian Film and Television School and is Vice Chairman of the Advisory Committee on the National Film and Sound Archive. His research interests center on the educational role of radio and television, and he has contributed several scholarly articles on this subject.

DOV SHINAR is a faculty member of the Communications Institute at the Hebrew University of Jerusalem. He is the author of *Communications in Old Age: Bringing the Mountain to Mohammed*. Currently, he is completing a manuscript on communications on the Palestinian West Bank.

BENNO SIGNITZER is Associate Professor and Head of Public Relations in the Department of Communications at Salzburg University. His research interests center on international communications. He is the author of *Reg-*

ulation of Direct Broadcasting from Satellites, Massenmedien in Öesterreich, and *Praxis in Öesterreich.*

THOMAS SZENDREY is a Professor of History at Gannon University. His research interests focus on East Central European politics and culture. He has authored several articles on Hungarian historiography and religion. Currently, he is completing a manuscript on Hungarian philosophy.

TIMOTHY C. TOMLINSON is an Assistant Professor at Northwestern College. Currently, he is working on his doctorate in the area of international broadcasting at the University of Minnesota.

FEI WANG is a Researcher at the Institute of Journalism of the Chinese Academy of Social Sciences. She has published several articles in the field of broadcasting and has coedited a book entitled *Selection of Laws of Journalism of Foreign Countries.*

DEZHEN ZOU is a Researcher with the Institute of Journalism of the Chinese Academy of Social Sciences. Formerly she was an editor with the Central People's Broadcasting Station and a reporter and commentator with Radio Beijing (formerly Radio Peiping). She has written a host of articles on international affairs. Presently she is conducting a study of television in various nations.